CUBA

THE COOKBOOK

CUBA
THE COOKBOOK

MADELAINE
VÁZQUEZ GÁLVEZ *and* IMOGENE
TONDRE

INTRODUCTION 8

THE CUBAN PANTRY 16

APPETIZERS AND SNACKS 26

SOUPS 62

RICE 100

PASTAS AND PIZZAS 134

FISH, POULTRY, AND MEAT 152

VEGETABLES AND LEGUMES 218

EGGS 258

SALADS 278

SAUCES AND DRESSINGS 308

SWEETS AND DESSERTS 326

DRINKS 376

GUEST CHEFS 408

INDEX 428

INTRODUCTION

Introducción

Cuba, the largest island of the Caribbean, covers 42,815 square miles (110,922 sq km) of land and has a population of more than eleven million. The fact that Cuba is an island does not influence its food as much as you might expect. Although some coastal regions and fishing communities— Gibara, Manzanillo, Caibarién, Cienfuegos—have a distinct food culture, for the most part, Cuban food has been more influenced by its migrant populations than by its geography. These various groups have contributed to the combinations of flavors and ingredients of Cuban cuisine, and this fusion can be seen as representative of the cultural and ethnic mixture of the country itself, and therefore symbolic of a national identity. According to renowned Cuban anthropologist Fernando Ortiz, "Cuba is an *ajiaco*. What is an *ajiaco*? The most typical and complex stew, made from various types of vegetables, which we call *vianda* (tubers), and different types of meat, all brought to a boil until producing a very thick and succulent broth that is seasoned with the very Cuban *ají* (pepper), for which it is named."

Ajiaco is seen as representative of the people of Cuba because the most significant ingredients that make up this dish (and the contributions to Cuban cuisine in general), come from the indigenous population of the island, the Spanish colonizers, and the African slaves brought to Cuba. It is important to note that, unlike other indigenous populations in Central and South America, the original inhabitants of Cuba were a relatively small and dispersed population, and they were almost entirely eradicated during the early colonial years. This caused Cuba's food culture to gradually move away from that of the native population. This divergence has come under observation in recent years by health-concerned critics who have noticed that many of the foods that have become incorporated into the traditional Cuban diet seem at odds with the extreme heat of the island. There are efforts being made by both national and international food organizations to rescue and grow crops in danger of extinction, and to integrate more Cuban native plants into the diet, such as the *gandul* and *caballero* beans and tropical fruits like *canistel, caimito,* and soursop.

Like many colonized lands, a significant culinary influence came from the colonizer. Pork and livestock production common in Spain displaced fishing, and bean soups and other stews were incorporated into the Cuban diet. Spices brought to Cuba by the Spanish included cinnamon, nutmeg, cloves, ginger, cumin, garlic, onion, parsley, oregano, basil, thyme, fennel, anise, marjoram, and cilantro (coriander), which are all customary in Cuban kitchens today. Examples of other Spanish products are olives, capers, raisins, and almonds.

The third major influence on Cuban cuisine came from slaves brought from Africa, and can be observed in the use of yams, plantains, taro root, and okra. In addition to the sugar plantations and other fieldwork that the African slaves were forced to do, they also began to cook in the plantation owners' kitchens, so it is very logical that their culinary practices would show up on the Cuban home table.

Other immigrant groups also contributed to Cuba's food culture. There was a wave of French immigrants that settled mostly on the Eastern side of the island after the Haitian Revolution of 1791. They founded many coffee plantations and were responsible for developing the harvest of that crop, which would eventually become known as Cuba's national drink. The French were also influential in the development of cocoa plantations.

Another influence on Cuban food comes from the Chinese, who began arriving in Cuba in 1847 as indentured servants. They were key in establishing small gastronomic businesses and incorporated vegetables such as bok choy, scallions (spring onions), and spinach in their recipes. The Chinese also introduced a dessert made from winter melon, fruit ice creams, and a dish made from a combination of cabbage and meat. There is documentation that rice was being cultivated in Cuba as early as 1600, but it is believed that it was the Chinese who popularized it and contributed to making it a staple of the Cuban diet today.

Of lesser influence are the waves of immigrant Haitians and Jamaicans to the Eastern side of Cuba between 1913 and 1917, which brought French and English cooking techniques and dishes, such as the use of coconut milk in various recipes, and dumplings. Beginning with the original mixture of food traditions of the indigenous population, Spanish colonizers, and African slaves, up through the twenty-first century, Cuba's culinary history has always included many examples of fusion food and outside influences.

The Republic of Cuba refers to the time period between 1902—when Cuba seceded from US rule in the aftermath of the Spanish-Cuban-American war, which ended in 1898—until the Cuban Revolution of 1959. Cuban scholars refer to this era as a "neo-colony," during which time Cuba enjoyed symbolic independence, but was essentially under control of the United States. At that time of American presence on the island, there was an exchange of influences between the two countries that carried over to the culinary arts. During the first half of the twentieth century, Cubans considered the United States to be the origin of modernity, and certain technologies and kitchen appliances were adopted in the Cuban kitchen. Many of these appliances, like pressure cookers and electric mixers, were sold accompanied with pamphlets of suggested recipes, which were integrated into Cuba's food culture. A linguistic analysis also shows the presence of culinary influences from the United States: hotcakes, sandwiches, hot dogs, and more. Instead of using the traditional Spanish term *torta* or *pastel*, Cubans refer to the "cake," an indispensable element of birthdays and other celebrations.

Our research of cookbooks published in the first half of the twentieth century revealed other examples of American presence in Cuban cuisine. Canned goods became very common, and cookbooks from the 1940s and '50s feature recipes including fruit preserves of products that were imported from the United States, such as pears, apricots, plums, and cherries, which were incorporated into the Cuban diet during that time.

There were other foreign influences during this era as well. More sophisticated culinary arts were developed starting in 1930, with the construction of major hotels in Havana, requiring more variety and an increased quality in the food. After World War II, these hotels were in the hands of the Spanish and French, who began incorporating olive oil, raisins, *turrones* (Spanish candies made of almonds, honey, and egg whites), wines, ciders, and French pastries.

Starting in the 1960s, there were close relations between Cuba and the former Soviet Union, which meant there were many Soviet products in the market in Cuba, such as meat, flour, fish preserves, cured meats and sausages, and milk products. Cubans of any generation born during the 1950s through the 1980s often remember nostalgically the Soviet products associated with their youth. Those products are now difficult or impossible to find. There were also thousands of Cuban students who studied in the USSR and were exposed to the food of that region. Some examples of this influence, such as borscht soup (page 73) and beef Stroganoff (page 202) can be found in this cookbook.

★

During the process of consolidation of the Cuban identity, which spanned from the end of colonization, to the independence

wars, and into the republic years, the island was divided into three regions: Western, Central, and Eastern. The Western and Central regions shared some similar culinary customs, such as the consumption of plain white rice and black beans without root vegetables. The traditions from the Eastern region were more distinct, and included the use of okra and a particular way of preparing rice and beans together with the addition of meat and root vegetables, and more use of herbs and spices, especially culantro. That part of the island is also known for some specific fermented drinks, such as *pru oriental* (Fermented Herb and Root Beverage, page 393) and *aliñado* (Fermented Fruit Beverage, page 392).

The city of Baracoa can easily be considered the place with the most authentic culinary traditions, due to its geography. Located on the northeastern tip of Cuba, this coastal region is isolated from the rest of the island on the other side by a mountain range. A road that created access to Baracoa was not built until 1964, which means that its geographical isolation led it to maintain a self-sufficient, sustainable food culture not found anywhere else in Cuba. The city of Camagüey was also of special significance at the beginning of the twentieth century for its unique gastronomy, such as the Port of Prince Stew (page 94) and the Camagüey-Style Meat and Fruit Salad (page 208), among other recipes.

It would be impossible to understand Cuba's food culture without acknowledging the impacts that the socioeconomic/political system has had over the past six decades. After the Revolutionary government came into power in 1959, an era of massive, collective food production and distribution began. The gastronomic structure, industrial food production networks, and agriculture were completely reconfigured with the intention of eradicating hunger and incorporating women into the workplace. Between 1961 and 1962, the Cuban Revolutionary government implemented a rationing system to provide many products to the population at subsidized prices.

The purpose of the ration system was never to completely fulfill the dietary requirements of the population, but rather to establish some of the most important staples as accessible to everyone. It was also intended to last for just a few years, but political and economic conditions led to the continuation of this system (in some form) until the present.

Another aspect of the socialized food systems are the dining halls (*comedores*) established in schools (including preschools and day cares), and workplaces. While there were elaborate regulations and guidelines established for these *comedores*, the quality and variety of the meals suffered because of the nature of mass production. The *comedores* still exist in many schools and workplaces, but some have been eliminated in the restructuring of Cuba's social and political system since 2011.

There were some excellent State restaurants, especially during the 1970s and '80s. Some of the most renowned restaurants at that time were 1830, Monseñor, La Torre, Emperador, La Roca, Cochinito, Conejito, Centro Vasco, and Rancho Luna. However, like many aspects of Cuban life, the economic crisis of the 1990s, known as the Special Period, which occurred after the collapse of the Soviet Union, dramatically shifted the country's gastronomy. Over the last twenty years, it has been more difficult to find good-quality restaurants, and Cuba's food has long been criticized by foreigners visiting the country (who perhaps did not have the opportunity to enjoy more delicious home-cooked meals). The State-owned restaurants have historically been plagued by limited variety, the pilfering of products by some employees, and mediocre quality. All that changed starting in 2010.

Paladares, or private restaurants run out of family homes, were initially legalized in the 1990s. These businesses have increased dramatically since 2011. While over one hundred different types of jobs in the private sector were legalized in an effort to transition a large portion of the population out of State jobs, the gastronomy category (both restaurants and food stands/cafeterias) is where one of the highest number of new, private businesses can be found. With this increase in privately owned restaurants, Cuba has experienced an absolute revitalization of its food culture. There are creative menus found in the hundreds of restaurants in

Havana and throughout the country, and a handful of new specialty restaurants have opened. While many of the private restaurants are pricey and geared toward tourists, there are also more affordable restaurants, and it has been argued that the Cuban population is eating out more frequently now, thus experiencing a shift in food culture. Some of the innovative recipes created by chefs in the *paladares* will be featured in this book (page 419), although the majority are home cooking recipes from the average Cuban household.

These days, a typical meal in a Cuban home consists of rice and beans; roasted or fried pork; boiled root vegetables; tostones; avocado, lettuce, and/or tomato salad; and some kind of dessert, usually a fruit marmalade. When meat is not available, it is common to eat rice and beans with a fried egg or egg scramble, though there is a general expectation that the *plato fuerte*, or main dish include meat.

The emphasis on meat can be traced back to the 1800s. An American traveler visiting Cuba in the nineteenth century observed, "Cubans eat meat for breakfast, lunch, and dinner." The meat-centered approach is also present in a more comprehensive cookbook published in 1956, called *¿Gusta, usted? Prontuario culinario y... necesario*. The introduction to the meat chapter extols the type of food as an important source of protein, while the chapters of fruit and vegetable recipes make no mention of the nutritional value of these foods. Though these days more Cubans incorporate fruits and vegetables into their diet, the heavy preference for meat is still prevalent.

In the case of a party or celebration, ham or chicken *croquetas* and *ensalada fría* (pasta salad) are considered essential. For New Year's Eve, roasted pork and rice and beans (along with root vegetables, salad, and fried plantains) is the standard meal. While the aforementioned *ajiaco* has historically been considered the national dish, it is not prepared as frequently because of its numerous ingredients and long and complicated preparation.

Street food options have increased dramatically in recent years, along with private restaurants. The most common street food is some kind of sandwich (with ham, cheese, omelet, croquette, pork, or hamburger). Fritters are also extremely popular. Pizza, an affordable option, has become ubiquitous among young people. A more typical traditional home meal sold as street food is *la cajita* (the little box), which consists of rice, beans, meat, a boiled root vegetable, and salad. Other common street food includes sweets, juices, *refrescos* (sodas from a packaged powder, carbonated drinks, or watered-down juice), and milkshakes.

There are many farmers' markets, known as *agromercados*, or *el agro*, that sell fruits and vegetables. They are located in every neighborhood in the city and throughout the island, and vary from a small stand with just a couple of products, to a larger market with up to thirty different vendors. These markets are both State-run and private. There are also *organopónicos*, small urban farms that sell fresh produce, and started in the 1990s in response to the severe economic crisis. The Cuban government passed laws and resolutions to encourage food production in and around the cities, and distributed resources to initiate and sustain this urban agriculture.

In life, each person feels that there are certain activities that attract him or her more than others. In my case, I loved watching my two grandmothers, Rosa and Teté, competing with each other to see who made the best flan or pudding, and observing their passion for cooking. As a young woman in 1978, I went to college in Ukraine, where I studied Technological Engineering of Social Food Systems. When I returned to Cuba, I worked in the Office of Social Food Systems and Gastronomy in the Ministry of Internal Trade with renowned chefs Laura Gil and Bartolo Cárdenas. My youngest daughter is named Laura in honor of this chef. I also took many cooking courses at that time. From 1992–2006, I was a Director and Chef at the Eco-Restorán El Bambú, the first vegetarian restaurant in Cuba, located at the Botanical Garden of Havana. It was there that I learned to cook with the enormous variety of edible plants that grow in my country, some of which have only recently been incorporated into the Cuban diet.

Given my experience with edible plants and as a food technologist, a television channel proposed that I host the cooking show *Con sabor* to demonstrate a type of healthy and natural cooking. This work gave me the opportunity to learn more about the food preferences of the Cuban people and broaden my knowledge about our culinary roots. I also demonstrated more than 350 recipes, which were well received by the viewers.

When I began my master's degree in Higher Education Sciences, I became involved with a program for elderly learners, and created a program about food culture for them. This was the field work for my thesis. I taught a workshop on traditional and current Cuban cooking seen through the eyes of our grandparents' generation. I learned so much from my students and am still close to many of them today. Through this work, I realized that I love teaching, and I continue giving food culture classes each year through the Biology Department at the University of Havana.

My environmental values led me to become involved with Slow Food International, and in 2012 I was elected the International Councilor for Cuba and the Caribbean. Our work includes intense exchanges between chefs and farmworkers. It has given me the chance to learn about other food cultures and ways of production. The phrase that American farmer and poet Wendell Berry said resonates with me: "Eating is an agricultural act." Two of the people I most admire are Carlo Petrini, the president of Slow Food, and Alice Waters, for her work promoting school gardens.

At home, I love cooking for everyone when I have the time. My husband Omar also loves cooking, and of my three children, Vasili, Olga, and Laura, I believe that Olga has a natural talent for the culinary arts. Vasili and Laura help critique my food with their refined palates. My brother, Ernesto, also cooks from the heart.

I truly enjoy the art of cooking and thinking about food. I have an extensive collection of food-related books. My father, in addition to his work as an architect, was also a book vendor all his life, so I grew up surrounded by thousands of books in our home. He patiently set aside any cookbooks that he came across, and today, they have turned into some of my greatest treasures. They have helped me understand Cuban cooking, which never stops finding new ways to transcend time and confront adversities.

FROM IMOGENE

I grew up in Oakland, California, and moved to Cuba as an adult, after visiting several times and deciding that I wanted to make it home. Soon after I moved there in 2010, it became clear to me how important food was as a source of pleasure to be shared among family and friends, as a topic of conversation, and as something that was not always easy to find. I was struck by how much people talked about food. This helped me at first as I got used to buying typical Cuban foods at the markets; I was always appreciative of a random stranger who would comment to me about the good or bad quality of a certain product, or point out the best way to select something. The challenge of obtaining the food one is looking for lends itself to increased communication about the topic. My neighbors are constantly telling me where they found perfect mangoes or good *vianda*. On the contrary, they also inform me when they have returned unsuccessful from an *agromercado* with limited selection, so I know not to bother with my food procurement at that particular market.

The interrogation that I received from almost everybody I met about being an American who moved to Cuba often included the question, "Do you know how to cook Cuban food?" When I replied that I was learning, the other person would generally offer me a selection of recommended recipes. What caught my attention was how strictly people seemed to follow most recipes, with little room for improvisation or substitution. I remember once roasting some beets in my oven when a neighbor came in and asked what I was doing. After I explained, she categorically informed me that beets are boiled, not roasted. Apparently, she thought there was only one way to prepare them. This strict attitude generally applies to the most classic recipes, such as bean soup, *congrí*, or *moros y cristianos*. However, this rigidity is in stark contrast to the enormous flexibility and creativity that Cubans show in the face of scarce ingredients and limited options. While there is often a diet of limited variety among the population, in recent years, the culinary arts in restaurants have evolved by leaps and bounds in Cuba.

In 2011, I helped organize a delegation of chefs from California that came to Cuba for a culinary exchange. The majority of these chefs had worked at Alice Waters's Berkeley, California, restaurant Chez Panisse, and were able to apply the food philosophy learned there to the workshops and meals created during their visit to Cuba. The importance of making delicious meals from the ripest produce obtainable is very applicable to Cuba. These chefs were taught to go to the market first to see what was available, and then create a meal from those products, instead of following a recipe. Through the activities of this delegation, I observed an interesting paradigm: The rigid food culture of many Cubans (who might not be willing to try new or different food) coexists with the blossoming innovations of new culinary styles, enjoyed by other parts of the population that have become more open-minded. The delegation of Californian chefs occurred around the beginning of a dramatic expansion of private restaurants in Cuba, and we worked with chefs from both the State and private sector.

The initial delegation of chefs from California was followed up with smaller delegations of chefs from the United States who taught workshops to Cuban chefs, generally very receptive to new approaches. A few years later, some of the people involved with the initial delegation, plus Madelaine and myself, went on a research trip to Baracoa, where the cuisine is unique as a result of the city's geographic location and isolation. This trip gave us a head start on research for this book before we had any idea we would be writing it. I continued food-related research when I got a master's degree in Interdisciplinary Studies of Cuba and the Caribbean at the University of Havana. My thesis examined the history of gastronomy in Cuba, specifically over the last thirty-five years, and the intersection of food culture and the growing private sector.

ABOUT THE BOOK

The respective food-related work that we had done prepared us to embark on the project of compiling *Cuba: The Cookbook*, which Phaidon commissioned us to create. We knew we wanted to focus on both traditional cooking and new culinary tendencies. It is important to note that many of the more traditional recipes have been lost over the years for various reasons, so we prioritized the recuperation of this valuable knowledge. We took advantage of Madelaine's extensive culinary library to rescue some of these treasures and interviewed Cuban chefs and the elderly, who have extensive knowledge and experience in home cooking. For more modern dishes, we used some recipes from *Con sabor,* Madelaine's cooking show. We had surveyed hundreds of people for our theses and other research.

In addition to the surveys and research, it is important to note that the constant conversation in our daily lives about food and recipes gave us lots of information. Considering our different backgrounds, we complemented each other well to achieve a balanced end product, and the research and writing of the book reinforced our recognition of the individuality of Cuban food. As we say before our meals here, "*¡Buen provecho!*"

THE CUBAN PANTRY

La despensa cubana

This book is a compilation of traditional home-cooking recipes, so the ingredients used are those typically found in Cuba. While some of the products are well known internationally, others are very specific to the region and may need explanation. We have offered alternatives for ingredients that might be hard to find outside Cuba, while maintaining the authenticity of the recipes.

The potatoes, onions, garlic, and tomatoes in Cuba are all smaller than in many countries. While the recipes usually specify the size, they should be adjusted accordingly with the general assumption that the Cuban products tend to be small.

Many of the recipes in this book call for cooking in a *baño de maría* (more commonly called by its French name, bain-marie). This is a method in which a pan or dish of food is placed in a larger pot or pan, which contains hot water that comes up the sides of the smaller pan. In the oven, the water bath tempers the heat and makes for gentler, more even cooking. On the stovetop, if the larger pot is tightly covered, the food is cooked with the even heat of steam. In classic Cuban cookbooks, the *baño de maría* is used both on the stovetop and in the oven. However, in Cuban home kitchens today, flans and other desserts are most frequently put into pans that close hermetically in water in a pressure cooker and cooked on the stovetop. The preference for the stovetop is because Cuban home kitchens have not historically had ovens. Even after they became more common, the custom to use the stovetop has remained very prevalent, and many Cubans use their ovens to store pots and pans, using them sporadically for special occasions.

Bitter orange (*Citrus aurantium*, also known as a Seville orange) is commonly grown in Cuba and used frequently for *mojo*, or dressings, poured over meats or cooked root vegetables. A very simple *mojo* can be made with garlic and bitter orange juice—a variation on the classic garlic and lime juice combination. Some chefs recommend mixing two parts sweet orange juice with one part grapefruit juice and one part lime juice, to imitate the flavor of the bitter orange.

BREAD

Cuban bread is an airier version of French bread, with a hard crust on the outside, and a soft inside. Soft rolls are also very common and distributed daily to all individuals by the State rationing system. There is also a long, soft bread in the shape of a baguette, but with the consistency of the soft roll. Other types of bread are produced on a smaller scale, but the recipes in this book generally call for one of the breads mentioned here.

CHEESE

The most commonly produced cheese in Cuba is *queso blanco criollo*, or Cuban white cheese, made by farmers and others who live in the countryside. It is made from the raw milk of a recently milked cow. The cleaned, salted, and dried stomach (a coagulant) of a slaughtered pig or cow is added after being salted and dried. This sours the milk, which is then put into a receptacle lined with cheesecloth, topped with a brick or weight of some kind, and then drained and aged for at least twelve hours. In the city, people make homemade cheese by boiling raw milk and adding vinegar and/or lime juice. This homemade white cheese has a mild taste and is similar to queso fresco, which can be found at any Latino grocery store.

The industrial production of cheese in Cuba began in 1920 in the former regions of Las Villas, Camagüey, and Oriente. Through 1965, the cheeses produced in Cuba included *patagrás*, an aged, cured and pressed cheese, and fresh cream cheese. Cheese production was further developed starting in 1968. The types of cheeses that have been produced and sold since then are: Azul Atabey, Mar Azul, and Guaicanamar, blue cheeses with a strong taste; Caribe, which has a compact, stretchy texture; mozzarella, made from cow's milk with a stringy texture; Cumanayagua, a yellow cheese with a hard outside, good for pastas or oven-roasted dishes; and Santa Cruz, a semi-hard cheese. The most commonly sold cheeses now are Caribe, Cuban "Gouda," cream cheese, and various processed cheeses.

CHICKEN

Many of the recipes in this book call for cooked chicken. In Cuba, it is most common to boil chicken legs in order to stretch the bird into two meals: the meat is used for preparations such as croquettes, pasta salads, and stews, and the broth is used for preparations such as soups, rice, and sauces. Typically, the chicken legs are combined with 6⅓ cups (50 fl oz/1.5 liters) salted water, garlic, onions, *chay* pepper, carrots, parsley, ground black pepper, cumin, bay leaf, and oregano and cooked, covered, over medium heat for 35 minutes. It is also fine to substitute with a store-bought roasted chicken or other chicken leftovers.

COCONUT

Various recipes call for grated or shredded coconut. This refers to the grated or shredded meat of a dry, but *fresh* coconut. The inside has dried naturally (the coconut water has evaporated while on the tree), but it has not been processed in any way. If fresh coconuts are not available, this ingredient can be substituted with the same amount of dried shredded coconut or flakes.

CUBAN LIME

Limón criollo, or Cuban lime, is a small lime with a yellowish color when ripe. It is very juicy and acidic and measures 1–1½ inches (2.5–3.5 cm) in diameter. It can be substituted with regular limes.

CUBAN OREGANO

Cuban oregano (Mexican mint) is a common herb in Cuba. It has a delicate flavor that is reminiscent of lemon or lime, and can be grown easily at home in pots.

CULANTRO

Culantro (*Eryngium foetidum*), not to be confused with cilantro (coriander), is a plant indigenous to Cuba that grows close to the ground in humid areas. It has long leaves with jagged edges, a strong smell, and is used to season soups, fish, and black beans.

FLOUR

The recipes call for all-purpose (plain) flour. In Cuba, white flour is less processed and coarser than in other countries. It has a low gluten content and is moist, because of the climate.

MAÍZ MOLIDO

Maíz molido, or ground corn, is commonly found at farmers' markets in Cuba. It is simply the fresh tender corn kernels of field corn ground into a moist, yellow paste. It is used for tamales both in husks and in bowls (a thick cornmeal stew served in a bowl, sometimes called a tamale or cornmeal casserole). It can be found in Latino grocery stores.

MILK

OIL

Cow's milk in Cuba used to be sold pasteurized (heated to 194°F/90°C), but it was recommended that consumers boil it again to kill possible remaining bacteria. During the economic crisis of the 1990s, people started to consume more powdered milk; this is still the most common option. Evaporated milk and sweetened condensed milk are also sold. Now it is possible to buy raw cow's milk directly from farmers, but it must be boiled. For the best results, use the type of milk called for in the recipe.

Most of the recipes call for vegetable oil without specifying what kind. Typical Cuban cooking does not use a lot of olive oil because it is quite expensive. While lard was extremely popular in the past, and is still used commonly in the countryside, most home cooking in the city is done with vegetable oil. It doesn't matter what type of vegetable oil you use in the recipes; it could be soy, sunflower, canola (rapeseed), or corn oil. And if you want, you can substitute olive oil for added flavor.

ONIONS

The onion most commonly grown in Cuba is white and small to medium in size, although a small red onion, which has a stronger flavor, is also used.

PEPPERS

Ají refers to many kinds of peppers. The most commonly used is the slightly sweet *chay* pepper, a cone-shaped green pepper 2–3-inches (5–7.5 cm) long that is harvested and used year-round. (In the United States the *ají* chay is called a cubanelle or Italian frying pepper.) Another very common pepper is the *pimiento*, which looks like a small green bell pepper (3–4 inches/8–10 cm) and is indigenous to the tropics. In Cuban cuisine, this pepper is used in pastas, sauces, salads, and is also prepared stuffed and grilled. The *cachucha* pepper is red-orange and is a lantern-shaped pepper as long (¾–1 inch/

2–2.5 cm) as it is wide (¾–1 inch/2–2.5 cm). It is very aromatic with a distinct flavor and a very slight bite. Although Cuban food is generally not spicy, there is one pepper native to Cuba that is used in some recipes. It is known popularly as the *guaguao* pepper (the onomatopoeic sound a barking dog makes). This pepper, which is indigenous to Cuba, is red when it is ripe and is an oblong shape that measures ¾ inch (2 cm) or less in length, and ¼ inch (6 mm) or less in width. Although this pepper is not used as commonly as the others, it is the go-to option for any dish that requires some spiciness.

PUMPKIN

Calabaza (Cucurbita moschata) is a dry, hard pumpkin. Some are round (about 8 inches/20 cm) in diameter, and others have an oblong shape and measure up to 16 inches (40 cm) long. The flesh is yellow-orange. It can be substituted with a butternut squash or other winter squash.

SOFRITO

One of the most important elements in Cuban cooking, referred to many times in the recipes in this book, is the sofrito. This is a basic sauté of onions, garlic, peppers, and tomatoes cooked separately and used to flavor beans, soup, meat, and vegetable dishes.

SUGAR

The white sugar in Cuba is less refined and coarser than sugar that is generally consumed in the international market. The brown sugar in Cuba is a lightly processed, very coarse sugar similar to what is internationally known as raw cane sugar, natural brown sugar, turbinado, or demerera.

TASAJO

Tasajo, dried or dehydrated beef, was originally prepared with horsemeat, but is now more commonly made with beef. To make *tasajo*, the meat is first submerged into brine, then drained, dried, salted, rinsed, and finally laid out in the sun. During this process of dehydration, the *tasajo* loses 50 percent of its moisture. This complex process was developed in Europe to transport large quantities of meat across the Atlantic Ocean to feed the slaves in the colonies. Although

tasajo was thought of as slave food, it eventually became incorporated into the diet of the elites, and has since been considered a very typical dish in Cuba.

The custom to prepare *tasajo* has been lost over the years due to problems with accessibility, but it can still be found in some specialty grocery stores and restaurants and is included because it was an important part of the Cuban diet for many years.

TOCINO

Tocino is best translated as salt pork. The cut always includes the skin and is dry-salted. A good substitute for *tocino* is salt pork or sliced bacon (streaky).

TOMATO SAUCE

Tomato sauce (seasoned passata) is extremely common in Cuban cooking. While there is a homemade version in the sauces and dressings chapter (page 323), the tomato sauce called for in the majority of the recipes refers to a canned sauce that has a medium density and is usually flavored with salt, garlic, and onions. Many Cubans also make homemade tomato paste (tomato puree) by boiling very ripe tomatoes, blending them with garlic, onion, and other spices, straining the mixture, and cooking it for about 10 minutes to thicken it.

VINEGAR

When the recipes call for vinegar, it generally refers to white vinegar, which is the most common in Cuba, but other types of vinegar can be used if desired. In Cuba, it is also very common to make homemade vinegars by fermenting banana or pineapple peels or rice.

PRESSURE COOKERS

A common kitchen appliance in an average Cuban home is the pressure cooker. Some homes still boast the pressure cookers from the era of Soviet presence on the island. These *ollas rusas*, or "Russian pots," had one pressure valve and one safety valve. Later, pressure cookers with three valves were sold across the island and now many homes have electric pressure cookers, which have the benefit of turning off automatically. The pressure cooker is very popular and is seen as extremely convenient because it greatly reduces the cooking time of a dish. It can cook soups in 10–15 minutes, several types of vegetables in around 6 minutes, various types of meats in 10–20 minutes, beans in about 45 minutes, lentils in 20 minutes, and chickpeas in 20–30 minutes. The legumes group is especially important because it is considered a staple of the Cuban diet and consumed daily by many families, but can require lengthy cooking times if cooked without pressure. When following the recipes in this book, it is important to account for the difference in cooking times if you are not using a pressure cooker, which can be up to an additional 2 hours for cooking beans.

CAFETERIA III CATEGORIA.
El Paradero

P/c HAMBURGUESA 2.00 127G	RON BARTOLOMÉ 57.00 700ML
P/c FRITA 97G 1.00	
PAN C/ CROQUETA 0.60 80 G	CIGARRO TITANI -U- 0.35
REF VITAMINADO 1.00 252 ML	CIGARRO TITANIC (c) 7.00
YOGOURT _BOLSA_ c/u 3.00	CIGARRO CRIOLLO (c) 7.00
YOGOUT 232ML 0.75	CIGARRO CRIOLLO 0.35 c/u
REF. DE LIMÓN 10.00 355 ML	CIGARRO POPULAR CAJA 7.00
REF TÚ KOLA 2LT 10.00	CIGARRO POPULAR c/u 0.35
	TABACO -U- 1.00
	VINO TINTO 50.00 750 ML

APPETIZERS AND SNACKS

Entrantes y meriendas

Most of the recipes in this chapter are for dishes that are served as appetizers in restaurants and in homes, or as snacks between meals. Some are often served at parties and social occasions, and others are purchased from food stands in the street. While Cuban food culture does not include as much snacking as in other countries, many of these dishes are often consumed between meals or instead of meals. The recipes for crepes and arepas in this chapter are considered snacks or breakfast foods. These recipes are important to Cuban food culture; however, it is important to note that a large percentage of the Cuban population does not commonly eat breakfast at home early in the morning, and instead consumes a cup of coffee and some kind of snack as a breakfast substitute at or near their workplace around 10:00 a.m. For those who do eat it (more likely people who don't work, or have a more leisurely schedule in the morning), a typical breakfast could consist of bread with butter and coffee with milk, and/or a fried egg or scramble of some kind. The custom of skipping breakfast (and the high consumption of sugar) can be traced back to the slaves in Cuba, who were only given *guarapo* (sugarcane water) or just a piece of sugarcane to chew on before working on the plantations.

While the consumption of fruit is both common and increasing among the Cuban population, it is often consumed as a snack at other times of day instead of for breakfast. Fruits are eaten in their natural form, but it is more common to prepare them in juices, smoothies, or bake them in sweets, while bananas are frequently eaten with lunch or dinner. Eggs are also very common in the Cuban diet (see pages 258–274) and are often consumed for lunch or dinner, as well as for breakfast.

The arepas and crepe recipes came to Cuba through foreign influences, specifically North American and Russian. Arepas are prepared in Cuban homes for both breakfast and snacks, while crepes are more likely to be found in restaurants.

Fruit and seafood cocktails are very common appetizers, both in restaurants and in homes. The fruit cocktails are an especially refreshing option to eat in the heat, and are often served at birthday parties.

The fried foods (fritters, croquettes, fried banana chips, and so on) are extremely common and popular. These dishes are found in both restaurants and in typical homes.

Sandwiches are an important part of the Cuban diet, although that term is not commonly used. Besides the famous Cuban sandwich, the other recipes are usually referred to as *pan con algo*, or "bread with something," and are seen as something eaten in lieu of a proper meal. For example, these options can be purchased at food stands when people need to eat something to take the place of a proper meal of rice, beans, meat, and salad. This category of snacks is also served at parties or taken on picnics or other outings.

FISH COCKTAIL WITH LIME

Cóctel de pescado al limón

In a medium container, combine the fish, salt, pepper, and lime juice. Set aside, covered, in the refrigerator.

Bring a medium pot of water to a boil. Cut an "x" into the skin at the blossom end of the tomatoes and submerge them in the boiling water for 1 minute. Transfer to a cutting board and remove the skin (peeling at the incision). Halve, seed, and finely dice. Transfer to a small bowl and add the mayonnaise, onion, and scallions (spring onions).

On a serving dish or in 4 individual cocktail glasses, arrange the spinach leaves. Top with the fish and drizzle with the sauce and tabasco sauce (if using). Garnish with orange supremes, lime slices, or parsley sprigs.

PREPARATION TIME: 15 MINUTES
COOKING TIME: 10 MINUTES
SERVES: 4

2 cups (460 g) cooked fish, such as red snapper, king mackerel, swordfish, or a freshwater fish, cut into ¾ inch (2 cm) pieces
½ teaspoon salt
¼ teaspoon ground black pepper
1 tablespoon lime juice
2 small tomatoes
½ cup (115 g) mayonnaise, store-bought or homemade (page 318)
1 small white onion, finely chopped
1 bunch scallions (spring onions), finely chopped
4 spinach leaves
A few drop of tabasco sauce (optional)
Orange supremes, lime slices, or sprigs parsley, for serving

FRESH FRUIT COCKTAIL

Cóctel de frutas naturales

PREPARATION TIME: 15 MINUTES, PLUS CHILLING TIME OF 2 HOURS

SERVES: 4–6

★

1 cup (165 g) diced mango
1 cup (140 g) diced pineapple
8 grapefruit supremes
10 orange supremes
1 cup (165 g) diced papaya
1 tablespoon lime juice
1 cup (8 fl oz/240 ml) Simple Syrup (page 323)
5 sprigs spearmint

In a large bowl, combine the mango, pineapple, grapefruit, orange, and papaya. Add the lime juice and simple syrup and stir gently with a wooden spoon. Refrigerate 2 hours, until cold.

Serve in wine or water glasses with a sprig of spearmint.

Note: Banana, guava, and melon can also be added.

FRUIT COCKTAIL WITH GUAVA JUICE

Cóctel de frutas con jugo de guayaba

PREPARATION TIME: 30 MINUTES

SERVES: 6

★

2 medium guavas (3½ oz/100 g each), peeled and cut into large pieces
2 cups (16 fl oz/500 ml) ice water
3 tablespoons raw cane sugar or honey
3 medium bananas, cut into small pieces
1 cup (140 g) diced pineapple
1 lime, halved
Mint leaves, for garnish

In a blender, combine the guavas, ice water, and raw sugar and blend until smooth. Strain the guava juice through a fine-mesh sieve.

In a serving bowl, gently toss together the bananas, pineapple, and guava juice. Squeeze the lime juice over the fruit and garnish with mint.

SHRIMP COCKTAIL

Cóctel de camarones

**PREPARATION TIME: 15 MINUTES,
PLUS 1 HOUR TO COOL
COOKING TIME: 5 MINUTES
SERVES: 4**

4 tablespoons ketchup
4 tablespoons mayonnaise, store-
bought or homemade (page 318)
1 teaspoon salt
40 medium shrimp (prawns)
(about 1 lb/450 g total),
peeled and deveined
1 lime, cut into 4 wedges

In a small bowl, combine the ketchup and mayonnaise. Set the sauce aside.

Bring a large pot of water with the salt to a boil. Add the shrimp (prawns) and cook for 3 minutes. Remove and refrigerate for 1 hour.

Divide the shrimp among 4 cups, pour the sauce on top of the shrimp, and finish with a squeeze of lime.

LOBSTER COCKTAIL

Cóctel de langosta

**PREPARATION TIME: 10 MINUTES
SERVES: 4**

4 tablespoons ketchup
4 tablespoons mayonnaise, store-
bought or homemade (page 318)
2 cups (1 lb/450 g) diced cooked
lobster
1 lime, cut into 4 wedges

In a small bowl, combine the ketchup and mayonnaise. Divide the lobster among 4 cocktail glasses, pour the sauce over the lobster and finish with a squeeze of lime.

CHICKEN COCKTAIL

Cóctel de pollo

In a large bowl, toss the chicken with the salt, black pepper, and lime juice. In a small bowl, combine the mayonnaise, tomato sauce (seasoned passata), onion, bell pepper, and scallions (spring onions).

On a platter or in 4 individual cocktail glasses, arrange the lettuce leaves. Top with the chicken and drizzle with the sauce and tabasco sauce (if using). Garnish with orange supremes, lime slices, or parsley sprigs.

PREPARATION TIME: 15 MINUTES
SERVES: 4

2 cups (460 g) diced cooked
chicken (see page 19)
½ teaspoon salt
¼ teaspoon ground black pepper
1 tablespoon lime juice
½ cup (115 g) mayonnaise, store-
bought or homemade (page 318)
2 tablespoons tomato sauce
(seasoned passata) or ketchup
1 medium white onion, diced
1 red bell pepper, diced
1 small bunch scallions (spring
onions), finely chopped
4 lettuce leaves
A few drops of tabasco sauce
(optional)
Orange supremes, lime slices,
or sprigs parsley, for serving

SPRING SALAD

Ensalada primavera

Divide the mayonnaise among three separate bowls. Stir the ketchup into one, the mustard into a second, the *cachucha* peppers into the third.

Arrange the tomatoes, cucumber, and greens on a serving tray and serve with the 3 dipping sauces.

PREPARATION TIME: 20 MINUTES
SERVES: 4

½ cup (115 g) mayonnaise, store-
bought or homemade (page 318)
1 teaspoon ketchup
½ teaspoon mild mustard
2 cachucha peppers or cubanelles,
thinly sliced
2 large tomatoes, quartered
1 small cucumber, halved
lengthwise and cut crosswise into
half-moons
2 cups (160 g) greens,
such as lettuce, bok choy,
collard greens, or cabbage

CORN AREPAS

Arepas de maíz

PREPARATION TIME: 10 MINUTES
COOKING TIME: 20 MINUTES
SERVES: 4

1 cup (400 g) maíz molido (ground
fresh corn, see page 20)
½ cup (4 fl oz/125 ml) whole milk
1 egg, whisked
2 tablespoons all-purpose
(plain) flour
1 teaspoon salt
5 tablespoons vegetable oil
1 cup (120 g) finely diced
vegetables (see Note)

Arepas are very similar to crepes, but are smaller in size.
They are consumed in Cuba for both breakfast and as
snacks, and probably come from the North American
culinary influence, which includes pancakes and hotcakes.
After the Cuban Revolution in 1959, the custom was taken up
again with the "boxed arepas," a common fast-food option
in the 1970s and 1980s, influenced by the presence
of the USSR.

In a medium bowl, combine the ground corn, milk, egg,
flour, salt, and 1 tablespoon of the oil and gently mix with
a wooden spoon. Set aside.

In a medium heavy-bottomed frying pan, heat 1 tablespoon
of the oil over medium heat. Add the vegetables and sauté
until they are cooked al dente, about 5 minutes. Transfer to
a bowl and set aside.

In the same frying pan, heat 2 tablespoons of oil, being
sure to spread it around to cover the whole pan, over
low-medium heat. Add the batter by tablespoons to make
arepas 2¾–3 inches (7–8 cm) in diameter and cook until
browned on each side, 2–3 minutes. Add the remaining
1 tablespoon oil as needed when the frying pan is dry.
Transfer to a plate and cover with the sautéed vegetables.
Serve hot.

*Note: Use carrot, pumpkin, bell pepper, scallions (spring
onions), onion, eggplant (aubergine), or potatoes, depending
on the season.*

STUFFED AREPAS

Arepas rellenas

**PREPARATION TIME: 10 MINUTES,
PLUS 30 MINUTES RESTING TIME
COOKING TIME: 30 MINUTES
MAKES: 15–18 AREPAS**

1 cup plus 2 tablespoons (160 g)
all-purpose (plain) flour
2 eggs
1 cup (8 fl oz/240 ml) whole milk
1 tablespoon (15 g) butter,
at room temperature
2 tablespoons raw cane sugar
¼ teaspoon salt
Vegetable oil, for cooking
4 oz (120 g) cream cheese
(see Note)
Honey or chocolate syrup,
for serving

Pour the flour into a wide, shallow bowl and make a well in the center of the mound. Crack the eggs and pour them into the well. Stir gently with a wooden spoon to break up the eggs. Begin incorporating some of the flour, stirring in enough to make a loose batter. Gradually pour in the milk while incorporating the rest of the flour, then add the softened butter, raw sugar, and salt. Mix until the dry ingredients are incorporated and a loose batter is achieved; there will be some lumps of soft butter. Set aside for 30 minutes.

In a medium heavy-bottomed frying pan, heat 1 tablespoon of the oil over medium-high heat. Add the batter in 2-tablespoon scoops to make arepas 2¾–3 inches (7–8 cm) in diameter and cook until browned on both sides, 2–3 minutes total. Transfer to a plate lined with paper towel and cover with a tea towel while you continue cooking the rest of the arepas, adding more oil as necessary.

Spread a generous 1 teaspoon of the cream cheese on half of the arepas and cover with the other half. Drizzle with honey or chocolate syrup and serve hot.

Note: Instead of cream cheese and honey or chocolate syrup, you can use jam, finely chopped sautéed vegetables, or vegetable puree.

STUFFED CREPES

Crepas rellenas

Pour the flour into a wide bowl and make a well in the center of the mound. Pour the whole egg and egg yolks into the well and stir gently with a wooden spoon. Gradually pour in the milk. Add 1 tablespoon (15 g) of the softened butter and ¼ teaspoon salt and mix to make a smooth batter. Strain through a fine-mesh sieve into a clean bowl and set aside to rest for 15 minutes.

In a nonstick medium frying pan, heat the remaining 2 tablespoons (30 g) butter over medium heat. Add the bread cubes and cook, stirring occasionally, until evenly browned, 12–14 minutes. Transfer to a medium bowl to cool slightly. Add the cheese and basil and toss gently to combine. Season to taste with salt. Set aside the filling.

Wipe out the frying pan and heat 2 teaspoons of the vegetable oil over medium heat. Pour in ¼ cup (60 ml) batter per crepe and cook until lightly browned on both sides, 1½–2 minutes. Transfer to a warm plate or baking sheet and cover with a dry tea towel while you continue making more crepes, using the remaining 1 teaspoon oil.

Fill each crepe with 4–5 tablespoons of filling, then roll up like a burrito and return them to the frying pan seam side down. Cook over low heat until the crepe is crispy and the cheese is melted, turning once, 6–8 minutes. Transfer to plates or a platter and garnish with the parsley. Serve hot.

PREPARATION TIME: 20 MINUTES, PLUS 15 MINUTES RESTING TIME
COOKING TIME: 30 MINUTES
MAKES: 8 CREPES

1 cup plus 2 tablespoons (160 g)
all-purpose (plain) flour
1 egg
2 egg yolks
1¼ cups (10 fl oz/295 ml)
whole milk
3 tablespoons (45 g) very soft butter
Salt
6 oz (170 g) bread, crusts
removed, cut into ½-inch (1.25 cm)
cubes
7 oz (200 g) Cuban white cheese
or queso fresco, cut into ¼-inch
(6 mm) dice
Leaves of 1 sprig basil, finely
chopped
3 teaspoons vegetable oil
Finely chopped parsley,
for serving

FISH CEVICHE
WITH VEGETABLES

Crudo de pescado con vegetales

**PREPARATION TIME: 45 MINUTES,
PLUS 9 HOURS 20 MINUTES
MARINATING TIME
SERVES: 4**

★

1 lb (460 g) red snapper (or other
white fish) fillets, diced
1½ cups (12 fl oz/375 ml) lime juice
2 chay peppers or cubanelles,
diced
1 medium white onion, diced
4 cloves garlic, minced
2 medium tomatoes, cut into
quarter rounds
1 cup (200 g) green beans, cut into
1 inch (2.5 cm) pieces
2 tablespoons vegetable oil
1 tablespoon salt
¼ teaspoon ground black pepper
1 tablespoon chopped cilantro
(coriander), parsley, or culantro
1 cup (75 g) mixed greens, such as
lettuce, cabbage, or bok choy

In a nonreactive container, combine the fish and lime juice. Cover and refrigerate for 8 hours.

Add the *chay* peppers, onion, garlic, tomatoes, beans, oil, salt, and black pepper and mix thoroughly. Cover and refrigerate for 1 hour.

Add the cilantro (coriander), adjust the seasoning, and set aside for 15–20 minutes.

Before serving, drain the fish and vegetable mixture. Serve on a bed of mixed greens.

Note: This recipe can also be prepared with a freshwater fish.

FRIED GREEN PLANTAINS

Tostones

**PREPARATION TIME: 15 MINUTES
COOKING TIME: 30 MINUTES
SERVES: 4**

★

2 cups (16 fl oz/500 ml)
vegetable oil, for deep-frying
3 large green plantains, peeled,
ends trimmed, and cut into slices
1¼ inches (3 cm) thick
½ teaspoon salt

According to Esteban Rodríguez Herrera, a famous Cuban linguist, the term *tostón* is used commonly in the Cuban province of Camagüey, while in Havana they historically called this dish *plátanos fritos a puñetazos* (punched fried plantains), in Vueltabajo they call it *ambuila* or *sambuila*, and in the Eastern provinces, they are known as *tostones* or *chatinos*.

★

In a medium heavy-bottomed pan, heat the oil over medium heat. Carefully add the plantains and fry until soft, about 5 minutes. Transfer to a plate lined with paper towels to drain the excess oil. Smash the plantains with the bottom of a glass or with your hand, using a paper towel to soak up the oil, until about ⅓ inch (1 cm) thick. Return to the pan and fry until browned, 1–2 minutes. Transfer to a serving plate and sprinkle with the salt. Serve hot.

GREEN PLANTAIN CHIPS

Chicharritas o mariquitas de plátano

PREPARATION TIME: 10 MINUTES,
PLUS 30 MINUTES TO SOAK
COOKING TIME: 30 MINUTES
SERVES: 6

★

2 teaspoons salt
2 large green plantains, peeled
and cut into slices ⅟₁₆ inches
(2 mm) thick
2 cups (16 fl oz/500 ml)
vegetable oil, for deep-frying

Fill a bowl with water and season with ½ teaspoon of the salt. Add the plantains and let soak for 30 minutes. This helps to prevent them from sticking to one another and also seasons them.

In a medium heavy-bottomed pan, heat the oil over high heat until very hot. (Drop a little piece of bread in the oil and it will begin to brown if the oil is hot enough.) Reduce the heat to medium so as not to burn the food and carefully add the plantains. Fry, stirring occasionally with a skimmer, until lightly browned, about 8 minutes. Transfer to a serving dish and sprinkle with the remaining 1½ teaspoons salt. Serve hot.

Note: The traditional way to prepare the plantains is by cutting them into rounds.

STUFFED FRIED PLANTAINS

Tostones rellenos

PREPARATION TIME: 20 MINUTES
COOKING TIME: 30 MINUTES
SERVES: 4

★

2 cups (16 fl oz/500 ml) vegetable
oil, for deep-frying
2 medium green plantains, peeled
and cut into slices 1¼ inches
(3 cm) thick
3 oz (80 g) ham, ground
2 oz (50 g) Cuban gouda or other
mild yellow cheese, grated

Preheat the oven to 350°F (180°C/Gas Mark 4). Line a baking sheet with parchment paper.

In a medium heavy-bottomed pan, heat the vegetable oil over medium heat. Carefully add the plantains and fry until softened but not browned, about 5 minutes. Remove, reserving the oil, and let cool.

Make an indent in each plantain (a very typical Cuban method is to put the plantain in a small coffee cup, and then smash it down with the top of a plastic water bottle; this creates the ideal indent and edges). In the same pan, heat the oil over high heat. Carefully add the plantains and fry until browned, 1 minute. Remove and fill each indent with ham and cheese. Transfer to the prepared baking sheet and bake until the cheese is melted, about 1 minute. Serve hot.

Note: The plantains can also be filled with an eggplant (aubergine) spread, avocado, ropa vieja (Shredded Beef, page 204), or vegetable sautés.

PUMPKIN FRITTERS

Frituras de calabaza

PREPARATION TIME: 20 MINUTES
COOKING TIME: 30 MINUTES
MAKES: 15 FRITTERS

1 lb (500 g) pumpkin, peeled,
cut into large pieces
2 cloves garlic, finely chopped
1 tablespoon butter
½ teaspoon salt
5 tablespoons all-purpose (plain)
flour
3 cups (24 fl oz/750 ml) vegetable oil,
for deep-frying

Bring a medium pot of water to a boil. Add the pumpkin and cook until soft, 10–15 minutes. Mash the pumpkin into a puree using a potato masher, fork, pestle, or another similar tool and transfer to a medium bowl. Stir in the garlic, butter, salt, and flour and mix to combine.

In a medium heavy-bottomed pan, heat the oil over medium heat until very hot. Add the pumpkin mixture in tablespoon-size balls and fry until browned on both sides, 3–4 minutes. Drain on paper towels. Serve hot.

TARO ROOT FRITTERS

Frituras de malanga

PREPARATION TIME: 15 MINUTES
COOKING TIME: 30 MINUTES
MAKES: 15 FRITTERS

2 cups (220 g) peeled grated taro
root
3 cloves garlic, finely chopped
1 bunch parsley, finely chopped
1 egg, whisked
½ teaspoon salt
3 cups (24 fl oz/750 ml) vegetable oil,
for deep-frying

In a medium bowl, combine the taro root, garlic, parsley, egg, and salt and gently stir.

In a medium heavy-bottomed pan, heat the oil over medium heat until very hot. Add the taro root mixture in tablespoon-size balls and fry until browned on both sides, 3–4 minutes. Drain on paper towels. Serve hot.

Note: You can add grated onion for more flavor.

TARO ROOT
AND SESAME FRITTERS

Frituras de malanga y ajonjolí

In a medium bowl, combine the taro root, egg, toasted sesame seeds, and salt and gently stir.

In a medium heavy-bottomed pan, heat the oil over medium heat until very hot. Add the taro root mixture in tablespoon-size balls and fry until browned on both sides, 3–4 minutes. Drain on paper towels. Serve hot.

PREPARATION TIME: 15 MINUTES
COOKING TIME: 30 MINUTES
MAKES: 15 FRITTERS

2 cups (200 g) grated peeled
taro root
1 egg, whisked
¼ cup (40 g) sesame seeds,
toasted
½ teaspoon salt
3 cups (24 fl oz/750 ml) vegetable oil,
for deep-frying

CHEESE FRITTERS

Frituras de queso

In a medium bowl, sift together the flour, baking powder, and salt. In another bowl, stir together the eggs and milk. Add the egg mixture to the flour mixture and gently stir. Add the cheese and stir to combine.

In a medium heavy-bottomed pan, heat the oil over medium heat until very hot. Add the batter in tablespoon-size balls and fry until browned on both sides, about 5 minutes. Drain on paper towels. Serve hot.

PREPARATION TIME: 15 MINUTES
COOKING TIME: 30 MINUTES
MAKES: 15 FRITTERS

1 cup (135 g) all-purpose (plain)
flour
1 teaspoon baking powder
1 teaspoon salt
2 eggs
1 cup (8 fl oz/240 ml) whole milk
1 cup (115 g) grated Cuban gouda
or other mild yellow cheese
3 cups (24 fl oz/750 ml) vegetable oil,
for deep-frying

SAVORY CORN FRITTERS

Frituras de maíz saladas

PREPARATION TIME: 15 MINUTES
COOKING TIME: 30 MINUTES
MAKES: 16 FRITTERS

1½ cups (600 g) maíz molido
(ground fresh corn, see page 20)
2 cloves garlic, finely chopped
2 chay peppers or cubanelles,
finely chopped
½ medium white onion, finely
chopped
1 bunch parsley, finely chopped
1 egg, whisked
½ teaspoon salt
3 cups (24 fl oz/750 ml) vegetable
oil, for deep-frying

In a medium bowl, combine the ground corn, garlic, *chay* peppers, onion, parsley, egg, and salt and gently stir with a wooden spoon.

In a medium heavy-bottomed pan, heat the vegetable oil over medium heat until very hot. Add the corn mixture in tablespoon-size balls and fry until browned on both sides, 3–4 minutes. Drain on paper towels. Serve hot.

BLACK-EYED PEA FRITTERS

Frituras de frijol carita

PREPARATION TIME: 5 MINUTES,
PLUS 2 DAYS BEAN SOAKING TIME
COOKING TIME: 30 MINUTES
MAKES: 10 FRITTERS

1 cup (165 g) dried black-eyed
peas (beans)
2 cloves garlic, roughly chopped
1 bunch scallions (spring onions),
roughly chopped
1 egg
1 teaspoon salt
3 cups (24 fl oz/750 ml) vegetable
oil, for deep-frying

This recipe owes its popularity to the Chinese vendors who sold it in plazas and markets during the first half of the twentieth century.

Soak the black-eyed peas (beans) in water for 2 days, changing the water 2 times per day.

In a blender, combine the black-eyed peas, garlic, scallions (spring onions), egg, and salt and blend until smooth. In a medium heavy-bottomed pan, heat the vegetable oil over medium heat until very hot. Add the mixture in tablespoon-size balls and fry until browned on both sides, about 5 minutes.

SALT COD FRITTERS

Frituras de bacalao

In the Eastern provinces, culantro is used instead of parsley. In Camagüey province, it is common to mix *salsa criolla* into the salt cod stew, which is then added to the fritter batter. In more modern adaptations of these recipes, the fritters can be accompanied with mustard mixed with honey.

★

Soak the salt cod in water for 24 hours, changing the water 3 or 4 times per day to remove the salt.

Bring a medium pot of water to a boil over medium heat. Add the salt cod and boil until softened, 20–25 minutes. Reserving ¼ cup (2 fl oz/60 ml) of the cooking water, drain the cod and set aside to cool. Once cool enough to handle, remove the skin and bones and discard; shred the meat and set aside.

In a frying pan, heat 2 tablespoons oil over medium-low heat. Add the onion and garlic and sauté until the onions are translucent, about 3 minutes. Add the shredded cod and cook for 10–12 minutes. Add the scallion (spring onion), parsley, and white pepper and cook for 1 minute. Add the wine, season to taste with salt, and cook for 1 minute more. Set aside.

In a large bowl, combine the flour, baking powder, and ⅛ teaspoon salt and mix well. Add the eggs, the cod mixture, and the reserved cooking water and stir until the mixture is smooth. Form little 2½ inch (6 cm) balls using 2 spoons.

In a medium heavy-bottomed pan, heat the remaining 3 cups (24 fl oz/750 ml) oil over medium-low heat. Add the cod balls and fry for 5 minutes. Increase the heat to medium and fry until browned, 5–7 minutes. This helps to avoid the fritters being cooked on the outside and raw on the inside. Drain on paper towels. Serve hot.

**PREPARATION TIME: 15 MINUTES,
PLUS 24 HOURS SOAKING TIME
COOKING TIME: 1 HOUR 15 MINUTES
MAKES: 15**

★

1 lb (500 g) salt cod
3 cups (24 fl oz/750 ml)
plus 2 tablespoons vegetable oil
1 large white onion, chopped
1 head garlic, chopped
1 scallion (spring onion), chopped
1 sprig parsley, chopped
1 teaspoon ground white pepper
1 tablespoon dry white wine
Salt
4⅓ cups (585 g) all-purpose
(plain) flour
1 teaspoon baking powder or
baking soda (bicarbonate of soda)
2 eggs, whisked

FISH AND PARSLEY CROQUETTES

Croquetas de pescado al perejil

PREPARATION TIME: 30 MINUTES
COOKING TIME: 45 MINUTES
MAKES: 50 CROQUETTES

1 cup (230 g) cooked ground (minced) fish
2 tablespoons salsa criolla (Cuban Sauce, page 311)
2 cups (16 fl oz/500 ml) stock or water
¼ teaspoon grated nutmeg
1 tablespoon salt
¼ teaspoon ground black pepper
2 cup (270 g) all-purpose (plain) flour
2 tablespoons vegetable oil, plus more for frying
2 eggs, whisked
2½ cups (300 g) dried breadcrumbs
1 cup (90 g) chopped parsley

Heat a small pan over medium heat. Add the ground (minced) fish and the *salsa criolla* and sauté for 2 minutes. Remove and set aside.

In a heavy-bottomed pot, bring the stock, nutmeg, salt, and pepper to a boil. Pour the flour in when the stock begins to boil. Stir with a wooden spoon, reduce the heat to medium, and add the 2 tablespoons oil around the edges of the pot. Add the ground fish and continue stirring until the mixture unsticks from the pot, about 5 minutes. Set the dough aside to cool.

Set up 2 bowls, one with the eggs and one with the breadcrumbs and parsley. Roll the dough into ovals ¾ inch (2 cm) thick and 2 inches (5 cm) long. Dip each cylinder into the eggs followed by the breadcrumb mixture.

In a large heavy-bottomed pot, heat 2 inches (5 cm) oil over medium heat until very hot. Working in batches, add the croquettes and fry, turning regularly, until golden-brown, 3–5 minutes. Drain on paper towels. Serve hot.

HAM CROQUETTES

Croquetas de jamón

PREPARATION TIME: 30 MINUTES,
PLUS 2 HOURS CHILLING TIME
COOKING TIME: 45 MINUTES
MAKES: 20 CROQUETTES

1 cup (8 fl oz/240 ml) whole milk
1¼ cups (165 g) all-purpose (plain) flour
½ teaspoon grated nutmeg
½ teaspoon salt
⅛ teaspoon ground black pepper
5 tablespoons (75 g) butter
¾ cup (120 g) finely diced white onion
1 tablespoon dry white wine
Generous 1¾ cups (230 g) finely chopped ham
2 eggs, whisked
1 cup (100 g) ground crackers (cracker meal)
Canola oil, for deep-frying

In a blender, combine the milk, flour, nutmeg, salt, and pepper and blend until smooth.

In a medium heavy-bottomed pot, heat the butter over low heat. Add the onion and sauté until translucent, about 7 minutes. Add the milk mixture and cook over low heat, stirring constantly with a wooden spoon, until very thick, about 3 minutes. Remove from the heat, add the wine and ham and stir to incorporate. Pour into a bowl and set aside to cool completely, then refrigerate for 2 hours.

Divide the ham mixture into 20 portions (about 1 oz/32 g each) and roll each into cylinders 1 inch (2.5 cm) wide and 2 inches (5 cm) long. Set up 2 bowls, one with the eggs and one with the ground crackers. Dip each cylinder into the eggs, let the excess drip away, then roll in the ground crackers and set aside.

Pour 2 inches (5 cm) oil into a large heavy-bottomed pot and heat to 350°F (180°C). Working in batches, fry the croquettes until golden brown, 3–5 minutes. Drain on paper towels. Serve hot.

CHICKEN CROQUETTES

Croquetas de pollo

PREPARATION TIME: 30 MINUTES
COOKING TIME: 45 MINUTES
MAKES: 50 CROQUETTES

★

1 cup (230 g) cooked ground (minced) chicken
2 tablespoons salsa criolla (Cuban Sauce, page 311)
2 cups (16 fl oz/500 ml) chicken stock
¼ teaspoon grated nutmeg
1 tablespoon salt
¼ teaspoon ground black pepper
2 cups (270 g) all-purpose (plain) flour
2 tablespoons vegetable oil, plus more for frying
2 eggs, whisked
2½ cups (300 g) dried breadcrumbs
1 cup (90 g) chopped parsley

Heat a small pan over medium heat. Add the ground (minced) chicken and the *salsa criolla* and sauté for 2 minutes. Remove and set aside.

In a large heavy-bottomed pot, bring the stock, nutmeg, salt, and pepper to a boil over medium-high heat. Pour the flour in when the stock begins to boil. Stir with a wooden spoon, reduce the heat to medium, and add the 2 tablespoons oil around the edges of the pot. Add the ground chicken and continue stirring until the mixture unsticks from the pot, about 5 minutes. Set the dough aside to cool.

Set up 2 bowls, one with the eggs and one with the breadcrumbs and parsley. Roll the dough into cylinders 1 inch (2.5 cm) thick and 2 inches (5 cm) long. Dip each cylinder into the eggs followed by the breadcrumb mixture.

In a large frying pan, heat 2 inches (5 cm) oil over medium heat until very hot. Working in batches, add the croquettes and fry, turning regularly, until golden-brown, 3–5 minutes. Drain on paper towels. Serve hot.

FRIED WONTONS

Maripositas chinas

In a small bowl, mix the ground (minced) beef or pork with ½ teaspoon salt and the pepper.

In a medium bowl, mound the flour. Make a well in the center of the mound and pour the oil into the well. Mix well with your hands. Add the egg, salt, and wine and gently mix until a soft, uniform texture is achieved. Divide the dough into 8–10 portions. Roll out each portion into a 3½-inch (9 cm) square. Arrange ½ teaspoon of the ground beef in one corner of each square. Form the dough into butterflies by rolling the dough from the corner with the ground beef and twisting the other corners in the opposite direction to form the wings.

In a medium frying pan, heat 2 inches (5 cm) oil over medium heat until very hot. Add the wontons and fry until browned, 3–5 minutes. Serve hot with the sweet and sour sauce.

Note: The filling can also be sautéed vegetables.

PREPARATION TIME: 30 MINUTES
COOKING TIME: 30 MINUTES
MAKES: 8–10 FRIED WONTONS

½ cup (115 g) cooked ground (minced) beef or pork (see Note)
1 teaspoon salt
¼ teaspoon ground black pepper
1 cup (135 g) all-purpose (plain) flour
1½ tablespoons vegetable oil
1 egg, whisked
1 tablespoon dry white wine
Vegetable oil, for deep-frying
Sweet and sour sauce, for serving

FRIED PORK RINDS

Chicharrones

There are various methods used to prepare chicharrones. Some people cook them with water (adding crushed garlic, orange juice, and salt) on low heat until all the water is evaporated. Then they are cooled and fried again. *Chicharrones de viento* or *chicharron de pellejo de puerco* are prepared with just the pig skin, using this same technique, but the pig skin is put out in the sun for several days until it turns into a thick, dry hide before being cooked slowly in lard or salted water. Another technique is to boil the pork rind first, then dry it in the sun, and then fry it in very hot lard just before consuming.

PREPARATION TIME: 20 MINUTES
COOKING TIME: 25 MINUTES
SERVES: 4

1 tablespoon vegetable oil
1 lb (460 g) pork rind, cut into 1–1½-inch (2.5–4 cm) squares
½ teaspoon salt

In a large heavy-bottomed pot, heat the oil over medium heat. Add the pork rind, cover, and cook, stirring occasionally, until all the fat has been rendered out, about 20 minutes. Remove and set aside to cool, reserving the pot with the rendered fat. (Some people put the chicharrones in the freezer for 30 minutes to cool them well.)

Heat the pot with the fat over high heat. Return the chicharrones to the pot and fry until browned, about 3 minutes. Drain off the fat (see Note). Sprinkle with the salt.

Note: The rendered fat can be used for cooking other dishes.

CUBAN TURNOVERS

Empanadillas criollas

**PREPARATION TIME: 25 MINUTES,
PLUS 15 MINUTES RESTING TIME
COOKING TIME: 15 MINUTES
MAKES: 8 TURNOVERS**

★

2½ oz (75 g) ground (minced) pork
1 tablespoon salsa criolla (Cuban
Sauce, page 311)
2 tablespoons dry white wine
2 tablespoons raw cane sugar
1 cup (135 g) all-purpose
(plain) flour
¼ teaspoon salt
5 tablespoons vegetable oil,
plus more for frying

Heat a pan over medium heat. Add the ground (minced) pork and *salsa criolla* and sauté for 2 minutes. Remove and set aside.

In a small pot, heat the wine, raw sugar, and 3 tablespoons water over medium heat until the sugar is dissolved. Set the syrup aside to cool.

In a medium bowl, pour the flour in a mound and add the salt. Make a well in the center and pour the syrup and 5 tablespoons oil in the well. Gently mix, then knead until a smooth dough forms and set aside for 15 minutes.

Divide the dough into 8 equal portions. Roll out each portion with a rolling pin until ⅛ inch (3 mm) thick. Cut out rounds using a small 4 inch (11 cm) coffee saucer. Fill one half of each round with 1 tablespoon of the ground pork, then fold the dough in half and press to seal using a fork.

In a large frying pan, heat 2 inches (5 cm) oil over medium heat until very hot. Working in batches, add the *empanadillas* and fry until golden-brown, 3-5 minutes. Serve hot.

Notes: The filling can also be made of a vegetable sauté, chicken, ham, or cheese. A teaspoon of baking powder can be added to the dough to make it crunchier.

SWEET TURNOVERS

Empanadillas dulces

**PREPARATION TIME: 25 MINUTES,
PLUS 1 HOUR RESTING TIME
COOKING TIME: 15 MINUTES
MAKES: 8–10 TURNOVERS**

★

1 cup (135 g) all-purpose (plain)
flour
1 teaspoon baking powder
¼ teaspoon salt
1 tablespoon raw cane sugar
2 eggs, whisked
2 tablespoons vegetable oil,
plus more for frying
3 tablespoons (45 g) butter,
melted
2 tablespoons dry white wine
⅓ cup (100 g) Guava Marmalade
(page 336)

In a medium bowl, combine the flour, baking powder, salt, and raw sugar and form a mound. Make a well in the center of the mound and place the eggs, 2 tablespoons oil, and melted butter in the well and mix. Add the wine. Knead until a smooth dough forms and set aside, covered, at room temperature for 1 hour. Knead again for a few seconds, adding more flour if the dough is sticky. Roll the dough out with a rolling pin until ⅛ inch (3 mm) thick. Cut out 8 rounds using a small 4 inch (11 cm) coffee saucer. Fill one half of each round with 1 tablespoon of the marmalade, then fold the dough in half and press to seal using a fork.

In a large frying pan, heat 2 inches (5 cm) oil over medium heat until very hot. Working in batches, add the *empanadillas* and fry until golden-brown, 3–5 minutes. Serve hot.

CUBAN FRITA

Frita cubana

PREPARATION TIME: 30 MINUTES
COOKING TIME: 35 MINUTES
MAKES: 14 FRITAS

½ cup (80 g) dried breadcrumbs
½ cup (120 ml) whole milk
1 lb (460 g) beef, cut into chunks
1 dried sausage (about 2 oz/60 g)
1 medium white onion,
coarsely chopped
1 egg, whisked
½ teaspoon paprika
1 teaspoon salt
⅓ cup (2½ fl oz/80 ml) vegetable oil
Small white rolls, ketchup, French
fries, and finely chopped onion, for
serving

According to Chef Jorge Junco Monserrat, the *frita* was created by Sebastián Carro, a Spaniard who sold coal, until he opened a *frita* stand in the 1940s at Zapata and A, in the Vedado neighborhood of Havana. It became extremely popular and spread across the country. *Fritas* were traditionally accompanied by very cold beer, soda, or *malta* (a nonalcoholic derivative of beer fermentation). The *frita* is, without a doubt, the "Cuban hamburger."

★

In a small bowl, combine the breadcrumbs and milk.
In a food processor, combine the beef, sausage, milk-soaked breadcrumbs, and onion and process until roughly ground. Transfer to a large bowl, add the egg, paprika, and salt and mix well with a wooden spoon. Form into 1¾–2 oz (50–55 g) balls. Flatten each ball into a 2⅓-inch (6 cm) patty.

In a medium frying pan, heat the oil over medium heat. Add the patties and fry until browned, about 4 minutes on each side.

Arrange each patty in a white roll with ketchup and top with the finely chopped onion. Serve with French fries on on top or on the side.

CUBAN SANDWICH

Sándwich cubano

PREPARATION TIME: 10 MINUTES
COOKING TIME: 10 MINUTES
SERVES: 3

3 tablespoons mustard
1 loaf Cuban bread (about
12 oz/360 g), ends cut off,
horizontally sliced lengthwise, then
cut crosswise into 3 even sections
about 7 inches (18 cm) each
6 slices ham (about 3½ oz/
95 g total)
9 slices roasted pork
(about 11 oz/320 g total)
9 slices Genoa salami
(about 1½ oz/45 g total)
9 slices Swiss cheese
(about 6 oz/180 g total)
9 slices pickle
½ tablespoon (10 g) butter, melted
6 lettuce leaves, cut into
smaller pieces
1 large tomato, sliced
½ small white onion, sliced
1 teaspoon vinegar
1 teaspoon olive oil
¼ teaspoon salt

There are various theories about the origin of the Cuban sandwich. In one version, the sandwich came from Ybor City, near Tampa, Florida, where there was a Cuban cigar factory in which immigrants from all over the world worked. They all contributed their influences to the sandwich they ate on their breaks; the Italians contributed the salami, the Cubans the roasted pork, the Spanish the ham, and the Germans the pickled cucumbers and mustard. The sandwich is not heated up; the Genoa salami, sweet ham, and pork are marinated in garlic; the cucumbers are pickled in vinegar with dill, and yellow mustard is used. The order in which the ingredients are placed on the bread is important to maximize the flavor. This sandwich was originally prepared to go.

In Miami, it is believed that the sandwich came from Cuba, and was sold in Havana throughout the twentieth century. In Cuba, the sandwich was registered in the food preparation volumes from the National Gastronomy Section of the Ministry of Domestic Commerce in the 1970s, where mortadella is specified instead of salami.

The "Cuban bread" called for is a type of white bread similar to a baguette, with a hard crust on the outside and a soft inside. It tends to be airier than a baguette, and it is the ideal bread for the typical Cuban sandwich (and other snacks).

Spread the mustard on the top half of the 3 sections of bread. On each bottom half, arrange 2 slices of ham, 3 slices of roasted pork, 3 slices of salami, 3 slices of Swiss cheese, and 3 slices of pickle. Finish with the top half of the bread. Brush the outsides of the sandwiches with the melted butter and grill or pan-fry over medium heat until the cheese melts, about 10 minutes.

Meanwhile, in a medium bowl, combine the lettuce, tomato, and onion. Dress with the vinegar, oil, and salt and gently toss.

Cut the sandwiches diagonally. Serve on plates with the salad on the side.

GRILLED CHEESE SANDWICH

Disco volador de queso

PREPARATION TIME: 5 MINUTES
COOKING TIME: 5 MINUTES
MAKES: 1

1 teaspoon butter
1 white bread roll
(about 1½ oz/40 g), split
1 thick slice (about 1 oz/30 g)
Cuban gouda or other mild
yellow cheese

This is a very popular snack in Cuba, frequently consumed by school-aged children. It is very common for Cuban kitchens to have a *platillo volador*, or *disquera* tool—a hinged metal sandwich press with long handles used to grill the sandwiches. Cheese is the most common (and most affordable) ingredient for a grilled sandwich, but other alternatives are: guava paste and white cheese; ham, roasted pork, mortadella, and cheese; ham and Swiss cheese; ground beef and yellow cheese; and turkey and mozzarella cheese. Pickled cucumbers can also be added.

Spread the butter on the outside of each half of the roll, add the cheese, and close the sandwich. Place the sandwich in a *platillo volador* (handheld sandwich press) and cook over medium-low heat until toasted, about 2 minutes on each side. (You can also make this in a panini press or on the stovetop in a frying pan.)

SALT COD SANDWICHES

Bacalao con pan

PREPARATION TIME: 10 MINUTES
SERVES: 4

4 lettuce leaves
8 Salt Cod Fritters (page 45)
4 slices tomato
4 hamburger buns, split open
4 tablespoons salsa criolla (Cuban
Sauce, page 311) or mojo picante
(Spicy Sauce, page 312)

This sandwich is served as a snack in the Eastern provinces, where it is accompanied by coffee or iced lemonade. It was traditionally popular among young people, but the custom to eat *bacalao con pan* has decreased in recent years. The famous song "Bacalao con pan," by the musical group Irakere, was inspired by this dish. Other types of bread (sliced bread, rolls, and so on) can be used. In some places, onion slices are added. In a more modern version of this dish, the *mojo* can be substituted with mustard and a few drops of honey.

Arrange the lettuce, fritters, and tomato on the bottom half of a bun. Brush with the *salsa criolla* or *mojo picante* and top with the other half of the bun.

BREAD WITH SUCKLING PIG

Pan con lechón

This is a very popular snack in Cuba, and is commonly served at parties. It is often accompanied with a cold beer. It is also common to find this snack sold at the Carnaval celebrations in Havana and Santiago de Cuba.

Arrange the pork on the bottom half of the baguettes. Spread the top halves with the *mojo criollo* and close the sandwich.

PREPARATION TIME: 10 MINUTES
SERVES: 4

½ lb (240 g) grilled suckling pig, thinly sliced
4 soft baguettes (about 2 oz/ 60 g each), split lengthwise
4 teaspoons mojo criollo (Cuban Dressing, page 311)

MIXED SNACK

Bocadito surtido

Spread all the bread with the butter. On each of 4 pieces of bread, arrange one-quarter of the ham, roasted pork, mortadella, and cheese. Top each with another slice of bread. Cut the crusts off the sandwich and cut on the diagonal into 2 triangles. Serve with the pickles and finely chopped greens on top.

PREPARATION TIME: 10 MINUTES
SERVES: 4

8 squares slices bread (about 1¼ oz/35 g each)
4 teaspoons (20 g) butter
2 oz (60 g) ham, thinly sliced
2 oz (60 g) roasted pork, thinly sliced
2 oz (60 g) mortadella, thinly sliced
2 oz (60 g) Cuban gouda or other mild yellow cheese, thinly sliced
12 slices pickled cucumber
1 cup (60–80 g) finely chopped lettuce, bok choy, or other greens

VEGETARIAN SNACK

Bocadito vegetariano

PREPARATION TIME: 20 MINUTES
COOKING TIME: 10 MINUTES
SERVES: 4

4 cloves garlic, finely chopped
1 cup (110 g) grated vegetables
(such as carrot, radish,
and cabbage)
Juice of 1 lime
Salt
¼ cup (40 g) raw peanuts
4 oz (120 g) cream cheese,
at room temperature
⅓ cup (80 g) mayonnaise, store-
bought or homemade (page 318)
4 soft white bread rolls
(about 3 oz/80 g each), split open
2 medium tomatoes, sliced
1 teaspoon vegetable oil
4 lettuce leaves, for serving

In a large bowl, mix together the garlic, grated vegetables, lime juice, and salt to taste. Set aside.

With a mortar and pestle or in a blender, roughly crush the peanuts. Transfer to a small bowl and mix in the cream cheese and mayonnaise.

Spread the cream cheese and mayonnaise mixture on the bottom half of each roll and top with the tomato slices and grated vegetables. Put the top half of the rolls on top.

In a large frying pan, heat the oil over low heat. Add the sandwiches and toast until lightly browned on both sides, about 4 minutes. Serve with the lettuce on the side.

CRACKER ASSORTMENT

Galleticas surtidas

PREPARATION TIME: 10 MINUTES
SERVES: 4

2 oz (60 g) ham, thinly sliced
2 oz (60 g) mortadella,
thinly sliced
2 oz (60 g) roasted pork,
thinly sliced
2 oz (60 g) Cuban gouda or other
mild yellow cheese, thinly sliced
16 soda crackers
12 slices pickle

Arrange the ham, mortadella, pork, and cheese on half of the crackers. Top with the remaining crackers and serve with the pickle slices.

BREAD WITH GUAVA PASTE

Pan con timba

This snack was very popular in poor neighborhoods during the nineteenth century and first half of the twentieth century. Its origin traces back to 1874, when the English arrived on the island to install the railroad system that would connect Bejucal to Havana. These Englishmen saw the Cubans eating this snack, and, because of the dark color of the guava paste (prepared with raw cane sugar), they called it "timber ties" in English, in reference to the dark pieces of wood greased with oil used to build the railway. This term was "Cubanized" and turned into *pan con "timba,"* which it is still called today. Despite being associated with economically precarious times, it is a really delicious snack—even better when prepared with Cuban white cheese or cream cheese. This sandwich can also be toasted before serving.

Arrange the guava paste on the bottom half of the baguette. Top with the other half and serve.

PREPARATION TIME: 5 MINUTES
SERVES: 4

1 soft baguette (about 8 oz/230 g),
split lengthwise and cut
into 4 pieces
4 slices guava paste
(about 6 oz/180 g), finely sliced

SOUPS

Sopas

In Cuba, soups are generally served at the beginning of a meal, although they sometimes function as a meal in themselves. Despite the hot climate of Cuba, the consumption of cold soups (from the Spanish influence) is not common, and the general preference is instead for heavy, hot soups.

Ajiaco, a traditional stew, is considered the most genuine and representative of all Cuban dishes. Don Fernando Ortiz (1881–1969), a renowned Cuban anthropologist, ethnologist, archeologist, and journalist, considered *ajiaco* a metaphor for the ethnic mixture of the people of Cuba. The *ají* (peppers) were used by the Taínos, the indigenous people of the island, in a soup they traditionally made during pre-Columbian times. They dipped their *casabe* (a flatbread made from yuca/cassava that served as the staple of the indigenous diet) in the soup. The Spanish culinary influence contributed various meats to this *ají*-based soup, such as pork, beef, dried beef, chicken, and fish. Other ingredients added to the stew come from African influences, including yam, sweet potato, green and ripe bananas, and yellow taro root. The seasonings added, which also have various origins, include onion, garlic, saffron, parsley, cumin, culantro, tomato, lime, and salt. As Ortiz argues, the contributions of the three main ethnic groups make this dish a symbolic melting pot of the Cuban population.

According to oral history, this stew was traditionally prepared collectively in Cuban neighborhoods on June 24 each year, as an initiation of the San Juan festivities.

The stew was prepared in patios or plazas in a large iron cauldron over a fire, and neighbors from the community would bring meat or vegetables to contribute to the dish.

The Villa de Puerto Príncipe seems to be the origin of the *ajiaco*, although a publication from 1956 (*¿Gusta, usted? Prontuario culinario y …necesario*) also refers to *ajiaco bayamés* (which features corn and banana dumplings), *ajiaco cardenense* (which is characterized by finely chopped meat and parsley), *ajiaco campestre* (which uses a dried beef called *Montevideo* and includes mashed pumpkin in the seasoning), and *ajiaco de monte* (with dried beef and lime juice poured over the vegetables). A modern-day version of the *ajiaco* is the *caldosa*, which contains similar ingredients.

Bean soups (*potajes*) are a staple of the Cuban diet. They are either prepared with whole beans in a thick broth or blended like a puree. Other typical Cuban soups are fish soups, which are made with noodles or rice and are most popular in the coastal zones. They are generally colored with *annatto* (achiote), and flavored with the typical sofrito (see page 22) and bay leaves. It is customary to add lime juice to the fish soup just before eating. Chicken noodle soup is also very common. Many Cubans cook chicken by boiling it (see page 19) and use the broth to make this soup. Flour-based cream soups became very popular in the pizza parlors established in the 1970s (see page 136), and are still popular in both restaurants and home cooking today.

HAVANA-STYLE SOUP

Sopa a la habanera

This is an old recipe from nineteenth-century Cuban cuisine, which is rarely prepared in current times. Some recipes suggest the addition of cloves and a cinnamon stick.

★

In a medium pot, heat the stock over medium heat. Add the crushed almonds and cook, stirring regularly, until the stock thickens, about 15 minutes. Arrange strips of bread on the bottom of each of 6 soup bowls and sprinkle with the cheese and parsley. Pour the stock over the bread and serve hot.

PREPARATION TIME: 15 MINUTES
COOKING TIME: 25 MINUTES
SERVES: 6

★

6⅓ cups (50 fl oz/1.5 liters)
beef stock
½ cup (115 g) blanched almonds,
toasted and finely crushed
into a powder
6 slices bread, cut into long 1 inch
(2.5 cm) strips and toasted
1½ cups (150 g) grated Cuban
gouda or other mild yellow cheese
2 tablespoons chopped parsley

ONION SOUP

Sopa de cebolla

In a medium pot, heat the butter over low heat. Add the onion and sauté until translucent, about 3 minutes. Add the stock, salt, and basil and cook over low heat for 15 minutes. Arrange the bread in a serving dish, pour the stock over the bread, and sprinkle with the cheese.

PREPARATION TIME: 15 MINUTES
COOKING TIME: 25 MINUTES
SERVES: 4

4 tablespoons (60 g) butter
1 large white onion, sliced
3 cups (24 fl oz/750 ml) chicken
stock
½ teaspoon salt
½ teaspoon dried basil
1 bread roll (about 2¾ oz/80 g),
cut into small pieces and toasted
4 tablespoons grated Cuban
gouda or other mild yellow cheese

PLANTAIN SOUP

Sopa de plátanos

PREPARATION TIME: 20 MINUTES
COOKING TIME: 45 MINUTES
SERVES: 6

3 medium green plantains,
unpeeled
2 tablespoons vegetable oil
1 medium white onion, diced
2 chay peppers or cubanelles,
finely chopped
4 cloves garlic, finely chopped
1 tablespoon lime juice
5 cups (40 fl oz/1.25 liters)
vegetable stock
2 tablespoons tomato sauce
(seasoned passata)
¼ teaspoon ground cumin
½ tablespoon salt
⅛ teaspoon ground black pepper
½ cup (30 g) chopped scallions
(spring onions)

Plantain soup is very representative of Cuban cuisine, and there are several ways of preparing it. In other recipes for plantain soup, egg yolks or toasted breadcrumbs are added. In the novel *Paradiso*, a work written by the famous Cuban author Jose Lezama Lima, there is a plantain soup served with tapioca and popcorn. This soup can be accompanied by croutons, butter, or grated cheese sprinkled on top.

Bring a large pot of water to a boil. Add the plantains and cook until soft, 15–18 minutes. Let cool, then peel and cut crosswise into pieces about ⅓ inch (1 cm) thick. Set aside.

In a medium frying pan, heat the oil over medium-low heat. Add the onion, *chay* peppers, and garlic and sauté until softend, about 3 minutes. Transfer the sofrito to a blender, add the boiled plantains, lime juice, and 2 cups (16 fl oz/ 500 ml) of the stock, and blend until smooth, about 1 minute. Set aside.

In a large pot, bring the remaining 3¼ cups (25 fl oz/750 ml) of the stock to a boil over medium-high heat. Add the plantain mixture and stir until dissolved, about 2 minutes. Reduce the heat to low and add the tomato sauce (seasoned passata), cumin, salt, and black pepper. Cook, stirring occasionally, until thickened, about 5 more minutes. Serve very hot topped with chopped scallions (spring onions).

CHICKEN NOODLE SOUP

Sopa de pollo con fideos

In a large pot, combine the chicken, onion, *chay* peppers, celery, garlic, ½ teaspoon salt, and 6 cups (48 fl oz/ 1.4 liters) water and cook over medium heat until the chicken is cooked through, about 30 minutes. Add the tomato sauce (seasoned passata) and annatto (achiote) seeds and cook for 3 minutes to blend the flavors. Remove the chicken, let it cool, then remove the meat from the bone and cut it into medium pieces. Strain the broth if you prefer. Return the broth and the chicken to the pot and bring to a boil. Add the carrot and pasta, and cook over medium-low heat until the pasta is al dente. Adjust the salt to taste. Serve hot.

PREPARATION TIME: 25 MINUTES
COOKING TIME: 45 MINUTES
SERVES: 6

½ chicken (about 1½ lb/700 g),
cut into 8 pieces
1 medium white onion, cut into
⅛ inch (3 mm) cubes
2 *chay* peppers or cubanelles,
cut into ⅛ inch (3 mm) cubes
1 stalk celery, cut into ⅛ inch
(3 mm) cubes
3 cloves garlic, finely chopped
Salt
1 tablespoon tomato sauce
(seasoned passata)
½ teaspoon annatto (achiote)
seeds
1 medium carrot, diced
2 handfuls (3½ oz/100 g)
angel-hair pasta

CHICKEN AND RICE SOUP

Sopa de pollo y arroz

In a large pot, combine the chicken, bell pepper, onion, garlic, celery, tomatoes, ½ teaspoon salt, and 6 cups (48 fl oz/1.4 liters) water, cover, and cook over medium heat until the liquid reduces to about 4 cups (32 fl oz/ 950 ml), about 30 minutes. Remove the chicken and let cool. Remove the meat from the bone and then cut it into small pieces. Strain the broth if you prefer.

Return the broth to the pot, bring to a boil, and add the rice. Cook, covered, over low heat until the rice is cooked, about 15 minutes. Add the chicken and cook for 3 minutes to warm through. Adjust the salt to taste, remove from the stove, and sprinkle parsley on top.

Divide the sliced hard-boiled eggs among 4 bowls and ladle the hot soup over them.

PREPARATION TIME: 20 MINUTES
COOKING TIME: 1 HOUR
SERVES: 4

1 large chicken leg quarter
(about 14 oz/400 g), skinned
1 large green bell pepper,
finely chopped
1 medium white onion,
finely chopped
3 cloves garlic, finely chopped
Leaves of 1 celery stalk,
finely chopped
2 medium tomatoes, diced
Salt
¼ cup (60 g) short-grain
white rice
2 tablespoons chopped parsley
4 hard-boiled eggs, sliced

TARO ROOT, PINEAPPLE, AND CUCUMBER SOUP

Sopa de malanga, piña y pepino

**PREPARATION TIME: 20 MINUTES,
PLUS CHILLING TIME
COOKING TIME: 15 MINUTES
SERVES: 4**

★

1 medium (7 oz/200 g) taro root,
peeled and roughly diced
7 oz (200 g) cucumber, peeled
and sliced, plus more for serving
1 large slice (7 oz/200 g)
pineapple, roughly diced,
plus more for serving
1 medium white onion, sliced
4 leaves fresh culantro
4 sprigs parsley
½ teaspoon salt
Ground black pepper (optional)

Cold soups are not traditionally common in Cuba, although they have become more popular at restaurants in recent years.

★

Place the taro root in a medium pot and add water to cover. Bring to a boil over medium heat and cook, covered, until soft, about 15 minutes. Reserving 1 cup (8 fl oz/240 ml) of the cooking water, drain the taro and let cool. When cool, transfer the taro root and reserved cooking water to a blender. Add the cucumber, pineapple, onion, culantro, and parsley and blend until smooth. Add the salt and black pepper (if using) and strain. Refrigerate to chill.

Serve cold and garnish with strips of cucumber and pineapple.

VEGETABLE SOUP

Sopa de vegetales

**PREPARATION TIME: 20 MINUTES
COOKING TIME: 1 HOUR
SERVES: 6**

★

2 tablespoons vegetable oil
1 medium white onion,
finely chopped
2 cloves garlic, crushed
1 bunch scallions (spring onions),
finely chopped
Salt
1 ear of corn, cut crosswise into
1-inch (2.5 cm) pieces
1 medium potato, peeled
and chopped
1 large carrot, peeled and diced
2 medium taro roots (14 oz/400 g
total), peeled and chopped
½ lb (230 g) unpeeled pumpkin,
cut into large pieces
1 teaspoon annatto (achiote) seeds
1 cup (80 g) chopped bok choy
1 sprig parsley, chopped
¼ teaspoon ground black pepper

In a medium frying pan, heat the oil over medium-low heat. Add the onion, garlic, and scallions (spring onions) and sauté until softened, about 2 minutes. Set aside.

In a large pot, bring 8 cups (64 fl oz/1.9 liters) water to a boil and add 1 tablespoon salt. Add the corn, potato, carrot, taro, and pumpkin. Cover and cook over low heat until the vegetables are soft, about 40 minutes. Add the onion mixture and the annatto (achiote) and cook for 3 minutes. Add the bok choy and parsley and cook for 1 minute more. Season with the pepper and salt to taste.

CHINESE SOUP

Sopa china

PREPARATION TIME: 25 MINUTES
COOKING TIME: 1 HOUR 5 MINUTES
SERVES: 4

★

½ small chicken (about 1¼ lb/
600 g), cut into large pieces
7 oz (200 g) pork loin or
tenderloin, cut into large pieces
½ cup (50 g) dried shrimp
1 medium white onion,
finely chopped
1 piece fresh ginger (about 1 oz/
25 g), finely chopped
1 teaspoon soy sauce
Salt
1 thick slice (about 5 oz/150 g)
ham, julienned
½ cup (40 g) chopped bok choy
1 small bunch scallions
(spring onions), finely chopped
2 oz (60 g) bean sprouts,
cut into small pieces

The Chinese influence in Cuban cuisine dates back to 1847, when the first wave of Chinese immigrants arrived on the island, and the establishment of gastronomic businesses in the Chinese community encouraged the general development of the *fondas* (food stands or small cafeterias) in Havana.

According to Cuban culinary legend Nitza Villapol, this dish can be served with or without egg. In the *fondas*, it was called an *especial* when an egg yolk was put on the bottom of the bowl. The dried shrimp can be substituted with fresh fish. Another variation uses winter melon and capellini instead of the bean sprouts. The noodles were put in the bottom of the bowl and the hot soup was poured over them.

In a large pot, combine the chicken, pork, shrimp, onion, ginger, and 8 cups (64 fl oz/1.9 liters) water. Cook over medium heat until the water reduces by half, about 1 hour, skimming the foam from the top. Strain the broth, setting aside the chicken, pork, and shrimp and discarding the onion and ginger.

Return the broth to the pot and add the soy sauce and ½ teaspoon salt. Cut the chicken and pork into smaller pieces. Return the chicken, pork, and shrimp to the pot and add the ham, bok choy, scallions (spring onions), and bean sprouts. Adjust the salt to taste and cook for 3 minutes to heat through. Serve hot.

PEANUT SOUP

Sopa de maní

PREPARATION TIME: 10 MINUTES
COOKING TIME: 25 MINUTES
SERVES: 4

2 tablespoons (30 g) butter
2 medium white onions,
finely chopped
2 cups (16 fl oz/500 ml) chicken
stock
5 tablespoons all-purpose (plain)
flour or 2½ tablespoon cornstarch
(cornflour)
2½ cups (20 fl oz/625 ml)
whole milk
½ cup (80 g) finely ground
raw peanuts
1 teaspoon salt
¼ teaspoon ground black pepper

In a medium frying pan, heat the butter over medium-low heat. Add the onion and sauté until translucent, about 2 minutes.

In a small bowl, stir ½ cup (4 fl oz/125 ml) of the stock into the flour. In a medium pot, combine the remaining stock and the milk, and heat over medium heat for 2 minutes. Add the flour and stock mixture, the sautéed onion, and ground peanuts and cook, stirring regularly to avoid lumps, over medium-low heat until thickened, 18–20 minutes. Season with the salt and pepper and strain through a fine-mesh sieve (optional). Serve hot.

CUBAN BORSCHT SOUP

Sopa borscht a la cubana

This soup was popularized in Cuba during their years of strong political ties with the Soviet Union, from the 1960s to 1989. During this era, Soviet culinary influences were more common. Today, this soup would most likely be found at a Russian restaurant, rather than on a standard Cuban menu or in a typical Cuban home. Beef or pork can be substituted for the chicken.

In a large pot, combine the chicken and 8 cups (64 fl oz/ 1.9 liters) water. Bring to a boil and cook until the chicken is tender, about 30 minutes. Remove the chicken and let it cool, then remove the meat from the bones. Strain the broth and measure out 6 cups (48 fl oz/1.4 liters).

In a small pan, heat the oil over low heat. Add the beet and sauté for 1 minute. Add 1 tablespoon vinegar, the raw sugar, and tomato paste (puree) and cook for about 20 minutes.

Meanwhile, in a large pot, combine the potatoes, bay leaf, and reserved 6 cups (48 fl oz/1.4 liters) chicken broth. Bring to a boil over medium-low heat and cook until the potatoes start to soften, about 10 minutes. Add the cabbage and cook, covered, until very soft and translucent, about 20 minutes.

In a medium pan, heat the butter over medium-low heat. Add the onion, carrot, garlic, scallions (spring onions), and chopped parsley and sauté until softened, about 3 minutes. Transfer the sautéed vegetables to the broth and add the chicken, the beet mixture, the salt, and pepper. Add vinegar to taste. Remove from the heat to cool slightly. Garnish with the remaining parsley and serve hot with 1 tablespoon sour cream per serving.

PREPARATION TIME: 30 MINUTES
COOKING TIME: 1 HOUR, 15 MINUTES
SERVES: 8

1 medium chicken (3½ lb/1.5 kg), cut into 8 pieces
1 tablespoon vegetable oil
1 small beet, peeled and sliced
1 tablespoon vinegar, plus more to taste
½ teaspoon raw cane sugar
⅓ cup (75 g) tomato paste (tomato puree)
2 large potatoes, peeled and cut into large pieces
1 bay leaf
3 cups (300 g) chopped green cabbage
2 tablespoons (30 g) butter
1 large onion, diced
1 medium carrot, sliced
4 cloves garlic, finely chopped
1 bunch scallions (spring onions), finely chopped
1 bunch parsley, leaves picked, half finely chopped, half for garnish
1 tablespoon salt
¼ teaspoon ground black pepper
Sour cream, for serving

BLACK BEAN SOUP

Potaje de frijoles negros

**PREPARATION TIME: 20 MINUTES,
PLUS 6 HOURS BEAN SOAKING TIME
COOKING TIME: 1 HOUR 15 MINUTES
SERVES: 6**

2 cups (440 g) dried black beans,
rinsed and soaked in water
to cover for 6 hours
4 cachucha peppers
or cubanelles—2 coarsely
chopped, 2 finely chopped
4 chay peppers or cubanelles—
2 coarsely chopped, 2 finely chopped
2 small white onions—1 coarsely
chopped, 1 finely chopped
6 cloves garlic—
3 finely chopped, 3 whole
3 tablespoons vegetable oil
½ teaspoon ground cumin
½ teaspoon ground oregano
1 bay leaf
1 leaf fresh culantro
½ tablespoon salt
⅛ teaspoon ground black pepper
(optional)
1 teaspoon raw cane sugar
1 tablespoon vinegar
4 tablespoons dry white wine
2 small (3 oz/85 g) roasted bell
peppers (optional)

In Cuban homes, cooked beans are typically served with lots of liquid in a bowl, almost like bean soup. Sometimes the beans are eaten alone in a bowl before the *plato fuerte*, or main course. After the beans are eaten as a soup, they are also served on top of the rice that is eaten with the main dish.

★

Drain the beans. In a pressure cooker (see Note), combine the beans and 6 cups (48 fl oz/1.4 liters) water. Add the coarsely chopped peppers and onions and the whole garlic cloves to the pressure cooker. Lock the lid and bring to pressure over medium heat. Cook at pressure until the beans are soft, about 45 minutes.

Meanwhile, in a medium pan, heat 2 tablespoons of the oil over medium-low heat. Add the finely chopped peppers, onion, and garlic, the cumin, and oregano and cook for about 3 minutes. Set the sofrito aside until the beans have cooked.

Quick-release the pressure on the pressure cooker, open the lid and add the bay leaf. Mash or blend 1 cup (60 g) of the cooked beans and return to the pressure cooker to thicken the soup. Transfer the sofrito to the pressure cooker and add the culantro leaf. Continue to cook the beans (without pressure) until completely softened, about 30 minutes. Add the salt, black pepper (if using), raw sugar, vinegar, and the remaining 1 tablespoon oil. Add the wine and cook for 2 more minutes. Add the roasted bell peppers (optional). Serve in soup bowls.

Note: If you don't have a pressure cooker, it is very important to soak the beans. Then cook them in a large pot with the peppers, onions, garlic, and 12 cups (96 fl oz/ 3 liters) water over medium-high heat for 1½–2 hours, depending on the quality of the beans. Make the sofrito as directed and add to the beans, then cover and continue cooking until tender, about 30 minutes. The step of mashing some of the beans to thicken the broth is important, and should be followed as direceted. Add the seasonings as directed.

RED BEAN SOUP

Potaje de prijoles colorados

**PREPARATION TIME: 30 MINUTES,
PLUS 6 HOURS BEAN SOAKING TIME
COOKING TIME: 1 HOUR 10 MINUTES
SERVES: 6**

¼ teaspoon whole oregano
¼ teaspoon cumin seeds
2 tablespoons vegetable oil
3½ oz (100 g) slab bacon (streaky)
or salt pork, chopped
2 chay peppers or cubanelles,
finely chopped
3 cloves garlic, finely chopped
1 medium white onion,
finely chopped
1 tomato, chopped
2 tablespoons tomato paste
(tomato puree)
Salt
1½ cups (340 g) dried red beans,
rinsed and soaked in water
to cover for 6 hours
1 bay leaf
1 large potato,
peeled coarsely diced
1 medium taro root (7 oz/200 g),
coarsely diced
1 dried sausage (about 3½ oz/
100 g), casings removed and cut
into slices ⅛ inch (3 mm) thick
3½ oz (100 g) pumpkin, peeled
and cut into small pieces

In Cuba, it once was common to soak the beans with pork bones and bacon skin (butchers sell bacon with the skin on, like salt pork). This step is not used as frequently today, except by the most traditional of home cooks.

In a small pan, toast the oregano and cumin seeds over medium heat until fragrant, about 1 minute. Transfer to a mortar and pestle and roughly crush. Set aside.

In a medium frying pan, heat the vegetable oil over medium heat. Add the bacon (streaky) and sauté until the fat is rendered, about 2 minutes. Add the *chay* peppers, garlic, and onion and cook until softened, about 3 minutes. Add the chopped tomato, tomato paste (puree), 1 teaspoon salt, and the toasted spices and stir with a wooden spoon. Cook until reduced, about 2 minutes. Set aside.

Drain the beans. In a pressure cooker (see Note), combine the beans, bay leaf, and 6 cups (48 fl oz/1.4 liters) water. Lock the lid and cook at pressure over medium heat until the beans are soft, about 45 minutes. Quick-release the pressure and add the potato, taro root, and sausage. Cook, uncovered, until the broth thickens, about 10 minutes. Add the pumpkin and cook until soft, about 10 minutes. Add the bacon mixture and cook to continue thickening the broth, about 5 minutes. Adjust salt to taste. Serve in soup bowls.

Note: If you don't have a pressure cooker, it is very important to soak the beans first. Cook in 12 cups (96 fl oz/ 3 liters) water in a large pot over medium-high heat for 1½–2 hours, depending on the quality, age, and type of beans. Then follow the rest of the instructions as directed.

GREEN SPLIT PEA SOUP

Potaje de chícharos

PREPARATION TIME: 30 MINUTES
COOKING TIME: 1 HOUR 10 MINUTES
SERVES: 6

2 tablespoons vegetable oil
3 chay peppers or cubanelles,
finely chopped
3 cloves garlic, finely chopped
1 medium white onion, diced
3 tomatoes, diced
2 tablespoons tomato sauce
(seasoned passata)
¼ teaspoon ground cumin
2 cups (440 g) green split peas,
rinsed
1 large potato, coarsely diced
1 slice ham (about 5 oz/150 g),
diced
5¼ oz (150 g) pumpkin,
cut into medium pieces
1 teaspoon salt
⅛ teaspoon ground black pepper

In the Eastern regions, it is common to add a ripe plantain 5 minutes before removing from the stovetop.

In a medium frying pan, heat the oil over medium-low heat. Add the peppers, garlic, and onion and sauté until softened, about 3 minutes. Add the tomatoes and cook until the juices reduce, about 2 minutes. Add the tomato sauce (seasoned passata) and cumin and cook for 1 minute more. Remove the sofrito from the heat and set aside.

In a pressure cooker (see Note), combine the split peas and 7 cups (56 fl oz/1.6 liters) water. Lock the lid and cook at pressure over medium heat until softened, about 45 minutes. Quick-release the pressure. Add the potato and ham and cook uncovered until tender, about 10 minutes. Add the pumpkin and cook until tender, about 10 minutes. Add the sofrito and cook for 5 minutes. Add the salt and pepper. Serve in soup bowls.

Note: If you don't have a pressure cooker, cook the split peas in a large pot with 12 cups (96 fl oz/ 3 liters) water over medium-high heat for 1½–2 hours, depending on the quality of the split peas. Then follow the recipe instructions to make the sofrito and add the remaining ingredients.

CHICKPEA SOUP

Potaje de garbanzos

**PREPARATION TIME: 30 MINUTES,
PLUS 6 HOURS CHICKPEA
SOAKING TIME
COOKING TIME: 1 HOUR 10 MINUTES
SERVES: 6**

2 cups (440 g) dried chickpeas,
rinsed

2½ oz (70 g) skin-on slab salt pork,
skin removed and meat diced

2 pork bones

3 tablespoons vegetable oil

2 chay peppers or cubanelles,
finely chopped

1 large white onion, finely chopped

4 cloves garlic, finely chopped

2 tomatoes, diced

2 tablespoons tomato sauce
(seasoned passata)

¼ teaspoon ground cumin

¼ teaspoon dried oregano

1 bay leaf

2 large potatoes, peeled and cut
into large pieces

1 pork sausage, casings removed
and cut into slices ⅓ inch
(1 cm) thick

1 teaspoon salt

In a large bowl or pot, combine the chickpeas, pork skin, pork bones, and 7 cups (56 fl oz/1.6 liters) water and let soak for 6 hours.

In a medium frying pan, heat 2 tablespoons of the oil over medium heat. Add the *chay* peppers, onion, and garlic and sauté until softened, about 3 minutes. Add the diced tomatoes and cook until the liquid begins to reduce, about 2 minutes. Add the tomato sauce (seasoned passata), cumin, oregano, and bay leaf and cook for 1 minute to blend the flavors. Remove the sofrito from the heat and set aside.

In another frying pan, heat the remaining 1 tablespoon oil over medium heat. Add the diced salt pork and fry until the fat is rendered out, about 2 minutes. Add the sofrito and cook for 1 minute. Set aside.

In a pressure cooker (see Note), cook the chickpeas in the soaking liquid. Lock the lid and cook at pressure over medium heat until tender, about 45 minutes. Quick-release the pressure. Add the potatoes and the sausage and cook uncovered until the potatoes are tender, about 15 minutes. Add the salt pork/sofrito mixture and cook until thickened, about 10 minutes. Add the salt. Serve in a soup bowl or a clay pot.

Note: If you don't have a pressure cooker, cook the chickpeas in a large pot with 7 cups (56 fl oz/1.6 liters) water for 1½–2 hours. Then follow the recipe instructions to make the sofrito and add the remaining ingredients.

GREEN SPLIT PEAS AND VEGETABLES

Olla de chícharos y vegetales

In a pressure cooker, combine the split green peas and vegetable stock and cook over medium heat until soft, 30–45 minutes. Add the taro root and cook (without pressure) until soft, about 10 minutes. Add the pumpkin and cook until soft, about 10 minutes.

In a frying pan, heat the oil over medium-low heat. Add the onion, *chay* peppers, garlic, and scallions (spring onions) and sauté until the onion becomes transluscent, about 3 minutes. Add the tomatoes, bay leaf, and 1 teaspoon salt and cook until the tomato softens, about 2 minutes.

Transfer the sofrito to the pot with the peas and add the bok choy and plantain. Adjust the salt to taste and cook until the plantain softens, about 5 minutes. Let cool slightly before serving.

PREPARATION TIME: 15 MINUTES
COOKING TIME: 1 HOUR 15 MINUTES
SERVES: 6

1 cup green split peas
8½ cups (68 fl oz/2 liters)
vegetable stock
1 large taro root (10 oz/300 g),
peeled and coarsely diced
7 oz (200 g) pumpkin,
coarsely diced
2 tablespoons oil
1 large white onion, diced
2 chay peppers or cubanelles,
diced
6 cloves garlic, finely chopped
1 bunch scallions (spring onions),
finely chopped
4 medium tomatoes
¼ teaspoon ground bay leaf
Salt
1½ cups (120 g) chopped bok choy
1 ripe medium plantain, cut into
¾ inch (2 cm) slices

GALICIAN SOUP

Caldo gallego

**PREPARATION TIME: 20 MINUTES,
PLUS 6 HOURS BEAN SOAKING TIME
COOKING TIME: 1 HOUR
SERVES: 6**

2 tablespoons olive oil
6 cloves garlic, finely chopped
1½ cups (330 g) dried white beans,
rinsed and soaked in water
to cover for 6 hours
10 oz (300 g) cured ham,
shredded
1 slice salt pork (about 3½ oz/
100 g), finely diced
1 lb (460 g) potatoes, peeled
and coarsely diced
1 cup (80 g) chopped collard greens
1 cup (100 g) chopped cabbage
½ teaspoon salt
⅛ teaspoon ground black pepper

This recipe was very popular during the colonial times (from the fifteenth century to the nineteenth century). It was not commonly prepared over the last several decades, but is currently being reincorporated into Cuban cuisine as a traditional recipe. In the original recipe, turnips were used instead of potatoes. In some versions of the recipe, the garlic and (skinless) salt pork are mashed together and the mixture added after the beans are softened—a technique derived from European culinary influences.

In a medium frying pan, heat the olive oil over medium heat. Add the garlic and sauté until fragrant, about 1 minute. Set aside.

Drain the beans. In a pressure cooker (see Note), combine the beans, ham, salt pork, and 7 cups (56 fl oz/1.6 liters) water. Lock the lid and cook at pressure over medium heat until softened, about 30 minutes. Quick-release the pressure. Add the potatoes and cook, covered and without pressure, until soft, about 20 minutes. Remove the top and add the collard greens and cabbage and stir. Add the sautéed garlic, salt, and pepper and cook until quite thick, about 10 minutes.

Note: If you don't have a pressure cooker, cook the beans, ham, salt pork in a large pot with 10 cups (84 fl oz/2.5 ml) water over medium heat until tender, about 1 hour 15 minutes. Then follow the recipe instructions as directed.

CORNMEAL WITH PORK

Harina de maíz con carne de cerdo

In a large bowl, combine the pork, orange juice, 3 cloves of the garlic, ¼ teaspoon of the salt, and the black pepper and let marinate for at least 30 minutes. Reserving the marinade, drain the pork.

In a large pan, heat the oil over high heat. Add the pork and cook, stirring with a wooden spoon, until lightly browned, about 5 minutes. Remove the pork and set aside. In the same pan, add the bell pepper, the remaining 2 cloves garlic, and the onion and sauté until the onion is translucent, about 2 minutes. Return the pork to the pan and stir in the tomato sauce (seasoned passata) and 2 tablespoons of the reserved marinade. Cover and cook over medium heat until the sauce is partially reduced, about 5 minutes. Add the cornmeal, 10½ cups (84 fl oz/2.5 liters) water, and remaining 2 teaspoons salt and cook over low heat, stirring regularly, until thickened, about 1 hour. Serve.

PREPARATION TIME: 45 MINUTES, PLUS 30 MINUTES MARINATING TIME
COOKING TIME: 1 HOUR 15 MINUTES
SERVES: 6

¾ lb (320 g) pork loin or tenderloin, diced into ½ inch (1 cm) cubes
½ cup (4 fl oz/125 ml) orange juice
5 cloves garlic, crushed
2¼ teaspoons salt
⅛ teaspoon ground black pepper
4 tablespoons vegetable oil
1 green bell pepper, finely chopped
1 medium onion, finely chopped
4 tablespoons tomato sauce (seasoned passata)
2 cups (490 g) cornmeal

CORNMEAL WITH CHICKEN

Harina de maíz con pollo

In a medium frying pan, heat the oil over medium-low heat. Add the *chay* peppers, garlic, and onion and sauté until softened, about 3 minutes. Stir in the chicken, then add the tomato sauce (seasoned passata), wine, paprika, sugar, salt, and pepper and cook until reduced, about 5 minutes. Remove from the flame and set aside.

In a medium pot, combine the cornmeal and the broth and cook over low heat, stirring regularly with a wooden spoon, until it begins to thicken, about 30 minutes. Add the chicken and cook until the cornmeal is completely cooked, about 30 minutes. Serve hot.

PREPARATION TIME: 12 MINUTES
COOKING TIME: 1 HOUR 10 MINUTES
SERVES: 4

3 tablespoons vegetable oil
4 chay peppers or cubanelles, finely chopped
4 cloves garlic, finely chopped
1 medium white onion, finely chopped
1 cup (230 g) cooked chicken (see page 19), cut into ½ inch (1.5 cm) pieces
½ cup (125 g) tomato sauce (seasoned passata)
½ cup (4 fl oz/125 ml) dry white wine
¼ teaspoon paprika
½ teaspoon raw cane sugar
½ tablespoon salt
⅛ teaspoon ground black pepper
1 cup (245 g) cornmeal
4 cups (32 fl oz/1 liter) chicken stock

LAS TUNAS-STYLE STEW

Caldosa tunera

PREPARATION TIME: 30 MINUTES
COOKING TIME: 1 HOUR 40 MINUTES
SERVES: 8

★

3 tablespoons vegetable oil
1 large white onion, finely chopped
4 chay peppers or cubanelles,
finely chopped
6 cloves garlic, finely chopped
½ chicken (1¾ lb/760 g),
cut into 2 or 3 sections
4 tablespoons tomato sauce
(seasoned passata)
1 teaspoon paprika
¼ teaspoon ground cumin
1 tablespoon mild mustard
2 tablespoons vinegar
Salt
3 small yuca (cassava) roots
(11 oz/325 g total), peeled and
coarsely diced
3 medium potatoes (1 lb/450 g
total), peeled and coarsely diced
1 large taro root (9 oz/250 g),
peeled and coarsely diced
2 small medium-ripe plantains
(5 oz/150 g each), cut into slices
1 tablespoon soy sauce
Cuban lime, for serving

In a large pot, heat the oil over medium heat. Add the onion, peppers, and garlic and sauté until softened, about 3 minutes. Add the chicken and cook over medium heat until lightly browned, about 3 minutes. Add the tomato sauce (seasoned passata), paprika, cumin, mustard, and vinegar and cook until reduced, about 2 minutes. Add ½ tablespoon salt and 7½ cups (60 fl oz/1.75 liters) water and cook until the chicken is completely soft, about 30 minutes.

Remove the chicken and let cool. Remove the meat from the bone and cut into thin strips, discarding the skin and bones. Return the chicken to the broth and add the yuca (cassava), potatoes, taro, and plantains. Cover the pot and cook until the tubers are very soft, about 30 minutes. Remove from the heat and add the soy sauce.

Serve with slices of Cuban lime.

Note: In this recipe, a regular chicken has been used instead of a stewing hen (the original base ingredient), as stewing hens are not easy to come by. In other versions of the dish, the plantains are fried separately, and ground corn (maíz molido, see page 20) is also added.

CORNMEAL WITH CRABS

Harina de maíz con cangrejos

PREPARATION TIME: 20 MINUTES
COOKING TIME: 40 MINUTES
SERVES: 4

1 ½ teaspoons salt, plus more for seasoning
3 cups (395 g) cornmeal
3 tablespoons olive oil
1 small green bell pepper, diced
1 small red bell pepper, diced
1 large white onion, diced
4 cloves garlic, crushed
2 tomatoes, diced
1 tablespoon dry white wine
1 bay leaf
½ teaspoon ground cumin
½ teaspoon paprika
¼ teaspoon ground black pepper
½ lb (230 g) cooked crabmeat
Lime juice
Green Plantain Chips (page 40), for serving

In a medium pot, combine 1 teaspoon of the salt and 6 cups (48 fl oz/1.4 liters) water and bring to a boil over medium heat. Gradually add the cornmeal, stirring frequently with a wooden spoon to avoid lumps. Reduce the heat to low and cook until the mixture thickens and separates slightly from the sides of the pot, 18–20 minutes. Remove the cornmeal from heat and set aside.

In another medium pot, heat the oil over medium heat. Add the bell peppers and sauté until softened, about 1 minute. Add the onion and sauté until translucent, 2 minutes. Stir in the garlic and sauté until lightly browned and fragrant, about 2 minutes. Add the tomatoes, wine, bay leaf, cumin, paprika, black pepper, and the remaining ½ teaspoon salt. Cook over low heat until the liquid reduces, about 8 minutes. Add the crabmeat and cook for about 5 minutes (be sure not to overcook, which makes the crab tough). Season to taste with salt and remove from the heat.

Serve the cornmeal in a bowl and top with the crab and lime juice to taste. If desired, serve with green plantain chips on the side.

Notes: In traditional recipes, crab was cooked live and its legs and claws were crushed and added to the sofrito.

SEAFOOD TAMALE

Tamal a la marinera

PREPARATION TIME: 15 MINUTES
COOKING TIME: 1 HOUR 10 MINUTES
SERVES: 4

2 tablespoons vegetable oil
4 chay peppers or cubanelles,
finely chopped
4 cloves garlic, crushed
1 medium white onion,
finely chopped
½ lb (230 g) cooked white fish
½ cup (125 g) tomato sauce
(seasoned passata)
½ cup (4 fl oz/125 ml) dry white
wine
¼ teaspoon ground allspice
½ teaspoon raw cane sugar
½ tablespoon salt
⅛ teaspoon ground black pepper
1 cup (250 g) cornmeal, rinsed
4 cups (32 fl oz/1 liter) stock
(vegetable, fish, or other type)

In a medium frying pan, heat the oil over medium heat. Add the *chay* peppers, garlic, and onion and sauté until the onion is translucent, about 3 minutes. Stir in the fish and add the tomato sauce (seasoned passata), wine, allspice, and raw sugar and cook until the sauce reduces, about 5 minutes. Add the salt and black pepper, then remove from the heat and set aside.

In a medium pot, combine the cornmeal and stock and cook over medium-low heat, stirring regularly, until smooth and thickend, about 30 minutes. Add the fish and tomato sauce mixture and cook until the cornmeal is completely cooked, about 30 minutes. Serve.

TAMALE CASSEROLE

Tamal en cazuela

PREPARATION TIME: 25 MINUTES
COOKING TIME: 1 HOUR 15 MINUTES
SERVES: 8

1 lb 2 oz (500 g) pork loin or
tenderloin, finely diced
1¼ teaspoons salt
⅛ teaspoon ground black pepper
3 tablespoons vegetable oil
5 chay peppers or cubanelles,
finely chopped
5 cloves garlic, finely chopped
1 large white onion, finely chopped
½ cup (125 g) tomato sauce
(seasoned passata)
⅛ teaspoon ground cumin
2 tablespoons vinegar
2⅓ cups (940 g) maíz molido
(ground fresh corn, see page 20)

Season the pork with the salt and black pepper. In a large pot, heat the oil over high heat. Add the pork and cook until lightly browned, about 2 minutes. Add the *chay* peppers, garlic, and onion and sauté, stirring with a wooden spoon, until the onion turns translucent, about 4 minutes. Add 1 cup (8 fl oz/240 ml) water, cover, and cook over medium heat until the meat is soft, about 15 minutes. Add the tomato sauce (seasoned passata), cumin, and vinegar, while stirring well, and cook until the sauce reduces slightly, about 2 minutes. Stir in the *maíz molido* and add 4 cups (32 fl oz/950 ml) water. Cook over high heat until it bubbles, about 5 minutes. Reduce the heat to low and cook, stirring occasionally, until the tamale thickens, about 45 minutes. Serve.

CORN AND CHEESE CREAM SOUP

Crema de maíz con queso

In a large bowl, combine the *maíz molido* and 3 cups (24 fl oz / 700 ml) water. Set a sieve over a large bowl and press the mixture through the sieve to achieve a thick liquid.

Transfer the corn liquid to a large pot and add the salt. Cook over low heat, stirring occasionally to avoid lumps, until thickened, about 45 minutes. Set aside.

In a medium frying pan, heat the oil over medium-low heat. Add the *chay* peppers, garlic, onion, and tomato and sauté until the onion turns translucent, about 4 minutes. Strain or blend the sofrito (optional). Add the sofrito to the creamed corn and cook for about 10 minutes. Add the wine and adjust the salt. Serve in a clay pot with the grated cheese on top.

PREPARATION TIME: 30 MINUTES
COOKING TIME: 45 MINUTES
SERVES: 6

2 cups (920 g) maíz molido
(ground fresh corn, see page 20)
½ tablespoon salt
2 tablespoons vegetable oil
2 chay peppers or cubanelles,
finely chopped
3 cloves garlic, finely chopped
1 medium white onion, finely chopped
1 large tomato, diced
2 tablespoons dry white wine
4 oz (115 g) Cuban gouda
(or other white cheese such as
white cheddar), grated

TARO ROOT, POTATO, AND CELERY SOUP

Crema de malanga, papa y apio

In a large pot, bring the chicken stock to a boil over medium heat. Add the salt, potatoes, and taro, then cover and cook over medium heat until softened, about 20 minutes. Set aside.

In a medium frying pan, heat the oil over medium heat. Add the onion, garlic, scallions (spring onions), and celery and sauté until the onion turns translucent, about 3 minutes. Transfer the sofrito to a blender. Add the potatoes, taro roots, stock, and nutmeg and blend until creamy. (If the soup is too thick, add a little water.) Return to the same pot and cook over low heat until thick and creamy, about 5 minutes. Adjust the salt and pepper to taste. Serve in bowls with chopped scallions or parsley sprinkled on top.

PREPARATION TIME: 25 MINUTES
COOKING TIME: 30 MINUTES
SERVES: 4–6

4 cups (32 fl oz/1 liter) chicken stock
1 teaspoon salt, plus more for
serving
3 large potatoes, peeled and cut
into medium pieces
2 medium taro roots
(14 oz/400 g total), peeled
and cut into medium pieces
2 tablespoons vegetable oil
1 large white onion, finely chopped
4 cloves garlic, finely chopped
1 bunch scallions (spring onions),
finely chopped
½ cup (45 g) chopped celery
¼ teaspoon grated nutmeg
Ground black pepper
Finely chopped scallions (spring
onions) or parsley, for serving

PUMPKIN AND TARO ROOT CREAM SOUP

Crema de calabaza y malanga

PREPARATION TIME: 30 MINUTES
COOKING TIME: 45 MINUTES
SERVES: 6

★

1 lb (460 g) taro root, peeled and
chopped
1 teaspoon salt,
plus more for seasoning
1 medium pumpkin (1 lb/460 g),
cut into medium pieces
2 medium white onions, diced
2 cups (16 fl oz/500 ml) whole milk
2 tablespoons (30 g) butter
¼ teaspoon grated nutmeg
2 tablespoons dry white wine
Croutons, for serving

In a medium pot, combine the taro root, water to cover, and ½ teaspoon salt. Bring to a boil over medium heat and cook until soft, about 20 minutes. Add the pumpkin and cook until soft, about 10 minutes. Remove from the heat and let cool.

Reserving the cooking water, drain the taro and pumpkin and transfer to a blender. Add the onions, milk, butter, nutmeg, and the remaining ½ teaspoon salt and blend until smooth. (If the soup is too thick, add some of the reserved cooking water, adding no more than 1 cup.)

Return the mixture to the pot and cook over low heat, stirring regularly until thick and creamy, 10 minutes. Adjust the salt to taste and add the wine. Serve with croutons (optional).

TARO ROOT AND PEANUT SOUP

Crema de malanga y maní

PREPARATION TIME: 25 MINUTES
COOKING TIME: 30 MINUTES
SERVES: 4

★

2 large taro roots (1¼ lb/600 g
total), peeled and cut into medium
pieces
½ tablespoon salt
2 tablespoons vegetable oil
1 small white onion, diced
2 cloves garlic, diced
1 tablespoon tomato sauce
(seasoned passata)
½ cup (80 g) unsalted roasted
peanuts
Croutons, for serving

In a medium pot, combine the taro roots, water to cover, and the salt. Cover, bring to a boil over medium heat, and cook until soft, about 20 minutes. Reserving the cooking water, drain the taro and set aside.

In a medium frying pan, heat the oil over medium-low heat. Add the onion and garlic and sauté until softened, about 3 minutes. Add the tomato sauce (seasoned passata) and cook until the sauce reduces slightly, about 1 minute. Transfer the sofrito to a blender and add the cooked taro roots and peanuts. Pour in just enough reserved cooking water to cover the ingredients and blend until creamy. Transfer to a medium pot and cook over medium heat for 2 minutes to heat through. Serve hot in bowls, accompanied by croutons.

CHICKEN AND CHEESE SOUP

Crema de queso con pollo

PREPARATION TIME: 15 MINUTES
COOKING TIME: 20 MINUTES
SERVES: 4

1 small white onion, diced
5 tablespoons all-purpose
(plain) flour
1 teaspoon salt
3 cups (24 fl oz/700 ml) whole milk
1½ cups (12 fl oz/350 ml) chicken
stock
4 tablespoons (60 g) butter
1 tablespoon vegetable oil
½ cup (115 g) shredded cooked
chicken (see page 19)
1 tablespoon salsa criolla
(Cuban Sauce, page 311)
½ cup (50 g) grated Cuban gouda
or other mild yellow cheese

In a blender, combine the onion, flour, salt, milk, and stock and blend until smooth.

In a medium pot, melt the butter over low heat. Pour the blended mixture into the pot and cook over medium-low heat, stirring frequently with a wooden spoon to avoid lumps, until thickened, about 20 minutes.

In a small frying pan, heat the oil over medium heat. Add the cooked chicken and the *salsa criolla* and cook for 1–2 minutes. Transfer to the soup and stir. Serve hot with grated cheese on top.

RICE AND CELERY CREAM SOUP

Crema de arroz y apio

PREPARATION TIME: 10 MINUTES
COOKING TIME: 45 MINUTES
SERVES: 4

¾ cup (170 g) short-grain
white rice
4 cups (32 fl oz/1 liter)
chicken stock
1 tablespoon vegetable oil
1 tablespoon (15 g) butter
1 large white onion, finely chopped
1 bunch celery, finely chopped
1 teaspoon salt
⅛ teaspoon ground black pepper

In a medium pot, combine the rice and stock and cook over low heat until the rice is cooked, about 35 minutes. Let cool, then transfer to a blender and blend until creamy. Return to the pot.

In a medium pan, heat the oil and butter over medium-low heat. Add the onion and sauté until softened, about 2 minutes. Transfer to the pot and add the celery, salt, and pepper and cook until it thickens slightly, about 5 minutes. Serve hot.

Note: The onion and celery can be mixed in the blender as well, if preferred.

QUIQUÍA'S SOUP

Sopa Quiquía

Quiquía was a fisherman from the fishing town of Regla, in Havana. This soup was his specialty, and was named after him.

Bring a small pot of water to a boil. Cut an "x" into the skin at the blossom end of the tomato and submerge it in the boiling water for 1 minute. Transfer to a cutting board to cool, then remove the skin (peeling at the "x"). Halve, seed, and dice.

In a medium pan, heat the oil over medium-low heat. Add the bell pepper, onion, and garlic and sauté until the onion is translucent, about 2 minutes. Add the diced tomato. Set the sofrito aside.

In a medium pot, combine the fish and stock, cover, and cook over medium heat until the fish is tender, about 15 minutes. Add the sofrito, potatoes, rice, paprika, and salt and cook over medium-low heat until very creamy, about 20 minutes. Serve hot.

PREPARATION TIME: 15 MINUTES
COOKING TIME: 40 MINUTES
SERVES: 4

1 small tomato
2 tablespoons vegetable oil
1 small green bell pepper,
finely chopped
1 medium white onion,
finely chopped
5 cloves garlic, finely chopped
1 lb 2 oz (500 g) skinless fish such
as red snapper or stone bass,
diced into ¾ inch (2 cm) cubes
6⅓ cups (50 fl oz/1.5 liters)
fish stock
2 medium potatoes,
peeled and sliced
½ cup (115 g) short-grain white rice
1 teaspoon paprika
1 teaspoon salt

STONE BASS HEAD SOUP

Sopa de cabeza de cherna

In a large pot, combine the fish head and 12 cups (96 fl oz/ 3 liters) water and bring to a boil. Cook for 15 more minutes. Remove the head and separate the meat from the head. Strain the broth and return to the pot.

Bring a medium pot of water to a boil. Cut an "x" into the skin at the blossom end of the tomatoes and submerge them in the boiling water for 1 minute. Transfer to a cutting board to cool, then remove the skin (peeling at the "x"). Halve, seed, and dice.

In a medium frying pan, heat the oil and sauté the *chay* peppers, onion, and garlic until the onion is translucent, about 3 minutes. Add the fish and cook for 2 minutes. Add the diced tomato and cook for 1 minute. Set aside.

Return the broth to the stove over medium-low heat. Add the bay leaf, 1 teaspoon salt, and the potatoes and cook for 10 minutes. Add the sofrito and the noodles and cook until the noodles are soft, 10 minutes. Adjust the salt and black pepper to taste. Serve with lime slices, chopped parsley, and toast.

PREPARATION TIME: 40 MINUTES
COOKING TIME: 45 MINUTES
SERVES: 10

1 wreckfish (stonebass) head
(2 lb 10 oz/1.2 kg),
rinsed and gills removed
3 small tomatoes
2 tablespoons vegetable oil
2 chay peppers
or cubanelles, diced
1 large white onion
(7 oz/200 g), diced
3 cloves garlic, finely chopped
1 bay leaf
Salt and ground black pepper
4 cups (1¾ lb/800 g)
diced potatoes
1 package (4 oz/120 g) fideos
or capellini
Lime slices, chopped parsley,
and toast, for serving

PORT OF PRINCE STEW

Ajiaco de Puerto Príncipe

**PREPARATION TIME: 40 MINUTES,
PLUS 12 HOURS DRIED BEEF
SOAKING TIME
COOKING TIME: 3–4 HOURS
SERVES: 10**

½ lb (230 g) tasajo
(salted dried beef)
1 bay leaf
3 tablespoons vegetable oil
2 small green bell peppers,
finely chopped
1 large white onion, finely chopped
4 cloves garlic, finely chopped
1 lb (460 g) pork, loin or tenderloin,
coarsely diced
½ small chicken (1 lb 5 oz/600 g),
coarsely diced
4 tablespoons lime juice
3 large tomatoes, diced
3 ears field corn, cut crosswise into
1 inch (2.5 cm) disks
1 yuca (cassava) root (7 oz/200 g),
peeled and chopped
2 large taro roots (1¼ lb/560 g
total), peeled and chopped
2 medium white or yellow sweet
potatoes (1 lb/445 g total), peeled
and chopped
½ small yam (3½ oz/100 g), peeled
and chopped
1 green plantain, peeled and
thinly sliced
1 tablespoon tomato paste
(tomato puree)
Salt
1 ripe plantain, peeled and
thinly sliced
½ lb (230 g) pumpkin, diced

This stew is commonly prepared at the end of June, for the Saint Juan and Saint Pedro festivities.

The "true" yam is a tuber in the *Dioscoreaceae* family and is not related to the yam of the American South (which is actually a sweet potato). It is considered a typical food in the rural zones of Cuba, and it was a staple in the diet of the slaves brought from Africa to work on the sugar plantations. The slaves who were forced to work in the kitchens of the sugar plantations incorporated this food into Cuban cuisine.

In older recipes of this traditional dish, the spices used were culantro, cumin, and saffron, to add color. Cuban *campesinos* (people who live in the countryside) add the *guaguao* pepper (a small, very spicy pepper).

In a container, combine the *tasajo* and enough water to cover. Let soak for at least 12 hours, changing the water every 4 hours, to remove the salt.

Drain the beef and cut in half. Transfer to a large pot and add water to cover. Bring to a boil, drain the water, add fresh water, and bring to a boil again to remove the salt. Drain and return the beef to the pot. Add water to cover 3 or 4 finger-widths above it. Add the bay leaf, cover, and cook over medium heat until softened, 1½–2 hours. Reserving the cooking water if desired (see Note), drain the beef and cut into medium pieces.

In a large pot, heat the oil over medium heat. Add the bell peppers, onion, and garlic and sauté until the onion turns translucent, about 2 minutes. Add the cooked beef, pork, chicken, and 2 tablespoons of the lime juice and sauté until lightly browned, about 5 minutes. Add the tomatoes and cook until the liquid reduces slightly, about 3 minutes. Add the corn and 8½ cups (68 fl oz/2 liters) water and cook until the meat is soft, about 30 minutes.

Add the yuca (cassava), taro, sweet potatoes, and yam. Dip the green plantain in the remaining 2 tablespoons lime juice to prevent it from darkening the broth, and add it to the pot. Cook until the root vegetables are soft, about 20 minutes. Add the tomato paste (puree), ½ tablespoon salt, the ripe plantain, and pumpkin and cook until thickened, about 30 minutes. Adjust the salt to taste and serve.

Note: One option for preventing the green plantain from discoloring the stew is to cook it separately in its peel in the beef cooking water.

BAYAMESE STEW

Ajiaco bayamés

PREPARATION TIME: 30 MINUTES
COOKING TIME: 1 HOUR 15 MINUTES
SERVES: 8

2 medium yuca (cassava) roots
(1 lb/450 g total), peeled and cut
into medium pieces
2 medium white or yellow sweet
potatoes (14 oz/400 g total),
peeled and cut into medium pieces
1 large taro root (12 oz/350 g),
peeled and cut into medium pieces
1 small yam (7 oz/200 g), peeled
and cut into medium pieces
½ lb (230 g) unpeeled pumpkin,
coarsely diced
½ cup (120 g) cornmeal
½ cup (4 fl oz/125 ml) beef stock
2 green plantains, ends trimmed
and the skin slit lengthwise
4 tablespoons vegetable oil
2 medium onions, finely chopped
8 cloves garlic, crushed
Juice of 1 bitter orange
(see page 18)
2 small green bell peppers,
finely chopped
3 medium tomatoes, diced
¼ teaspoon ground cumin
2 leaves fresh culantro, halved
1½-pound (650 g) pork, loin
or tenderloin, cut into ¾ inch
(2 cm) cubes
Salt

Soak the yuca (cassava), sweet potatoes, taro root, and yam in a large bowl with water to prevent them from browning. Soak the pumpkin in a medium bowl with water separately.

Meanwhile, in a medium bowl, combine the cornmeal and stock and stir. Roll the moist cornmeal into 1-inch (2.5 cm) balls.

In a large pot, combine the plantains and water to cover, bring to a boil, and cook until softened, about 20 minutes. Let cool then peel and mash them into a puree with a fork. In a small frying pan, heat 2 tablespoons of the oil over medium heat until warm. Transfer to a medium bowl and add half the onions and garlic, and the bitter orange juice and stir. Transfer to the plantain puree and roll the puree into 20 small (1 inch/2 cm) balls.

In a medium frying pan, heat the remaining 2 tablespoons oil over medium heat. Add the bell peppers and the remaining onions and garlic and sauté until softened, about 3 minutes. Add the tomatoes and cook until the liquid reduces slightly, about 5 minutes. Add the cumin and culantro and stir. Set aside the sofrito.

In a large pot, combine the pork with 8 cups (64 fl oz/1.9 liters) water. Cook, covered, over medium heat until the meat is semisoftened, about 25 minutes, skimming the foam from the surface. Add the drained yuca (cassava), sweet potatoes, taro, and yam, the cornmeal balls, and the plantain balls. Cover and cook over medium-low heat until the vegetables are tender, about 20 minutes. Add the pumpkin and the sofrito and cook until the stew thickens, about 10 minutes. Season to taste with salt and serve.

EASTERN-STYLE SOUP

Sopa oriental

Renowned Cuban chef Gilberto Smith Duquesne argues that this soup has always been prepared in all of Cuba, despite its name, which suggests it is from the Eastern provinces.

★

In a medium frying pan, heat 2 tablespoons of the oil over medium heat. Add the *chay* peppers, onions, garlic, and parsley and sauté until softened, about 2 minutes. Add ½ teaspoon of the salt, the black pepper, paprika, and tomato sauce (seasoned passata), and cook for 1 minute more. Set the sofrito aside.

In a medium frying pan, heat the remaining 1 tablespoon oil over high heat. Add the beef and cook, stirring regularly, until lightly browned, about 4 minutes. Add half the sofrito and cook over low heat for 6 minutes. Set aside.

In a medium pot, bring 6 cups (48 fl oz/1.4 liters) water to a boil and add the potatoes and the other half of the sofrito, and cook for 5 minutes. Reduce the heat, add the beef mixture, and cook until the potatoes are soft, about 5 more minutes. Add the noodles and cook until soft, about 5 minutes. Add the remaining 1 teaspoon salt.

PREPARATION TIME: 15 MINUTES
COOKING TIME: 40 MINUTES
SERVES: 4

3 tablespoons vegetable oil
5 chay peppers or cubanelles,
finely chopped
2 small onions (120 g),
finely chopped
5 cloves garlic, crushed
1 sprig parsley, finely chopped
1½ teaspoons salt
⅛ teaspoon ground black pepper
1 teaspoon paprika
2 tablespoons tomato sauce
(seasoned passata)
9 oz (250 g) ground (minced) beef
2 large potatoes (14 oz/400 g),
peeled and diced
1 package (4 oz/120 g) fideos
or capellini

RICE
Arroz

In Cuba, rice is considered a staple that is consumed almost every day—if not every single day—by most families. The servings are abundant, to the point where foreigners visiting the island are often surprised by the mountains of rice heaped onto plates. To give an idea of the high consumption of rice, it is helpful to know that as part of the rationing system, each Cuban individual is allotted five pounds (2.3 kg) of rice every month. The national production of rice does not meet the demand, so Cuba also imports rice from Brazil, Vietnam, and other countries. The type of rice generally consumed is short-grain white rice. Although brown rice is gaining popularity among the more health-conscious segments of the population, it is far less common than white rice.

The general preference among Cubans is to serve rice topped with stews, heavy sauces, and bean soups. There is even the common expression *"mojar el arroz,"* which means "to wet the rice," as a reference to a sauce or a liquid of some kind. When the rice is served as a side dish, it is usually plain white rice or either *moros y cristianos* or *congrí,* two very common dishes. When rice is combined with meat or vegetables, it is often served as the main dish in home cooking and in restaurants. Rice is also found in salads, desserts, and drinks. Rice is so deeply entrenched in Cuban culture that it is used in some common sayings, such as *"arroz con mango,"* which refers to a commotion of some kind.

RED BEANS AND RICE

Arroz congrí

**PREPARATION TIME: 20 MINUTES,
PLUS 6 HOURS BEAN SOAKING TIME
COOKING TIME: 1 HOUR 15 MINUTES
SERVES: 4**

¾ cup (165 g) dried red beans,
rinsed and soaked in water to
cover for 6 hours
2 tablespoons vegetable oil
2 small white onions
(4 oz/120 g total), finely chopped
5 cachucha peppers or cubanelles,
finely chopped
6 cloves garlic, crushed
2 cups (460 g) short-grain white rice
¼ teaspoon ground cumin
¼ teaspoon dried oregano
1 bay leaf
2 tablespoons tomato sauce
(seasoned passata)
1 teaspoon salt
¼ cup (2 fl oz/60 ml) dry white wine
¾ cup (10 g) fried pork rind,
finely chopped (optional)

Serve this dish alongside stewed, fried, and roasted meats.

In a large pot, combine the beans and 5 cups (40 fl oz/ 1.25 liters) water. Cook over medium heat until tender, about 45 minutes. Reserving 2 cups (16 fl oz/475 ml) of the cooking water, drain the beans.

In a large pot, heat the oil over medium heat. Add the onions, *cachucha* peppers, and garlic and cook until softened, about 2 minutes. Add the rice and cook for 2 minutes, stirring regularly. Stir in the drained beans, cumin, oregano, bay leaf, and tomato sauce (seasoned passata). Add the reserved bean liquid and the salt. Cover and cook over high heat until it comes to a boil, then lower the heat to low and cook for 12 minutes. Fluff the mixture, stir in the wine, cover, and let steam for 10 more minutes, adding the pork rind (if using) after 5 minutes.

RICE AND PORK

Arroz con cerdo

In a container, combine the crushed garlic, ½ tablespoon salt, and the bitter orange juice. Add the pork and let marinate for 1 hour in the refrigerator.

In a large heavy-bottomed pot, heat the oil over high heat. Add the pork and cook until lightly browned, about 6 minutes. Remove the pork and set aside. In the same pot, add the onion, *chay* peppers, and chopped garlic and sauté over medium-low heat until softened, about 2 minutes. Add the tomato, cumin, and oregano and cook until the juice from the tomato is absorbed, about 2 minutes. Return the pork to the pot and stir, then add the stock, cover, and cook over medium heat until the meat is tender, about 25 minutes.

Add the rice, bring to a boil, then reduce the heat to medium-low, cover, and cook until the rice is tender, about 15 minutes. Season to taste with salt. Reduce the heat to low, cover, and cook until the rice is done, 10 more minutes. Stir in the wine.

PREPARATION TIME: 20 MINUTES, PLUS 1 HOUR MARINATING TIME
COOKING TIME: 1 HOUR, 10 MINUTES
SERVES: 6

6 cloves garlic—5 crushed and 1 finely chopped
Salt
3 tablespoons bitter orange juice (see page 18)
1 lb 5 oz (600 g) pork loin or tenderloin, cut into medium pieces
4 tablespoons vegetable oil
1 large white onion, finely diced
3 chay peppers or cubanelles, finely diced
1 large tomato, coarsely diced
¼ teaspoon ground cumin
¼ teaspoon dried oregano
4 cups (32 fl oz/1 liter) beef stock
2½ cups (575 g) short-grain white rice, rinsed
3 tablespoons dry white wine

EASTERN-STYLE RICE AND BEANS

Congrí oriental

PREPARATION TIME: 20 MINUTES
COOKING TIME: 1 HOUR 15 MINUTES
SERVES: 4

1 cup (220 g) dried red beans, rinsed

4 tablespoons vegetable oil

½ lb (230 g) boneless pork shoulder, diced

2 small white onions, chopped

5 cachucha peppers or cubanelles, chopped

6 cloves garlic, crushed

2 cups (460 g) short-grain white rice, rinsed

¼ teaspoon ground cumin

¼ teaspoon dried oregano

1 bay leaf

2 tablespoons tomato sauce (seasoned passata)

1 teaspoon salt

This is a very common dish for Christmas and other family gatherings. According to Cuban anthropologist Fernando Ortiz, the name of this dish demonstrates the Franco-Haitian influence in Cuban cuisine. It is thought that the term *congrí* was created by a combination of African and French languages: *congó*, an African word for beans, and *riz*, the French word for rice.

In a pressure cooker (see Note), combine the beans with water to cover by 2 inches (5 cm). Lock the lid and bring to pressure over medium heat. Cook at pressure until soft, about 45 minutes (be careful not to overcook them). Quick-release the pressure. Reserving 2½ cups (20 fl oz/590 ml) of the cooking water, drain the beans.

In a medium frying pan, heat 2 tablespoons of the oil over medium-high heat. Add the pork and cook until lightly browned, about 8 minutes. Set aside.

In a large heavy-bottomed pot, heat the remaining 2 tablespoons oil over medium heat. Add the onions, *cachucha* peppers, and garlic and sauté until softened, about 3 minutes. Return the pork to the pan, add the rice, and cook for 2 minutes. Stir in the drained beans, cumin, oregano, bay leaf, and tomato sauce (seasoned passata). Add the reserved cooking water and the salt. Bring to a boil, then reduce the heat to low, cover, and cook until the rice is done, about 12 minutes. Stir and cook for 6 more minutes.

Note: If you don't have a pressure cooker, it is very important to soak the beans first. Cook in 12 cups (96 fl oz/ 3 liters) water in a large pot over medium-high heat for 1½–2 hours, depending on the quality, age, and type of beans. Then follow the rest of the instructions as directed.

RICE WITH CHICKEN AND VEGETABLES

Arroz con pollo y vegetales

PREPARATION TIME: 20 MINUTES
COOKING TIME: 40 MINUTES
SERVES: 4

2 tablespoons vegetable oil
1 medium green bell pepper,
finely chopped
5 cachucha peppers or cubanelles,
finely chopped
1 medium white onion,
finely chopped
4 cloves garlic, finely chopped
1 lb (400 g), cooked chicken
(see page 19), cut into ½ inch
(1 cm) pieces
1 cup (240 g) tomato sauce
(seasoned passata)
2 tablespoons dry white wine
1 tablespoon vinegar
Salt
1½ cups (345 g) short-grain white
rice, rinsed
1 cup (240 g) cooked corn kernels
1 cup (110 g) diced carrot or
peeled pumpkin
1 cup (100 g) chopped cabbage
1½ cups (12 fl oz/375 ml) chicken
stock
1 cup (60 g) chopped scallions
(spring onions)

In a medium frying pan, heat the oil over medium-low heat. Add the bell pepper, *cachucha* peppers, onion, and garlic and sauté until softened, about 3 minutes. Stir in the cooked chicken. Add the tomato sauce (seasoned passata), wine, vinegar, and salt to taste and cook until the sauce reduces, about 5 minutes.

Transfer the mixture to a large pot and add the rice, corn, carrot, cabbage, and stock. Bring to a boil over medium-high heat, then reduce the heat to medium-low and cook until the rice swells, about 12 minutes. Stir in the scallions (spring onions) and cook until the rice is completely done, about 5 minutes. Serve in a bowl or clay pot.

TRADITIONAL MOORS AND CHRISTIANS

Moros y cristianos tradicional

The name *moros y cristianos*, or Moors and Christians, comes from the era of Arab or Mozarabic domination in Spain, and refers to the black beans (Moors/blacks or Arabs) and rice (Christians/whites). Rice was introduced to Spain by the Arabs. In the traditional recipe, the dressing added at the end is cooked in lard. In this recipe, it is cooked in the wine to make the dish lighter.

★

In a pressure cooker (see Note), combine the beans and the large pieces of bell pepper and add water to cover by 2 inches (5 cm). Lock the lid and bring to pressure over medium heat. Cook at pressure until tender, about 40 minutes (be careful not to overcook them). Quick-release the pressure. Reserving 3 cups (24 fl oz/700 ml) of the cooking water, drain the beans and pepper.

Meanwhile, in a small frying pan, combine ¼ cup (2 fl oz/ 60 ml) of the wine, 3 cloves of the garlic, 1 onion, and half the julienned pepper. Bring to a boil over medium heat and cook for 1 minute. Set the dressing aside.

In a large heavy-bottomed pot, heat the lard over low heat. Add the remaining onion, the remaining julienned pepper, the remaining 7 cloves garlic, the bay leaf, cumin, and oregano and cook until fragrant, about 1 minute. Add the rice and stir over medium heat for 3–4 minutes. Add the drained beans, reserved bean liquid, salt, and sugar. Increase the heat to medium-high and bring to a boil. When it begins to boil, reduce the heat to medium-low and cook, covered, until the liquid is absorbed, about 12 minutes. Reduce the heat to low and add the chicharrones and the remaining ¾ cup (6 fl oz/180 ml) wine. Stir, cover, and cook until the rice swells, about 10 minutes. Stir again and cook over low heat until the rice is completely done, about 5 minutes, adding the dried parsley in the last minute (optional). Uncover, add the dressing, and stir. Remove from the heat and let sit for 15 minutes before serving.

Note: If you don't have a pressure cooker, it is very important to soak the beans first. Cook in 12 cups (96 fl oz/ 3 liters) water in a large pot over medium-high heat for 1½–2 hours, depending on the quality, age, and type of beans. Then follow the rest of the instructions as directed.

PREPARATION TIME: 20 MINUTES
COOKING TIME: 1 HOUR 45 MINUTES
SERVES: 8

★

1½ cups (330 g) dried black beans, rinsed
2 small green bell peppers—
1 cut into large, irregular pieces and 1 julienned
1 cup (8 fl oz/240 ml) dry white wine
10 cloves garlic, crushed
2 small white onions, finely chopped
⅓ cup (80 g) lard
1 bay leaf
1 teaspoon ground cumin
½ teaspoon dried oregano
3⅓ cups (760 g) short-grain white rice, rinsed
2½ teaspoons salt
½ teaspoon sugar
½ cup (80 g) chicharrones (Fried Pork Rinds, page 49)
4 tablespoons dried parsley (optional)

MOORS AND CHRISTIANS WITH SOFRITO

Moros y cristianos con sofrito

PREPARATION TIME: 10 MINUTES
COOKING TIME: 1 HOUR 15 MINUTES
SERVES: 4

¾ cup (165 g) black beans, rinsed

1½ cups (345 g) short-grain white rice, rinsed

1 teaspoon salt

4 tablespoons vegetable oil

1 large green bell pepper, diced (see Note)

1 large white onion, diced

6 cloves garlic, finely chopped

¼ teaspoon ground cumin

⅛ teaspoon dried oregano

1 bay leaf

It is common in the Eastern Region of Cuba to briefly sauté the rice in a little oil before mixing it with the beans and broth.

★

In a pressure cooker (see Note), combine the beans and water to cover by 2 inches (5 cm). Lock the lid and bring to pressure over medium heat. Cook at pressure until tender, about 30–45 minutes (be careful not to overcook them). Quick-release the pressure. Reserving 1½ cups (12 fl oz/ 350 ml) of the cooking liquid, drain the beans.

In a medium heavy-bottomed pot, combine the drained beans, the rice, ½ teaspoon of the salt, and reserved bean liquid. Cook over high heat until it comes to a boil, then reduce the heat to medium-low and cook until the rice is tender and the water is absorbed, about 12 minutes. Stir and cook until the rice is done, 6 more minutes.

Meanwhile, in a medium frying pan, heat the oil over medium-low heat. Add the bell peppers, onion, and garlic and sauté until softened, about 3 minutes. Add the cumin, oregano, and bay leaf and cook for 1 minute. Add the remaining ½ teaspoon salt.

Add the sofrito to the rice and beans and cook over low heat until the rice absorbs the flavors of the sofrito, about 3 minutes.

Notes: If you don't have a pressure cooker, it is very important to soak the beans first. Cook in 12 cups (96 fl oz/ 3 liters) water in a large pot over medium-high heat for 1½–2 hours, depending on the quality, age, and type of beans. Then follow the rest of the instructions as directed.

The bell pepper can be roasted instead of sautéed, or it can be substituted with cachucha pepper.

Another variation adds the sofrito just before serving.

CAMAGÜEY-STYLE RICE

Arroz a la camagüeyana

PREPARATION TIME: 30 MINUTES
COOKING TIME: 1 HOUR 15 MINUTES
SERVES: 4

2 medium tomatoes

4 tablespoons vegetable oil

1 lb (500 g) pork belly, trimmed
and cut into 1¼-inch (3 cm) pieces

4 cloves garlic, finely chopped

1 medium white onion,
finely chopped

3 cachucha peppers or cubanelles,
finely chopped

2 leaves fresh culantro,
torn into smaller pieces

½ cup (4 fl oz/120 ml) dry white wine

2 leaves fresh Cuban oregano
(Mexican mint) or regular oregano

1 bay leaf

3 cups (24 fl oz/700 ml) chicken stock

7 oz (200 g) pumpkin,
peeled and diced

1 large ripe plantain, peeled and
cut into diagonal slices ⅓ inch
(1 cm) thick

2 cups (460 g) short-grain white
rice, rinsed

½ teaspoon salt

¼ teaspoon ground black pepper

¼ teaspoon ground cumin

Avocado or tomato, cabbage,
and cucumber, for serving

Bring a medium pot of water to a boil. Cut an "x" into the skin at the blossom end of the tomatoes and submerge them in the boiling water for 1 minute. Transfer to a cutting board to cool, then remove the skin (peeling at the "x"). Halve, seed, and dice finely.

In a medium pot, heat the oil over high heat. Add the pork belly and cook until browned, about 5 minutes. Reduce the heat to medium, add the garlic, onion, *cachucha* peppers, and culantro and sauté until softened, about 3 minutes. Add ¼ cup (2 fl oz/60 ml) of the wine, then add the tomatoes and cook until the liquid begins to evaporate, about 6 minutes. Add the oregano and bay leaf, pour in the chicken stock, cover, and cook over medium heat until the meat is semi-soft, 20–25 minutes.

Add the pumpkin and plantain and cook until they begin to soften, about 5 minutes. Set a colander over a bowl and strain the broth into it. Pour the broth into a measuring cup, then measure out rice in a 1:1 ratio, or a 1:1½ ratio (by volume), depending on the variety of rice. Return the broth to the pot and bring to a boil. Add the rice, the remaining ¼ cup (2 fl oz/60 ml) wine, the salt, black pepper, and cumin. Cover and cook over low heat until the rice swells, about 12 minutes. Stir and cook until the rice is completely cooked, 6 more minutes.

Serve accompanied by a tomato, cabbage, and cucumber salad or thick avocado wedges.

Note: Many people add 1 tablespoon annatto (achiote) seed to the broth to add an orange color.

RICE WITH CHICKEN-VEGETABLE SAUCE

Arroz con salsa de vegetales y pollo

PREPARATION TIME: 25 MINUTES, PLUS 2 HOURS FOR MARINATING
COOKING TIME: 1 HOUR 15 MINUTES
SERVES: 4

4 medium skinless chicken thighs (about 5½ oz/160 g each)
3 teaspoons salt
¼ cup (2 fl oz/60 ml) bitter orange juice (see page 18)
8 cloves garlic, finely chopped
1 cup (200 g) green beans, cut into ¾ inch (2 cm) pieces
2 tablespoons vegetable oil, plus more for deep-frying
1 medium green bell pepper, diced
1 large white onion, diced
½ lb (230 g) pumpkin or carrots, cut into medium pieces
1 cup (240 g) tomato sauce (seasoned passata)
2 tablespoons dry white wine
1 tablespoon vinegar
1 tablespoon raw cane sugar
¼ teaspoon ground cumin
1½ cups (345 g) short-grain white rice, rinsed
Chopped parsley or scallions (spring onions), for serving

In a medium container, combine the chicken, 1 teaspoon of the salt, the bitter orange juice, and half the garlic. Let marinate for 2 hours. Drain and discard the marinade.

Meanwhile, bring a medium pot of water to a boil over high heat. Add the green beans and cook uncovered until they are cooked al dente, about 10 minutes. Drain and set aside. In a medium frying pan, heat 2 inches (5 cm) oil over medium heat. Add the chicken and fry until browned and cooked through, about 30 minutes. Set aside.

In another large frying pan, heat 2 tablespoons of oil over medium heat. Add the bell pepper, onion, remaining garlic, the pumpkin, and green beans and sauté until they begin to soften, about 5 minutes. Add the tomato sauce (seasoned passata), wine, vinegar, raw sugar, cumin, and 1 teaspoon of the salt. Add the chicken and cook until the sauce thickens, about 3 minutes. Set aside.

In a medium pot, combine the rice with the remaining 1 teaspoon salt and 1½ cups (12 fl oz/350 ml) water. Cook over medium-low heat until tender, about 15 minutes. Add the sautéed vegetables and chicken, stir so that the rice absorbs the sauce, and cook for 3 minutes to warm through. Serve with parsley or scallions (spring onions) on top.

CHICKEN RICE STEW

Ensopada de pollo

Bring a medium pot of water to a boil. Add the chicken, half the *chay* peppers, onions, garlic, and parsley, then add ½ tablespoon salt and the annatto (achiote) seeds. Cook over medium heat until the chicken is cooked through, about 25 minutes. Remove the chicken and strain the broth, reserving 2½ cups (20 fl oz/590 ml). Let cool, then remove the meat from the bone and shred into ¾ inch (2 cm) long pieces.

In a large pan, heat the oil over medium-low heat. Add the chicken and the remaining *chay* peppers, onions, garlic, and parsley, along with the tomatoes, and cook until the vegetables soften, about 2 minutes. Add the cumin, tomato sauce (seasoned passata), and rice and cook until the sauce colors the rice, about 2 minutes. Add the reserved broth and salt to taste, and cook until the rice puffs up, about 15 minutes. Continue cooking over low heat until the rice is completely done, about 10 more minutes. Add the wine, stir, and cook for 2 more minutes. Serve with parsley or scallions (spring onions) on top.

PREPARATION TIME: 40 MINUTES
COOKING TIME: 1 HOUR 10 MINUTES
SERVES: 4

4 medium chicken thighs (about 5½ oz/160 g each)
4 chay peppers or cubanelles, finely chopped
2 medium white onions or 1 cup (60 g) scallions (spring onions), finely chopped
6 cloves garlic, finely chopped
1 bunch parsley, finely chopped
Salt
½ teaspoon annatto (achiote) seeds
2 tablespoons vegetable oil
2 medium tomatoes, diced
¼ teaspoon ground cumin
1 tablespoon tomato sauce (seasoned passata)
1½ cups (345 g) short-grain white rice, rinsed
2 tablespoons dry white wine
Chopped parsley or scallions (spring onions), for serving

RICE WITH CHICKEN "A LA CHORRERA"

Arroz con pollo a la Chorrera

PREPARATION TIME: 20 MINUTES
COOKING TIME: 1 HOUR 50 MINUTES
SERVES: 5

½ lb (230 g) chicken giblets
2 medium green bell peppers,
cut into irregular pieces
2 medium white onions—
½ cut into irregular chunks
and 1½ finely chopped
4 cloves garlic, finely chopped
1 teaspoon annatto (achiote) seeds
4 tablespoons olive oil
2 large boneless, skinless chicken
breasts (1 lb 5 oz/600 g total),
each cut into 3 pieces
4 medium chicken thighs (about
5½ oz/160 g each)
1 medium red bell pepper,
finely chopped
⅓ cup (80 g) tomato sauce
(seasoned passata)
¼ teaspoon ground cumin
¼ teaspoon bay leaf
1½ teaspoons salt
2½ cups (575 g) short-grain white
rice, rinsed
1 cup (8 fl oz/240 ml) light beer
2 tablespoons dry white wine
¼ cup (80 g) canned peas
½ cup (115 g) chopped canned
mushrooms
1 large pickled morrón pepper,
cut into strips

According to famous Cuban chef Gilberto Smith Duquesne, this dish owes its name to a restaurant of the same name, at the Fuente de la Chorrera, at the mouth of the Almendares River in the Vedado neighborhood in Havana. Chef Acela Matamoros writes that in this spot, where a small fishing community was situated, a two-story wooden hotel was built in 1905. This hotel included a restaurant that offered this dish as its main attraction.

In a large pot, combine the chicken giblets, bell peppers, the onion chunks, half the garlic, the annatto (achiote) seeds, and 5 cups (40 fl oz/1.2 liters) water. Bring to a boil over medium-high heat, then reduce to low and cook for 30 minutes. Strain the broth and discard the solids.

In the same pot, heat 3 tablespoons of the oil over high heat. Add the chicken breasts and thighs and sauté, stirring regularly, until browned, about 5 minutes. Reduce the heat to medium and add the finely chopped onion, red bell pepper, remaining garlic, tomato sauce (seasoned passata), cumin, and bay leaf. Cook until the sauce begins to reduce, about 5 minutes. Add the strained broth and salt, cover, and cook until the chicken is tender, about 20 minutes.

Add the rice and bring to a boil over high heat. Reduce the heat to low, cover, and cook until the rice is tender, about 12 minutes. Add the beer, cover, and cook over low heat until the beer begins to evaporate, about 10 minutes. Add the remaining 1 tablespoon oil and the wine and cook for 2 more minutes. Remove from the heat and add the peas, mushrooms, and pickled pepper. Serve hot.

IMPERIAL RICE
WITH CHICKEN

Arroz imperial con pollo

PREPARATION TIME: 20 MINUTES
COOKING TIME: 40 MINUTES
SERVES: 4–6

★

3 tablespoons vegetable oil
3 medium white onions, diced
4 cloves garlic, finely chopped
¼ teaspoon ground cumin
2½ cups (575 g) short-grain white
rice, rinsed
1 tablespoon salt
1 teaspoon annatto (achiote) seeds
4 tablespoons dry white wine
1 cup (230 g) cooked chicken
(see page 19), cut into ½ inch
(1 cm) pieces
1 carrot, diced
2 green bell peppers, diced
2 tablespoons tomato sauce
(seasoned passata)
¾ cup (170 g) mayonnaise, store-
bought or homemade (page 318)
1 cup (100 g) grated Cuban gouda
or other mild yellow cheese,
for serving (optional)
Green or red bell peppers, hard-
boiled eggs, or parsley (optional),
for serving

This recipe was created in a former sugar mill, called
Violeta, in 1921.

★

In a medium pot, heat 2 tablespoons of the oil over medium
heat. Add one-third of the onions and half the garlic and
sauté until the onion turns translucent, about 3 minutes.
Add the cumin and stir, then add the rice and stir.
Add 2½ cups (20 fl oz/590 ml) water, the salt, and annatto
(achiote) seeds, cover, and cook over high heat until the
water begins to be absorbed, about 12 minutes. Reduce
the heat to medium-low and continue cooking, covered,
until the rice is done, about 15 minutes. Stir gently, then
add 2 tablespoons of the wine and remove from the heat.
Set aside covered.

In a medium pan, heat the remaining 1 tablespoon oil over
medium-low heat. Add the chicken, the remaining onion
and garlic, the carrot, and bell peppers and sauté until the
chicken is lightly browned, about 3 minutes. Add the tomato
sauce (seasoned passata) and remaining 2 tablespoons
wine and cook until the wine begins to evaporate, about
2 minutes.

In a casserole dish, spread out a ¾ inch (2 cm) layer each
of rice, chicken, and mayonnaise. Continue alternating,
finishing with a layer of rice. If desired, top with grated
cheese. Garnish with peppers, hard-boiled eggs, or parsley
(optional). Serve hot.

HOMEMADE FRIED RICE

Arroz frito casero

Season the whisked eggs with the salt. In a small frying pan, heat ½ tablespoon of the oil over medium-low heat. Add one-third of the whisked eggs and cook for 1 minute on each side. Transfer to a plate. Add ½ tablespoon oil and make 2 more omelets. Slice the omelets into thin strips and set aside.

In a large frying pan, heat the remaining 3 tablespoons oil over high heat. Add the chicken and sauté until it browns lightly, about 3 minutes. Lower the heat and cook until the chicken is soft, 5 more minutes. Add the ham and cook 1 minute. Add the onions and pepper and cook until softened, about 2 minutes. Add the rice and stir gently. Pour in the soy sauce and stir to achieve an even color. Add the omelet strips, scallions (spring onions), and bean sprouts and cook, stirring regularly, until all the ingredients are mixed well, about 3 minutes.

PREPARATION TIME: 40 MINUTES
COOKING TIME: 25 MINUTES
SERVES: 4

★

3 eggs, whisked
½ teaspoon salt
4 tablespoons vegetable oil
1 large chicken quarter (1 lb/
460 g), bones and skin removed,
cut into strips
1 lb (460 g) ham, cut into strips
2 medium white onions, sliced into
half-moons
1 large green bell pepper,
cut into strips
3 cups (600 g) cooked rice
2 tablespoons dark soy sauce
1 bunch scallions (spring onions),
finely chopped
½ lb (230 g) bean sprouts,
cut into small pieces

CUBAN FRIED RICE

Arroz frito a la cubana

PREPARATION TIME: 45 MINUTES
COOKING TIME: 20 MINUTES
SERVES: 6

★

6 tablespoons vegetable oil

4 eggs, whisked

½ lb (230 g) pork loin or
tenderloin, cut into thin strips

1 lb (460 g) shrimp (prawns),
peeled and deveined

½ lb (230 g) ham, cut into thin strips

1 cup (230 g) cooked chicken
(see page 19), cut into ¾ inch
(2 cm) segments

6 cups (1 kg) cooked rice

3 tablespoons dark soy sauce

1 bunch scallions (spring onions),
finely chopped

5 oz (150 g) bean sprouts,
finely chopped

This dish is influenced by Chinese cooking, in which the technique of sautéing the ingredients of a dish all together is commonly used.

★

In a medium frying pan, heat 1 tablespoon of the oil over medium-low heat. Add half of the whisked eggs and cook for 1 minute on each side. Transfer to a plate. Add 1 tablespoon oil to the pan, and make another omelet with the other half of the eggs. Slice the omelets into thin strips and set aside.

In a large frying pan, heat the remaining 4 tablespoons oil over high heat. Add the pork and sauté until lightly browned, about 8 minutes. Add the shrimp (prawns) and sauté until pink and opaque, about 1 minute. Add the ham and chicken and cook until lightly browned, about 2 minutes. Reduce the heat to medium-low, add the rice, and stir to combine. Pour in the soy sauce and mix with a fork until the rice is a uniform color. Add the strips of omelet, scallions (spring onions), and bean sprouts. Stir and cook for 3 minutes.

EXQUISITE PILAF

Arroz pilaf exquisito

PREPARATION TIME: 20 MINUTES
COOKING TIME: 25 MINUTES
SERVES: 4

2 tablespoons vegetable oil
1 carrot, thinly sliced
1 red bell pepper, thinly sliced
3 cloves garlic, finely chopped
1 medium white onion,
    finely chopped
3 leaves fresh oregano, cut into
    thin slivers
1½ cups (345 g) short-grain white
    rice, rinsed
¼ teaspoon ground cumin
2 cups (16 fl oz/500 ml)
    vegetable stock
½ teaspoon salt
Finely chopped parsley,
    for serving

In a medium pot, heat the oil over medium heat. Add the carrot, bell pepper, garlic, onion, and oregano and sauté until softened, about 3 minutes. Add the rice and cumin and cook until the rice absorbs the condiments, about 2 minutes. Add the stock and salt and cook, covered, over medium-high heat until the rice puffs up, about 11 minutes. Stir, then cover and cook over low heat until the rice is tender, about 6 minutes. Serve garnished with the chopped parsley.

RICE WITH FRIED RIPE PLANTAINS

Arroz con plátano maduro

PREPARATION TIME: 20 MINUTES
COOKING TIME: 40 MINUTES
SERVES: 4

6 tablespoons vegetable oil
3 cloves garlic, finely chopped
1 medium white onion, finely chopped
1 carrot, grated
1½ cups (345 g) short-grain white
    rice, rinsed
¼ teaspoon ground cumin
⅛ teaspoon dried oregano
1 bay leaf
1 teaspoon salt
2 cups (16 fl oz/500 ml) vegetable
    stock
½ lb (230 g) bean sprouts
2 medium ripe plantains, cut
    diagonally
Finely chopped parsley, for serving

In a medium pot, heat 2 tablespoons of oil over medium heat. Add the garlic, onion, and carrot and sauté until they begin to soften, about 3 minutes. Add the rice, cumin, oregano, bay leaf, and salt and cook for 2 minutes. Pour in the stock and bring to a boil, then reduce the heat to low, cover, and cook until the rice swells, about 10 minutes. Stir and cook until the rice is tender, 5 more minutes. Stir in the bean sprouts and cook until softened, about 2 minutes.

In a medium pan, heat the remaining 4 tablespoons oil over medium-high heat. Add the plantains and fry until browned on both sides, about 5 minutes total.

Serve the rice with finely chopped parsley and top with the fried plantains.

RICE WITH DRIED SHRIMP

Arroz con camarones secos

This combination is reminiscent of Chinese cuisine in Cuba. Fried plantains go nicely with this dish.

★

Soak the shrimp in 1½ cups (12 fl oz/355 ml) of water for 30 minutes. Drain.

In a medium pot, heat the oil over medium-high heat. Add the shrimp and sauté until they turn a reddish-orange color, about 1 minute. Add the *salsa criolla*, salt, and rice and cook for 3 minutes. Add 2 cups (16 fl oz/475 ml) of the fish stock and bring to a boil. Reduce the heat to low, cover, and cook until the rice is tender, about 15 minutes. Serve garnished with parsley, egg, and pickled peppers.

PREPARATION TIME: 10 MINUTES, PLUS 30 MINUTES SHRIMP SOAKING TIME
COOKING TIME: 20 MINUTES
SERVES: 4

★

1 cup (3½ oz/100 g) dried shrimp
2 tablespoons vegetable oil
⅔ cup (5 fl oz/150 ml) salsa criolla
(Cuban Sauce, page 311)
½ teaspoon salt
1½ cups (345 g) short-grain white
rice, rinsed
1½–2 cups (12–16 fl oz/375–475 ml)
fish stock
Parsley, finely chopped for garnish
Hard-boiled egg, quartered,
for garnish
Pickled peppers, sliced, for garnish

YELLOW RICE

Arroz amarillo

In a medium heavy-bottomed pot, heat the oil over medium heat. Add the ham and sausage and sauté until lightly browned, about 2 minutes. Add the *cachucha* peppers, garlic, and onions and cook, stirring, until softened, about 2 minutes.

Add the rice to the ham/sausage mixture. Cook over medium heat until the rice absorbs the flavors of the sauté, about 3 minutes. Stir in the salt, annatto (achiote) seed, and 2 cups (16 fl oz/475 ml) water. Cook, covered, until the rice swells, about 12 minutes. Stir and cook until the rice is tender, 6 more minutes. Add the wine and parsley, cover, and let steam for 4 minutes.

PREPARATION TIME: 15 MINUTES
COOKING TIME: 35 MINUTES
SERVES: 4

★

3 tablespoons vegetable oil
5 oz (150 g) ham, diced
1 dried sausage (about 2 oz/60 g),
diced
3 cachucha peppers or cubanelles,
finely chopped
5 cloves garlic, crushed
2 small white onions,
finely chopped
2 cups (460 g) short-grain white
rice, rinsed
1 teaspoon salt
1 teaspoon annatto (achiote) seeds
⅓ cup (2½ fl oz/80 ml)
dry white wine
1 bunch parsley, finely chopped

CURRY RICE

Arroz al curry

PREPARATION TIME: 10 MINUTES
COOKING TIME: 25 MINUTES
SERVES: 4

★

2 tablespoons vegetable oil
1 large white onion, finely chopped
4 cloves garlic, finely chopped
1 cup (230 g) chopped cooked
chicken (see page 19)
1½ cups (345 g) short-grain white
rice, rinsed
2 cups (16 fl oz/500 ml) chicken
stock
2 teaspoons curry powder
½ teaspoon salt
½ cup (4 fl oz/125 ml) dry white wine
¼ cup chopped scallions (spring
onions) or parsley, for serving
(optional)

Curry is not a spice typically found in traditional Cuban cooking, but some people have started incorporating it into their home cooking.

★

In a medium pot, heat the oil over medium heat. Add the onion and garlic and sauté until softened, about 2 minutes. Add the chicken and cook for 1 minute. Stir in the rice, stock, curry powder, and salt. Bring to a boil, then reduce the heat to low, cover, and cook until the rice is tender, about 15 minutes. Add the wine and cook for 2 more minutes. Serve hot, preferably garnished with scallions (spring onions) or parsley.

RICE AND VEGETABLES

Arroz con vegetales

PREPARATION TIME: 20 MINUTES
COOKING TIME: 25 MINUTES
SERVES: 6

2 tablespoons vegetable oil
2 chay peppers or cubanelles,
finely chopped
4 cloves garlic, finely chopped
1 medium white onion,
finely chopped
7 oz (200 g) pumpkin, diced
1 cup (200 g) cooked corn kernels
2 tablespoons tomato sauce
(seasoned passata)
1½ cups (345 g) short-grain white
rice, rinsed
1 tablespoon salt
1 cup (200 g) cooked green beans,
cut into ¾ inch (2 cm) pieces
½ cup (60 g) chopped scallions
(spring onions)
1 tablespoon (15 g) butter
2 tablespoons dry white wine

In a medium pot, heat the oil over medium heat. Add the *chay* peppers, garlic, onion, pumpkin, and corn and sauté until the onion turns translucent, about 3 minutes. Add the tomato sauce (seasoned passata) and cook until it begins to reduce, about 1 minute. Add the rice, 2 cups (16 fl oz/475 ml) water, and the salt and stir. Cook, covered, over medium-low heat until the rice is tender, about 15 minutes. Stir in the green beans, scallions (spring onions), and butter. Add the wine and cook until the rice absorbs the liquid, about 3 more minutes.

RICE WITH PIGEON PEAS AND COCONUT

Arroz con frijol gandul y coco

In Cuba, the *gandul* bean has traditionally been grown in home gardens and consumed by the rural population. Over the last six decades, this population has migrated to the cities in large numbers and, as a result, the *gandul* bean has been gradually disappearing due to low production. In an effort to save it from extinction, agronomists, specialists in urban farming, families who grow food in their gardens, and farmers in the countryside are making efforts to plant this bean.

★

In a pressure cooker (see Note), combine the beans and 4 cups (1 liter) water. Lock the lid and bring to pressure over medium heat. Cook at pressure until soft, about 25 minutes. Quick-release the pressure. Reserving 2 cups (16 fl oz/ 475 ml) of the cooking water, drain the beans.

In a medium pot, heat the coconut oil over low heat. Add the garlic, onion, *chay* peppers, tomatoes, and culantro and cook until softened, about 5 minutes. Add the rice, salt, and white pepper and stir a few times. Stir in the drained beans, coconut milk, and reserved bean liquid. Cover and cook over high heat until the water begins to be absorbed, about 6 minutes. Reduce the heat to low and continue cooking until the liquid is fully absorbed, about 10 minutes. Stir gently and cook until the rice is completely done, about 5 minutes. Serve as a side dish.

Notes: If you don't have a pressure cooker, it is very important to soak the beans first. Cook in 12 cups (96 fl oz/ 3 liters) water in a large pot over medium-high heat for 1 hour, depending on the quality, age, and type of beans. Then follow the rest of the instructions as directed.

To make coconut milk, blend 1 cup (75 g) grated fresh coconut with 1 cup (8 fl oz/ 240 ml) hot water in a blender. Strain the mixture through a sieve lined with cheesecloth, then squeeze the cheesecloth hard to get out as much coconut milk as possible.

PREPARATION TIME: 25 MINUTES
COOKING TIME: 53 MINUTES
SERVES: 4

1 cup (220 g) gandul beans
(pigeon peas), rinsed
¼ cup (68 g) coconut oil
5 cloves garlic, finely chopped
1 medium white onion,
finely chopped
2 chay peppers or cubanelles,
finely chopped
2 medium tomatoes,
finely chopped
5 leaves fresh culantro,
finely chopped
2 cups (460 g) long-grain white rice
½ teaspoon salt
¼ teaspoon ground white pepper
½ cup (4 fl oz/125 ml) coconut
milk, store-bought or homemade
(see Note)

ORANGE RICE
WITH SAUTÉED VEGETABLES

Arroz a la naranja con vegetales salteados

PREPARATION TIME: 15 MINUTES
COOKING TIME: 35 MINUTES
SERVES: 6

★

1 tablespoon julienned orange zest
1 tablespoon vegetable oil
2 tablespoons (30 g) butter
1 carrot, julienned
1 large white onion, julienned
½ cup (120 g) cooked corn kernels
Generous 2 cups (460 g)
short-grain white rice, rinsed
2¼ cups (18 fl oz / 550 ml)
orange juice
1 teaspoon salt
⅛ teaspoon ground black pepper

Bring a small pot of water to a boil over high heat.
Add the orange zest and blanch for 3 minutes. Set aside.

In a medium frying pan, heat the oil and butter over
medium heat. Add the carrot, onion, and corn and sauté
until the onion turns translucent, about 3 minutes. Set aside.

In a medium pot, combine the rice, orange juice, salt,
and pepper, and bring to a boil over medium-high heat.
Reduce the heat to low, cover, and cook until the rice swells,
about 12 minutes. Carefully stir in the sautéed vegetables,
and cook until the rice is tender, 6 more minutes. Serve hot,
garnished with the orange zest.

*Note: This dish can also be garnished with orange supremes
instead of or in addition to the orange peel.*

RICE SAUTÉED
WITH VEGETABLES

Arroz salteado con vegetales

PREPARATION TIME: 25 MINUTES
COOKING TIME: 15 MINUTES
SERVES: 4

★

3 tablespoons vegetable oil
1 bunch scallions (spring onions),
finely chopped
4 cloves garlic, finely chopped
1 carrot, sliced thinly
1 large green bell pepper,
sliced thinly
2 medium white onions,
sliced thinly
1 cup (80 g) chopped bok choy
3 cups (600 g) cooked rice
2 tablespoons dark soy sauce
5 oz (150 g) bean sprouts,
cut into ¾-inch (2 cm) pieces
2 tablespoons dry white wine

In a large frying pan, heat the oil over medium-high heat.
Add the scallions (spring onions) and garlic and sauté until
fragrant, about 1 minute. Add the carrot, bell pepper, onions,
and bok choy and sauté, stirring with a wooden spoon, over
medium heat until softened, about 5 minutes. Reduce the
heat to medium-low, add the rice, and stir. Gradually stir in
the soy sauce and mix with a fork until it is an even color.
Add the bean sprouts and wine and stir. Cook, uncovered,
until the bean sprouts soften, about 3 minutes.

COUNTRY-STYLE RICE WITH CORN

Arroz con maíz a la campesina 📷

PREPARATION TIME: 30 MINUTES
COOKING TIME: 1 HOUR 15 MINUTES
SERVES: 4

★

1 cup (240 g) field corn kernels
2 tablespoons vegetable oil
5 cloves garlic, finely chopped
1 large white onion, finely chopped
3 chay peppers or cubanelles, finely chopped
1 cup (60 g) finely chopped scallions (spring onions)
1 teaspoon annatto (achiote) seeds
3 tablespoons tomato sauce (seasoned passata)
7 oz (200 g) unpeeled pumpkin, diced
1½ cups (345 g) short-grain white rice, rinsed
2 cups (16 fl oz/500 ml) vegetable stock
1 teaspoon salt
¼ cup (2 fl oz/60 ml) dry white wine

Bring a medium pot of water to a boil over high heat. Add the corn kernels and cook, covered, until softened, about 45 minutes. Drain well and set aside.

In a medium pot, heat the oil over medium heat. Add the garlic, onion, *chay* peppers, and scallions (spring onions) and sauté until softened, about 3 minutes. Stir in the corn, annatto (achiote) seeds, and tomato sauce (seasoned passata) and cook for 2 minutes. Add the pumpkin, rice, stock, and salt and stir. Cook, covered, over low heat until the rice swells, about 15 minutes. Stir, add the wine, and cook until the rice is tender, about 5 minutes.

RICE WITH POTATOES

Arroz con papas

PREPARATION TIME: 20 MINUTES
COOKING TIME: 25 MINUTES
SERVES: 4

★

7 oz (200 g) potatoes, peeled and diced
1 teaspoon salt
1½ cups (345 g) short-grain white rice, rinsed
2 tablespoons vegetable oil
1 large white onion, finely chopped
4 cloves garlic, crushed
2 chay peppers or cubanelles, finely chopped

This recipe was created by Cuban cooks during the Special Period and has been passed down orally.

★

In a medium pot, combine the potatoes, salt, and 2 cups (16 fl oz/500 ml) water. Bring to a boil over high heat. Add the rice, reduce the heat to low, cover, and cook until the rice is tender, about 15 minutes.

Meanwhile, in a medium frying pan, heat the oil over medium-low heat. Add the onion, garlic, and *chay* peppers and sauté until softened, about 3 minutes.

Stir the sofrito into the rice and cook for 2 minutes.

RICE WITH PEANUTS AND HERBS

Arroz con maní y finas hierbas

PREPARATION TIME: 15 MINUTES
COOKING TIME: 30 MINUTES
SERVES: 4

★

2 cups (460 g) short-grain white
rice
1 teaspoon salt
2 tablespoons (30 g) butter
1 tablespoon vegetable oil
2 cloves garlic, finely chopped
1 large white onion, finely chopped
1 leaf fresh culantro,
finely chopped
3 tablespoons chopped parsley,
plus sprigs for garnish
4 tablespoons unsalted roasted
peanuts, roughly crushed

In a medium pot, combine the rice, salt, 1 tablespoon (15 g) of the butter, and 2 cups (16 fl oz/475 ml) water. Cook, covered, over high heat until the water begins to be absorbed. Reduce the heat to low and continue cooking, covered, until the rice is tender, about 15 minutes. Stir gently, then cook until the rice is fluffy, about 2 minutes. Remove from the heat and set aside.

In a saucepan, heat the remaining 1 tablespoon (15 g) butter and the oil over medium heat. Add the garlic, onion, culantro, and parsley, and sauté until softened, about 3 minutes. Add the peanuts and cook over low heat for 2 minutes. Add this mixture to the rice and mix gently. Let cool slightly, then serve garnished with a sprig of parsley.

RICE WITH PEANUTS

Arroz con maní

PREPARATION TIME: 15 MINUTES
COOKING TIME: 30 MINUTES,
PLUS 1 HOUR 30 MINUTES
TO COOK THE PEANUTS
SERVES: 4

★

½ cup (80 g) raw peanuts
2 tablespoons vegetable oil
1 carrot, diced
1 small green bell pepper, diced
1 medium white onion, diced
3 cloves garlic, finely chopped
1 bunch scallions (spring onions),
finely chopped
2 cups (460 g) short-grain white
rice, rinsed
4 tablespoons tomato sauce
(seasoned passata)
¼ teaspoon ground cumin
¼ teaspoon dried oregano
1 teaspoon salt
1 bay leaf
2 tablespoons dry white wine

This recipe became popular during the Special Period in the 1990s, a severe economic crisis in Cuba following the collapse of the Soviet Union. Home cooks became very innovative, creating new recipes within the context of great scarcities.

★

In a large pot, combine the peanuts and 8 cups (64 fl oz/ 1.9 liters) water. Bring to a boil over medium-high heat and cook until softened, about 1 hour 30 minutes. Reserving 2½ cups (20 fl oz/590 ml) of the cooking water, drain the peanuts and set aside.

In a large pot, heat the oil over medium heat. Add the carrot, bell pepper, onion, and garlic and sauté until the onion turns translucent, about 3 minutes. Add the scallions (spring onions) and cook, until softened, 1 minute.
Add the drained peanuts, rice, tomato sauce (seasoned passata), cumin, and oregano and cook for 3 minutes. Add the reserved peanut cooking liquid, the salt, and bay leaf. Bring to a boil, then reduce the heat to low, cover, and cook until the rice swells, about 12 minutes. Stir and cook until the rice is tender and the liquid has been absorbed into the rice, 5 minutes. Add the wine and cook for 2 more minutes. Serve hot in a bowl or clay pot.

CUBAN PAELLA

Paella a la cubana

PREPARATION TIME: 20 MINUTES
COOKING TIME: 35 MINUTES
SERVES: 8

6 tablespoons olive oil

1 dried sausage (about 2½ oz/
75 g), thinly sliced

5 cups (40 fl oz/1.2 liters) fish stock

1 teaspoon saffron

1 teaspoon paprika

½ teaspoon ground white pepper

4 cloves garlic, finely chopped

1 sprig parsley, finely chopped

1 medium white onion,
finely chopped

1 large pickled pepper (140 g),
julienned

9 oz (250 g) boneless, skinless
chicken breast cut into strips

7 oz (200 g) pork loin
or tenderloin, diced

6 oz (180 g) squid, cleaned

¾ cup (5 oz/150 g) chopped octopus

10 oz (300 g) crabmeat

11 oz (300 g) peeled, deveined
shrimp (prawns)

10 oz (300 g) swordfish steaks, cut
into ¾–1½-inch (2–3 cm) cubes

3½ cups (800 g) Valencia rice

1 tablespoon vinegar

1 cup (8 fl oz/240 ml) dry white
wine

1½ tablespoons salt

½ cup (120 g) tomato sauce
(seasoned passata)

2 dried bay leaves

1 large cooked lobster tail
(7½ oz/220 g)

10 mussels

Lime slices, for garnish

This dish can be accompanied with sliced bread toasted in a frying pan with olive oil and garlic.

In a large wok, heat 5 tablespoons of the olive oil over medium-low heat. Add the sausage and sauté, stirring regularly, until the fat begins to render, about 3 minutes. Transfer the sausage to a blender (set the wok aside). To the blender add 1 cup (8 fl oz/240 ml) of the stock, the saffron, paprika, white pepper, garlic, and parsley. Blend these ingredients and set them aside.

Return the wok to medium-low heat. Add the onion and sauté until it turns translucent, about 2 minutes. Add the pickled pepper and sauté for 1 minute. Add the chicken and pork and cook until lightly browned, about 2 minutes. Add the squid, octopus, crab, and shrimp (prawns) and sauté until lightly browned, 1 minute. Add the fish and stir. Pour the rice over all these other ingredients and cook, stirring with a wooden spoon, for 2 minutes. Gradually pour in the remaining 4 cups (32 fl oz/950 ml) fish stock, the vinegar, wine, and 1 tablespoon of the salt. (The stock should completely cover the rice.) Add the sausage and tomato sauce (seasoned passata) and cook for 7 more minutes. Add the bay leaves. Put the lobster tail in the middle of the paella, and surround it with the mussels. Add the remaining ½ tablespoon salt.

Reduce the heat, cover, and cook until the rice is fluffy, about 10 minutes. Remove from heat and let the paella sit, covered, for 5 minutes. Drizzle the remaining 1 tablespoon olive oil over the top. Serve hot in a bowl or clay pot decorated with lime slices.

Notes: Other seafood can also be used. Peas can be added just before removing the paella from the stove.

JUGO de MANGO 3.00

REFRESCO GASEADO 2.00   JUGO de TAMARINDO 3.00

PAN con HAMBURGUESA 10.00   PAN con BISTEC 10.00

PAN con PERRO 10.00

PAN con JAMON y QUESO 10.00

PAN con JAMON y QUESO 5.00   PAN con CROQUETA y QUESO 5.00

PIZZA BAMBINA 5.00

BAMBINA de JAMON 7.00   PAN con MINUTA 5.00

PIZZA de QUESO 10.00   PIZZA de PERRO 15.00

PIZZA de JAMON 15.00

PASTAS AND PIZZAS

Pastas y pizzas

Pastas and pizzas have been so incorporated into the Cuban diet that it is logical to include them in this cookbook. Although originally from Asia, pastas are most frequently associated with Italian cuisine, which made its way to some hotels in Cuba during the first half of the twentieth century. Various cookbooks and informational pamphlets published in the United States and distributed in Cuba in the 1950s featured elbow noodles and other short noodles, but it was not until the 1970s that both pastas and pizzas were vastly popularized in Cuba with the establishment of a chain of government-owned fast-food restaurants. As the private gastronomic sector gradually opened up throughout the 1990s, and over the last several years, pastas and pizzas clearly became the protagonists in the menus of these small businesses, and they are currently the most common type of "fast food" consumed by Cubans. Some food culture and culinary experts have even expressed concern that young people in Cuba prefer pastas and pizzas over traditional Cuban food, which could be in danger of being displaced due to that preference. In addition to being served at many restaurants and food stands, pastas and pizzas are also frequently consumed in Cuban homes.

The following are general tips for preparing pastas: The sauce should be added to the pasta very soon after it is cooked, with the exception of pastas cooked in the oven; pastas should ideally be cooked al dente, but not overcooked (although Cubans usually prefer well-cooked or even overcooked pastas); the water should be six times the volume of the pasta, and the pastas should be stirred occasionally while being cooked; and the pastas should be added to salted, boiling water, at a ratio of 1½ tablespoons salt per 5 quarts (5 liters) water.

SPAGHETTI
AND MEATBALLS

Espaguetis con albondiguillas

In a bowl, mix the ground (minced) beef with the egg and breadcrumbs. Season with ½ teaspoon salt and the paprika. Roll the mixture into meatballs about 1½ inches (4 cm) in diameter.

In a medium frying pan, heat the oil over medium heat. Add the bell pepper, onion, and garlic and sauté until softened, about 3 minutes. Add the tomato sauce (seasoned passata) and raw sugar and cook until the mixture comes to a boil, about 3 minutes. Carefully add the meatballs, reduce the heat to low, cover, and cook for 10 minutes. Add the wine and adjust the salt. Remove from the heat and set aside.

Bring a large pot of lightly salted water to a boil. Add the spaghetti and cook until al dente according to the package directions. Drain and serve with the sauce and meatballs on top, sprinkled with grated cheese.

PREPARATION TIME: 25 MINUTES
COOKING TIME: 25 MINUTES
SERVES: 4

1 cup (230 g) ground (minced) beef
1 egg, whisked
3 tablespoons dried breadcrumbs
Salt
½ teaspoon paprika
2 tablespoons vegetable oil
1 large green bell pepper, diced
1 medium white onion, diced
4 cloves garlic, finely chopped
1 cup (240 g) tomato sauce (seasoned passata)
1 teaspoon raw cane sugar
¼ cup (2 fl oz/60 ml) dry white wine
1 package (14 oz/400 g) spaghetti
4 oz (115 g) Cuban white cheese or queso fresco, grated

SPAGHETTI
WITH PEPPER AND ONION

Espaguetis con pimiento y cebolla

Bring a large pot of lightly salted water to a boil.

In a frying pan, heat the oil over medium heat. Add the bell peppers and onions and sauté until translucent, about 3 minutes. Add the tomato sauce and cook until it comes to a boil, about 5 minutes. Add ½ teaspoon salt and the black pepper. Remove from the heat and set aside.

Add the spaghetti to the boiling water and cook until al dente according to the package directions. Drain the spaghetti and serve covered with the sauce and grated cheese.

PREPARATION TIME: 10 MINUTES
COOKING TIME: 15 MINUTES
SERVES: 4

Salt
2 tablespoons vegetable oil
6 green bell peppers, cut into strips
2 medium white onions, cut into rings
1 cup (250 g) Tomato Sauce (page 323)
¼ teaspoon ground black pepper
1 package (14 oz/400 g) spaghetti
4 oz (115 g) Cuban gouda or other mild yellow cheese, grated

SPAGHETTI WITH VEGETABLE SAUCE

Espaguetis con salsa de vegetales

PREPARATION TIME: 15 MINUTES
COOKING TIME: 20 MINUTES
SERVES: 4

★

Salt
1 package (14 oz/400 g) spaghetti
1 cup (240 g) tomato sauce
(seasoned passata)
1 tablespoon (15 g) butter
2 tablespoons vegetable oil
1 carrot, diced
1 green bell pepper, diced
2 cloves garlic, finely chopped
1 white onion, diced
1 small bunch parsley, finely
chopped, plus more for serving
2 tablespoons fresh basil,
finely chopped
1 leaf fresh Cuban oregano
(Mexican mint) or regular oregano,
finely chopped
3 oz (80 g) bok choy, sliced
¼ cup (25 g) grated Cuban gouda
or another mild yellow cheese

Bring a large pot of lightly salted water to a boil. Add the spaghetti and cook until al dente according to the package directions. Reserving ½ cup (4 fl oz/120 ml) of the cooking water, drain the pasta.

In a medium bowl, combine the tomato sauce (seasoned passata) and reserved cooking water. Stir and set aside.

Meanwhile, in a medium frying pan, melt the butter and oil over medium-low heat. Add the carrot, bell pepper, garlic and onion and sauté until softened, about 4 minutes. Add the parsley, basil, oregano, and bok choy. Pour in the tomato sauce and cook until the sauce thickens, about 5 minutes. Adjust the salt.

Serve the spaghetti quite hot, with the sauce in the middle, and the cheese grated in a circle around the sauce. Garnish with parsley.

SAUTÉED SPAGHETTI

Espaguetis salteados

PREPARATION TIME: 25 MINUTES
COOKING TIME: 30 MINUTES
SERVES: 6

★

Salt
1 package (14 oz/400 g) spaghetti
3 tablespoons vegetable oil
2 eggs, whisked
1 medium white onion,
cut into crescents
1 bunch scallions (spring onions),
finely chopped
1 tablespoon vinegar
2 tablespoons soy sauce
7 oz (200 g) pumpkin, julienned
½ lb (230 g) bean sprouts,
finely chopped

The technique of sautéing and the use of omelet, scallions (spring onions), and bean sprouts are derived from the Chinese culinary influence in Cuba.

★

Bring a large pot of lightly salted water to a boil. Add the spaghetti and cook until al dente according to the package directions. Drain and set aside to cool.

In a medium pan, heat 1 tablespoon of the oil over medium-low heat. Add the eggs and cook until set, 1 minute on each side. Let the omelet cool then cut it into strips and set aside.

In a large frying pan, heat the remaining 2 tablespoons oil over medium heat. Add the onion and scallions (spring onions) and sauté until softened, 3 minutes. Add the spaghetti, vinegar, and soy sauce and mix. Stir in the omelet strips and bean sprouts and serve.

ELBOW MACARONI WITH VEGETABLES AND CHEESE

Coditos con vegetales y queso

PREPARATION TIME: 20 MINUTES
COOKING TIME: 25 MINUTES
SERVES: 6

Salt
2 tablespoons vegetable oil
1 tablespoon (15 g) butter
½ cup (30 g) finely chopped
scallions (spring onions)
4 cloves garlic, finely chopped
6 oz (175 g) okra,
cut into small slices
1 tablespoon lime juice
3 oz pumpkin (75 g) or carrot,
cut into medium cubes
1 large green bell pepper,
finely diced
1 tablespoon dried basil
⅛ teaspoon dried oregano
1 cup (240 g) tomato sauce
(seasoned passata)
1 package (14 oz/400 g) elbow
macaroni
4 oz (120 g) Cuban white cheese
or queso fresco, grated
Chopped parsley, for garnish

Bring a large pot of lightly salted water to a boil.

Meanwhile, in a medium frying pan, heat the oil and butter over medium heat. Add the scallions (spring onions) and garlic and sauté until softened and fragrant, about 1 minute. Add the okra and the lime juice and cook until the okra is crisp-tender, about 5 minutes. Add the pumpkin and bell pepper and stir until the bell pepper softens, about 2 minutes. Add the basil, oregano, and tomato sauce (seasoned passata) and cook until the sauce thickens, about 5 minutes.

Add the pasta to the boiling water and cook until al dente according to the package directions. Drain and return to the pot over low heat. Add the vegetable sauce and mix gently. Add the grated cheese, stir, and cook until the cheese begins to melt, about 5 minutes. Serve the noodles very hot, garnished with parsley.

ELBOW MACARONI WITH CHICKEN

Coditos con pollo

PREPARATION TIME: 15 MINUTES
COOKING TIME: 15 MINUTES
SERVES: 4

★

Salt

2 tablespoons vegetable oil

2 chay peppers or cubanelles, diced

1 medium onion, diced

2 cloves garlic, finely chopped

1 cup (230 g) cooked chicken (see page 19), cut into 1 inch (2.5 cm) pieces

1 tablespoon chopped fresh basil

1 cup (240 g) Tomato Sauce (page 323)

1 package (14 oz/400 g) elbow macaroni

1 bunch scallions (spring onions), finely chopped

Bring a large pot of lightly salted water to a boil.

Meanwhile, in a frying pan, heat the oil over medium heat. Add the *chay* peppers, onion, and garlic and sauté until the onion is translucent, about 3 minutes. Stir in the chicken and sprinkle in the basil. Add the tomato sauce and cook until the sauce begins to reduce, about 3 minutes. Season to taste with salt.

Add the pasta to the boiling water and cook al dente according to the package directions. Drain and serve hot, covered with the sauce and scallions (spring onions).

HOME-STYLE LASAGNA

Lasaña casera

In a medium bowl, combine the flour and egg to make a cohesive dough, then transfer to a clean surface and knead until it is smooth and pliable, 8–10 minutes; if the dough seems too tight to knead, cover with a towel and let rest for 10 minutes before continuing to knead. Wrap tightly in plastic wrap (clingfilm) and refrigerate at least 1 hour or overnight.

On a lightly floured surface, roll out the dough to a 7 x 21-inch (18 x 53 cm) rectangle and cut it into three 7-inch (18 cm) squares with a knife or a pasta cutter.

Bring a large pot of lightly salted water to a boil. Cook the noodles one at a time until each is al dente and rises to the surface, 30–60 seconds. Carefully remove the noodles from the water and let them drain on a clean, dry tea towel.

In a medium bowl, combine the ground (minced) beef and 1 cup (250 g) of the béchamel sauce.

Preheat the oven to 375°F (190°C/Gas Mark 5). Lightly oil an 8-inch (20 cm) square baking pan.

Spread 2 tablespoons of the béchamel sauce over the bottom of the oiled pan. Add one lasagna noodle, then half of the beef mixture, followed by one-third of the grated cheese. Arrange another noodle, the remaining beef mixture, and another one-third of the grated cheese. Arrange the last noodle on top, then spread the remaining béchamel sauce over it. Pour the tomato sauce evenly over the top and finish with the remaining cheese.

Bake until the cheese is melted and the juices are bubbling, about 5 minutes. Serve hot.

Note: The beef can be replaced with ground ham or sautéed vegetables.

**PREPARATION TIME: 35 MINUTES,
PLUS 1 HOUR DOUGH CHILLING TIME
COOKING TIME: 20 MINUTES
SERVES: 2–4**

¾ cup (100 g) all-purpose (plain) flour, plus more for dusting
1 egg, whisked
Salt
¾ (140 g) cup Cuban Ground Beef (page 206)
1½ cups (12 fl oz/350 g) Béchamel Sauce (page 322)
Vegetable oil, for greasing
1 cup (4¼ oz/120 g) grated Cuban gouda or other mild yellow cheese
½ cup (132 g) Tomato Sauce (page 323)

SWEET POTATO GNOCCHI

Ñoquis de boniato 📷

**PREPARATION TIME: 25 MINUTES,
PLUS 1 HOUR RESTING TIME
COOKING TIME: 1 HOUR
SERVES: 4**

★

2 medium white sweet potatoes
(1 lb/460 g total)
Salt
½ cup (120 g) cream cheese
2 tablespoons (30 g) butter,
softened
2 egg yolks, whisked
1 cup (135 g) all-purpose (plain) flour
¼ teaspoon ground black pepper
¼ teaspoon grated nutmeg
1 tablespoon vegetable oil
1 small bunch basil, chopped
½ cup (30 g) chopped scallions
(spring onions)
½ cup (125 g) tomato sauce
(seasoned passata)
½ cup (4 fl oz/125 ml) vegetable
stock
¼ cup (2 fl oz/60 ml) dry white wine
1 teaspoon raw cane sugar
1 teaspoon Cuban lime juice

In a medium pot, combine the sweet potatoes, ½ teaspoon salt, and 5 cups (40 fl oz/1.25 liters) water. Bring to a boil and cook, covered, until soft, about 30 minutes. Drain and let cool. Peel and transfer to a large bowl.

Mash the sweet potatoes using a fork. Add the cream cheese, 1 tablespoon (15 g) of the butter, the egg yolks, ½ cup (65 g) flour, ½ teaspoon salt, the pepper, and nutmeg and mix to combine. Transfer to a floured surface and knead, adding the remaining ½ cup (65 g) flour, until the dough is smooth. Roll the dough into long ropes 1 inch (2.5 cm) thick, then cut them crosswise into ½-inch (1 cm) pieces. Roll each piece into a ball and squish with a fork. Transfer to a floured baking sheet and set aside for 1 hour.

Meanwhile, in a medium pan, heat the remaining 1 tablespoon (15 g) butter and the oil. Add the basil and scallions (spring onions) and sauté until softened, 1 minute. Add the tomato sauce (seasoned passata), stock, wine, raw sugar, and lime juice, and cook over medium-low heat until the sauce reduces, 10 minutes. Remove and set aside.

Bring a large pot of lightly salted water to a boil. Working in batches, add the gnocchi to the water and cook until they rise to the surface, 4–5 minutes. Remove with a slotted spoon and let drain. Transfer to a serving dish and pour the sauce over the gnocchi.

TARO ROOT GNOCCHI

Ñoquis de malanga

**PREPARATION TIME: 25 MINUTES,
PLUS 1 HOUR RESTING TIME
COOKING TIME: 50 MINUTES
SERVES: 4**

★

2 medium taro roots (14 oz/400 g
total), peeled and coarsely diced
Salt and ground black pepper
3½ oz (100 g) cheese, grated
2 egg yolks, whisked
2 tablespoons butter (30 g), melted
1 cup (135 g) all-purpose (plain) flour
¼ teaspoon grated nutmeg
1 cup (8 fl oz/240 ml) salsa criolla
(Cuban Sauce, page 311)
Fresh basil leaves, for garnish

In a medium pot, combine the taro roots, 2¼ teaspoons salt, and 5 cups (40 fl oz/1.25 liters) water. Bring to a boil and cook until soft, 20 minutes. Transfer to a bowl and mash with a fork. Add the cheese, egg yolks, butter, ½ cup (65 g) flour, 1 teaspoon salt, ¼ teaspoon pepper, and nutmeg. Transfer to a floured surface and knead, adding the remaining ½ cup (65 g) flour, until smooth. Roll the dough into long ropes 1 inch (2 cm) thick, then cut them crosswise into ½-inch (1 cm) pieces. Roll each piece into a ball and squish with a fork. Transfer to a floured baking sheet and set aside for 1 hour.

Bring a large pot of lightly salted water to a boil. Working in batches, add the gnocchi to the water and cook until they rise to the surface, 4–5 minutes. Remove with a slotted spoon and let drain. Transfer to a serving dish and pour the *salsa criolla* over the gnocchi. Garnish with basil leaves.

SIMPLE PIZZA DOUGH

Masa de base sencilla

**PREPARATION TIME: 15 MINUTES,
PLUS 35 MINUTES RISING TIME
MAKES: 4 INDIVIDUAL 9-INCH
(23 CM) PIZZAS**

★

3 cups (450 g) all-purpose (plain)
flour, plus more for rolling out
½ teaspoon salt
1 tablespoon instant (fast-action)
yeast
1 teaspoon sugar
¼ cup (2 fl oz/60 ml) vegetable oil,
plus more for greasing

In a large bowl, combine the flour, salt, yeast, and sugar. Make a well in the center, then pour the oil and 1 scant cup (7 fl oz/210 ml) tepid water into the middle. Gently knead until a dough is formed and roll the dough into a ball. Return to the bowl and cover with a slightly damp tea towel. Let rise until doubled in size with lots of bubbles, about 35 minutes.

Cut the dough into 4 equal portions, roll into balls, then roll each out on a floured surface to a round about 9 inches (23 cm) across and a scant ¼ inch (5 mm) thick.

Place each one uncovered in a greased 9 inch (23 cm) pizza pan with ¾ inch (2 cm) tall edges and let rise 25 minutes before adding toppings and baking in the oven.

ONION PIZZA

Pizza de cebolla

**PREPARATION TIME: 15 MINUTES,
PLUS 1 HOUR RISING TIME
COOKING TIME: 10 MINUTES
SERVES: 4**

★

4 pizza crusts made with Simple
Pizza Dough (page 146)
½ cup (125 g) tomato sauce
(seasoned passata)
8 oz (240 g) Cuban gouda or
other mild yellow cheese, grated
1 large white onion, cut into semi-
rounds (see Note)

Make the pizza crusts through the rising on the pans. Preheat the oven to 400°F (200°C/Gas Mark 6).

Spread the tomato sauce (seasoned passata) over each pizza dough and sprinkle the cheese over the sauce. Top with the onion. Bake until the cheese melts, about 7 minutes.

Note: The onion can be sautéed before adding to the pizza, if preferred.

BELL PEPPER PIZZA

Pizza de pimiento

**PREPARATION TIME: 15 MINUTES,
PLUS 1 HOUR RISING TIME
COOKING TIME: 10 MINUTES
SERVES: 4**

★

4 pizza crusts made with Simple
Pizza Dough (page 146)
½ cup (125 g) tomato sauce
(seasoned passata)
8 oz (240 g) Cuban gouda or
other mild yellow cheese, grated
1 large red bell pepper, julienned
(see Note)

Make the pizza crusts through the rising on the pans.
Preheat the oven to 400°F (200°C/Gas Mark 6).

Spread the tomato sauce over each pizza dough and
sprinkle the cheese over the sauce. Top with the pepper.
Bake until the cheese melts, about 7 minutes.

*Note: The pepper can be sautéed before adding to the pizza,
if preferred.*

BASIL PIZZA

Pizza de albahaca

**PREPARATION TIME: 30 MINUTES,
PLUS 30 MINUTES RISING TIME
COOKING TIME: 10 MINUTES
SERVES: 2**

★

1½ cups (205 g) all-purpose (plain)
flour
1 tablespoon active dried yeast
½ teaspoon salt
1 egg, whisked
6 tablespoons lukewarm whole
milk
4 tablespoons vegetable oil
⅓ cup (80 g) tomato sauce
(seasoned passata)
½ cup (50 g) grated Cuban gouda
or other mild yellow cheese
1 medium white onion,
cut into crescent moons
2 medium tomatoes, cut into
half-moons
Leaves from 1 small bunch basil

In a large bowl, sift the flour and add the yeast and salt.
Make a mound and pour the egg, milk and oil in the middle.
Gently knead until smooth and homogenous. Transfer to a
medium bowl and cover with a damp tea towel. Let rise until
doubled in size, about 30 minutes.

Preheat the oven to 400°F (200°C/Gas Mark 6).

Divide the dough in half, and roll each half out on a floured
surface until ½ inch (1 cm) thick. Place each one uncovered
in a greased 9 inch (23 cm) pizza pan with ¾ inch (2 cm)
tall edges and let rise 25 minutes. Spread the tomato sauce
(seasoned passata) and sprinkle the cheese over the dough.
Add the onion, tomato, and basil leaves on top. Bake until
the cheese melts and the dough is cooked, about 7 minutes.

FISH, POULTRY, AND MEAT

Pescado, pollo y carne

To understand this chapter, it is important to remember the history of the original inhabitants of the island, and how that history has impacted the food customs of Cuba. The indigenous people survived on the natural resources of the island by hunting and gathering. They captured various types of fish and crustaceans on the coasts and in the rivers, but they fished with very rustic techniques. When Cuba was colonized by the Spanish, the indigenous population was wiped out and the new inhabitants imposed their food customs, such as livestock and poultry production.

Starting in the seventeenth century, half the population on the island consisted of slaves from Africa. The necessity to feed this population meant that the Spanish started to systematically import *tasajo* (salted dried beef or horsemeat), salt cod, and rice. The slaves had a significant influence on the food culture, such as their preferences for fried and sweet food, still present in Cuban homes. The single-crop production of sugar and the development of livestock were responsible for the evolution of the Cuban palate. The preference for red meat (pork and beef)—seasoned with the ever-present onion, garlic, pepper, tomato, bitter orange juice, and cumin—are some of the features that define Cuban food to this day. This history helps to partially explain why there is not a large consumption of fish and other seafood in Cuba. This deeply established preference is reinforced by the current reality, in which a large proportion of the seafood is designated for export or for the tourist industry, and therefore less accessible to the Cuban people. This dynamic has some influence on the relatively low fish consumption; however, the partiality to red meat dates back to the days of colonization. Currently, pork and chicken are the most commonly consumed meat options.

In this chapter, we have included some regional plates, such as the *bolitas de pescado macabí*, *liseta frita*, and *pescado salsa perro*, which are important because they are traditional dishes that have remained popular in their original form. Others, such as *ropa vieja*, *vaca frita*, and *picadillo alcaparrado* are modern adaptations of traditional recipes.

Meats in Cuba are frequently marinated with garlic, salt, and bitter orange juice, while fish is usually marinated with salt, pepper, and lime juice, although garlic can also be added. Ground black pepper is used in many of the recipes in this book; however, it is important to note that this condiment is more frequently used in restaurants than in traditional home cooking. Chicken is usually seasoned with salt, pepper, lime juice or bitter orange juice, and garlic. Wine, bay leaves, oregano, and onions are generally added to stewed chicken. The typical Cuban sofrito—garlic, onion, *chay* pepper, and tomato—is prevalent in the majority of the following recipes, and tomato sauce (seasoned passata) is also quite common.

Visitors to Cuba often expect spicier flavors, perhaps because of the association with other Caribbean and Latin American countries. However, spicy food is not common in Cuba, with the exception of a couple of recipes that include the *guaguao* chili, which is native to the island. The indigenous and slave populations consumed this chili in some dishes, but the custom of eating spicy food was mostly eliminated during the twentieth century.

There is a prevalence of breaded recipes, specifically with fish fillets and chicken. The meat in Cuba is usually well cooked and served in very large portions, and Cubans often classify the quality of a menu or meal based on the size of the meat portion. Cubans generally feel like a meal is not complete without *la proteína* (the protein) or *el plato fuerte* (the main dish), a meat component. Although there is a tendency among some to try to diversify their diet, food culture in Cuba remains very meat-centered.

LOBSTER IN PEPPER SAUCE

Enchilado de langosta

In a large frying pan, heat the oil over medium-high heat. Add the lobster and sauté, stirring constantly, until the lobster turns light red, about 5 minutes. Sprinkle with the salt, add the onion, and sauté until translucent, about 2 minutes. Add the bell pepper and garlic and sauté until softened, about 3 minutes. Stir in the tomato sauce (seasoned passata) and ketchup. Add the dry wine, the wine, vinegar, bay leaf, and black pepper and stir. Add the soy sauce and stir. Add the parsley, cover, and cook over medium heat until the sauce begins to reduce, about 5 minutes. Uncover and cook until the sauce thickens, about 5 minutes. Add the hot sauce (if using) just before removing the pan from the heat. Serve with white rice and fried plantains.

PREPARATION TIME: 20 MINUTES
COOKING TIME: 25 MINUTES
SERVES: 4

½ cup (8 fl oz/120 ml) vegetable oil
4 small cooked lobster tails (about 14 oz/400 g total), shells removed and cut into rounds
1 teaspoon salt
1 medium white onion, sliced
1 large red bell pepper, sliced
3 cloves garlic, crushed
1 cup (240 g) tomato sauce (seasoned passata)
½ cup (120 g) ketchup
¼ cup (2 fl oz/60 ml) dry white wine
¼ cup (2 fl oz/60 ml) white wine
1 tablespoon vinegar
1 bay leaf
½ teaspoon ground black pepper
1 teaspoon soy sauce
2 tablespoons chopped parsley
1 tablespoon hot sauce, such as Tabasco sauce (optional)
White rice and Fried Sweet Plantains (page 244), for serving

VARADERO LOBSTE.

Langosta Varadero

This dish was invented by a group of chefs, including Ramón Pedreira and Pedro Pablo Martínez, at the beginning of the Revolution. It was created to replace other recipes that called for ingredients that were not available at the time. They named this dish Varadero lobster after the most beautiful and famous beach in Cuba. Serve with white rice and Sautéed Vegetables (page 221).

Season the lobster tails with the salt and pepper. In a large frying pan, heat the oil over high heat. Add the lobster and sauté until softened, about 3 minutes. Add the rum to the pan and carefully light with a long fireplace match. Let the flames extinguish, then add the wine and cook for 2 minutes. Add the *salsa criolla*, cover, and cook over medium heat until the sauce reduces, about 3 minutes.

PREPARATION TIME: 15 MINUTES
COOKING TIME: 10 MINUTES
SERVES: 4

6 sma   oked lobster tails (about 18   500 g), cut into ro   s
1 teaspoo   alt
¼ teaspoon ground b   k pepper
4 tablespoons vegeta   e oil
4 tablespoons Ron Carta   ite rum or añejo dark rum
4 tablespoons dry white wine
1½ cup (12 fl oz/350 ml) salsa criolla (Cuban Sauce, page 311)

SQUID IN ITS INK

Calamares en su tinta

PREPARATION TIME: 30 MINUTES
COOKING TIME: 1 HOUR 10 MINUTES
SERVES: 6

★

½ cup (4 fl oz/120 ml) olive oil
10 squid (about 2¼ lb/1 kg
total), head, tentacles, and body
separated, ink sacs removed from
the head, tentacles discarded, quill
removed, and body cut into rings
1 large white onion, finely chopped
4 cloves garlic, finely chopped
4 tablespoons chopped parsley
1 cup (8 fl oz/240 ml) dry white wine
1 teaspoon vinegar
1½ teaspoons salt
⅛ teaspoon ground black pepper

This is considered an emblematic dish in Cuban cuisine. It appears in cookbooks dating back to the beginning of the twentieth century, and is always included among the dishes that are representative of Cuba.

★

In a large frying pan, heat the oil over medium heat. Add the squid, onion, and garlic and sauté until the onion turns translucent, about 3 minutes. Add the parsley, wine, vinegar, salt, and pepper and cook over medium-high heat until the wine begins to reduce, about 3 minutes. Transfer ½ cup (120 ml) of the sauce to a small bowl and add the ink sacs. Strain into the pan with the squid, cover, and cook over low heat until the squid are soft, about 1 hour.

CUBAN SALMON WITH SHRIMP

Salmón con camarones a la cubana

PREPARATION TIME: 25 MINUTES,
PLUS 1 HOUR MARINATING TIME
COOKING TIME: 25 MINUTES
SERVES: 4

★

1 large fillet (about 1 lb 14 oz/845
g) salmon, cut into 4 pieces
Salt
¼ teaspoon ground black pepper
4 cloves garlic, finely chopped
Juice of 2 small Cuban limes
¼ cup (2 fl oz/60 ml) dry white
wine
2 tablespoons olive oil
24 large shrimp (prawns), peeled
and deveined
2 tablespoons (30 g) butter

Serve with roasted potatoes and white rice.

★

In a large bowl, combine the salmon, ½ teaspoon salt, the pepper, garlic, lime juice, wine, and olive oil and let marinate in the refrigerator for 1 hour. Reserving the marinade, drain the salmon.

Bring a large pot of lightly salted water to a boil. Add the shrimp (prawns) and cook until pink and opaque, 3–5 minutes. Drain and set aside (see Note).

In a large frying pan, melt the butter over medium heat. Add the salmon and cook, sprinkling with all of the marinade, until the salmon is cooked, about 8 minutes on each side. Add the shrimp on top of the salmon about 2 minutes before removing it to heat through.

Note: After boiling the shrimp in water, they can be sautéed for 1 minute in the oil from cooking the salmon to add additional flavor.

ARIMAO RIVER SHRIMP

Camarones Río Arimao

PREPARATION TIME: 15 MINUTES,
PLUS 1 HOUR MARINATING TIME
COOKING TIME: 5 MINUTES
SERVES: 4

★

24 large shrimp (prawns),
peeled and deveined
½ teaspoon salt
¼ teaspoon ground cumin
3 cloves garlic, finely chopped
1 small white onion, finely chopped
2 spicy chilies, such as the
guaguao pepper, finely chopped,
2 tablespoons lime juice
⅔ cup (5 fl oz/150 ml) aguardiente
(see Note)
2 tablespoons vegetable oil
Tostones (Fried Green Plantains,
page 38), lime slices, and guaguao
pepper slices (optional), for serving

Season the shrimp (prawns) with the salt and cumin.
In a large bowl, combine the shrimp, garlic, onion, chilies,
lime juice, and *aguardiente* and let marinate for 1 hour. Drain,
discarding the marinade, and set the shrimp aside.

In a medium frying pan, heat the oil over medium heat.
Add the shrimp and sauté until pink and opaque, about
3 minutes. Serve with tostones and garnish with lime slices
and guaguao pepper slices (if using).

Note: Aguardiente *is a distilled alcoholic beverage made
from sugarcane*.

MACABÍ FISH DUMPLINGS

Bolitas de pescado macabí

PREPARATION TIME: 1 HOUR
COOKING TIME: 40 MINUTES
MAKES: 40 DUMPLINGS

★

1 whole (2¼ lb/1 kg) headless,
gutted macabí (bonefish)
3 bread rolls, crusts removed, torn
1 cup (8 fl oz/240 ml) whole milk
2 tablespoons vegetable oil, plus
more for deep-frying
1 medium white onion,
finely chopped
4 scallions (spring onions),
finely chopped
2 eggs, whisked
2 tablespoons dry white wine
2 tablespoons lime juice
Salt and ground black pepper
All-purpose (plain) flour,
for dusting
1½ cups (12 fl oz/350 ml) salsa
criolla (Cuban Sauce, page 311)
4 tablespoons chopped parsley

Tenderize the fish with a wooden mallet a few times. Make
a lengthwise incision on the top, and fold the skin down
to remove the backbone. Use a spoon to extract the fish.
Repeat this procedure on the other side, and put all the fish
in a bowl.

In a large bowl, soak the bread in the milk. Squeeze out the
excess milk.

Pass the fish and the bread together through a meat grinder
and into a large bowl.

In a medium frying pan, heat the 2 tablespoons oil over
medium-low heat. Add the onion and scallions (spring
onions) and sauté until the onion turns translucent, about
3 minutes. Let cool for 2 minutes, then transfer to the fish
mixture and add the eggs, wine, lime juice, 1 teaspoon salt,
and ⅛ teaspoon pepper. Knead the mixture and form small
balls. Dust with flour.

In a small, heavy-bottomed pan, heat 2 inches (5 cm) oil
until very hot. Add the dumplings and fry until browned,
about 5 minutes. Pour the *salsa criolla* overtop and garnish
with parsley.

TETÍ WITH FRESH COCONUT MILK

Tetí con leche de coco

PREPARATION TIME: 25 MINUTES
COOKING TIME: 35 MINUTES
SERVES: 4

3 cups (345 g) grated fresh
coconut
1 lb (455 g) tetí fish, rinsed
2½ teaspoons salt
2 tablespoons lime juice
All-purpose (plain) flour,
for dusting
2 tablespoons vegetable oil,
plus more for deep-frying
2 chay peppers or cubanelles,
finely chopped
1 medium red onion,
finely chopped
5 leaves fresh culantro,
finely chopped
2 leaves fresh oregano,
finely chopped
1 tablespoon ground annatto
(achiote)
¼ teaspoon ground black pepper

Tetí is a fish that can only be found seven days after the full moon between July and January in the mouths of the Duaba, Toa, and Miel rivers in Baracoa, the most Eastern province of Cuba. It is a tiny, transparent fish of no more than ¾ inch (2 cm) in length. During its season, fishermen, men, women, and children come out at night to catch them. The people from this region believe that these fish have aphrodisiac properties and eat them with tomatoes (fried, dried, in stew, in empanadas), and as part of a traditional Baracoan dish called *bacan*.

In a large bowl, combine the grated coconut and 3 cups (24 fl oz/710 ml) tepid water and stir. Line a sieve with cheesecloth and set over a bowl. Scoop the coconut and water into the bowl, catching the coconut milk beneath. Squeeze the cheesecloth to get out as much liquid as possible (discard the solids). Set the coconut milk aside.

Season the *tetí* with 1½ teaspoons of the salt and the lime juice, then dust with flour. In a small, heavy-bottomed pan, heat 2 inches (5 cm) oil until very hot. Add the fish and fry until browned, about 3 minutes. Transfer to a serving dish.

In a medium frying pan, heat the 2 tablespoons oil over medium heat. Add the *chay* peppers, onion, culantro, and oregano and sauté until softened, about 3 minutes. Add the coconut milk and annatto (achiote) and cook over low heat, stirring with a wooden spoon, until it reduces, about 10 minutes. Add the remaining 1 teaspoon salt and the black pepper. Serve the sauce over the *tetí*.

FISH IN PEPPER SAUCE

Enchilado de pescado

Serve this with white rice or boiled root vegetables, such as taro root, yuca (cassava), or sweet potato.

Season the fish with the lime juice, 1 teaspoon salt, and the black pepper, and set aside.

Roast the bell peppers directly over the flame of a gas stove (or under a hot broiler [grill] if you don't have a gas stove), turning regularly, until the skin blackens, about 5 minutes. Let cool, then rinse, peel, and dice.

In a medium frying pan, heat the oil over medium heat. Add the fish and cook until lightly browned, about 2 minutes. Add the *chay* peppers, garlic, and onion, and sauté until softened, about 3 minutes. Add the tomato sauce (seasoned passata), wine, vinegar, bay leaf, and raw sugar and cook down for 5 minutes. Add the roasted bell peppers and scallions (spring onions) and season to taste with salt.

PREPARATION TIME: 20 MINUTES
COOKING TIME: 15 MINUTES
SERVES: 4

1½ cups (345 g) shredded cooked white fish
1 tablespoon lime juice
Salt
¼ black ground pepper
1 large green bell pepper
1 large red bell pepper
2 tablespoons olive oil
2 chay peppers or cubanelles, diced
4 cloves garlic, finely chopped
1 medium white onion, diced
¾ cup (185 g) tomato sauce (seasoned passata)
¼ cup (2 fl oz/60 ml) white wine
1 tablespoon vinegar
¼ teaspoon ground bay leaf
1 teaspoon raw cane sugar
1 bunch scallions (spring onions), finely chopped

SHREDDED FISH

Aporreado de pescado

PREPARATION TIME: 15 MINUTES
COOKING TIME: 25 MINUTES
SERVES: 4

1 whole (2¼ lb/1 kg) gutted fish,
head and tail removed
Salt
1 bay leaf
3 tablespoons vegetable oil
3 chay peppers or cubanelles,
finely chopped
1 medium white onion,
finely chopped
6 cloves garlic, finely chopped
3 tablespoons tomato sauce
(seasoned passata)
1 tablespoon paprika
⅛ teaspoon ground black pepper
¼ cup (2 fl oz/60 ml) dry white wine

This dish is very representative of Cuban cuisine and can be made with any kind of white fish. It is typically served with white rice and boiled root vegetables, such as taro root or sweet potato, and can be accompanied by fried bread slices. In the past, sectors of the population of a low socio-economic status would boil the fish head and use the broth for a soup and the fish meat from the head to prepare this dish.

★

In a large frying pan, combine the fish, 1 teaspoon salt, bay leaf, and 7 cups (56 fl oz/1.7 liters) water and cook until the fish softens, about 10 minutes. Remove the fish from the broth and let cool. Crumble into smaller pieces, removing the bones and skin, and set aside. Strain the broth and reserve 1 cup (8 fl oz/240 ml).

In a medium frying pan, heat the oil over medium heat. Add the *chay* peppers, onion, and garlic and sauté until softened, about 3 minutes. Add the tomato sauce (seasoned passata), paprika, black pepper, and reserved broth and cook over low heat until the sauce begins to reduce, about 5 minutes. Add the fish and cook for 5 minutes. Season to taste with salt, add the wine, and cook for 1 more minute.

FISH CHOP SUEY

Chop suey de pescado

PREPARATION TIME: 15 MINUTES
COOKING TIME: 10 MINUTES
SERVES: 4

4 tablespoons vegetable oil
2 cup (460 g) shredded cooked
saltwater fish, such as red snapper
1 inch (2.5 cm) fresh ginger, grated
4 tablespoons dry white wine
1 bunch scallions (spring onions),
finely chopped
1 head bok choy, cut into strips
3 medium white onions,
finely chopped
⅔ lb (300 g) bean sprouts,
cut into small pieces
2 tablespoon dark soy sauce
1 teaspoon salt
White rice, for serving

Chop suey recipes are representative of the Chinese influence in Cuba cuisine, and can be made with pork, chicken, fish, or vegetables.

In a medium pan, heat the oil over medium heat. Add the fish, ginger, and wine and sauté until the wine begins to reduce, about 3 minutes. Add the scallions (spring onions), bok choy, and onions and sauté until softened, about 3 minutes. Add the bean sprouts, soy sauce, and salt to taste and cook until the bean sprouts soften, about 3 minutes. Serve with white rice.

FISH ESCABECHE

Escabeche

**PREPARATION TIME: 20 MINUTES,
PLUS 24 HOURS CHILLING TIME
COOKING TIME: 30 MINUTES
SERVES: 4**

1 cup (16 fl oz/240 ml)
plus 2 tablespoons vegetable oil,
for frying
2 medium white onions, sliced
2 small green bell peppers, cut into
strips
1½ cups (12 fl oz/375 ml) vinegar
1 teaspoon salt
¼ teaspoon ground black pepper
½ teaspoon paprika
4 kingfish steaks (6 oz/170 g each)
All-purpose (plain) flour,
for dredging
1 can (3¾ oz/106 g) pitted green
olives
1½ cups (12 fl oz/350 ml) olive oil

Escabeche is the name for a number of dishes in Mediterranean and Latin American cuisines that can be made with fish, chicken, rabbit, or pork. They are marinated and cooked in an acidic mixture (vinegar) and usually colored with *pimentón* (Spanish paprika) or saffron. The dish is common in Spain and has evolved with local modifications in various former Spanish colonies.

The origin of the word *escabeche* is Persian and was brought to Spain by Arabs during the Moorish conquests. The word derives from *al-sikbaj*, the name of a popular meat dish cooked in a sweet and sour sauce, usually with vinegar and honey or date molasses.

In a medium frying pan, heat 2 tablespoons of the oil over medium heat. Add the onions and bell peppers and sauté until softened, about 2 minutes.

In a small bowl, combine the vinegar, salt, black pepper, and paprika.

Coat the fish in the flour. In a second medium frying pan, heat the remaining 1 cup (16 fl oz/240 ml) oil over medium-high heat. Add the fish and fry until browned, about 7½ minutes on each side. Transfer to an earthenware, ceramic, or glass dish and cover with the sautéed onions and peppers, the olives, vinegar mixture, and the olive oil. Cover and refrigerate for 24 hours. Serve cold.

FRIED LISETA MULLET

Liseta frita

This dish is typical of the city of Manzanillo, where it is accompanied by a cold beer. It is said that any passerby who eats the fish head will stay in the city of Manzanillo forever. Serve with fried root vegetables, such as potatoes, taro root, plantains, or sweet potatoes.

★

In a large container, combine the mullets, salt, pepper, and lime juice. Cover and let marinate for 20 minutes.

Coat the fish with the flour. In a medium frying pan, pour 2 inches (5 cm) of oil and heat over medium heat. Add the fish and fry until browned on one side, about 2½ minutes. Flip and fry on the other side for another 2½ minutes. Serve garnished with lime slices.

PREPARATION TIME: 45 MINUTES
COOKING TIME: 20 MINUTES
SERVES: 4

★

8 whole liseta mullets (about 3½ oz/100 g each), gutted and scaled
1 teaspoon salt
¼ teaspoon ground black pepper
2 tablespoons lime juice
5 tablespoons all-purpose (plain) flour
Vegetable oil, for frying
Lime slices, for serving

LISETA MULLET WITH CHEESE

Liseta Nápoles

This is a typical recipe from the city of Manzanillo. Serve with fried potatoes, taro root, plantains, or sweet potatoes.

★

In a large container, combine the mullets, salt, pepper, and lime juice and let marinate for 20 minutes.

Coat the fish with the flour. In a medium frying pan, pour 2 inches (5 cm) of oil and heat over medium heat. Add the fish and fry until browned, about 2½ minutes on each side. Place each fillet over a strip of cheese to melt it. Serve garnished with lime slices.

PREPARATION TIME: 45 MINUTES
COOKING TIME: 25 MINUTES
SERVES: 4

★

8 whole liseta mullets (about 3½ oz/ 100 g each), gutted and scaled
1 teaspoon salt
¼ teaspoon ground black pepper
2 tablespoons lime juice
5 tablespoons all-purpose (plain) flour
8 thin 2 inch (5 cm) long strips Cuban gouda or other mild yellow cheese
Vegetable oil, for frying
Lime slices, for serving

TROPICAL FISH FILLETS

Filete de pescado tropical 📷

PREPARATION TIME: 15 MINUTES
COOKING TIME: 20 MINUTES
SERVES: 4

★

4 fish skinless fillets (about
4 oz/115 g each), such as wreckfish
(stonebass), red snapper, kingfish,
swordfish, or a freshwater fish
1 teaspoon salt
¼ teaspoon ground black pepper
2 tablespoons lime juice
2 tablespoons chopped parsley
1 tablespoon chopped scallions
(spring onions)
1 tablespoon (15 g) butter
3 tablespoons vegetable oil
1 1.8 oz (50 g) slice pineapple,
diced
1 1.8 oz (50 g) small slice papaya,
diced
8 orange supremes
3 tablespoons orange juice
2 tablespoons dry white wine
1 teaspoon raw cane sugar
All-purpose (plain) flour, for
dredging

In a dish, combine the fish, salt, pepper, lime juice, parsley, and scallions (spring onions). Cover and let marinate in the refrigerator for 1 hour.

In a medium frying pan, melt the butter and ½ tablespoon of the oil over medium heat. Add the pineapple, papaya, orange supremes, orange juice, wine, and raw sugar and cook down for 2 minutes. Set aside.

Dredge the fish in the flour. In a medium pan, heat the remaining 2½ tablespoons oil over medium-high heat. Cook the fish until browned, about 3½ minutes on each side. Serve with the fruit sauce.

Note: The fruit sauce can be made thicker with the addition of cornstarch. Diced mango or other fruit can also be added.

OVEN-BAKED COASTAL FILLET

Filete costero al horno

PREPARATION TIME: 10 MINUTES
COOKING TIME: 25 MINUTES
SERVES: 4

★

2 tablespoon vegetable oil
4 skinless saltwater fish fillets
(about 6 oz/175 g each), such as
red snapper
½ teaspoon salt
¼ teaspoon ground black pepper
2 tablespoon lime juice
⅔ cup (160 g) salsa criolla (Cuban
Sauce, page 311)
4 large cooked shrimp (prawns)

Preheat the oven to 350°F (180°C/Gas Mark 4). Grease a baking pan with the vegetable oil.

In a medium bowl, combine the fish, salt, pepper, and lime juice and let marinate. Cover and let marinate in the refrigerator for 1 hour.

Transfer the fish to the prepared pan and bake until cooked through, about 25 minutes, adding the *salsa criolla* 2 minutes before removing from the oven. Serve garnished with the cooked shrimp (prawns).

FISH, POULTRY, AND MEAT

Pescado, pollo y carne

TURIGUANÓ FISH FILLET

Filete de pescado Turiguanó

PREPARATION TIME: 25 MINUTES
COOKING TIME: 30 MINUTES
SERVES: 4

★

8-inch (20 cm) skinned red snapper
fillet (about 1½ lb/690 g), cut
crosswise into 4 serving portions
1 teaspoon salt
¼ teaspoon ground black pepper
All-purpose (plain) flour,
for dusting
14 oz (400 g) shrimp (prawns),
peeled and deveined
2 tablespoons (30 g) butter
5 cloves garlic, finely chopped
1 medium white onion,
finely chopped
1 bay leaf
⅓ cup (2½ fl oz/80 ml) dry white
wine
Vegetable oil, for frying

This recipe became famous in Cuban gastronomy in the
1970s, an era when culinary competitions became popular.
It is named after the peninsula Turiguanó. It is always served
with tostones, green plantain chips, and fried sweet plantains.

★

Season the fish with ½ teaspoon salt and ⅛ teaspoon pepper.
Dust with flour.

Season the shrimp (prawns) with the remaining ½ teaspoon
salt and ⅛ teaspoon pepper.

In a medium frying pan, melt the butter over medium heat.
Add the shrimp and sauté until pink and opaque, about
2 minutes. Add the garlic, onion, and bay leaf and cook
until the onion turns translucent, about 2 minutes. Add
the wine and cook until the wine begins to reduce, about
3 minutes. Set aside.

In a large frying pan, heat ½ cup (4 fl oz/125 ml) oil over
medium heat. Add the fish and fry until it begins to brown,
about 10–12 minutes. Serve topped with the shrimp.

SPICED FISH

Pescado sobre uso

PREPARATION TIME: 35 MINUTES
COOKING TIME: 20 MINUTES
SERVES: 4

★

4 skinless tilapia fillets (7 oz/
200 g each)
1 small head garlic, separated into
cloves and chopped
½ teaspoon salt
⅛ teaspoon ground white pepper
5 tablespoons lime juice
3 large tomatoes
4 tablespoons vegetable oil
1 large white onion, sliced
2 tablespoons chopped parsley
¼ cup (2 fl oz/60 ml) dry white
wine

The *sobre uso* in the title means to add a sofrito to an already
cooked food, so it usually refers to spicing up leftovers. Serve
with mashed potatoes, yuca (cassava), or taro root with *salsa
criolla* (Cuban Sauce, page 311) on top.

★

In a large container, combine the tilapia, garlic, salt, pepper,
and lime juice and marinate for 20 minutes. Reserving the
marinade, drain the fish.

Meanwhile, bring a medium pot of water to a boil. Cut an
"x" into the skin at the blossom end of the tomatoes and
submerge them in the boiling water for 1 minute. Transfer
to a cutting board to cool, then remove the skin (peeling at
the "x"). Halve, seed, and dice.

Preheat the oven to 325°F (160°C/Gas Mark 3).

In a large frying pan, heat the oil over medium-high heat.
Add the tilapia and cook until lightly browned, 3 minutes
on each side. Transfer to a baking dish. Add the reserved
marinade and cover with the onion, tomato, parsley, and
wine. Bake until the fish is cooked through, about 12 minutes.

FISH FILLET FROM BARACOA

Filete de pescado a la baracoense

PREPARATION TIME: 20 MINUTES
COOKING TIME: 10 MINUTES
SERVES: 4

★

4 skinless catfish fillets
(about 4 oz/115 g each)
1 tablespoon salt
¼ teaspoon ground black pepper
2 tablespoons lime juice
1 bunch parsley, finely chopped
1 cup (120 g) grated fresh coconut
1 bunch scallions (spring onions),
finely chopped
1 stalk celery, finely chopped
5 tablespoons all-purpose (plain)
flour
1 egg, whisked
5 tablespoons vegetable oil

Serve with boiled root vegetables (such as sweet potatoes or taro roots) or cooked vegetables (such as steamed carrots or roasted eggplant).

★

In a large bowl, combine the fish, salt, pepper, and lime juice. Cover and let marinate in the refrigerator for 1 hour. Squeeze the parsley in a thin tea towel or cheesecloth to soften its taste (optional). Transfer to a large shallow bowl and add the grated coconut, scallions (spring onions), and celery. Set up three shallow bowls for dredging: one with the flour, the second with the egg, and the third with the coconut mixture. Dip the fish into the flour, then the egg, then the coconut mixture. Use a knife to smooth out any uneven areas.

In a medium frying pan, heat the oil over medium heat. Add the fish and cook until browned on both sides, about 3½ minutes on each side.

HONEY FISH FILLET

Filete de pescado a la miel

PREPARATION TIME: 15 MINUTES,
PLUS 4 HOURS MARINATING TIME
COOKING TIME: 15 MINUTES
SERVES: 4

★

4 white skinless fish fillets (about
6 oz/175 g each), such as red
snapper, king fish, sword fish
1 large white onion, finely chopped
4 cloves garlic, finely chopped
½ cup (4 fl oz/125 ml) cognac
1 teaspoon salt
¼ teaspoon ground black pepper
8 tablespoons vegetable oil
6 tablespoons (120 g) honey
Fried Sweet Potato (page 247), for
serving

It is Cuban tradition to use homemade wine as the alcohol in this recipe. It is a fermented drink made from Cuban grapes, pineapple, and tamarind. It is substituted with cognac in this recipe.

★

In a large bowl, combine the fish, onion, garlic, cognac, salt, and pepper and marinate in the refrigerator for 4 hours.

Preheat the oven to 350°F (180°C/Gas Mark 4).

Pour 4 tablespoons of the oil into a 9 x 14 inch (24 cm x 36 cm) baking dish. Arrange the fish in the dish and top with the honey and the remaining 4 tablespoons oil. Bake until well cooked, but still juicy, about 15 minutes. Serve with fried sweet potatoes.

FISH IN RED SAUCE

Masas de pescado enchiladas

**PREPARATION TIME: 25 MINUTES,
PLUS 10 MINUTES MARINATING TIME
COOKING TIME: 45 MINUTES
SERVES: 5**

½ spicy chili, such as guaguao
or jalapeño
Juice of 1 Cuban lime
Salt
5 skinless fish fillets (about
7 oz/200 g each), such as hake,
red snapper, tilapia, or catfish,
cut into 1¼-inch (3 cm) squares
All-purpose (plain) flour,
for dredging
5 tablespoons vegetable oil
1 tablespoon (15 g) butter
1 small red bell pepper, finely diced
1 small green bell pepper,
finely diced
2 cloves garlic, finely chopped
1 small red onion, finely diced
2 medium tomatoes, finely diced
¼ teaspoon ground bay leaf
4 tablespoons tomato sauce
(seasoned passata)
½ cup (4 fl oz/125 ml) fish stock
White rice and tostones
(Fried Green Plantains, page 38),
for serving

In a mortar with pestle, crush the chili. Add the lime juice and 1 teaspoon salt. Transfer to a large bowl, add the fish, and marinate for 10 minutes.

Coat the fish with the flour. In a medium frying pan, heat 4 tablespoons of the oil over medium-high heat. Add the fish and fry until browned, 1½ minutes on each side. Transfer to a plate lined with paper towels to absorb excess oil.

In a medium pot, heat the remaining 1 tablespoon oil and the butter over medium heat. Add the bell peppers, garlic, and onion, and sauté until the onions turn translucent, about 3 minutes. Add the tomatoes and cook until softened, about 3 minutes. Stir in the bay leaf, tomato sauce (seasoned passata), and fish stock and cook over low heat until reduced, about 5 minutes. Season to taste with salt.

Carefully add the fish to the pot, without stirring, and cook for 10 minutes. Remove from the heat and let cool for 2–3 minutes. Serve with white rice and fried green plantains.

FRIED RED SNAPPER

Parguito frito

**PREPARATION TIME: 10 MINUTES,
PLUS 10 MINUTES MARINATING TIME
COOKING TIME: 15 MINUTES
SERVES: 4**

1 whole (about 2 lb 10 oz/1.2 kg)
red snapper, fins removed
1 teaspoon salt
1 teaspoon ground black pepper
2 tablespoons lime juice
All-purpose (plain) flour,
for dusting
Vegetable oil, for frying
Lime slices, for serving

Serve with a side of white rice and Sautéed Vegetables (page 211), boiled root vegetables (such as yuca, sweet potato, or taro root), or salad (such as lettuce, kale, watercress, or cabbage).

★

Make 2 superficial slits on each side of the fish. In a large container, combine the fish, salt, pepper, and lime juice and let marinate for 10 minutes.

Dust the fish with the flour. In a large frying pan, heat 1 cup (240 ml) oil over high heat. Add the fish and fry until browned, 7 minutes on each side. Serve garnished with lime slices.

BREADED FISH
WITH FINE HERBS

Pescado empanado a las finas hierbas

**PREPARATION TIME: 35 MINUTES,
PLUS 1 HOUR MARINATING TIME
COOKING TIME: 30 MINUTES
SERVES: 4**

4 skinless catfish fillets
(about 4 oz/115 g each), cut into
strips ¾ inch (2 cm) wide
2 tablespoons lime juice
1 teaspoon salt
¼ teaspoon ground black pepper
4 cloves garlic, finely chopped
1 bunch parsley, finely chopped
1 bunch scallions (spring onions),
finely chopped
Leaves of 1 sprig basil,
finely chopped
1 cup (150 g) dried breadcrumbs
2 eggs, whisked
2 tablespoons whole milk
½ cup (70 g) all-purpose (plain)
flour
½ cup (4 fl oz/120 ml) vegetable
oil
Salsa criolla (Cuban Sauce, page
311) and lime slices, for serving

Claria, a type of catfish found in Cuba, is often used for this recipe. It is both farmed in Cuba and found wild.

★

In a medium container, combine the fish, lime juice, salt, and pepper. Cover and let marinate in the refrigerator for 1 hour.

Set up three bowls for dredging: In one bowl, combine the garlic, parsley, scallions (spring onions), basil, and breadcrumbs. In a second bowl, combine the eggs and milk. In a third place the flour.

Coat the fish first with the flour, then dip them in the egg/milk mixture, then in the parsley/breadcrumb mixture. In a medium frying pan, heat the oil over high heat until very hot. Add the fish and fry until browned on both sides, about 7 minutes. Serve with *salsa criolla* and garnished with a slice of lime.

FISH WITH "DOG" SAUCE

Pescado salsa perro

PREPARATION TIME: 20 MINUTES
COOKING TIME: 1 HOUR 30 MINUTES
SERVES: 4

1 wreckfish (stonebass) head
(1¼ lb /600 g)
5 potatoes, peeled—2 cut into
irregular chunks and 3 cut into
slices ⅓ inch (1 cm) thick
4 cloves garlic—3 peeled but left
whole and 1 chopped
4 small white onions—1 peeled but
left whole and 3 thinly sliced
4 small green bell peppers—
1 cut into irregular pieces
and 3 cut into strips
1 bunch chives, finely chopped
1 large tomato, chopped
Salt
1 guaguao pepper or other hot
chili (optional)
3 tablespoons olive oil
4 wreckfish (stonebass) rounds
(about 7 oz/220 g each)
White rice, for serving

This dish emerged at the beginning of the twentieth century at the España hotel, founded in 1912 in the city of Caibarién, a port town in the central zone of the island. It was made at the hotel's restaurant with a *perro* or "dog" fish (hogfish in English). The story is that the restaurant's cook, Ladislao, put the hogfish on the stove to make a fish broth with potato slices. He put it on low heat and forgot about it while he worked on other orders. He offered it to a diner much later that night and was told it was delicious.

It is a typical dish in the Villa Clara region and can be made with other fish as well. It can also be accompanied by a light spicy sauce made with a *guaguao* pepper, vinegar, oil, and salt to taste. Others prefer it with just lime juice, or with both.

In a large pot, combine the fish head, the chunks of potato, 3 cloves of garlic, the whole onion, pieces of bell pepper, one-third of the chopped chives, the tomato, 1 teaspoon salt, and 8½ cups (68 fl oz/2 liters) water. Cook, covered, over low heat until thickened, about 1 hour. Let cool. Strain the broth into a bowl. Discard the fish head. Transfer the cooked onion, bell pepper, garlic, chives, and potato to a blender and add the remaining garlic, the *guaguao* pepper (if using), and 1 tablespoon of the oil. Add 2 cups (16 fl oz/ 475 ml) of the reserved broth and blend until thick, then add enough broth to measure 4¼ cups (34 fl oz/1 liter). Set the sauce aside.

In a tall pot, arrange a layer of half the potato slices, top with 2 of the fish steaks, cover with half the sliced onions, half the remaining chives, and half the bell pepper strips. Repeat this process to make a second layer. Add the reserved sauce, the remaining 2 tablespoons oil, and 1 teaspoon salt. Cook, covered, over low heat, without stirring, until the fish softens completely, about 10 minutes. Increase the heat and bring to a boil and cook, covered, without stirring, until the broth thickens, about 20 minutes. Season to taste with salt. Remove from the heat and let sit for a few minutes. Serve with white rice.

Note: This recipe follows the traditional steps. In more modern adaptations, the potatoes are first cooked for 10 minutes, then the fish is added and cooked until soft. The sauce is thickened by mashing some of the potatoes and adding them to the sauce.

GARLIC CHICKEN
Pollo al ajillo

Season the chicken with the salt and pepper. Refrigerate for 30 minutes.

In a large pot, heat the oil over high heat. Add the chicken and sauté, stirring regularly with a wooden spoon, until lightly browned, about 3 minutes. Add the garlic, stir, cover, and cook over low heat until the chicken is cooked through, about 15 minutes. Increase the heat to high, add the wine, and cook until the wine begins to reduce, about 2 minutes.

**PREPARATION TIME: 15 MINUTES,
PLUS 30 MINUTES CHILLING TIME
COOKING TIME: 25 MINUTES
SERVES: 4**

1½ lb (700 g) boneless, skinless
chicken breasts, cut into pieces
¾-inch (2 cm) long and ⅔ inch
(1.5 cm) wide
½ teaspoon salt
¼ teaspoon ground black pepper
3 tablespoons olive oil
1 small head garlic, separated into
cloves and chopped
2 tablespoons dry white wine

CHICKEN IN BUTTER AND SOY SAUCE
Pollo a la barbacoa

Serve with boiled root vegetables (such as potato or taro root) or Steamed Vegetables (page 222).

★

In a large bowl, combine the chicken, salt, garlic, and bitter orange juice and marinate in the refrigerator for 1 hour. Drain.

In a medium pot, melt the butter over low heat. Add the chicken and pour in the soy sauce, stirring gently. Cook, covered and flipping the chicken regularly, until softened, about 35 minutes.

**PREPARATION TIME: 10 MINUTES,
PLUS 1 HOUR MARINATING TIME
COOKING TIME: 35 MINUTES
SERVES: 4**

2 large chicken leg quarters
(about 1¾ lb/800 g total),
halved and skinned
½ teaspoon salt
3 cloves garlic, finely chopped
4 tablespoons bitter orange juice
(see page 18)
4 tablespoons (60 g) butter
2 teaspoons soy sauce

COUNTRY-STYLE CHICKEN

Pollo a la guajira

**PREPARATION TIME: 25 MINUTES,
PLUS 1 HOUR MARINATING TIME
COOKING TIME: 35 MINUTES
SERVES: 4**

4 boneless, skinless chicken thighs
(about 5½ oz/160 g each)
1 tablespoon salt
½ cup (4 fl oz/125 ml) bitter orange
juice (see page 18)
5 medium tomatoes
2 large green bell peppers
All-purpose (plain) flour, for
dusting
2 cups (16 fl oz/500 ml) plus
2 tablespoons vegetable oil
4 cloves garlic, finely chopped
2 medium white onions, finely
chopped
½ cup (4 fl oz/125 ml) dry white
wine
1 cup (8 fl oz/240 ml) chicken
stock
½ cup (30 g) finely chopped
scallions (spring onions)
¼ cup (22 g) chopped parsley
Mashed Potatoes (page 232), for
serving

In a medium container, combine the chicken, salt, and bitter orange juice. Cover and marinate in the refrigerator for 1 hour.

Meanwhile, bring a large pot of water to a boil. Cut an "x" into the skin at the blossom end of the tomatoes and submerge them in the boiling water for 1 minute. Transfer to a cutting board to cool, then remove the skin (peeling at the "x"). Halve, seed, and dice.

Roast the bell peppers directly over the flame of a gas stove (or under a hot broiler [grill] if you don't have a gas stove), turning regularly, until the skin blackens, about 5 minutes. Let cool, then rinse, peel, and cut them into thin strips. Dust the chicken with the flour. In a large frying pan, heat 2 cups (16 fl oz/500 ml) of the oil over high heat until very hot. Add the chicken and fry until browned on both sides, about 15 minute. Set the pan aside.

In a medium frying pan, heat the remaining 2 tablespoons oil over medium heat. Add the garlic and onions and sauté until softened, about 3 minutes. Add the diced tomatoes and cook over medium heat until the sauce begins to reduce, about 5 minutes.

Pour the sofrito over the chicken, add the wine, and cook over medium heat until the wine begins to reduce, about 5 minutes. Add the stock, roasted peppers, and scallions (spring onions) and cook, covered, until the chicken is tender, about 15 minutes. Serve garnished with parsley and accompanied with mashed potatoes.

CHICKEN STEAK
WITH ONIONS

Bistec de pollo encebollado

In a bowl, combine the chicken, salt, pepper, garlic, and vinegar. Cover and marinate in the refrigerator for 1 hour.

In a medium frying pan, heat the oil over medium heat. Add the onion and sauté until translucent, about 5 minutes. Remove and set aside. Add the chicken to the pan and cook over high heat until browned on both sides, about 10 minutes. Reduce the heat to low, cover, and cook until the chicken is cooked through, about 25 minutes. Serve garnished with the onion and parsley.

PREPARATION TIME: 25 MINUTES, PLUS 1 HOUR MARINATING TIME
COOKING TIME: 30 MINUTES
SERVES: 4

★

2 large boneless chicken legs quarters (about 14 oz/400 g), halved and skinned
½ teaspoon salt
¼ teaspoon ground black pepper
4 cloves garlic, finely chopped
4 tablespoons vinegar
2 tablespoons vegetable oil
3 medium onions, thinly sliced
Finely chopped parsley, for serving

CHICKEN WITH FRESH
TOMATO SAUCE

Pollo con salsa natural

Serve the chicken with white rice and boiled root vegetables, such as potatoes, taro root, or sweet potatoes.

In a large pot, combine the chicken, ½ tablespoon salt, and 6⅓ cups (50 fl oz/1.5 liters) water and bring to a boil. Cover and cook until the chicken is tender, about 30 minutes. Reserving the broth, drain the chicken. Pull the chicken meat off the bone and shred. Transfer to a medium bowl and add the bitter orange juice and set aside to marinate while you make the sauce.

In a blender, combine the onion, garlic, *cachucha* peppers, tomatoes, ½ tablespoon salt, and ½ cup (4 fl oz/120 ml) reserved broth and blend until smooth. Strain (optional).

In a medium frying pan, heat the oil over medium heat. Add the chicken and sauté until browned, about 5 minutes. Add the tomato sauce and cook until it begins to reduce, about 5 minutes. Season to taste with salt and stir in the bay leaf. Serve garnished with chopped scallions (spring onions).

PREPARATION TIME: 25 MINUTES
COOKING TIME: 40 MINUTES
SERVES: 4

★

2 large (1 lb 12 oz/800 g) chicken legs (drumstick and thigh), skinned and separated into drumsticks and thighs
Salt
4 tablespoons bitter orange juice (see page 18)
1 large white onion, coarsely chopped
5 cloves garlic, coarsely chopped
2 cachucha peppers or cubanelles, coarsely chopped
3 medium tomatoes, coarsely chopped
2 tablespoons vegetable oil
¼ teaspoon ground bay leaf
Finely chopped scallions (spring onions), for garnish

CHICKEN AND SWEET POTATO STEW

Aporreado de pollo con boniato

**PREPARATION TIME: 30 MINUTES,
PLUS 1 HOUR MARINATING TIME
COOKING TIME: 25 MINUTES
SERVES: 4**

12 oz (345 g) cooked chicken (see
page 19), cut into ¾-inch
(2 cm) pieces (1½ cups)
4 tablespoons bitter orange juice
(see page 18)
1 tablespoon salt
⅛ teaspoon ground black pepper
2 tablespoons raw cane sugar
2 medium white or yellow sweet
potatoes (1 lb/460 g total), peeled
and cut into medium cubes
3 tablespoons vegetable oil
2 large green bell peppers,
finely chopped
2 chay peppers or cubanelles,
finely chopped
5 cloves garlic, finely chopped
1 large red onion, finely chopped
½ cup (45 g) finely chopped
parsley
3 medium tomatoes,
seeded and diced
½ cup (30 g) chopped scallions
(spring onions)

In a large bowl, combine the chicken, bitter orange juice, ½ tablespoon of the salt, and the black pepper and let marinate for 1 hour.

Bring a medium pot of water with the sugar and the remaining ½ tablespoon salt to a boil. Add the sweet potatoes and cook until soft, about 8 minutes. Drain and set aside.

In a medium frying pan, heat 2 tablespoons of the oil over medium heat. Add the bell peppers, *chay* peppers, garlic, onion, and parsley and sauté until softened, about 5 minutes. Add the tomatoes and cook until reduced, about 5 minutes. Add the chicken with the marinade and cook until lightly browned, about 5 minutes.

In another medium pan, heat the remaining 1 tablespoon oil over mediun heat. Add the sweet potatoes and scallions (spring onions) and sauté until the sweet potatoes are lightly browned, about 3 minutes.

Serve the chicken with the sweet potatoes.

STUFFED CHICKEN

Ballotina de pollo

This dish comes from the French culinary influence, which mostly spread to Cuba when French colonizers moved to escape the Revolution in Haiti in 1791. The term *ballotina* (which comes from the French *ballotine*) refers to a boneless piece of meat or fish that is stuffed, rolled up, tied, and cooked.

Preheat the oven to 350°F (180°C/Gas Mark 4). Grease a rimmed baking sheet with 1 tablespoon of the oil.

Bone out the thighs, leaving the drumsticks. Trim excess fat. Season the chicken with ½ teaspoon salt and the pepper.

In a small bowl, combine the breadcrumbs and milk.

In a small frying pan, heat the remaining 1 tablespoon oil over medium heat. Add the onion and sauté until translucent, about 2 minutes.

In a meat grinder, grind the pork loin with the ham hock, moistened breadcrumbs, and sautéed onion. Transfer to a large bowl. Add the egg, salt to taste, and wine and mix well. Divide into 4 equal portions.

Stuff the chicken quarters with the filling and cover with the skin. Pull the skin tight to ensure the stuffing stays in the chicken and wrap underneath. Stick toothpicks through the chicken skin to secure. Wrap in foil and transfer to the prepared baking sheet. Bake the *ballotinas* until cooked through, about 1 hour 10 minutes. If the chicken needs to brown more, open the foil and cook, uncovered, until browned, about 10 minutes. Serve hot or cold.

PREPARATION TIME: 45 MINUTES
COOKING TIME: 1 HOUR 30 MINUTES
SERVES: 4

★

2 tablespoons vegetable oil
4 chicken leg quarters
(about 3 lb/1.4 kg total)
Salt
¼ teaspoon ground black pepper
½ cup (75 g) fresh breadcrumbs
¼ cup (2 fl oz/60 ml) whole milk
1 small white onion, finely chopped
5 oz (150 g) pork loin,
coarsely diced
5 oz (150 g) boneless ham hock
1 egg, whisked
1 tablespoon dry white wine

QUEEN-STYLE CHICKEN SUPREMES

Suprema de pollo a la reina 📷

**PREPARATION TIME: 20 MINUTES,
PLUS 30 MINUTES MARINATING TIME
COOKING TIME: 25 MINUTES
SERVES: 6**

★

2 large boneless, skinless chicken
breasts (1 lb 5 oz/600 g total),
each cut horizontally into 2 even
pieces, then julienned lengthwise
Salt
⅛ teaspoon white ground pepper
⅓ cup (2½ fl oz/80 ml)
Cuban lime juice
1 tablespoon vegetable oil
2 tablespoons (30 g) butter
½ pineapple (7 oz/200 g),
thickly julienned
1½ cups (12 fl oz/375 ml) pineapple
juice

Serve this with a rice pilaf and Sautéed Vegetables (page 221).

★

In a large bowl, combine the chicken, ½ teaspoon salt, the pepper, and lime juice and marinate in the refrigerator for 30 minutes. Drain and set aside.

In a large frying pan, heat the oil and butter over high heat. Add the chicken and sauté until lightly browned on both sides, about 5 minutes. Add the pineapple and sauté until translucent, about 5 minutes. Reduce the heat to low, add the pineapple juice, and cook, stirring occasionally, until the liquid begins to reduce and the chicken is cooked through, about 15 minutes. Season to taste with salt.

VEGETABLE CHICKEN CHOP SUEY

Chop suey de vegetales y pollo

**PREPARATION TIME: 20 MINUTES
COOKING TIME: 12 MINUTES
SERVES: 4**

★

3 tablespoons vegetable oil
2 cups (460 g) diced cooked
chicken (see page 19)
1 inch (2.5 cm) fresh ginger, grated
1 cup (60 g) chopped scallions
(spring onions)
2 cups (160 g) sliced bok choy
1 large green bell pepper,
thinly sliced
2 medium white onions, chopped
¾ lb (345g) bean sprouts,
cut into ¾-inch (2 cm) pieces
1½ tablespoon dark soy sauce
Sea salt
3 tablespoons dry white wine

In a large pan, heat the oil over medium-high heat. Add the chicken and ginger and sauté until lightly browned , about 3 minutes. Reduce the heat to medium, add the scallions (spring onions), bok choy, bell pepper, onions, and bean sprouts, and cook until softened, about 4 minutes. Add the soy sauce and salt to taste, then add the wine and cook for 2 minutes.

Note: If you'd like a thicker sauce, dissolve 1½ teaspoon cornstarch (cornflour) in the wine before adding to the pan.

BRAISED CHICKEN

Pollo en pricasé

PREPARATION TIME: 25 MINUTES
COOKING TIME: 1 HOUR
SERVES: 4

1 whole chicken (about 3¾ lb/
1.7 kg), cut into 8 pieces
1 teaspoon salt
¼ teaspoon ground black pepper
3 tablespoons vegetable oil
1¾ oz (50 g) salt pork,
finely chopped
1 head garlic, separated into
cloves, peeled, and crushed
1 small green bell pepper,
finely chopped
3 chay peppers or cubanelles,
finely chopped
1 medium white onion,
finely chopped
1 sprig parsley, finely chopped
½ cup (125 g) tomato sauce
(seasoned passata)
¼ teaspoon ground cumin
¼ teaspoon dried oregano
4 leaves fresh culantro
2 tablespoons vinegar
4 large potatoes (1 lb 5 oz/600 g
total), peeled and diced
2 large carrots, diced
2 bay leaves
12 stuffed olives
1 tablespoon (15 g) butter

Season the chicken with ½ teaspoon salt and ⅛ teaspoon black pepper.

In a large pot, heat the oil over high heat. Add the salt pork and sauté until browned, about 2 minutes. Add the chicken and cook, stirring regularly, until browned, about 5 minutes. Stir in the garlic, then add the bell pepper, *chay* peppers, onion, and parsley and sauté until softened, about 3 minutes. Add the tomato sauce (seasoned passata), cumin, oregano, culantro, vinegar, and the remaining ½ teaspoon salt and ⅛ teaspoon pepper and cook until the sauce begins to reduce, about 2 minutes. Add the potatoes, carrots, bay leaves, olives, and 2 cups (16 fl oz/500 ml) water and bring to a boil. Reduce the heat to medium-low, cover, and cook, stirring occasionally, until the potatoes are tender and the chicken is cooked through, about 40 minutes. Uncover, add the butter, and cook until the sauce thickens, about 3 minutes.

CHICKEN WITH FRUIT

Pollo con frutas

In a bowl, combine the chicken, 1 tablespoon salt, and the bitter orange juice and marinate for 15 minutes.

In a small saucepan, combine the pineapple, papaya, mango, orange (if using), raw sugar, and 1½ tablespoons water and cook over high heat until syrupy, about 5 minutes. Set aside.

In a medium frying pan, heat the oil over high heat. Add the chicken and sauté, turning with a wooden spoon, until browned, about 5 minutes. Remove the chicken and set aside. In the same pan, cook the garlic and onions until softened, about 3 minutes. Add the tomato sauce (seasoned passata) and stock, return the chicken to the pan, cover, and cook over medium heat until the chicken is cooked through, about 25 minutes. Add the fruits and stir. Adjust the salt, add the wine, and cook for 5 minutes. Serve.

PREPARATION TIME: 15 MINUTES,
PLUS 15 MINUTES MARINATING TIME
COOKING TIME: 45 MINUTES
SERVES: 4

2 large (14 oz/400 g) chicken legs (drumstick and thigh), skinned and cut into 2 pieces
Salt
½ cup (4 fl oz/125 ml) bitter orange juice (see page 18)
½ cup (70 g) diced pineapple
½ cup (80 g) diced papaya
½ cup (70 g) diced mango
12 orange supremes (optional)
3 tablespoons raw cane sugar
2 tablespoons vegetable oil
2 cloves garlic, finely chopped
2 medium onions, finely chopped
2 tablespoons tomato sauce (seasoned passata)
1 cup (8 fl oz/240 ml) chicken stock
2 tablespoons dry white wine

DRUNKEN CHICKEN THIGHS

Muslos de pollo borrachos

Season the chicken thighs with the salt and pepper.

In a large pot, heat the salt pork and sausage over medium heat until all the fat is rendered, about 5 minutes. Transfer to a plate. In the same pot, heat the oil over high heat. Add the chicken and cook, flipping regularly, until browned, about 8 minutes. Return the salt pork and sausage to the pot, add 2 tablespoons of the rum, and carefully light with a long fireplace match. Let the flames extinguish, then add the wine and stock, cover, and cook over low heat until the chicken is cooked through, about 25 minutes. Add the remaining 2 tablespoons rum and cook for 5 minutes. Serve hot.

PREPARATION TIME: 15 MINUTES
COOKING TIME: 50 MINUTES
SERVES: 4

8 large chicken thighs (about 12 oz/365 g each)
½ teaspoon salt
⅛ teaspoon ground black pepper
¼ lb (120 g) salt pork, thinly sliced
4 oz (120 g) dried sausage, thinly sliced
4 tablespoons vegetable oil
4 tablespoons white rum
3 tablespoons dry white wine
1⅓ cups (10½ fl oz/310 ml) chicken stock

MARINATED BRAISED CHICKEN WITH TARO ROOT

Pollo en fricasé con malanga

PREPARATION TIME: 25 MINUTES,
PLUS 1 HOUR MARINATING TIME
COOKING TIME: 40 MINUTES
SERVES: 4

2 large (1 lb 12 oz/800 g) chicken
legs (drumstick and thigh),
skinned and cut into 2 sections
2 tablespoons lime juice
3 tablespoons red wine
½ teaspoon salt
2 cup (16 fl oz/500 ml) plus
2 tablespoons vegetable oil
2 medium taro roots
(1 lb/460 g total), peeled
and cut into large pieces
½ cup (4 fl oz/125 ml) chicken
stock
¾ cup (6 fl oz/175 ml) salsa criolla
(Cuban Sauce, page 311)
½ teaspoon paprika
White rice and finely chopped
parsley, for serving

This recipe was inspired by a recipe called Pollo Farola, from a place called Alto de Cotilla near the Farola road, which goes from the Guantánamo province to Baracoa. In the 1950s, a well-known cook named La India lived near that road and opened a food stand. One day, she decided to try a new dish. She chopped the chicken, marinated it with various ingredients, added the fried taro root and *salsa criolla*, and slow-cooked it. When she was serving the plate to a driver named Pablo San Miguel Silo, a little red wine spilled on it. The meal was delicious and was dubbed Pollo Farola de Baracoa.

In a large bowl, combine the chicken, lime juice, red wine, and salt and marinate for 1 hour.

In a large frying pan, heat the 2 cups (16 fl oz/500 ml) oil over medium-high heat. Add the taro and fry until browned, about 5 minutes. Remove and set aside.

In a large pot, heat the remaining 2 tablespoons oil over medium-high heat. Add the chicken and sauté, turning it regularly with a wooden spoon, until browned, about 10 minutes. Add the chicken stock and the *salsa criolla*, then add the taro and paprika and stir. Cover and cook over medium heat until the chicken is tender, about 25 minutes. Serve with white rice and garnish with parsley.

CHICKEN SLICES WITH COCONUT

Lonjas de pollo al coco

PREPARATION TIME: 25 MINUTES
COOKING TIME: 25 MINUTES
SERVES: 4

2 large (14 oz/400 g) chicken legs
(drumstick and thigh), skinned,
boned, and cut into thin strips
Salt
2 tablespoons lime juice
2 tablespoons vegetable oil
3 cloves garlic, finely chopped
1 medium onion, sliced
1 cup (8 fl oz/240 ml) coconut milk,
store-bought or homemade
(see Note)
1 teaspoon ground annatto (achiote)
1 tablespoon all-purpose
(plain) flour
½ cup (4 fl oz/125 ml) dry white
wine
¼ teaspoon grated nutmeg

In a bowl, combine the chicken, ½ teaspoon salt, and the lime juice.

In a medium frying pan, heat the oil over high heat until very hot. Add the chicken and cook until browned, about 5 minutes. Reduce the heat to medium, add the garlic and onion, and cook, stirring with a wooden spoon, until the onion turns translucent, about 3 minutes. Add the coconut milk and annatto (achiote), sprinkle with the flour, and stir. Add the wine and nutmeg and adjust the salt. Cover and cook over low heat until the sauce thickens and the chicken softens, about 12 minutes. Serve hot.

Note: To make coconut milk, blend 1 cup (75 g) grated fresh coconut with 1 cup (8 fl oz/ 240 ml) hot water in a blender. Strain the mixture through a sieve lined with cheesecloth, then squeeze the cheesecloth hard to get out as much coconut milk as possible.

ORANGE CHICKEN THIGHS

Muslos de pollo con naranja

PREPARATION TIME: 15 MINUTES,
PLUS 1 HOUR MARINATING TIME
COOKING TIME: 55 MINUTES
SERVES: 4

4 chicken thighs (about 5½ oz/
160 g each), skinned
½ cup (4 fl oz/125 ml) orange juice
½ cup (4 fl oz/125 ml) dry white
wine
1 tablespoon salt
1 large white or yellow sweet
potato, peeled, sliced, and kept
in a bowl of water
1 tablespoon raw cane sugar
2 tablespoons vegetable oil
4 cloves garlic, finely chopped
½ cup (45 g) chopped parsley
2 tablespoons (30 g) butter

In a large bowl, combine the chicken, orange juice, wine, and salt and marinate in the refrigerator for 1 hour. Reserving the marinade, drain the chicken.

In a medium pot, combine the sweet potato, raw sugar, and enough water to cover by 1 inch (2.5 cm). Cover and cook over medium heat until soft, about 15 minutes. Set aside.

In a large frying pan, heat the oil over high heat until very hot. Add the chicken and cook until browned, 5 minutes on each side. Reduce the heat to low, cover, and cook, basting regularly with the marinade, until the chicken is tender, about 30 minutes. When the chicken is almost completely cooked, add the garlic and parsley.

Meanwhile, in another large frying pan, melt the butter over medium heat. Add the drained sweet potato and sauté until browned, about 5 minutes.

Serve with the sweet potatoes on the side.

LITTLE POT OF CHICKEN AND VEGGIES

Cazuelita de pollo y verduras

In a large bowl, combine the chicken, lime, 1 teaspoon salt, and ⅛ teaspoon black pepper.

In a small bowl, combine the vegetable stock and the cornstarch (cornflour) and whisk to dissolve.

In a medium pan, heat the butter and oil over high heat. Add the chicken and sauté until browned, about 5 minutes. Reduce the heat to low, cover, and cook until the chicken softens, about 10 minutes. Transfer the chicken to a plate. Add the bell peppers and onion to the pan and cook over medium-low heat until softened, about 5 minutes. Add the bok choy, soy sauce, and thyme, then add the vegetable stock mixture and cook, stirring constantly with a wooden spoon, until thickened, about 3 minutes. Adjust the salt. Return the chicken to the pan and add the pumpkin or carrots. Add the wine and cook until the liquid begins to reduce, about 3 minutes. Garnish with parsley and serve.

PREPARATION TIME: 30 MINUTES
COOKING TIME: 25 MINUTES
SERVES: 4

★

2 large (14 oz/400 g total) chicken legs (thigh and drumstick), skinned, boned, and cut into thin strips
1 tablespoon lime juice
Salt and ground black pepper
½ cup (4 fl oz/125 ml) vegetable stock
1 teaspoon cornstarch (cornflour)
2 tablespoons (30 g) butter
1 tablespoon vegetable oil
2 medium green bell peppers, diced
1 medium onion, diced
1 head bok choy (8 oz/230 g), thinly sliced
1 teaspoon soy sauce
¼ teaspoon dried thyme
7 oz (200 g) pumpkin or carrots, cooked and chopped
1 tablespoon dry white wine
Chopped parsley, for serving

PINEAPPLE CHICKEN THIGHS

Muslos de pollo con piña

Season the chicken with 1 tablespoon salt and coat with the flour.

In a large frying pan, heat 2 tablespoons of the oil over high heat. Add the chicken and cook until browned on each side, 5 minutes total. Reduce the heat to low, add the carrots, bell pepper, and garlic and stir. Add the stock, cover, and cook over low heat, stirring occasionally and adding stock to prevent the pan from drying up, until the chicken is cooked through, about 30 minutes. Season to taste with salt.

In a small pan, heat the remaining 1 tablespoon oil. Add the pineapple and cook until lightly browned, about 4 minutes.

Serve the chicken with the vegetables and pineapple.

PREPARATION TIME: 15 MINUTES
COOKING TIME: 45 MINUTES
SERVES: 4

★

4 chicken thighs (about 5½ oz/ 160 g each), skinned
Salt
3 tablespoons all-purpose (plain) flour
3 tablespoons vegetable oil
2 large carrots, diced
1 large green bell pepper, diced
4 cloves garlic, finely chopped
1 cup (8 fl oz/240 ml) chicken stock
4 slices pineapple (3 oz/85 g each), halved

TAMALE-STUFFED CHICKEN

Pollo relleno con tamal

PREPARATION TIME: 25 MINUTES
COOKING TIME: 2 HOURS
SERVES: 4

★

1 whole chicken (3 lb/1.3 kg)
Salt and ground black pepper
1 medium white onion, chopped
5 cloves garlic
1 small green bell pepper, chopped
1¾ oz (50 g) salt pork
¾ cup (300 g) maíz molido
(ground fresh corn, see page 20)
¼ teaspoon dried oregano
¼ teaspoon ground cumin
¼ teaspoon ground bay leaf
3 cups (24 fl oz/750 ml) chicken
stock

Preheat the oven to 350°F (180°C/Gas Mark 4).

Season the chicken with ½ teaspoon salt and ⅛ teaspoon black pepper.

In a meat grinder, grind the onion, garlic, bell pepper, and salt pork. In a bowl, combine the ground mixture with the *maíz molido* and add the oregano, cumin, bay leaf, ½ teaspoon salt, and ⅛ teaspoon black pepper. Stuff the chicken with this filling and sew it up with a cooking needle and thread. Transfer breast side up to a Dutch oven (casserole) and add the stock to come halfway up the chicken. Bake until browned, about 1 hour 40 minutes. Flip it over, pour the juice from the pot overtop, and bake until cooked through, 20 more minutes.

HAVANA-STYLE CHICKEN STEW

Pollo guisado a la habanera

PREPARATION TIME: 25 MINUTES
COOKING TIME: 45 MINUTES
SERVES: 4

5 tablespoons vegetable oil
1 medium half-ripe plantain,
peeled and thinly sliced
1 whole chicken (about 3 lb/1.4 kg),
cut into 8 pieces, skinned
7 oz (200 g) ham, julienned
1 small green bell pepper,
finely chopped
3 cloves garlic, finely chopped
1 medium white onion, finely chopped
½ bunch parsley, finely chopped
2 whole cloves
Salt and ground black pepper
2 tablespoons vinegar
1 tablespoon tomato sauce
(seasoned passata)
2 cups (16 fl oz/500 ml) chicken stock
½ cup (50 g) almonds
⅓ cup (50 g) raisins
White rice, for serving

In a medium frying pan, heat 2 tablespoons of the oil over medium heat. Add the plantain and fry until browned, about 2 minutes on each side. Transfer to a plate lined with paper towels to absorb excess oil.

In a large frying pan, heat 1 tablespoon of the oil over high heat. Add the chicken and sauté until browed, about 3 minutes. Add the ham, stir, and cook until lightly browned, about 2 minutes. Set aside.

In a large pot, heat the remaining 2 tablespoons oil over medium heat. Add the bell pepper, garlic, onion, and parsley and sauté until softened, about 3 minutes. Add the chicken, ham, cloves, ½ teaspoon salt, ⅛ teaspoon black pepper, vinegar, tomato sauce (seasoned passata), and stock and stir. Cover and cook for 10 minutes. Add the almonds, raisins, and plantain. Cover and cook until the chicken is cooked through, about 15 minutes. Reduce the heat to low and cook until the sauce thickens, about 5 minutes. Serve with white rice.

BRAISED PORK

Fricasé de cerdo

In a bowl, season the pork with ½ teaspoon salt and ⅛ teaspoon black pepper.

In a large Dutch oven (casserole), heat the oil over high heat. Add the pork and cook, stirring regularly, until browned, about 5 minutes. Reduce the heat to medium and add the *chay* peppers, garlic, onion, tomato, carrot, cumin, oregano, paprika, and raw sugar and cook, stirring constantly, until the vegetables soften, about 10 minutes. Stir in the tomato sauce (seasoned passata), pour in 1½ cups (12 fl oz/350 ml) water, and bring to a boil over high heat. Add the potatoes, cover, and cook for 30 minutes. Add the wine and cook for 1 more minute.

Serve decorated with olives, pickled peppers, or green peas.

PREPARATION TIME: 20 MINUTES
COOKING TIME: 50 MINUTES
SERVES: 4

1¾ lb (800 g) pork tenderloin, cut into 1¼-inch (3 cm) cubes
Salt and ground black pepper
3 tablespoons vegetable oil
3 chay peppers or cubanelles, finely chopped
5 cloves garlic, crushed
1 medium white onion, diced
1 large tomato, diced
1 large carrot, diced
¼ teaspoon ground cumin
¼ teaspoon dried oregano
½ tablespoon paprika
½ teaspoon raw cane sugar
½ cup (125 g) tomato sauce (seasoned passata)
10 oz (300 g) potatoes, peeled and diced
3 tablespoons dry white wine
Olives, pickled peppers, or green peas, for garnish

PORK STEAK IN SAUCE

Filete de cerdo en cazuela

In a large bowl, combine the pork, 1 teaspoon salt, the pepper, garlic, and bitter orange juice and marinate for 1 hour. Reserving the marinade, drain the pork.

In a large Dutch oven (casserole), heat the lard over medium heat. Add the onions, oregano, and cumin and sauté until the onion is translucent, about 3 minutes. Add the pork and sauté until browned, about 10 minutes. Add the reserved marinade and wine, cover, and cook until the pork is tender, about 6 minutes. Season to taste with salt and stir.

PREPARATION TIME: 15 MINUTES,
PLUS 1 HOUR MARINATING TIME
COOKING TIME: 25 MINUTES
SERVES: 4

1 lb (460 g) pork steak, cut into strips crosswise
Salt
¼ teaspoon ground black pepper
⅓ cup (2½ fl oz/80 ml) bitter orange juice (see page 18)
5 cloves garlic, finely chopped
3 tablespoons (45 g) lard
2 medium white onions, sliced
¼ teaspoon dried oregano
¼ teaspoon ground cumin
¼ cup (2 fl oz/60 ml) dry white wine

SHREDDED PORK

Carne de cerdo ripiá

PREPARATION TIME: 15 MINUTES
COOKING TIME: 1 HOUR 15 MINUTES
SERVES: 4

8 cloves garlic, peeled

2 teaspoons salt

2 tablespoons bitter orange juice
(see page 18)

4 small white onions—1 coarsely
diced and 3 sliced

1 small carrot, chopped

1 bunch chives, finely chopped

3 tablespoons chopped parsley

2 bay leaves

1¾ lb (800 g) pork tenderloin,
cut into 3 large pieces

¼ teaspoon ground white pepper

½ teaspoon ground cumin
(optional)

1 tablespoon olive oil

4 tablespoons vegetable oil or lard

⅓ cup (2½ fl oz/80 ml) dry white
wine

This dish is a mixture of *ropa vieja* (Shredded Beef, page 204) and *vaca frita* (Tender Shredded Beef, page 210). It can be prepared with another type of pork cut, which makes it more affordable and more common in Cuban home cooking.

In a medium bowl, crush the garlic with 1 teaspoon of the salt. Add the orange juice and stir.

In a medium pot, bring 6 cups (48 fl oz/1.4 liters) water to a boil. Add the coarsely diced onion, carrot, chives, 2 tablespoons of the parsley, and the bay leaves. Add the pork and stir. Cover, and cook until the meat is tender, about 50 minutes. Reserving ½ cup (4 fl oz/120 ml) of the broth, drain the pork. The leftover broth can be used for other recipes.

When the meat is cool enough to handle, shred it with a fork and transfer to a large bowl. Add the remaining 1 teaspoon salt, the white pepper, cumin (if using), and olive oil and let marinate while you prepare the onion sauce. In a medium frying pan, heat 2 tablespoons of the vegetable oil over medium-low heat. Add the sliced onions and sauté until translucent, about 2 minutes. Add the garlic/orange mixture and sauté until it begins to reduce, about 1 minute. Add ¼ cup (2 fl oz/60 ml) of the reserved broth and the wine. Cover and cook for 3 minutes. Transfer the onion sauce to a small bowl and set aside.

In a large frying pan, heat the remaining 2 tablespoons vegetable oil over high heat. Add the pork and sauté until browned, about 1 minute. Add the onion sauce and stir. Reduce the heat to low and add the remaining ¼ cup (2 fl oz/60 ml) broth and the remaining 1 tablespoon parsley. Cook until the liquid begins to reduce, about 3 minutes.

FRIED PORK

Masas de cerdo fritas

According to chefs Bartolo Cardenas and Laura Gil, in the past, especially in rural zones that lacked adequate refrigeration, it was common to fry the pork and put it in various containers, covered with lard. This meat was stored for long periods of time and periodically removed and fried over low heat to be eaten in small portions. The meat would also be stored in *catauros* (boxes of palm leaves) hung in people's homes for preservation. This recipe is often served with yuca (cassava) or another cooked root vegetable.

Crush the garlic with ¼ teaspoon salt in a mortar and pestle. Set the mortar aside.

Season the pork with the remaining 1 teaspoon of salt and the pepper. In a Dutch oven (casserole), heat the lard over high heat until very hot. Add the meat and brown, stirring constantly, for 5 minutes. Reduce the temperature to medium, cover, and cook until tender, about 30 minutes. Uncover, increase the heat to high, and cook until the meat is lightly bronwed, about 5 minutes. Scoop the meat onto a serving plate. Pour the hot lard from the pan into a bowl.

Pour the bitter orange juice into the mortar and mix with the crushed garlic. Add 2 tablespoons of very hot lard. Cover and let to sit for 5 minutes.

Pour the sauce over the pork and serve hot.

PREPARATION TIME: 20 MINUTES
COOKING TIME: 40 MINUTES
SERVES: 4

3 cloves garlic
1¼ teaspoons salt
2¾ lb (1.25 kg) fresh ham
(pork leg) or pork loin, cut into
2-inch (5 cm) chunks
⅛ teaspoon ground black pepper
1 cup (8 oz/230 g) lard
¼ cup (4 fl oz/125 ml) bitter
orange juice (see page 18)

OVEN-ROASTED PORK TENDERLOIN

Lomito de cerdo al horno

PREPARATION TIME: 25 MINUTES
COOKING TIME: 1 HOUR
SERVES: 6

4 large potatoes (6 oz/175 g each)
4½ teaspoons salt
1 large tomato
1 pork tenderloin (2 lb/900 g)
½ teaspoon ground black pepper
6 tablespoons olive oil
1 medium white onion, sliced
3 cloves garlic, thinly sliced
1 carrot, julienned
1 bay leaf
¼ cup (2 fl oz/60 ml) red wine
1 cup (8 fl oz/240 ml) white wine
1 cup (8 fl oz/240 ml) beef stock
1 large green bell pepper
1 sprig parsley, chopped

Peel the potatoes and slice them lengthwise. Put them in a container and add water to cover and 1½ teaspoons of the salt. Bring a small pot of water to a boil. Cut an "x" into the skin at the blossom end of the tomato and submerge it in the boiling water for 1 minute. Transfer to a cutting board to cool, then remove the skin (peeling at the "x"). Halve, seed, and dice.

Season the tenderloin with ½ teaspoon of the salt and the black pepper. In a large frying pan, heat 3 tablespoons of the olive oil over medium heat for 3 minutes. Add the tenderloin and brown both sides, about 6 minutes total. Remove the pork from the pan and set aside.

In the same pan, add 2 tablespoons of the olive oil. Drain the potatoes and add them to the pan, sprinkling them with 1¼ teaspoons of the salt. Cook until browned, about 7 minutes. Remove the potatoes from the pan and set aside.

In the same pan, sauté the onion over medium heat until translucent, about 2 minutes. Add the garlic, carrot, bay leaf, and tomato and cook until softened, about 3 more minutes. Add the red wine and cook down for a few seconds. Add the white wine and cook down for 1 minute. Add the beef stock and the remaining 1¼ teaspoons salt and cook for 2 more minutes to bring to a light boil.

Preheat the oven to 400°F (200°C/Gas Mark 6).

Put the tenderloin in a 9¾ x 11¾ inch (25 x 30 cm) pan with 2¾ inch (7 cm) high sides and spread the potatoes around it. Put the whole bell pepper next to the pork. Pour the vegetable sauce over the pan and roast for 25 minutes. Check that the potatoes are tender, and increase the oven temperature to 425°F (220°C/Gas Mark 7). Cook until the tenderloin is browned, about 5 more minutes.

Sprinkle the parsley over the meat and potatoes. Take the bell pepper out, and when cool enough to handle, seed and cut it into thin strips.

Cut the tenderloin into slices and put it on a serving dish with the roasted potatoes and the rest of the vegetables. Decorate with the strips of bell pepper and the remaining 1 tablespoon olive oil (if desired).

CORN STEW WITH PORK

Guiso de maíz con cerdo

PREPARATION TIME: 20 MINUTES
COOKING TIME: 1 HOUR
SERVES: 4

★

1¾ lb (800 g) pork loin or tenderloin,
cut into 1½-inch (4 cm) cubes
Salt
¼ teaspoon ground black pepper
3 tablespoons vegetable oil
1½ cups (360 g) corn kernels
1 green bell pepper, diced
5 cloves garlic, crushed
1 white onion, diced
¼ teaspoon ground cumin
¼ teaspoon dried oregano
1 teaspoon raw cane sugar
½ cup (125 g) tomato sauce
(seasoned passata)
¾ lb (340 g) potatoes,
peeled and coarsely diced
¼ cup (2 fl oz/60 ml) dry white wine

Season the pork with ½ teaspoon salt and the black pepper. In a large Dutch oven (casserole), heat the oil over high heat. Add the pork and sauté until browned, about 4 minutes. Add the corn and cook for 2 minutes. Add the bell pepper, garlic, and onion and sauté until the onion turns translucent, another 2 minutes. Add the cumin, oregano, raw sugar, and tomato sauce (seasoned passata). Reduce the heat and cook for 5 minutes. Salt to taste. Add 2 cups (16 fl oz/500 ml) water, bring to a boil, and add the potatoes. Cover and cook over medium heat until the meat and potatoes cook, about 40 minutes. Add the wine and cook down for a few minutes, until the sauce thickens.

PORK STEW

Estofado de carne

PREPARATION TIME: 15 MINUTES
COOKING TIME: 1 HOUR 10 MINUTES
SERVES: 4

★

3 tablespoons (45 g) butter
1 6 oz (160 g) jar white
mushrooms, chopped
2 tablespoons all-purpose
(plain) flour
3 tablespoons vegetable oil
1½ lb (690 g) pork leg
or tenderloin, cut into ½-inch
(1.5 cm) dice
½ teaspoon salt
⅛ teaspoon ground black pepper
⅛ teaspoon dried thyme
½ cup (4 fl oz/125 ml) light beer
10 fl oz (300 ml) whipping cream

This recipe can be found in home cooking recipes from the 1950s and shows the influence of Russian cuisine. Thyme is now less common in Cuban cooking. The original recipe uses sour cream and beef. This adaptation of the recipe is prepared with pork, a more affordable option. Serve with white rice and salad.

★

In a medium frying pan, melt the butter over medium heat. Add the mushrooms and sauté for 4 minutes. Add the flour and stir gently with a wooden spoon. Gradually stir in 1 cup (8 fl oz/240 ml) water. Cook until the sauce thickens, about 2 minutes. Set aside.

In a large pot, heat the oil over medium-high heat. Add the pork and cook, stirring occasionally with a wooden spoon, until browned, about 15 minutes. Add the salt, pepper, and thyme. Add 1 cup (8 fl oz/240 ml) water and the beer and bring to a boil. Reduce the heat to medium-low, cover, and cook until the meat is tender, about 40 minutes. Add the mushroom sauce and the whipping cream and cook for 2 minutes.

FISH, POULTRY, AND MEAT

ROASTED PORK LEG

Pierna de cerdo asada

**PREPARATION TIME: 30 MINUTES,
PLUS 12 HOURS MARINATING TIME
COOKING TIME: 3 HOURS 30 MINUTES
SERVES: 14–16**

1 whole (14 lb/6.4 kg) fresh ham
(pork leg joint)
2 heads garlic, separated into
cloves and peeled
1 tablespoon salt
1 cup (8 fl oz/240 ml) bitter orange
juice (see page 18)
2 teaspoons ground cumin
1 tablespoon dried oregano

Pig roast (pork leg and the entire pig) is an important tradition in Cuba and can be prepared in various ways. The roasting of the pig is a ritual in some rural zones, where the tradition of slaughtering the pig the same day is maintained, especially by those who raise the pigs. It is especially common to prepare this meal for New Year's celebrations.

On the eastern side of the island, the pig is stuffed with Moors and Christians (page 107) and marinated, while on the western side it is common to roast it without marinating it, then serving it with a dressing from the cooking juices. In cities, it is common to roast pigs in the oven in the house or in a large bakery oven. They can also be cooked on a large grill.

Other popular pork recipes include: *cerdo ahogado* (drowned pork), which is a suckling pig fried in a frying pan covered completely in oil, and *cerdo asado en púa* (spit-roasted pork), which is pork spit-roasted over hot coals in a hole the size of the pig (the process takes at least 4 hours, so people usually take turns roasting, and it is a tradition to drink rum or beer during this time).

Make several 1½–2 inch (4–5 cm) incisions 3 inches (8 cm) apart and ⅔ inch (1.5 cm) deep in the pork and place in an extra large container.

In a mortar with a pestle, crush the garlic with the salt. Transfer to a medium bowl and add the bitter orange juice, cumin, and oregano. Pour over the pork and let marinate for 12 hours.

Preheat the oven to 350°F (180°C/Gas Mark 4).

Reserving the marinade, transfer the pork to a 12½ x 17 inch (32 x 44 cm) baking pan. Roast in the oven, pouring half the marinade over little by little until the pork cooks and browns on one side, about 1 hour 30 minutes. Flip the leg, pour the rest of the marinade over it, and roast until it cooks and browns on the other side, about 1 hour 30 minutes. Let rest before carving.

Note: Another (quicker) way to prepare this recipe is to wrap the marinated leg in foil and bake in a 350°F (180°C/ Gas Mark 4) oven for 1 hour. Then remove the foil and bake for 30-40 minutes on one side, and another 30-40 minutes on the other side. Increase the oven temperature to 500°F (260°C/Gas Mark 10) and cook for 5 minutes to make the skin crispy.

PORK ROLLS

Pulpeta de carne de cerdo

This is a very traditional recipe that is generally prepared with beef. This adaptation of the recipe is prepared with pork, a more affordable option. Serve with crackers, *casabe* (cassava-based flatbread), or vegetable salad.

In a bowl, beat together the raw egg, milk, and wine. Add the breadcrumbs and stir to moisten. Finely chop the cooked egg.

In a medium frying pan, heat the oil over medium heat. Add the *chay* peppers, garlic, onion, and parsley and sauté until softened, about 2 minutes. Remove from the heat and set aside.

In a meat grinder, grind the pork and sausage and transfer to a bowl. Add the chopped egg, moistened breadcrumbs, and sautéed vegetables. Stir with a wooden spoon. Add 1 teaspoon of the salt and the pepper. Divide the pork mixture into two portions. Put one portion onto a length of cheesecloth and roll into a long tube 6–7 inches (16–18 cm) long and 2 inches (6 cm) wide. Wrap the cheesecloth around it and tie at the ends. Repeat this procedure with the other half of the mixture.

In a large pan, combine the beef stock, bay leaf, oregano, and remaining ½ teaspoon salt. Bring to a simmer over medium heat. Put the rolls in the stock, cover, and cook over low heat until cooked through, about 40 minutes. Cool and cut into slices.

Notes: The pulpetas *(pork rolls) can also be wrapped in plastic wrap (clingfilm) or a plastic bag, but the traditional technique uses cheesecloth.* Pulpetas *can also be pan-fried or baked.*

PREPARATION TIME: 30 MINUTES
COOKING TIME: 45 MINUTES
SERVES: 4

2 eggs—1 raw and 1 hard-boiled
⅓ cup (2½ fl oz/80 ml) milk
2 tablespoons dry white wine
⅔ cup (100 g) dried breadcrumbs
1 tablespoon vegetable oil
4 chay peppers or cubanelles, chopped
6 cloves garlic, chopped
1 small white onion, chopped
1 sprig parsley, chopped
1 lb 2 oz (500 g) pork loin or tenderloin, cut into medium pieces
3 oz (80 g) dried sausage or ham, casings removed
1 ½ teaspoons salt
¼ teaspoon ground black pepper
8½ cups (68 fl oz/2 liters) beef stock
1 bay leaf
½ teaspoon dried oregano

CUBAN PIG'S FEET

Patica de cerdo a la criolla

PREPARATION TIME: 30 MINUTES
COOKING TIME: 1 HOUR 10 MINUTES
SERVES: 4

2¼ lb (1 kg) pig's feet (trotters)
1 bay leaf
2 small white onions, f
inely chopped
1 small carrot, sliced
1 sprig parsley, finely chopped
3 leaves fresh culantro, or more to
taste
2 tablespoons vegetable oil
4 cloves garlic, finely chopped
5 cachucha peppers or cubanelles,
finely chopped
2 medium tomatoes, seeded and
cut into medium chunks
4 tablespoons tomato paste
(tomato puree)
⅓ cup (2½ fl oz/80 ml) dry white wine
¼ teaspoon ground cumin
⅛ teaspoon ground black pepper
⅛ teaspoon paprika
½ teaspoon salt
Parsley, for garnish

Serve with boiled sweet potatoes and boiled corn.

Clean the pig's feet and cut them into large pieces. Add them to a large pot, add 3½ quarts (3.5 liters) room-temperature water, and bring to a boil over medium-high heat. When it begins to boil, add the bay leaf, half the onions, the carrot, parsley, and culantro. Cover and cook over medium heat until the meat has softened, about 50 minutes. Reserving a generous ¾ cup (6 fl oz/200 ml) of the broth, drain the pig's feet. (Save the rest of the broth for adding to beans or other pork stews.)

In a medium frying pan, heat the vegetable oil over medium heat. Add the garlic and remaining onion and sauté until the onion turns translucent, about 2 minutes. Add the softened pig's feet stirring gently, then add the *cachucha* peppers and tomatoes. Cook, stirring regularly, until the liquid begins to reduce, 3 minutes. Dilute the tomato paste (puree) in the reserved broth and add to the pan along with the wine, cumin, black pepper, paprika, and salt. Continue cooking until the sauce thickens, about 12 minutes.

Garnish with a sprig of parsley.

SANTIAGO-STYLE POT ROAST

Boliche mechado a la santiaguera

Make 8–10 2 inch (5 cm) long incisions in the beef. Stuff each opening with the ham, sausage, and salt pork.

In a large container, add the beef, salt, pepper, oregano, lime juice, onions, and garlic. Leave to marinate in the refrigerator for 12 hours. Reserving the marinade, drain the beef.

In a large Dutch oven (casserole), heat the oil over high heat. Add the beef and brown on both sides, about 5 minutes total. Reduce the heat to medium and stir in the wine, tomatoes, carrot, and reserved marinade. Pour the beef stock into the pot, cover, and cook over medium-low heat until the beef is cooked through, about 2 hours. Remove from the heat. Transfer the meat to a cutting board and let cool slightly before slicing. Strain the sauce. Serve hot with the sauce poured ontop.

PREPARATION TIME: 40 MINUTES, PLUS 12 HOURS MARINATING TIME
COOKING TIME: 2 HOURS 5 MINUTES
SERVES: 8

(3 lb/1.4 kg) beef eye round (topside) roast, trimmed
3 oz (90 g) ham, cut into strips 2 inches (5 cm) long and ⅓-inch (1 cm) wide
3 oz (90 g) dried sausage, cut into strips 2 inches (5 cm) long and ⅓-inch (1 cm) wide
3 oz (90 g) salt pork, cut into strips 2 inches (5 cm) long and ⅓-inch (1 cm) wide
½ teaspoon salt
⅛ teaspoon ground black pepper
¼ teaspoon dried oregano
3 tablespoons lime juice
2 medium white onions, finely chopped
6 cloves garlic, finely chopped
3 tablespoons vegetable oil
6 tablespoons dry white wine
2 tomatoes, diced
1 carrot, sliced
1½ cups (12 fl oz/375 ml) beef stock

BEEF STROGANOFF

Carne de res a la Stroganov

PREPARATION TIME: 30 MINUTES
COOKING TIME: 45 MINUTES
SERVES: 6

1¾ lb (800 g) beef eye round (topside) roast, cut into strips 1–1½ inches (3–4 cm) long and ¼–⅓ inch (5–8 mm) wide
Salt
¼ teaspoon ground black pepper
1⅔ cups (13 fl oz/395 ml) whipping cream
1 tablespoon lime juice
1 tablespoon vinegar
5 tablespoons vegetable oil
1 medium white onion, halved and thinly sliced
1 jar white mushrooms(160 g)
¼ cup (60 g) tomato sauce (seasoned passata)
7 small pickles (3½ oz/100 g), cut into small pieces
1 teaspoon paprika
3 tablespoons chopped parsley, for garnish

This dish comes from the Russian influence in Cuba after 1959. Its creation is credited to Alexander Stroganov (1795–1891), an important intellectual and political figure. It was a popular dish at the famous Restaurante Moscú in Havana, and is often served with pilaf rice, onion rings, quail eggs, French fries, or potato croquettes.

Season the beef with 1 teaspoon salt and the black pepper and let sit until time to cook.

In a bowl, with an electric mixer, combine the cream, lime juice, vinegar, and ¼ teaspoon salt and beat well to achieve a sour cream.

In a medium frying pan, heat 2 tablespoons of the oil over medium heat. Add the onion and sauté for 1 minute, until translucent. Add the mushrooms and cook for 2 more minutes. Pour the cream and tomato sauce (seasoned passata) into the pan and add the pickles and paprika. Cover and cook over low heat, stirring occasionally with a wooden spoon, until the sauce thickens, about 15 minutes. Salt to taste. Set the sauce aside.

In a large Dutch oven (casserole), heat the remaining 3 tablespoons oil over high heat. Add the strips of beef and cook, stirring constantly, until lightly browned, about 4 minutes. Reduce the heat, cover, and cook until the beef is cooked through, about 15 minutes. Add the sauce, stir, and remove from the heat. Serve with parsley sprinkled on top.

Note: This can be made with beef filet, with a shorter cooking time, or with pork. Another variation is to use half whipping cream and half smetana, a sour cream.

HAVANA-STYLE GROUND BEEF

Picadillo a la habanera

This recipe is a very popular and very traditional Cuban dish. Serve with French fries and white rice.

In a large frying pan, heat the oil over medium heat. Add the beef and cook until it begins to brown, about 4 minutes. Add the bell pepper, garlic, and onion and cook until the onion turns translucent, about 3 minutes. Add the tomatoes and cook until softened, about 2 more minutes. Add the tomato sauce (seasoned passata), wine, salt, and olives. Reduce the heat and cook until the liquid reduces, about 15 minutes. Serve with French fries and white rice.

Note: If you prefer peeled tomatoes, bring a medium pot of water to a boil. Cut an "x" into the skin at the blossom end of the tomatoes and submerge in the boiling water for 1 minute. Transfer to a cutting board to cool, then remove the skin (peeling at the "x").

PREPARATION TIME: 25 MINUTES
COOKING TIME: 30 MINUTES
SERVES: 4

3 tablespoons vegetable oil
1½ lb (690 g) ground (minced) beef
1 large green bell pepper, diced
6 cloves garlic, crushed
1 medium white onion, diced
2 medium tomatoes, peeled (optional; see Note) and diced
½ cup (60 g) tomato sauce (seasoned passata)
¼ cup (2 fl oz/60 ml) dry white wine
1 teaspoon salt
20 pitted green olives
French fries and white rice, for serving

HAVANA-STYLE SALTED DRY BEEF

Aporreado de tasajo estilo habanero

Tasajo was traditionally made with horsemeat, and is now made with either horsemeat or beef. Serve this with white rice and boiled sweet potato.

Soak the *tasajo* in water for at least 12 hours, changing the water every 4 hours if possible.

Drain and divide the *tasajo* in two. Add to a medium pot and add water to cover by 3–4 finger-widths above it. Add the bay leaves and bring to a boil. Reduce the heat to medium, cover, and cook until softened, 1½–2 hours. Reserving 1½ cup (12 fl oz/360 ml) of the broth, drain the beef. When cool enough to handle, shred the beef.

In a medium frying pan, heat the oil over medium heat. Add the beef and sauté until lightly browned, 1 minute. Add the *salsa criolla* and reserved broth. Cover and cook over medium heat for 15 minutes to reduce the sauce. Add the wine and cook for 1 more minute.

PREPARATION TIME: 15 MINUTES,
PLUS 12 HOURS SOAKING TIME
COOKING TIME: 2 HOURS 20 MINUTES
SERVES: 4

14 oz (400 g) tasajo (salted dried beef)
2 bay leaf
4 tablespoons vegetable oil
1 cup (8 fl oz/240 ml) salsa criolla (Cuban Sauce, page 311)
6 tablespoons dry white wine

SHREDDED BEEF

Ropa vieja

PREPARATION TIME: 55 MINUTES
COOKING TIME: 1 HOUR 20 MINUTES
SERVES: 4

★

1¾ lb (800 g) beef skirt steak
(bavette), cut into large pieces
2 bay leaves
2 medium white onions—1½ sliced
and ½ left whole
3 cloves garlic—1 whole and
2 cloves crushed
1 sprig parsley, finely chopped
½ teaspoon dried oregano
½ teaspoon ground black pepper
2 tablespoons olive oil
1 small carrot, sliced
1 red bell pepper, thinly sliced
1 green bell pepper, thinly sliced
1 chive, finely chopped
1 teaspoon paprika
½ teaspoon ground cumin
Salt
⅓ cup (2½ fl oz/80 ml) dry white
wine

This recipe, which has its origins in Spain, is considered a classic Cuban dish and is still popular today. Serve with an avocado salad and white rice, black beans, tostones (Fried Green Plantains, page 38), or Fried Sweet Plantains (page 244).

★

In a medium pot, bring 6 cups (48 fl oz/1.4 liters) water to a boil. Add the meat and cook, skimming the foam from the surface, until tender, about 1 hour. After removing the foam two or three times, add 1 of the bay leaves, the ½ onion, the whole garlic clove, half the parsley, the oregano, and ¼ teaspoon of the black pepper.

Remove from the heat. With a slotted spoon, transfer the meat to a plate to cool. Strain the broth and set aside 2 cups (16 fl oz/475 ml). Shred the meat into thin strips.

In a large frying pan, heat the oil over medium heat. Add the carrot, bell peppers, crushed garlic, sliced onions, and chives and cook until the onion turns translucent, about 3 minutes. Add the meat, stir, and add the reserved 2 cups (16 fl oz/475 ml) broth. Add the paprika, cumin, 1 teaspoon salt, the remaining bay leaf, remaining ¼ teaspoon black pepper, and the wine. Cover and cook over low heat for 5 minutes. Add the remaining parsley and salt to taste. Cook for 2 more minutes.

ITALIAN-STYLE LIVER

Hígado a la italiana

PREPARATION TIME: 15 MINUTES,
PLUS 30 MINUTES MARINATING TIME
COOKING TIME: 20 MINUTES
SERVES: 4

★

1 lb (460 g) cow liver
4 cloves garlic, crushed
Salt
¼ teaspoon ground bay leaf
⅛ teaspoon ground black pepper
2 tablespoons vinegar
2 tablespoons dry white wine
3 tablespoons vegetable oil
1 medium white onion, sliced
1 large green bell pepper,
thinly sliced
1 tablespoon all-purpose (plain) flour

Serve with white rice and tostones (Fried Green Plantains, page 38).

★

Remove the membrane around the liver, cut it into strips ⅓ inch (1 cm) wide, and put them in a glass bowl. Add the garlic, ½ teaspoon salt, the bay leaf, pepper, vinegar, and wine and leave to marinate for 30 minutes.

In a medium frying pan, heat the oil over medium heat. Add the onion and bell pepper and cook until the onion turns translucent, about 3 minutes. Sprinkle the flour over and stir. Increase the heat to high, add the liver and its marinade, and cook, stirring with a wooden spoon, until it begins to harden, about 3 minutes. Reduce the heat to low, cover, and cook until cooked through, about 10 minutes. Salt to taste.

CUBAN GROUND BEEF

Picadillo a la criolla

PREPARATION TIME: 25 MINUTES
COOKING TIME: 30 MINUTES
SERVES: 6

★

3 tablespoons vegetable oil
1½ lb (690 g) ground (minced) beef
1 large green bell pepper, diced
6 cloves garlic, crushed
1 medium white onion, diced
2 medium tomatoes, peeled
(optional; see Note) and diced
½ cup (60 g) tomato sauce
(seasoned passata)
¼ cup (2 fl oz/60 ml) dry white wine
1 teaspoon salt
20 pitted green olives
6 fried eggs, 12 Fried Sweet
Plantains (page 244), and white
rice, for serving

This dish is very similar to the Havana-Style Ground Beef (page 203), however it is served differently. In this case, the ground beef is served with fried eggs, fried sweet plantains, and white rice, all of which are integral to this traditional Cuban meal.

★

In a large frying pan, heat the oil over medium heat. Add the beef and cook until it begins to brown, about 4 minutes. Add the bell pepper, garlic, and onion and cook until the onion turns translucent, about 3 minutes. Add the tomatoes and cook until softened, about 2 more minutes. Add the tomato sauce (seasoned passata), wine, salt, and olives. Reduce the heat and cook until the liquid reduces, about 15 minutes. Serve with the fried eggs, fried sweet plantains, and white rice.

Note: If you prefer peeled tomatoes, bring a medium pot of water to a boil. Cut an "x" into the skin at the blossom end of the tomatoes and submerge in the boiling water for 1 minute. Transfer to a cutting board to cool, then remove the skin (peeling at the "x").

SALTED DRY BEEF WITH SWEET POTATO

Tasajo con boniato

PREPARATION TIME: 30 MINUTES,
PLUS 12 HOURS SOAKING TIME AND
1 HOUR MARINATING TIME
COOKING TIME: 2 HOURS 35 MINUTES
SERVES: 4

★

14 oz (400 g) tasajo
(salted dried beef)
2 bay leaves
6 cloves garlic, finely chopped
1 cup (8 fl oz/240 ml) bitter orange
juice (see page 18)
Salt
4 medium white or yellow sweet
potatoes (6 oz/175 g each), peeled
and cut into thick slices
4 tablespoons vegetable oil
2 medium white onion, chopped

Soak the *tasajo* in water for at least 12 hours, changing the water every 4 hours.

Drain the *tasajo* and transfer to a medium pot. Add the bay leaves and enough water to cover by 3–4 finger-widths above it, and bring to a boil. Reduce the heat to medium, cover, and cook until softened, 1½–2 hours. Drain. When cool enough to handle, slice, then pound with a meat tenderizer.

In a medium container, combine the *tasajo*, garlic, and orange juice and marinate for 1 hour.

In a medium pot of salted boiling water, cook the sweet potatoes, covered, until softened, about 20 minutes. Drain.

In a large frying pan, heat the oil over medium heat. Add the *tasajo* and sauté until it begins to brown, 4 minutes on each side. Reduce the heat to low, add the onion, and cook until translucent, 2 minutes. Serve with the sweet potatoes on the side and the sautéed onions on top.

GROUND BEEF AND CAPERS

Picadillo alcaparrado

PREPARATION TIME: 20 MINUTES
COOKING TIME: 30 MINUTES
SERVES: 4

★

2 tablespoons olive oil
1 lb (460 g) ground (minced) beef
1 cup (8 fl oz/240 ml) salsa criolla
(Cuban Sauce, page 311)
20 green pitted olives,
halved, plus 2 tablespoons
brine from the jar
½ cup (86 g) raisins
2 tablespoons capers
Salt
½ cup (4 fl oz/125 ml) dry white wine

Serve with Mashed Potatoes (page 232) or with white rice and Black Bean Soup (page 74).

★

In a medium frying pan, heat the oil over medium heat. Add the beef and cook until it begins to brown, about 3 minutes. Reduce the heat to low, add the *salsa criolla*, cover, and cook until the beef softens, about 15 minutes. Add the olives, olive brine, raisins, and capers. Continue cooking, uncovered, for 5 minutes. Salt to taste. Add the wine and cook until the wine reduces, 5 more minutes.

CAMAGÜEY-STYLE MEAT AND FRUIT SALAD

Salpicón camagüeyano

PREPARATION TIME: 15 MINUTES
SERVES: 4

★

3 tablespoons vinegar
2 tablespoons vegetable oil
½ teaspoon salt
⅛ teaspoon ground black pepper
3 lettuce leaves
1 lb (500 g) roast beef or pork, cut
into thin strips
1 small pineapple, peeled and
diced
1 cup (150 g) orange supremes,
halved

Salpicón is a term that usually refers to a food cooked in the shape of a roll, however, the 1956 book *¿Gusta, usted?* specifies that the *salpicón* from Camagüey refers to a salad made of cooked meat, sweet peppers, orange, and avocado slices, tossed with an oil and vinegar dressing and sprinkled with sugar. This dish is inspired by a recipe from Chef Gilberto Smith Duquesne.

It was traditionally prepared with leftovers, and can include pieces of bread (fried or not).

★

In a glass bowl, mix together the vinegar, oil, salt, and pepper. Put the lettuce leaves on a serving dish and put the meat over the lettuce. Pour the dressing on top, and place the fruits around the leaves.

TENDER SHREDDED BEEF

Vaca frita

PREPARATION TIME: 25 MINUTES
COOKING TIME: 1 HOUR 5 MINUTES
SERVES: 4

8 cloves garlic, peeled
2 teaspoons salt
2 tablespoons bitter orange juice
(see page 18)
1 medium white onion—¼ cut into
chunks and ¾ sliced
1 small carrot, chopped
2 chives, finely chopped
2 tablespoons chopped parsley
2 bay leaves
1¾ lb (800 g) brisket
6 tablespoons (90 g) lard
⅓ cup (2½ fl oz/80 ml) dry white wine
¼ teaspoon ground white pepper
½ teaspoon ground cumin
(optional)
1 tablespoon olive oil

This is an emblematic dish in Cuban cuisine. It is accompanied by white rice and French fries, or with Moors and Christians (page 107) and tostones (Fried Green Plantains, page 38).

In a mortar and pestle, crush the garlic with 1 teaspoon of the salt. Pour the bitter orange juice over it.

In a medium pot, bring 6⅓ cups (50 fl oz/1.5 liters) water to a boil. Add the onion chunks, carrot, chives, 1 tablespoon of the parsley, the bay leaves, and the meat and cook, covered, over medium heat until the meat is tender, about 45 minutes. Reserving ¼ cup (2 fl oz/60 ml) of the broth, drain the beef.

In a medium frying pan, heat 3 tablespoons (45 g) of the lard over medium-low heat. Add the sliced onion and cook until translucent, about 2 minutes. Add the garlic mixture and sauté for 1 minute until fragrant. Add the reserved broth and the wine. Cover and cook until the wine reduces and becomes fragrant, about 3 more minutes. Pour this dressing into a small bowl.

Cut the meat into steaks and pound them with a meat tenderizer. Place them in a medium container and season with the remaining 1 teaspoon salt, white pepper, cumin (if using), and olive oil. (Tear the meat slightly so that the seasonings spread out over it.)

In a large frying pan, heat the remaining 3 tablespoons (45 g) lard over medium heat. Fry the steaks until browned on both sides, about 5 minutes per side.

Put the meat on a serving dish and cover with the dressing. Sprinkle the remaining 1 tablespoon parsley on top.

CATALAN-STYLE BEEF MEATBALLS

Albóndigas de res a la catalana

PREPARATION TIME: 25 MINUTES,
PLUS 2 HOURS RAISIN SOAKING TIME
COOKING TIME: 45 MINUTES
SERVES: 6

3 tablespoons raisins
¼ cup (2 fl oz/60 ml) Moscatel wine
4 tablespoons vegetable oil
1 medium white onion,
finely chopped
⅔ cup (100 g) dried breadcrumbs
½ cup (4 fl oz/125 ml) whole milk
1 lb 7 oz (650 g) ground (minced)
beef
2 egg yolks, lightly beaten
Salt
All-purpose (plain) flour, for dusting
1 cup (8 fl oz/240 ml) salsa criolla
(Cuban Sauce, page 311)
1 teaspoon raw cane sugar
White rice and tostones
(Fried Green Plantains, page 38),
for serving

This recipe was very common in Cuban cuisine in the first half of the twentieth century. An important detail is the addition of a little bit of sugar to the sauce.

Soak the raisins in the wine for 2 hours. Drain, reserving the wine, and set aside.

In a small frying pan, heat 1 tablespoon of the oil over medium-low heat. Add the onion and sauté until translucent, about 3 minutes.

In a bowl, moisten the breadcrumbs with the milk. Put the ground (minced) beef in a stainless steel bowl. With a slotted spoon, lift the breadcrumbs out of the milk and add to the meat along with the drained raisins, sautéed onion, egg yolks, and ½ teaspoon salt and mix to make an even mixture. Form meatballs 1-½ inches (3–4 cm) in diameter and dust them with flour.

In a medium frying pan, heat the remaining 3 tablespoons oil over medium heat. Add the meatballs and cook, turning them carefully with a fork, until browned all over, about 4 minutes. Remove them from the frying pan and put them on a serving plate.

In a large frying pan, mix the *salsa criolla*, ¾ cup (6 fl oz/ 185 ml) water, and the raw sugar and bring to a boil. Salt to taste. Carefully place the meatballs in the boiling sauce. Cover and cook over low heat until they are cooked, about 12 minutes. Add the reserved wine. Serve with white rice and fried plantains.

GOAT IN RED SAUCE

Chilindrón de chivo

This is a very typical Cuban recipe, often accompanied with Red Beans and Rice (page 102) and tostones (Fried Green Plantains, page 38).

Cut the goat into 2¾-inch (7 cm) chunks, trimming it well. In a large container, pour the bitter orange juice over the goat and marinate in the refrigerator for 3 hours.

Bring a large pot of water to a boil. Cut an "x" into the skin at the blossom end of the tomatoes and submerge them in the boiling water for 1 minute. Transfer to a cutting board to cool, then remove the skin (peeling at the "x"). Halve, seed, and dice.

Drain the pieces of goat and season them with the black pepper. In a large Dutch oven (casserole), heat the oil over medium-high heat for 3 minutes. Add the goat and sauté until browned, about 18 minutes. Remove the goat and set aside. Add the bell pepper to the pot and cook until it softens, about 3 minutes. Add the garlic and onions and cook until fragrant, about 2 minutes. Add the tomatoes, tomato paste (puree), stock, wine, oregano, cumin, and bay leaf. Cook over low heat, stirring all the ingredients, until the sauce reduces, 7 minutes.

Return the goat to the pot and stir well. Add the parsley and ½ tablespoon salt. Cover and cook over medium-low heat until the meat is tender, about 1 hour 30 minutes, stirring occasionally. Pour in the beer and cook for 5 more minutes. Salt to taste. Let sit for 10 minutes before serving.

Note: If preferred, the goat can be boiled before being marinated to soften its strong taste. In some recipes, the goat is flamed with rum. Another variation of this recipes is to cook it with lamb instead of goat.

**PREPARATION TIME: 35 MINUTES, PLUS 3 HOURS MARINATING TIME
COOKING TIME: 2 HOURS 10 MINUTES
SERVES: 4**

4½ lb (2 kg) goat leg or shoulder
Juice of 1 bitter orange
(see page 18)
3 medium tomatoes
½ teaspoon ground black pepper
4 tablespoons vegetable oil
1 large green bell pepper, diced
4 cloves garlic, crushed
2 medium white onions, diced
2 tablespoons tomato paste
(tomato puree)
⅓ cup (2½ fl oz/80 ml) beef stock
½ cup (4 fl oz/125 ml) dry white wine
½ teaspoon dried oregano
¼ teaspoon ground cumin
1 bay leaf
1 bunch parsley, finely chopped
Salt
¾ cup (6 fl oz/180 ml) beer

OXTAIL STEW

Rabo de res encendido

PREPARATION TIME: 25 MINUTES
COOKING TIME: 1 HOUR
SERVES: 6

2 oxtails (3¼ lb/1.5 kg total)
¾ cup (180 g) tomato sauce
(seasoned passata)
1 cup (8 fl oz/240 ml) dry white wine
4 tablespoons vegetable oil
1½ medium white onions,
finely chopped
1 head garlic, separated into
cloves, peeled, and finely chopped
1 large carrot, diced
2 tablespoons chopped parsley
2 bay leaves
⅓ cup (2½ fl oz/80 ml) white rum
½ teaspoon ground cumin
½ teaspoon dried oregano
6 cups (48 fl oz/1.4 liters) beef
stock
½ teaspoon salt
1 hot chili, such as guaguao
pepper

Serve with white rice and Mashed Plantain (page 230).

Clean the oxtails and cut them at the joints. Dilute the tomato sauce (seasoned passata) in 2 tablespoons of the wine.

In a large Dutch oven (casserole), heat the oil over high heat. Add the oxtails and sauté until they begin to harden, about 6 minutes. Add the onions, garlic, carrot, parsley, and bay leaves, and cook until the onion is translucent, 2 minutes. Add the diluted tomato sauce, the remaining ¾ cup (6 fl oz/ 180 ml) plus 2 tablespoons wine, and the rum. Sprinkle in the cumin and oregano. Stir for 1 minute, then add the stock and salt. Reduce the heat to medium, cover, and cook until the oxtails are tender, about 35 minutes, making sure that the liquid does not evaporate completely. Add the chili, increase the heat to medium-high and cook the stew down until it has the consistency of a sauce, 5–7 minutes.

VEGETABLES AND LEGUMES

Verduras y legumbres

In Cuba, the most frequently cooked vegetables are pumpkin, okra, bell pepper, and cabbage. Eggplant (aubergine), carrots, green beans, and beets are also consumed with some regularity.

Roots are ubiquitous in Cuba, where they are known as *vianda*. This category includes the indigenous yuca (cassava) and sweet potato, taro root (which existed indigenously on a small scale; its cultivation increased due to African influence), potatoes (brought from South America), and yams (brought from Africa). In Cuba, the term *vianda* also includes plantains (brought from Africa). *Vianda* is a very important part of the Cuban diet, and represents a traditional way of eating that is still valued today. These foods are boiled and mashed into excellent homemade baby food, and many Cubans also cook and feed their dogs sweet potato, because processed dog food is both hard to find and expensive.

Legumes are also extremely important to the Cuban diet. Beans are most commonly prepared in *potajes*, or bean soups, that are poured over white rice. Those recipes are found in the soup chapter. The other common way to prepare beans are mixed with rice, such as the Red Beans and Rice (page 102) and Moors and Christians (page 107) recipes, found in the rice chapter. It is not as common to mix beans with other vegetables, but there are some examples of that combination, found in the following chapter. Corn is most commonly used to make tamales, but is used in other recipes as well.

The most popular preparation for all the ingredients in this chapter is fried—after that, boiled, in stews, or sautés. It is less common to steam the vegetables.

While Cubans frequently eat many of the following dishes, the general preference is to consume them as a side dish that complements the *plato fuerte*, or main dish, which consists of meat.

SAUTÉED VEGETABLES

Vegetales salteados

Bring a large pot of water to a boil. Cut an "x" into the skin at the blossom end of the tomatoes and submerge them in the boiling water for 1 minute. Transfer to a cutting board to cool, then remove the skin (peeling at the "x"). Halve, seed, and dice.

In a medium frying pan, heat the oil and butter over medium-low heat. Add the bell peppers, onion, and garlic and sauté until the onion is translucent, about 4 minutes. Add the pumpkin and mix well. Cook over low heat until the pumpkin is soft, about 7 minutes. Add the tomatoes and cook until softened, about 12 minutes. Adjust the salt. Serve garnished with parsley.

PREPARATION TIME: 20 MINUTES
COOKING TIME: 25 MINUTES
SERVES: 4

5 large tomatoes
2 tablespoons vegetable oil
1 tablespoon (15 g) butter
3 medium green bell peppers, diced
1 medium white onion, diced
3 cloves garlic, finely chopped
1 lb 2 oz (500 g) pumpkin or carrots, cut into medium chunks
Salt
2 tablespoons chopped parsley, for garnish

VEGETABLES WITH BASIL

Vegetales a la albahaca

In a steamer basket over a pan of boiling water, cover and steam the pumpkin and cabbage until softened, about 10 minutes. Set aside.

In a medium frying pan, heat the butter and oil over medium-low heat. Add the onion, basil, and scallions (spring onions) and sauté until softened, about 2 minutes. Add the tomato sauce (seasoned passata), stock, wine, raw sugar, and lime juice. Salt to taste and cook until the sauce reduces, about 10 minutes.

Serve the pumpkin and cabbage on a plate and pour the hot dressing over it.

Note: 1 tablespoon dried basil can be used instead of the fresh basil.

PREPARATION TIME: 25 MINUTES
COOKING TIME: 25 MINUTES
SERVES: 4

1 lb (460 g) pumpkin, peeled and cut into large chunks
½ medium cabbage, quartered
1 tablespoon (15 g) butter
2 tablespoons vegetable oil
1 large white onion, diced
Leaves of 4 sprigs basil, finely chopped
1 bunch scallions (spring onions), finely chopped
½ cup (125 g) tomato sauce (seasoned passata)
½ cup (4 fl oz/125 ml) vegetable stock
¼ cup (2 fl oz/60 ml) dry white wine
1 teaspoon raw cane sugar
1 teaspoon lime juice
Salt

STEAMED VEGETABLES

Vegetales al vapor 📷

PREPARATION TIME: 15 MINUTES
COOKING TIME: 15 MINUTES
SERVES: 4

★

1 medium eggplant (aubergine),
sliced
2 medium carrots, sliced
2 tablespoons vegetable oil
1 large white onion, thinly sliced
4 cloves garlic, finely chopped
½ teaspoon soy sauce
1 tablespoon vinegar
1 tablespoon dry white wine
1 tablespoon raw cane sugar
Salt

In a steamer basket set over a pan of boiling water, cover and steam the eggplant and carrots until soft, about 10 minutes. Drain and set aside.

In a medium frying pan, heat the oil over medium-low heat. Add the onion and garlic and sauté until the onion is translucent, about 3 minutes. Add the soy sauce, vinegar, wine, and raw sugar. Add salt to taste and cook the sauce until it reduces, about 2 minutes.

Serve the vegetables on a dish with the sauce on top.

Note: Aromatic herbs, such as thyme, parsley, oregano, and rosemary can be added to the water used to steam.

VEGETABLE STEW

Guiso de vegetales

PREPARATION TIME: 15 MINUTES
COOKING TIME: 10 MINUTES
SERVES: 4

★

3 tablespoons tomato sauce
(seasoned passata)
2 tablespoons dry white wine
3 tablespoons vegetable oil
2 chay peppers or cubanelles,
finely chopped
1 stalk celery, finely chopped
1 small white onion, quartered
and thinly sliced
4 cloves garlic, finely chopped
½ head bok choy (3½ oz/200 g),
thinly sliced
1 cup (100 g) cooked diced carrot
½ cup (100 g) cooked diced
potatoes
1 cup (200 g) cooked diced green
beans
Salt

In a small bowl, combine the tomato sauce and 1 tablespoon of the wine. Set aside.

In a medium frying pan, heat the oil over medium heat. Add the *chay* peppers, celery, onion, and garlic and sauté until softened, about 2 minutes. Add the bok choy and cook until its leaves soften, about 1 minute. Add the carrot, potatoes, and green beans, and gently stir with a wooden spoon. Add the diluted tomato sauce (seasoned passata) and cook until the sauce thickens, about 2 minutes. Salt to taste and add the remaining 1 tablespoon wine.

STUFFED BELL PEPPERS

Pimientos rellenos

PREPARATION TIME: 30 MINUTES
COOKING TIME: 1 HOUR
SERVES: 6

★

10½ oz (300 g) ground (minced)
beef
Salt
½ teaspoon paprika
2 tablespoons vegetable oil
1 medium white onion,
finely chopped
6 cloves garlic, finely chopped
2 tablespoons dry white wine
3 tablespoons tomato sauce
(seasoned passata)
1 cup (200 g) cooked rice
2 eggs, whisked
1 cup (8 fl oz/240 ml) salsa criolla
(Cuban Sauce, page 311)
½ cup (4 fl oz/125 ml) vegetable
stock
6 large green bell peppers,
the tops cut off and reserved,
stemmed and seeded (see Note)

Season the ground (minced) beef with ½ teaspoon salt and the paprika. Set aside.

In a medium frying pan, heat the oil over medium heat. Add the onion and garlic and sauté until the onion is translucent, about 2 minutes. Add the ground beef and cook for 3 minutes. Pour in the wine and tomato sauce (seasoned passata) and cook for 8 minutes to reduce and thicken the sauce. Stir in the rice, then stir in the eggs and cook until firm, about 3 minutes. Season to taste with salt and remove from the stove.

In a small bowl, combine the *salsa criolla* and the stock. Fill the bell peppers with the ground beef filling, then cover with the reserved tops. Arrange in a large pot and pour the *salsa criolla* mixture ontop. Cover and cook over low heat until soft, about 40 minutes.

Note: Though the traditional way to prepare this recipe is by cutting the tops off, the peppers can also be sliced in half lengthwise.

ORANGE-FLAVORED CARROTS

Zanahoria a la naranja

PREPARATION TIME: 15 MINUTES
COOKING TIME: 20 MINUTES
SERVES: 4

★

4 medium carrots, cut into ⅓-inch
(1 cm) slices
1 cup (8 fl oz/240 ml) orange juice
2 tablespoons (30 g) butter
1 tablespoon raw cane sugar
½ oz (15 g) fresh ginger, slivered
½ teaspoon salt

This is an excellent side dish to accompany fish or roasted meats.

★

In a medium frying pan, combine the carrots, orange juice, butter, raw sugar, ginger, and salt. Cover and cook over low heat until softened, about 20 minutes.

STEWED CABBAGE AND HAM

Col guisado con jamón

PREPARATION TIME: 30 MINUTES
COOKING TIME: 50 MINUTES
SERVES: 4

★

2 tablespoons vegetable oil
2 small white onions, quartered
4 cloves garlic, crushed
½ lb (230 g) ham, cut into 2 inch
(5 cm) long strips
1 small green cabbage (1¼ lb/560
g), cut into ⅓-inch (1 cm) strips
Salt
½ cup (125 g) tomato sauce
(seasoned passata)
2 tablespoons dry white wine
½ teaspoon ground cumin
1 teaspoon raw cane sugar
1 tablespoon vinegar
1 bunch parsley, finely chopped

In a medium frying pan, heat the oil over medium heat. Add the onions and garlic and sauté until softened, about 2 minutes. Add the ham and cook for 2 minutes. Add the cabbage, stir with a wooden spoon, and season to taste with salt. Stir in the tomato sauce (seasoned passata), wine, cumin, raw sugar, and vinegar. Cover and cook over very low heat until the cabbage is very soft, about 40 minutes. Garnish with the finely chopped parsley.

Note: If the tomato sauce used is very thick, it can be diluted with 1 tablespoon dry white wine.

CUBAN EGGPLANT

Berenjena a la cubana

PREPARATION TIME: 45 MINUTES
COOKING TIME: 25 MINUTES
SERVES: 6

★

2 medium eggplants (aubergines),
sliced ½ inch (1.25 cm) thick
Sea salt
6 cloves garlic, finely chopped
½ cup (4 fl oz/125 ml) bitter orange
juice (see page 18)
2 tablespoons vegetable oil, plus
more for frying the eggplant
All-purpose (plain) flour, for dredging
1 large white onion, sliced ¼ inch
(6 mm) thick
¼ teaspoon ground cumin
¾ cup (185 g) tomato sauce
(seasoned passata)
¼ cup (2 fl oz/60 ml) dry white wine
½ cup (4 fl oz/125 ml) vegetable stock
½ cup (2 oz/60 g) coarsely grated
gouda or mild yellow cheese

In a large bowl, submerge the eggplants (aubergines) in cold water with 1 teaspoon salt for 30 minutes. Drain, rinse the bowl, and return the eggplant to the bowl. Add 1½ teaspoons salt, half the garlic, and the bitter orange juice and stir. Let marinate for 10 minutes. Drain well.

Pour 2 inches (5 cm) oil into a medium heavy-bottomed frying pan and heat over high heat until very hot. Working in batches, dredge the eggplant in the flour and add to the pan, cooking until evenly browned, 3–4 minutes per side. Transfer to a plate lined with paper towels to absorb the excess oil.

In a large pot, heat the 2 tablespoons oil over medium-high heat. Add the onion and ½ teaspoon salt and sauté until the onions begin to sweat and wilt, about 3 minutes. Add the remaining garlic and cook until the onions are softened and translucent, about 1 minute more. Add the cumin, tomato sauce (seasoned passata), wine, and vegetable stock and bring to a simmer. Adjust the salt, then add the eggplant (aubergine) slices, stir well and cook until the liquid is mostly absorbed, about 2 minutes. Sprinkle with the cheese and serve hot.

BREADED EGGPLANT WITH BELL PEPPER

Berenjena rebozada con pimiento

In a medium bowl, submerge the eggplant (aubergine) slices in water with 1 teaspoon salt for 30 minutes. Drain and transfer to a large bowl. Season with ½ teaspoon salt, the black pepper, garlic, cumin, and lime juice and stir. In a small bowl, combine the flour and egg whites. Add the eggplant slices and toss.

Preheat the oven to 250°F (120°C/Gas Mark ½). Line a baking sheet with paper towels.

Pour 2 inches (5 cm) oil into a medium heavy-bottomed frying pan and heat over high heat until very hot. Working in batches, fry the eggplant until evenly browned, about 5 minutes per side. Transfer the slices to the lined baking sheet to absorb the excess oil and keep warm in the oven while you prepare the peppers.

Wipe out the frying pan and heat 2 tablespoons oil over medium-high heat until it shimmers. Add the bell peppers and onion and sauté, stirring frequently, until the onions are very wilted and the peppers are tender, about 10 minutes. Add the raw sugar, vinegar, mint, and salt to taste. Reduce the heat to low and cook until the sauce reduces, about 5 minutes.

Serve the eggplant with the pepper sauté on the side.

PREPARATION TIME: 30 MINUTES
COOKING TIME: 25 MINUTES
SERVES: 4–6

1 medium eggplant (aubergine), halved lengthwise and cut crosswise into slices ¼ inch (6 mm) thick
Salt
¼ teaspoon ground black pepper
3 cloves garlic, minced
¼ teaspoon ground cumin
1 tablespoon lime juice
4 tablespoons all-purpose (plain) flour
2 egg whites, whisked until frothy
2 tablespoons vegetable oil, plus more for frying the eggplant
3 large red bell peppers, cut into strips ½ inch (1.25 cm) wide
1 large white onion, halved and thinly sliced
¼ teaspoon raw cane sugar
1 tablespoon white vinegar or apple cider vinegar
¼ cup (22 g) finely chopped fresh mint leaves

OKRA WITH PLANTAIN AND CHICKEN

Quimbombó con bolas de plátano y pollo

PREPARATION TIME: 20 MINUTES
COOKING TIME: 35 MINUTES
SERVES: 4

★

1 large (10½ oz/300 g) half-ripe
plantain
Salt
2 tablespoons vegetable oil
2 chay peppers or cubanelles,
finely chopped
3 cloves garlic, finely chopped
1 medium red onion,
finely chopped
2 medium tomatoes, diced
1 cup (230 g) cooked chicken
(see page 19)
2 cups (350 g) sliced okra
1 tablespoon lime juice
½ cup (4 fl oz/125 ml) chicken
stock
1 tablespoon toasted sesame
seeds
2 tablespoons dry white wine

Make a lengthwise cut through the peel of the plantain. Bring a large pot of lightly salted water to a boil. Add the plantain and boil until softened, about 12 minutes. Drain and when cool enough to handle, peel the plantain and transfer to a ceramic pot. Mash the plantain with a fork and add ½ teaspoon salt. Roll the mashed plantains into balls about 1¼ inches (3 cm) in diameter. Set the dumplings aside.

In a large frying pan, heat the oil over high heat. Add the *chay* peppers, garlic, and onion and sauté until fragrant, about 2 minutes. Add the tomatoes and cook, stirring regularly, until softened, about 2 minutes. Stir in the cooked chicken and okra. Add the lime juice and stir over medium heat for 4 minutes. Add the chicken stock, sesame seeds, and wine and cook over low heat until the okra softens, about 12 minutes. Adjust the salt.

Arrange the plantain dumplings in the stew and gently stir. Remove from the heat and allow to cool slightly. Serve with white rice.

SWEET AND SOUR PUMPKIN

Calabaza agridulce

PREPARATION TIME: 15 MINUTES
COOKING TIME: 20 MINUTES
SERVES: 4

★

Salt
1 whole pumpkin (2¼ lb/1 kg),
peeled and diced
2 tablespoons vegetable oil
1 medium white onion,
finely chopped
4 cachucha peppers or cubanelles,
finely chopped
4 cloves garlic, crushed
½ cup (4 fl oz/125 ml) vinegar
1 ¾ inch (2 cm) slice fresh ginger,
grated
2 tablespoons raw cane sugar
Leaves of 1 sprig basil

Bring a large pot of lightly salted water to a boil. Add the pumpkin, cover, and cook until soft, about 10 minutes. Drain well.

In a medium frying pan, heat the oil over medium-low heat. Add the onion, *cachucha* peppers, and garlic, and sauté until softened, about 3 minutes. Add the pumpkin, vinegar, ginger, raw sugar, and basil and let cook until it thickens slightly, about 5 minutes. Season to taste with salt.

SWEET AND SOUR BEETS

Remolacha agridulce

PREPARATION TIME: 20 MINUTES
COOKING TIME: 1 HOUR 15 MINUTES
SERVES: 4

★

4 medium beets (4 oz/115 g each)
3 tablespoons raw cane sugar
1 tablespoon cornstarch (cornflour)
or all-purpose flour
¼ cup (2 fl oz/60 ml) vinegar
1 teaspoon salt
⅛ teaspoon ground black pepper
2 tablespoons (30 g) butter
1 medium white onion, halved
and sliced

In a large pot, combine the beets and 8 cups (1.9 liters) water. Cook, covered, for 1 hour on medium heat. Drain, reserving ¼ cup (2 fl oz/60 ml) of the cooking water. Let cool, then peel and cut into strips. Set aside.

In a small bowl, combine the raw sugar, cornstarch (cornflour), vinegar, salt, pepper, and the reserved cooking water. Set aside.

In a medium frying pan, heat the butter over medium-low heat. Add the onion and sauté until translucent, about 2 minutes. Add the sugar/vinegar mixture and cook, stirring regularly with a wooden spoon, until the sauce thickens, about 4 minutes. Add the beets, stir, and cook for 2 more minutes.

MASHED PLANTAIN

Fufú de plátano

PREPARATION TIME: 15 MINUTES
COOKING TIME: 45 MINUTES
SERVES: 6

★

4 medium green plantains
(7 oz/200 g each)
1½ teaspoons salt
2 tablespoons vegetable oil
10 oz (300 g) pork belly, diced into
1 ½ centimeter pieces
4 cloves garlic, crushed
2 tablespoons lime juice,
plus ½ lime for garnish

According to Cuban anthropologist Fernando Ortiz, the British also brought African slaves (specifically Ghanaian slaves) to Cuba during their brief rule. When the British fed the slaves their food, usually boiled and mashed plantains, they would say "Food, food," which is the origin of the name of this dish.

★

Trim the ends of the plantains and make a lengthwise slit in the peel of each one. Bring a medium pot of water with 1 teaspoon salt and the lime juice to a boil. Add the plantains and cook until softened, about 20 minutes. Drain and peel. Transfer to a medium bowl and mash with a fork.

In a medium frying pan, heat the oil over medium heat. Add the pork belly and fry until the fat is rendered and the meat is browned, about 15 minutes. Remove the chicharrones, reserving the rendered pork fat, and set aside.

In the same frying pan, heat 2 tablespoons of the reserved rendered pork fat over medium-high heat. Add the garlic and sauté until fragrant, about 1 minute.

Add the chicharrones and the garlic to the mashed plantains and gently mix. Add the remaining ½ teaspoon salt. Serve hot, accompanied with a slice of lime, or with lime squeezed over the dish.

SWEET AND SOUR MASHED PLANTAINS AND SWEET POTATO

Fufú agridulce

PREPARATION TIME: 20 MINUTES
COOKING TIME: 35 MINUTES
SERVES: 4

★

3 medium half-ripe burro plantains
Salt
1 medium white or yellow sweet
potato, peeled and chopped
2 tablespoons vegetable oil
1 large white onion, finely chopped
4 cloves garlic, finely chopped
2 tablespoons seedless tamarind
pulp
Thinly sliced scallions (spring
onions), for garnish

Trim the ends of the plantains and make a lengthwise slit through the peel of each. Bring a medium pot of lightly salted water to a boil. Add the plantains and cook until softened, 12–15 minutes. Drain and set aside.

Bring another medium pot of lightly salted water to a boil. Add the sweet potato, cover, and cook until softened, about 20 minutes. Reserving the cooking water, drain and set aside.

In a ceramic pot, combine the plantains and sweet potato and mash with a fork. Add 3–5 tablespoons of the reserved cooking water, or enough to achieve a smooth puree.

In a medium frying pan, heat the oil over medium-low heat. Add the onion and garlic and sauté until fragrant, about 3 minutes. Transfer to the puree, add the tamarind pulp, and gently mix. Season to taste with salt and garnish with the scallions (spring onions).

MASHED POTATOES

Puré de papas

PREPARATION TIME: 15 MINUTES
COOKING TIME: 25 MINUTES
SERVES: 6

★

6 large potatoes (2 lb/920 g total),
peeled and cut into small pieces
1 teaspoon salt
½ cup (2 fl oz/60 ml) whole milk
2 tablespoons (30 g) butter
⅛ teaspoon ground black pepper

Mashed potatoes are very popular in Cuban cuisine, especially when accompanied by Ground Beef and Capers (page 208).

★

In a medium pot, combine the potatoes and ½ teaspoon salt and add water to cover by 1 inch (2.5 cm). Bring to a boil, then reduce the heat to medium, cover, and cook until softened, about 25 minutes. Drain, return the potatoes to the pot, and mash into a puree.

Meanwhile, in a small pot, heat the milk over low heat. Add the milk, butter, remaining salt, and pepper to the mashed potatoes and mix well. Serve hot.

YUCA IN SAUCE

Yuca con mojo

PREPARATION TIME: 20 MINUTES
COOKING TIME: 1 HOUR
SERVES: 4

2 medium yuca (cassava) roots
(9 oz each/250 g each), peeled
and cut crosswise into 1 inch
(2.5 cm) long pieces 1 inch
(2.5 cm) thick
Salt
10 cloves garlic, crushed to a paste
¼ cup (2 fl oz/60 ml) bitter orange
juice (see page 18)
2 tablespoons vegetable oil

This is a very traditional Cuban dish, which is always present for New Year's Eve dinners and other holidays.

Yuca (cassava) is native to Cuba and the Caribbean, and was the base of the diet of the indigenous people. The yuca harvested in the winter months is especially soft and delicious.

Cut an "x" into the flesh on both cut sides of the yuca (cassava) pieces (this will help them cook faster). Bring a medium pot of lightly salted water to a boil. Add the yuca and cook until soft, about 1 hour. Set aside in the pot with the hot cooking water.

In a small bowl, combine the crushed garlic, bitter orange juice, and ½ teaspoon salt.

In a small frying pan, heat the oil over high heat. Add the garlic/orange mixture, cover, and remove the *mojo* from the heat.

Drain the yuca and serve dressed with the *mojo*.

TARO ROOT, PUMPKIN, AND BOK CHOY PUREE

Puré de malanga, calabaza y acelga

PREPARATION TIME: 25 MINUTES
COOKING TIME: 30 MINUTES
SERVES: 4

★

4 medium taro roots (14 oz/400 g total), peeled and cut into small pieces
7 oz (200 g) pumpkin, cut into small pieces
1 cup (80 g) chopped bok choy
1 tablespoon (15 g) butter
1 tablespoon vegetable oil
2 small white onions, finely chopped
1 bunch scallions (spring onions), finely chopped
2 cloves garlic, finely chopped
⅛ teaspoon grated nutmeg
1 teaspoon salt
Finely chopped parsley, for serving

This puree is often prepared as a homemade baby food. Though *acelga* is usually translated as Swiss chard, in Cuba it refers to bok choy.

★

In a large pot, combine the taro root and 4 cups (32 fl oz/ 950 ml) water. Bring to a boil, then reduce the heat to medium and cook, covered, until the taro root is semi-soft, about 15 minutes. Add the pumpkin and cook until both the pumpkin and taro root completely soften, about 10 minutes. Add the bok choy just before removing the pot from the stovetop.

In a medium frying pan, heat the butter and oil over medium heat. Add the onions, scallions (spring onions), and garlic and sauté until fragrant, about 2 minutes.

In a blender, combine the drained taro root, pumpkin, and bok choy mixture, and the sautéed onion mixture. Blend until smooth. Return to the pot and cook over medium-low heat until it comes to a light boil, about 2 minutes. Add the nutmeg and salt. Stir and remove from the heat. Serve garnished with parsley.

MASHED PLANTAINS WITH PORK

Machuquillo

PREPARATION TIME: 25 MINUTES
COOKING TIME: 1 HOUR
SERVES: 4

★

2 green burro plantains
2 ripe burro plantains
Salt
5 chicharrones (fried pork rinds)
4 tablespoons vegetable oil
14 oz (400 g) porkloin or tenderloin, diced into ½ inch (1 cm) pieces
8 cloves garlic, crushed
3 tablespoons lime juice

Make a lengthwise slit down the peel of the plantains. Bring a large pot of lightly salted water to a boil over medium heat. Add the green plantains and cook until semi-soft, about 15 minutes. Add the ripe plantains and continue cooking until the peel begins to separate, about 10 minutes. Drain and let cool. Peel and grind the plantains with the chicharrones in a food grinder (or finely chop the chicharrones, mash the plantains, and mix together with a fork if you don't have a food grinder).

In a medium frying pan, heat 2 tablespoons of the oil over medium heat. Add the pork and sauté until browned, about 10 minutes. Reduce the heat to low and sauté until cooked through, about 3 minutes. Set aside.

In a large pot, heat the remaining 2 tablespoons oil over medium heat. Add the garlic and sauté until fragrant, about 1 minute. Add the plantain puree and stir with a wooden spoon. Add the lime juice and ½ teaspoon salt and cook for 3 minutes. Serve hot.

JUAN IZQUIERDO-STYLE OKRA WITH SHRIMP

Quimbombó con camarones
al estilo de Juan Izquierdo

There is a reference to this recipe in the novel *Paradiso*, by the famous Cuban writer José Lezama Lima. In the book, a cook named Juan Izquierdo and the woman he works for, Señora Rialta, have a debate about this dish. The chef wants to include the dried shrimp, but Rialta argues that the ingredient does not blend well with traditional Cuban cuisine.

In a medium bowl, soak the dried shrimp (prawns) in room-temperature water for 30 minutes. Drain and set aside.

Season the fresh shrimp with ½ teaspoon salt and the pepper. In a medium frying pan, heat the oil and butter over medium heat. Add the fresh shrimp and sauté until pink and opaque, about 2 minutes. Remove and set aside.

In the same pan, in the same oil, sauté the okra, scallions (spring onions), garlic, and lime juice (if using) until softened, about 6 minutes. Add the tomatoes and cook until the juices reduce, about 3 minutes. Add 1 cup (8 fl oz/ 240 ml) water, the tomato sauce (seasoned passata), and 1 teaspoon salt. Cover and cook over medium-low heat for 8 minutes. Drain the dried shrimp, add to the sauce, and cook until the sauce thickens, about 3 minutes. Just before removing the pan from the heat, add the sautéed fresh shrimp and the parsley. Salt to taste, add the wine, and cook for 1 more minute.

Note: Lime juice reduces the slimy texture of the okra.

**PREPARATION TIME: 25 MINUTES,
PLUS 30 MINUTES SHRIMP
SOAKING TIME
COOKING TIME: 25 MINUTES
SERVES: 4**

½ cup (80 g) dried shrimp
(prawns), also known as
Chinese shrimp
½ lb (230 g) fresh shrimp
(prawns), peeled and deveined
Salt
⅛ teaspoon ground black pepper
2 tablespoons vegetable oil
1 tablespoon (15 g) butter
25 okra pods (1 lb/460 g), cut into
1-inch (2.5 cm) lengths
1 bunch scallions (spring onions),
finely chopped
5 cloves garlic, crushed
A few drops lime juice (see Note)
4 medium tomatoes, diced
2 tablespoons tomato sauce
(seasoned passata)
1 bunch parsley, finely chopped
2 tablespoons dry white wine

YUCA "DRUM" CASSEROLE

Tambor de yuca

PREPARATION TIME: 25 MINUTES
COOKING TIME: 30–40 MINUTES
SERVES: 6

Salt
4 medium yuca (cassava) roots
(10½ oz/300 g each), peeled and
cut into large, even chunks
1 tablespoon (15 g) butter
2½ tablespoons vegetable oil
1 small green bell pepper, diced
2 medium white onions, diced
3 cloves garlic, finely chopped
2 cups (230 g) chopped cooked
chicken (see page 19)
¼ teaspoon ground cumin
¼ teaspoon dried oregano
½ cup (125 g) tomato puree
(passata)
1 egg, whisked
3 tablespoons grated Cuban
gouda or other mild yellow cheese
Red bell pepper, sliced carrot,
or other colorful ingredient, for
garnish

This dish was inspired by the classic *tambor de papas*, which is the same dish made with potatoes instead of yuca (cassava).

Bring a large pot of lightly salted water to a boil. Add the yuca (cassava), return to a boil, then reduce the heat to medium and cook until softened, about 40 minutes. Drain and let cool. Transfer to a large bowl and mash into a puree with a fork, mixing in the butter. Taste for seasoning. Set aside.

Meanwhile, preheat the oven to 350°F (180°C/Gas Mark 4). Grease a 12 x 10-inch (30 x 25 cm) baking dish with ½ tablespoon of the oil.

In a medium frying pan, heat the remaining 2 tablespoons oil over medium heat. Add the bell pepper, onions, and garlic and sauté until tender, about 5 minutes. Add the chicken, cumin, oregano, and tomato puree (passata) diluted with 2 tablespoons water. Cook over high heat, stirring regularly, until it is thick and rich, about 3 minutes. Adjust the salt.

In the prepared baking dish, spread out a layer of half the mashed yuca, then all the ground chicken mixture, then the remaining yuca. Brush with the egg and sprinkle with the cheese. Bake until heated through and the cheese on top is golden, 10 minutes. Serve garnished with red bell pepper or sliced carrot.

Note: The cooked chicken can be substituted with cooked ground (minced) beef, ground ham, cook sausage removed from its casing, or cooked or canned mushrooms.

ROASTED POTATOES WITH SAUTÉED VEGETABLES

Papas asadas con salteado de vegetales

This makes an excellent side dish to accompany roasted meat.

★

Preheat the oven to 350°F (180°C/Gas Mark 4). Grease a 16½ x 12½-inch (44 cm x 32 cm) pan with ½ tablespoon of the oil.

In a large frying pan, heat 3½ tablespoons of the oil over medium heat. Add the potatoes and fry until lightly browned, about 7 minutes on each side. Transfer to paper towels to soak up excess oil.

In a medium frying pan, heat the remaining 2 tablespoons oil over medium heat. Add the bell pepper and carrot and sauté until the pepper softens, about 2 minutes. Add the garlic and stir. Add the onion and cook until translucent, about 1 minute. Add the tomato and cook until it softens and releases some of its juices, about 4 minutes. Add the wine and cook until it begins to reduce, about 2 minutes.

Arrange the potatoes in the prepared pan. Sprinkle with the salt and pepper and cover the potatoes with the bell pepper/carrot mixture. Bake until the potatoes soften, making sure the sauce does not dry up, about 25 minutes. Garnish with parsley.

PREPARATION TIME: 25 MINUTES
COOKING TIME: 40 MINUTES
SERVES: 4

6 tablespoons olive oil
4 large potatoes (2¼ lb/1 kg total), peeled and sliced lengthwise ⅓ inch (1 cm) thick
1 large green bell pepper, chopped
1 large carrot, chopped
4 cloves garlic
1 large white onion, finely chopped
1 large tomato, diced
⅓ cup (2½ fl oz/80 ml) dry white wine
½ teaspoon salt
⅛ teaspoon ground black pepper
2 tablespoons chopped parsley

MASHED TARO ROOT WITH COCONUT MILK

Puré de malanga con leche de coco

PREPARATION TIME: 20 MINUTES
COOKING TIME: 25 MINUTES
SERVES: 4

Salt

4 medium taro roots (14 oz/400 g total), peeled and chopped

¾ cup (6 fl oz/180 ml) coconut milk, store-bought or homemade (see Note)

1 tablespoon (15 g) butter

1 tablespoon vegetable oil

1 medium green bell pepper, finely diced

1 medium white onion, finely diced

2 cloves garlic, finely chopped

This is considered a fine side dish to serve with roasts or fish.

Bring a medium pot of lightly salted water to a boil. Add the taro roots, cover, and cook until softened, about 20 minutes. Drain and let cool. Transfer to a ceramic pot and mash into a puree with a fork or potato masher, while mixing in the coconut milk. Adjust the salt.

In a medium frying pan, heat the butter and oil over medium heat. Add the bell pepper, onion, and garlic and sauté until the onion is translucent, about 3 minutes.

Serve the mashed taro root with the sautéed pepper and onion mixture on top.

Notes: To make coconut milk, blend 1 cup (75 g) grated fresh coconut with 1 cup (8 fl oz/ 240 ml) hot water in a blender. Strain the mixture through a sieve lined with cheesecloth, then squeeze the cheesecloth hard to get out as much coconut milk as possible.

If you prefer, the sautéed seasonings can be mixed with the puree.

POTATOES WITH PEPPERS AND ONIONS

Papa con pimiento y cebolla

PREPARATION TIME: 25 MINUTES
COOKING TIME: 45 MINUTES
SERVES: 4

★

3 tablespoons vegetable oil
4 medium potatoes (14 oz/400 g total), peeled and cut into wedges
1 small green bell pepper, sliced
2 small red bell peppers, sliced
1 medium white onion, quartered
2 tablespoons chopped parsley
1 teaspoon salt
⅛ teaspoon ground black pepper

This recipe shows the culinary influence of the former Soviet Union, where thousands of Cuban students studied and became familiar with the food from that region.

★

In a medium pot, heat the oil over low heat. Add the potatoes, bell peppers, onion, and parsley and cook, covered, stirring every 10 minutes, until the potatoes are soft, about 40 minutes. Add the salt and black pepper.

POTATOES WITH CHEESE AND CUBAN OREGANO

Papas con queso y orégano francés

PREPARATION TIME: 30 MINUTES
COOKING TIME: 30 MINUTES
SERVES: 4

★

3 tablespoons vegetable oil
5 medium potatoes (4 oz/120 g each), peeled and cut into slices ⅓ inch (1 cm) thick
2 chay peppers or cubanelles, thinly sliced
1 medium white onion, chopped
4 tablespoons dry white wine
½ tablespoon salt
¼ teaspoon ground black pepper
¼ teaspoon ground cumin
1 cup (8 fl oz/240 ml) stock or water
6 leaves fresh Cuban oregano (Mexican mint) or regular oregano, thinly sliced
½ cup (50 g) grated Cuban gouda or other mild yellow cheese
Bell peppers, hard-boiled egg, or parsley, for garnish

In a medium frying pan, heat the oil over medium heat. Add the potatoes and sauté until browned, about 7 minutes. Add the *chay* peppers and onion, and sauté until the onion turns translucent, about 2 minutes. Add the wine, salt, black pepper, and cumin. Add the stock, cover, and cook over medium heat until the potatoes are semi-soft, about 8 minutes. Reduce the heat to low and cook until the potatoes are soft , about 10 minutes. Add the oregano and stir gently. Sprinkle the cheese over the potatoes and let melt. Serve hot, garnished with peppers, hard-boiled egg, or parsley.

FRIED SWEET PLANTAINS

Plátano maduro frito

PREPARATION TIME: 10 MINUTES
COOKING TIME: 25 MINUTES
SERVES: 6

★

5 ripe medium plantains (7 oz/
200 g each)
¼ cup (2 fl oz/60 ml) vegetable oil

This recipe has its roots in the culinary influences brought by the African slaves. The fried plantains make an excellent side dish, especially to accompany Cuban-style ground meats, pork, and beef steaks, and combined rice dishes.

★

Peel the plantains and cut them in long diagonal slices. In a medium frying pan, heat the oil over medium-high heat. Fry the plantain slices until browned on both sides, about 5 minutes. Drain on paper towels and serve hot.

STUFFED PLANTAINS

Bolas de plátano rellenas

PREPARATION TIME: 25 MINUTES
COOKING TIME: 20 MINUTES
SERVES: 6

★

Salt
4 medium half-ripe plantains,
unpeeled, cut crosswise into 2 or
3 pieces
2 tablespoons vegetable oil
1 cup (230 g) Chicken and Sweet
Potato Stew (page 180)

Bring a large pot of lightly salted water to a boil. Add the plantains and cook until softened, about 20 minutes. Reserving the cooking water, drain and let cool for a few minutes. Remove the peels while still a little hot and remove the line of seeds in the middle (optional). Transfer to a large bowl and mash with a fork until you achieve an even texture, using 2 tablespoons of the water used to cook the plantains. Stir in ½ teaspoon salt and the oil. Roll into balls 1½ inches (4 cm) in diameter, then fill each one with the chicken and sweet potato stew.

Note: The plantain balls can also be filled with a vegetable sauté, shredded fish, or cheese. They can also be breaded and fried.

POTATO SALAD IN SWEET AND SOUR SAUCE

Papas en escabeche

**PREPARATION TIME: 15 MINUTES,
PLUS 12 HOURS CHILLING TIME
COOKING TIME: 35 MINUTES
SERVES: 6**

6 medium potatoes (3½ oz/100 g
each), peeled and cut into slices
⅓ inch (1 cm) thick
½ cup (4 fl oz/150 ml) vegetable oil
2 medium white onions,
quartered and sliced
2 large green bell peppers, cut into
strips
4 cloves garlic, peeled but whole
8 tablespoons vinegar
2 tablespoons raw cane sugar
3 leaves fresh Cuban oregano
(Mexican mint) or regular oregano,
cut into strips
1 teaspoon salt
5 black peppercorns

This recipe calls for a technique usually used to prepare fish, but can also be applied to vegetables and roots.

In a medium pot, bring 6 cups (48 fl oz/1.4 liters) water to a boil. Add the potatoes, cover, and cook until the potatoes are semi-soft, about 20 minutes. Drain well.

In a large pan, heat 2 tablespoons of the oil over medium heat. Add the onions, bell peppers, and garlic cloves and sauté until the onion turns translucent, about 3 minutes. Add the potatoes and continue cooking until the potatoes have browned slightly on both sides, about 6 minutes. Cover with ¾ cup (6 fl oz/185 ml) water and the vinegar and add the raw sugar, oregano, salt, and peppercorns. Cover and bring to a boil over high heat, then remove from the heat. Add the remaining 6 tablespoons oil and let cool. Transfer to a glass or ceramic dish and refrigerate for 12 hours before serving.

Notes: ½ teaspoon paprika, ½ teaspoon rosemary, or 2 whole cloves can be added along with the water and vinegar.

The bell peppers can be substituted with carrots or green beans.

SWEET POTATO AND FISH DUMPLINGS

Bolas de boniato y pescado

**PREPARATION TIME: 25 MINUTES
COOKING TIME: 25 MINUTES
MAKES: 24 DUMPLINGS**

3 eggs, whisked
2 cups (200 g) finely ground
crackers (cracker meal) or dried
breadcrumbs
1 teaspoon salt
2 tablespoons raw cane sugar
4 medium white or yellow sweet
potatoes, peeled and diced
1 cup (175 g) Shredded Fish
(page 162)
All-purpose (plain) flour,
for shaping
Vegetable oil, for deep-frying

Set up 2 shallow bowls for dredging: 1 with the eggs and 1 with the ground crackers or breadcrumbs. Set aside.

Bring a large pot of water to a boil and season with the salt and sugar. Add the sweet potatoes, cover, and simmer until tender, about 15 minutes. Drain and let cool. Transfer to a large bowl and mash with a fork. Season to taste. With lightly floured hands, roll into balls 1½ inches (4 cm) in diameter. Make an indent into each ball using your thumb, then press the fish into it and seal the potato around the fish. Dip the balls in the egg, letting the excess drip, then roll in the ground crackers or breadcrumbs.

Pour 2 inches (5 cm) oil into a large, heavy-bottomed frying pan and heat over medium-high heat. Working in batches, add four or five dumplings and deep-fry until browned, about 4 minutes. Lift from the oil with a slotted spoon, drain on paper towels. Serve hot.

STUFFED POTATOES

Papas rellenas

This is a typical dish from Guanabacoa, a municipality of Havana, where the cafeteria El Faro is famous for its stuffed potatoes. This dish has continued to be popular in Cuban cuisine over the years.

Bring a large pot of lightly salted water to a boil. Add the potatoes and cook until soft, about 30 minutes. Drain and let cool. Peel and transfer to a large bowl.

Set up 3 shallow bowls for dredging: whisk the eggs and ¼ teaspoon salt in one, pour the flour in a second, and the breadcrumbs in the third. Set aside.

Mash the potatoes with a fork or potato masher. Add ¾ teaspoon salt, the white pepper, and the butter and mix. Divide into 12 equal portions, then roll each portion into a ball and fill with a spoonful of ground beef. Roll each ball to cover up the filling. Dip the potato balls in the flour, then egg, and then the breadcrumbs.

Pour 2 inches (5 cm) oil into a medium, heavy-bottomed pan and heat over medium-high heat. Add the potatoes and fry until browned, 3 minutes. Transfer to a plate lined with paper towels to drain the excess oil. Serve hot with ketchup.

Notes: The potatoes can be substituted with yuca (cassava) or sweet potato.

The ground beef can be substituted with ham, fish, or cheese.

PREPARATION TIME: 45 MINUTES
COOKING TIME: 15 MINUTES
SERVES: 6–8

Salt
3¼ lb (1.5 kg) medium potatoes
2 eggs
½ cup (70 g) all-purpose
(plain) flour
1 cup (150 g) dried breadcrumbs
¼ teaspoon ground white pepper
2 tablespoons (30 g) butter
1 cup (230 g) Havana-Style
Ground Beef (page 203)
Vegetable oil, for frying
Ketchup, for serving

FRIED SWEET POTATO

Boniato frito

Pour 2 inches (5 cm) oil into a medium heavy-bottomed pan and heat over medium-low heat until a piece of bread sizzles. Fry the sweet potatoes until completely soft, about 5 minutes. Increase the heat to high and continue frying until browned, about 3 minutes. Sprinkle with the salt and serve hot.

Note: The sweet potatoes can also be cut in long sticks, like French fries.

PREPARATION TIME: 15 MINUTES
COOKING TIME: 30 MINUTES
SERVES: 6

Vegetable oil, for deep-frying
3 medium white or yellow sweet
potatoes, peeled and cut into
slices ½ inch (1.25 cm) thick
½ teaspoon salt

CARAMELIZED SWEET POTATOES

Boniatos en tentación

PREPARATION TIME: 10 MINUTES
COOKING TIME: 20 MINUTES
SERVES: 4

1 tablespoon salt
1 large white or yellow sweet potato, peeled and cut into slices ⅓ inch (1 cm) thick
4 tablespoons raw cane sugar
½ cup (4 fl oz/125 ml) dry white wine
2 tablespoons (30 g) butter
3 cinnamon sticks

This recipe is an adaptation of the famous Cuban dish *plátanos en tentación*, or caramelized bananas.

★

In a medium pot, combine 3 cups (24 fl oz/700 ml) water and the salt and bring to a boil over medium heat. Add the sweet potato, reduce the heat to low, cover, and cook until softened, about 10 minutes. Reserving about 1 cup (8 fl oz/240 ml) of the cooking water, drain the sweet potatoes and put back in the pot. Return to the stovetop and add the raw sugar, wine, butter, cinnamon sticks, and the 1 cup (8 fl oz/240 ml) reserved cooking water. Continue cooking over low heat, turning the sweet potatoes carefully, until softened and lightly caramelized, 6–8 minutes.

SWEET AND SOUR BEANS

Frijoles agridulces

PREPARATION TIME: 10 MINUTES
COOKING TIME: 15 MINUTES
SERVES: 4

★

2 tablespoons vegetable oil
1 medium red onion, diced
2 cups (480 g) cooked red beans (canned or homemade)
4 tablespoons vinegar
3 tablespoons honey
2 tablespoons dry white wine
1 ¾ inch (2 cm) thick slice fresh ginger, grated
Salt

In a medium frying pan, heat the oil over medium-low heat. Add the onion and sauté until translucent, about 3 minutes. Stir in the beans. Add the vinegar, honey, wine, and ginger. Cook, stirring regularly, over medium heat, until the sauce thickens, about 10 minutes. Salt to taste.

SPICY GREEN BEANS

Habichuelas picantes

This recipe comes from a 1925 book called *Delicias de la mesa*, by master Chef María Antonieta Reyes Gavilán y Moenck. This and other books published by this chef set the standards for Cuban home cooking. This recipe is especially interesting, because it is rare to find spicy dishes in typical Cuban cuisine.

Bring a large pot of lightly salted water to a boil. Add the green beans and cook until crisp-tender, about 10 minutes. Drain and let cool. Set aside.

In a medium frying pan, heat the oil over high heat. Add the garlic, chili, and bay leaf and sauté until fragrant, about 1 minute. Transfer to a large bowl and set aside.

In the same pan, add the green beans, onion, ½ teaspoon salt, and vinegar and sauté, stirring constantly, for 3 minutes. Transfer to the bowl with the garlic mixture and gently stir. Serve hot.

PREPARATION TIME: 20 MINUTES
COOKING TIME: 10 MINUTES
SERVES: 4

Salt
1 lb (500 g) green beans,
cut into 1 inch (2.5 cm) pieces
3 tablespoons vegetable oil
2 cloves garlic, crushed
1 small guaguao chili,
finely chopped
1 bay leaf
1 medium white onion,
finely chopped
2 tablespoons vinegar
1 bunch parsley, finely chopped

COUNTRY-STYLE STEW

Guiso a la guajira

In a medium bowl, combine the cooked chicken, garlic, bitter orange juice, wine, 1 teaspoon salt, and the pepper. Marinate for 1 hour.

In a large heavy-bottomed frying pan, heat the oil over medium heat. Add the scallions (spring onions) and mint and sauté until fragrant, about 1 minute. Add the corn and beans, and cook for 1 minute. Add the chicken and the marinade and cook until the liquid is absorbed, about 10 minutes. Salt to taste. Serve.

PREPARATION TIME: 10 MINUTES,
PLUS 1 HOUR MARINATING TIME
COOKING TIME: 10 MINUTES
SERVES: 4

1 cup (230 g) cooked chicken (see
page 19), cut into ½ inch (1 cm)
pieces
4 cloves garlic, crushed
½ cup (4 fl oz/125 ml) bitter
orange juice (see page 18)
¼ cup (2 fl oz/60 ml) dry white
wine
Salt
⅛ teaspoon ground black pepper
2 tablespoons vegetable oil
1 cup (60 g) finely chopped
scallions (spring onions)
6 leaves fresh mint
1 cup (400 g) corn kernels
1 cup (240 g) cooked red beans
(canned or homemade)

FRIED CHICKPEAS

Garbanzos fritos

**PREPARATION TIME: 20 MINUTES,
PLUS 12 HOURS CHICKPEA
SOAKING TIME
COOKING TIME: 1 HOUR 20 MINUTES
SERVES: 8**

2⅓ cups (500 g) dried chickpeas,
soaked for 12 hours in tepid water
3 large tomatoes
2 tablespoons olive oil
3½ oz (100 g) slab bacon (streaky)
or salt pork, chopped
1 large white onion, finely chopped
1 teaspoon paprika
½ lb (230 g) dried sausage, thinly
sliced
1 bunch parsley, finely chopped
1 teaspoon salt

Drain the chickpeas. In a pressure cooker (see Note), combine the chickpeas and 6⅓ cups (50 fl oz/1.5 liters) water. Lock the lid and bring to pressure over medium heat. Cook at pressure until softened, about 1 hour. Quick-release the pressure. Drain (see Note) and set aside.

Meanwhile, bring a large pot of water to a boil. Cut an "x" into the skin at the blossom end of the tomatoes and submerge them in the boiling water for 1 minute. Transfer to a cutting board to cool, then remove the skin (peeling at the "x"). Halve, seed, and dice.

In a large frying pan, heat the oil over medium heat. Add the bacon (streaky) and sauté until the fat has rendered, about 1 minute. Add the onion and sauté until the onion is translucent, about 3 minutes. Add the tomato and cook until soft and its liquids reduce, about 8 minutes. Stir in the paprika, sausage, chickpeas, parsley, and salt. Cook over high heat, stirring regularly, until the water is absorbed, about 5 minutes. Serve hot.

Notes: If you don't have a pressure cooker, cook the chickpeas covered in a large pot with 3 quarts (3 liters) of water for 1½–2 hours over medium heat.

The water used to cook the chickpeas can be saved and used to add flavor to a soup.

BEANS WITH PEPPERS

Frijoles enchilados

PREPARATION TIME: 20 MINUTES
COOKING TIME: 1 HOUR 10 MINUTES
SERVES: 6

★

1 cup (220 g) dried red, white,
black, or pinto beans, rinsed
3 tablespoons vegetable oil
3 chay peppers or cubanelles,
finely chopped
1 cup (60 g) chopped scallions
(spring onions)
4 cloves garlic, finely chopped
6 oz (180 g) ham, finely diced
½ cup (125 g) tomato sauce
(seasoned passata)
1 half-ripe burro plantain, peeled
and sliced
1 tablespoon raw cane sugar
1 bay leaf
¼ teaspoon ground cumin
Salt and ground black pepper
1 tablespoon vinegar

In a pressure cooker (see Note), combine the red beans and 8½ cups (68 fl oz/2 liters) water. Lock the lid and bring to pressure over medium heat. Cook at pressure until soft, about 50 minutes.

In a medium frying pan, heat the oil over medium heat. Add the *chay* peppers, scallions (spring onions), and garlic and sauté until the garlic becomes fragrant, about 2 minutes. Add the ham and cook until it browns lightly, about 1 minute. Add the tomato sauce (seasoned passata), plantain, raw sugar, bay leaf, cumin, ½ teaspoon black pepper, vinegar, and ½ cup (4 fl oz/120 ml) water and cook until the sauce thickens, about 10 minutes. Salt to taste.

Note: If you don't have a pressure cooker, it is very important to soak the beans first. Cook in 12 cups (96 fl oz/ 3 liters) water in a large pot over medium-high heat for 1½–2 hours, depending on the quality, age, and type of beans. Then follow the rest of the instructions as directed.

CORN AND GROUND BEEF PUDDING

Pudín de maíz relleno con picadillo

PREPARATION TIME: 25 MINUTES
COOKING TIME: 1 HOUR 5 MINUTES
SERVES: 6

★

3 tablespoons (45 g) butter
1 tablespoon flour, for dusting
1 small white onion, finely chopped
1 cup (400 g) maíz molido (ground
fresh corn, see page 20)
4 eggs, whisked
1 teaspoon salt
¼ teaspoon ground black pepper
⅛ teaspoon grated nutmeg
1 cup (150 g) dried breadcrumbs
⅓ cup (2.5 fl oz/83 ml) vegetable
stock
½ cup (115 g) Havana-Style Ground
Beef (page 203)

Grease a 7 inch (18 cm) round 3 inch (7.5 cm) deep pan with 1 tablespoon of the butter and dust with the flour.

In a small frying pan, heat the remaining 2 tablespoons butter over medium-low heat. Add the onion and sauté until softened, about 2 minutes.

In a blender, combine the maíz molido, sautéed onion, eggs, salt, pepper, nutmeg, breadcrumbs, and stock and blend. Pour half of the mixture into the prepared pan, add the ground beef, and cover with the remaining ground corn mixture. Cover the pan tightly. It is very important to cover the pan tightly; if you do not have a pan that closes hermetically, cover tightly with foil.

Transfer the pan to a pot wide enough to hold the pan with room on the sides and pour water halfway up the sides of the pan. Cover the pot tightly and cook over medium heat. Steam the pudding until set and a knife comes out clean, about 1 hour. Serve.

CHICKEN TAMALE IN A HUSK

Tamal en hojas con pollo

PREPARATION TIME: 40 MINUTES
COOKING TIME: 55 MINUTES
SERVES: 5

★

4 tablespoons vegetable oil
3 cachucha peppers or cubanelles, finely chopped
1 large white onion, finely chopped
3 cloves garlic, finely chopped
1 cup (230 g) chopped cooked chicken (see page 19)
2 tablespoons tomato sauce (seasoned passata)
2¼ cups (960 g) maíz molido (ground fresh corn, see page 20)
2 tablespoons raw cane sugar
Salt
6 fresh corn husks
Ketchup, for serving

In a medium frying pan, heat the oil over medium-low heat. Add the *cachucha* peppers, onion, and garlic and sauté until softened, about 3 minutes. Add the chicken and tomato sauce (seasoned passata), and cook until it begins to reduce, about 3 minutes. Transfer to a large bowl, add the maíz molido, raw sugar, and ½ tablespoon salt and stir well.

Take one corn husk and holding it wide side up, fold in the sides and then fold the pointed end up to make a little pouch. Holding the pouch in one hand with the opening up, spoon ½ cup (100 g) of the ground corn mixture into the pouch. Take a second corn husk, wide side down, and wrap it around the pouch, then fold the pointed end down over the opening to enclose the filling and make a neat bundle. With a torn, thin strip of another husk, tie the bundle as you would tie a package, to secure the corn husks. Repeat to make a total of 5 tamales.

Bring a large pot of lightly salted water to a boil. Add the tamales and boil until soft, 45 minutes. Serve with ketchup.

BEET SALAD IN SWEET AND SOUR SAUCE

Remolacha en escabeche

PREPARATION TIME: 25 MINUTES,
PLUS 12 HOURS CHILLING TIME
COOKING TIME: 1 HOUR 25 MINUTES
SERVES: 8

★

6 medium beets
(1½ lb/660 g total)
⅔ cup (5 fl oz/150 ml) vegetable oil
2 medium white onions (7 oz/200 g total), thinly sliced
2 large green bell peppers, thinly sliced
3 cloves garlic, peeled
⅔ cup (5½ fl oz/165 ml) vinegar
2 tablespoons raw cane sugar
¼ teaspoon dried oregano
1 teaspoon salt

In a large pot of boiling water, cook the unpeeled beets, covered, until tender, about 1 hour 15 minutes. When cool enough to handle, peel the beets and cut them into ¼ inch (½ cm) thick slices. Put them in a ceramic or glass bowl.

In a medium saucepan, heat 2 tablespoons of the oil over medium-low heat. Add the onions, bell peppers, and whole garlic cloves and sauté until the onion turns translucent, about 3 minutes. Add ½ cup (4 fl oz/125 ml) water and the vinegar. Add the raw sugar, oregano, and salt. Cover, bring to a boil, and cook until thickened, 5 minutes. Remove from the heat. Add the remaining generous ½ cup (4½ fl oz/ 130 ml) oil. Set the dressing aside to cool, then pour it over the beets, cover, and refrigerate for 12 hours.

Notes: Spices such as paprika, rosemary, black pepper, or cloves can be added to the dressing.

The bell peppers can be substituted with pre-cooked, julienned carrots or green beans cut into 1 inch (2.5 cm) pieces.

VEGETARIAN
OFFER

Che

OTRAS TIERRAS DEL MUNDO
RECLAMAN E CONCURSO DE MIS

EGGS

Huevos

It would be impossible to write a Cuban cookbook without including eggs. The food culture in Cuba places a lot of emphasis on animal protein and following this logic, when meat is not available, eggs are the next best thing. Eggs are often seen as the *plato fuerte*, or main course, as a substitution for the always-coveted meat. The food scarcities that sometimes affect the average home have led many Cubans to refer to eggs as "the Cuban salvation" or "the lifesaver of the Cubans." It might be easy to assume that the consumption of eggs is a by-product of the food scarcities of more recent times, but the incorporation of eggs as an important part of the diet predates any rationing or food shortages or distribution problems that have taken place since the Revolution. The book *¿Gusta, usted? Prontuario culinario y ... necesario*, published in 1956, includes an entire chapter devoted to eggs, demonstrating their historical presence in the Cuban diet.

Eggs are still subsidized by the State as part of the monthly rations (five eggs per person), but they can also be bought in the open market, and it is very common to see people walking down the street balancing one or even two cartons of eggs, each containing thirty eggs.

In Cuba, it is common to eat eggs for breakfast, lunch, or dinner. Eggs are also fast and easy to prepare, which make them a great option for a quick meal. They are almost always served hot, with the exception of *huevos rellenos*, a cold egg dish similar to deviled eggs, which are sometimes served at parties.

The omelets in Cuba are generally prepared *a la española*, or "Spanish style," meaning in a round shape (like a frittata), as opposed to the half-moon shape of a French-style folded omelet.

SCRAMBLED EGGS WITH ONION

Revoltillo con cebolla

PREPARATION TIME: 5 MINUTES
COOKING TIME: 10 MINUTES
SERVES: 4

★

8 eggs
1 teaspoon salt
4 tablespoons vegetable oil
2 medium white onions,
finely chopped
6 tablespoons salsa criolla
(Cuban Sauce, page 311)

In a small bowl, whisk together the eggs and salt.

In a medium frying pan, heat the oil over medium-low heat. Add the onion and sauté until fragrant, about 2 minutes. Add the eggs and cook, stirring constantly with a wooden spoon, until they begin to form curds, about 2 minutes. Add the *salsa criolla* and continue stirring until cooked but not dry, about 4 minutes. Serve hot.

SCRAMBLED EGGS WITH BELL PEPPERS

Revotillo con pimientos

Roast the bell peppers directly over the flame of a gas stove (or under a hot broiler [grill] if you don't have a gas stove), turning regularly, until the skin blackens, about 5 minutes. Let cool, then rinse, peel, and cut into strips.

In a small bowl, whisk together the eggs and salt.

In a medium frying pan, heat the oil over medium-low heat. Add the peppers and sauté for 2 minutes. Add the eggs and cook, stirring regularly with a wooden spoon, until cooked but not dry, 2–3 minutes. Serve hot.

PREPARATION TIME: 10 MINUTES
COOKING TIME: 20 MINUTES
SERVES: 4

3 medium red bell peppers
3 medium green bell peppers
6 eggs
½ teaspoon salt
2 tablespoons vegetable oil

SPANISH TORTILLA

Tortilla española

In a medium bowl, whisk together the eggs and salt.

In a medium frying pan, heat 2 inches (5 cm) vegetable oil over medium-high heat. Add the potatoes and fry until they are cooked and browned, about 5 minutes. Let cool, then add to the egg mixture.

In the same pan, heat the olive oil over high heat until very hot. Pour the egg and potato mixture into the pan, cover, reduce to very low heat and cook until the edges firm up, about 5 minutes. Flip and cook on the second side until set, about 3 minutes.

PREPARATION TIME: 10 MINUTES
COOKING TIME: 25 MINUTES
SERVES: 4

4 eggs
⅛ teaspoon salt
Vegetable oil, for frying
1½ cups (345 g) diced potato
1 tablespoon olive oil

ONION AND BELL PEPPER OMELET

Tortilla con cebolla y pimiento

PREPARATION TIME: 10 MINUTES
COOKING TIME: 5 MINUTES
SERVES: 4

8 eggs, whisked
1 tablespoon salt
2 medium white onions, diced
2 small green bell peppers, diced
3 tablespoon vegetable oil

In a medium bowl, whisk together the eggs and salt. Stir in the onions and bell peppers.

In a medium frying pan, heat 1½ tablespoons of the oil over medium-low heat. Add half the egg mixture and cook until it firms up, about 1½ minutes. Flip and cook on the second side until it is done, another 1½ minutes. Add the remaining 1½ tablespoon oil to the pan and repeat the same procedure with the remaining egg mixture. Serve hot.

Note: The onion and bell pepper can be sautéed first for a less crunchy texture.

POTATO AND BELL PEPPER OMELET

Tortilla de papa y pimiento

PREPARATION TIME: 15 MINUTES
COOKING TIME: 20 MINUTES
SERVES: 4

Salt
4 small potatoes (5 oz/150 g total), diced
4 tablespoons vegetable oil
2 small green bell peppers, cut into strips
2 small white onions, chopped
8 eggs, whisked

Bring a small pot of lightly salted water to a boil. Add the potatoes and cook until softened, about 5 minutes. Drain and set aside.

In a medium frying pan, heat 2 tablespoons of the oil over medium heat. Add the bell peppers and onions and sauté until softened, about 2 minutes. Transfer to a large bowl and let cool for 3 minutes before adding the eggs, potatoes, and 1 teaspoon salt.

In a medium frying pan, heat 1 tablespoon of the oil over medium-low heat. Add half the egg mixture and cook the omelet until it firms up, about 2 minutes. Flip and cook on the second side until it is done, about 2 minutes. Add the remaining 1 tablespoon oil to the pan and repeat the same procedure with the remaining egg mixture. Serve hot.

GRATED POTATO OMELET

Tortilla de papas ralladas

Serve with a green salad.

In a medium bowl, combine the potatoes, eggs, and salt.

In a medium frying pan, heat 1 tablespoon (15 g) of the butter and 2 tablespoons of the oil over medium-low heat. Pour in half the potato and egg mixture and press it down with a fork into a thin omelet. Cover and cook over low heat until set, about 10 minutes. Flip and cook on the second side until browned on the bottom, about 5 minutes. Heat the remaining 1 tablespoon (15 g) butter and 2 tablespoons oil and repeat the same procedure with the remaining egg mixture. Garnish with parsley. Serve hot.

PREPARATION TIME: 10 MINUTES
COOKING TIME: 30 MINUTES
SERVES: 4

14 oz (400 g) potatoes,
peeled and grated
4 eggs
1 teaspoon salt
2 tablespoon (35 g) butter
4 tablespoons vegetable oil
Finely chopped parsley,
for garnish

OMELET WITH A VEGETABLE CROWN

Tortilla con corona de vegetales

Bring a medium pot of lightly salted water to a boil. Add the green beans and cook uncovered until al dente, about 10 minutes. Drain and set aside.

Meanwhile, bring another medium pot of lightly salted water to a boil. Add the potatoes and carrot, cover, and cook until softened, about 5 minutes. Drain and set aside.

In a small pot, combine the garlic, parsley, vinegar, 3 tablespoons of the oil, 1 teaspoon salt, and the pepper. Bring to a boil over high heat, reduce the heat to low, and let cook until reduced, 6–7 minutes. Set the dressing aside.

In a medium frying pan, heat the butter and 1 tablespoon of the oil over medium heat. Add the onion and sauté until translucent, about 2 minutes. Transfer to a small bowl and let cool for 2 minutes before adding the eggs and grated cheese.

In a medium frying pan, heat the remaining 1 tablespoon oil over medium-low heat. Pour in the egg mixture and cook until set on the bottom, about 1 minute. Flip and cook on the second side until set, about 1 minute. Set aside to cool. Roll the omelet up and cut crosswise into thin strips.

Arrange the green beans, carrot, and potatoes in a crown or circle around the edge of a serving plate. Place the strips of omelet in the center. Drizzle with the dressing.

PREPARATION TIME: 25 MINUTES
COOKING TIME: 35 MINUTES
SERVES: 4

Salt
7 oz (200 g) green beans, cut into
⅓–¾-inch (1–2 cm) lengths
7 oz (200 g) potatoes, peeled and
cut into ⅓-inch (1 cm) dice
1 medium carrot, cut into ⅓-inch
(1 cm) dice
4 cloves garlic, finely chopped
1 small bunch parsley, finely
chopped
4 tablespoons vinegar
5 tablespoons vegetable oil
⅛ teaspoon ground black pepper
1 tablespoon (15 g) butter
1 large white onion, thinly sliced
3 eggs, whisked
4 tablespoons grated Cuban
gouda other mild yellow cheese

OMELET WITH FRIED RIPE PLANTAINS

Tortilla con plátano maduro frito

PREPARATION TIME: 10 MINUTES
COOKING TIME: 15 MINUTES
SERVES: 4

★

8 eggs
1 teaspoon salt
6 tablespoons vegetable oil
2 small ripe plantains, peeled and
sliced diagonally

In a small bowl, whisk together the eggs and salt.

In a medium frying pan, heat 4 tablespoons of the oil over medium heat. Add the plantains and cook until browned on both sides, about 4 minutes. Remove the plantains from the pan and let cool for 3 minutes before transfering to the bowl with the egg mixture and gently mix.

In the same frying pan, heat 1 tablespoon of the oil over medium-low heat. Pour in half the egg and plantain mixture and cook until set, about 2 minutes. Flip and cook on the second side until it is done, about 2 minutes. Add the remaining 1 tablespoon oil to the pan and repeat the same procedure with the remaining egg and plantain mixture. Serve hot.

CRACKER OMELET

Tortilla de galletas

PREPARATION TIME: 5 MINUTES
COOKING TIME: 5 MINUTES
SERVES: 4

★

8 eggs, whisked
20 saltine or cream crackers,
crumbled
1 teaspoon salt
4 tablespoon vegetable oil

In a small bowl, combine the eggs, crackers, and salt.

In a small frying pan, heat 2 tablespoons of the oil over medium-low heat. Add half the egg mixture and cook until it begins to set, about 1 minute. Flip and cook on the second side until it is done, about 1 minute. Add the remaining 2 tablespoons oil to the pan and repeat the same procedure with the remaining egg mixture. Serve hot.

IMPERIAL OMELET

Tortilla imperial

PREPARATION TIME: 20 MINUTES
COOKING TIME: 10 MINUTES
SERVES: 6

★

6 eggs
Salt
½ cup (70 g) finely chopped
and cooked bok choy
½ medium white onion, diced
1 medium green bell pepper, diced
1 ½ tablespoons vegetable oil
4 tablespoons mayonnaise, store-
bought or homemade (page 318)
2 tablespoons chopped scallions
(spring onions)

In each of three small bowls, whisk together 2 eggs and ¼ teaspoon salt. In the first bowl, stir in the bok choy, in the second bowl, add the onion, and in the third bowl add the bell pepper.

In a medium frying pan, heat ½ tablespoon of the oil over medium-low heat. Pour in one bowl of the egg mixture and cook until it browns, 1 minute. Flip and cook on the second side until it is done, 1 minute. Transfer the first omelet to a plate and spread with 2 tablespoons of the mayonnaise. Add another ½ tablespoon of the oil to the pan and make a second omelet the same way and stack on top of the first omelet. Spread with the remaining 2 tablespoons mayonnaise. Add the remaining ½ tablespoon oil and make the third omelet and set on top. Serve hot, garnished with scallions (spring onions).

Note: Tomato sauce (seasoned passata), Sautéed Vegetable (page 221), or grated cheese can be added on top of the omelet stack.

SAUTÉED VEGETABLES AND HARD-BOILED EGGS

Guiso de huevos con vegetales

PREPARATION TIME: 15 MINUTES
COOKING TIME: 15 MINUTES
SERVES: 4

★

2 tablespoons vegetable oil
1 medium green bell pepper,
finely chopped
4 cloves garlic, finely chopped
1 medium white onion,
finely chopped
½ cup (100 g) finely diced
pumpkin
1 cup (200 g) cooked green beans,
cut into 1 inch (2.5 cm) pieces
4 tablespoons tomato sauce
(seasoned passata)
½ cup (4 fl oz/125 ml) dry white wine
⅛ teaspoon ground cumin
1 teaspoon salt
⅛ teaspoon ground black pepper
½ cup (45 g) chopped parsley
4 hard-boiled eggs, peeled
and quartered lengthwise

This recipe was common during the Special Period.

★

In a medium frying pan, heat the oil over medium heat. Add the bell pepper, garlic, and onion and sauté until softened, about 3 minutes. Stir in the pumpkin and green beans. Add the tomato sauce (seasoned passata) and wine and cook until it begins to reduce, about 5 minutes. Add the cumin, salt, black pepper, and parsley and cook until the sauce thickens, about 2 minutes. Add the eggs, stirring carefully, and cook for 1–2 more minutes.

OMELET "LASAGNA"

Lasaña de tortilla

In each of 3 small bowls, whisk together 2 eggs and ¼ teaspoon salt. Add the bok choy to one bowl and the potatoes to the second bowl. Add the grated pumpkin, onion, and scallions (spring onions) to the third.

Making one omelet at a time, in a medium frying pan, heat 1 tablespoon of the oil over medium heat. Pour in one bowl of the egg mixture and cook until it begins to set, about 1 minute. Flip and cook on the second side until it is done, about 1 minute. Transfer the first omelet to a plate and spread with one-third of the tomato sauce (seasoned passata). Add another 1 tablespoon of the oil to the pan and make a second omelet the same way. Stack on top of the first omelet and spread with another one-third of the tomato sauce. Add the remaining 1 tablespoon oil and make the third omelet, set on top, and spread with the remaining tomato sauce. Sprinkle with the grated cheese and serve hot.

PREPARATION TIME: 15 MINUTES
COOKING TIME: 10 MINUTES
SERVES: 6

6 eggs
Salt
½ cup (70 g) cooked
shredded bok choy
½ cup (100 g) cooked
diced potatoes
⅓ cup (35 g) grated pumpkin
or carrot
½ medium white onion,
finely chopped
2 tablespoons finely chopped
scallions (spring onions)
3 tablespoons vegetable oil
5 tablespoons tomato sauce
(seasoned passata)
3 tablespoons grated Cuban
gouda or other mild yellow cheese

RUM OMELET

Tortilla al ron

In a small bowl, whisk together the eggs, lime zest, and 1 tablespoon sugar.

Heat a medium cast-iron skillet over medium-low heat while you prepare the omelet.

In a medium frying pan, heat 1 tablespoon of the oil over medium heat. Add half the egg mixture and cook until set, about 1 minute. Flip and cook on the second side until it is done, about 1 minute. Sprinkle 1½ tablespoons sugar and cover with the heated cast-iron skillet to melt the sugar. Transfer the omelet to a plate. Add the remaining 1 tablespoon oil to the pan and repeat the same procedure with the remaining egg mixture.

Transfer both omelets to a serving dish and pour the rum ontop. Light the rum with a long fireplace match and serve, with the flames, and let extinguish at the table.

PREPARATION TIME: 5 MINUTES
COOKING TIME: 5 MINUTES
SERVES: 4

6 eggs
1 teaspoon grated lime zest
4 tablespoons sugar
2 tablespoons vegetable oil
4 tablespoons aged white rum

EGGS "IN THEIR BEDS"

Huevos en su lecho

PREPARATION TIME: 20 MINUTES
COOKING TIME: 35 MINUTES
SERVES: 4

Salt

2 lb (920 g) taro roots, peeled
and cut into small pieces

1 tablespoon (15 g) butter

1½ tablespoons vegetable oil

2 medium white onions,
finely chopped

2 cups (160 g) chopped bok choy

¼ teaspoon grated nutmeg

4 eggs

4 tablespoons grated Cuban
gouda or other mild yellow cheese

Bring a medium pot of lightly salted water to a boil. Add the taro, cover, and cook over medium heat until soft, about 20 minutes. Drain and let them cool a little. Transfer to a medium bowl and mash into a puree with a fork.

In a medium frying pan, heat the butter and 1 tablespoon of the oil over medium heat. Add the onions and bok choy and sauté until the onions turn translucent, about 3 minutes. Transfer to the bowl with the pureed taro root. Add the nutmeg and ½ teaspoon salt and gently stir.

In a medium frying pan, heat the remaining ½ tablespoon oil. Pour in the vegetable mixture and make 4 shallow indentations with a spoon. Crack an egg into each hole. Cover and cook over medium-low heat until the egg yolks are firm, about 12 minutes. Sprinkle with the cheese and serve hot.

Note: Potatoes or yuca (cassava) can be used instead of the taro root. The eggs can also be cooked in the oven for 5 minutes at 225°F (110°C/Gas Mark ¼).

SANTIAGO-STYLE EGGS

Huevos fritos a la santiaguera

PREPARATION TIME: 10 MINUTES
COOKING TIME: 15 MINUTES
SERVES: 4

★

3 tablespoons vegetable oil
3 chay peppers or cubanelles, diced
2 medium white onion, diced
6 cloves garlic, finely chopped
¾ cup (185 g) tomato sauce (seasoned passata)
1 teaspoon salt
¼ teaspoon ground black pepper
¼ teaspoon ground bay leaf
1 teaspoon raw cane sugar
4 eggs
Finely chopped parsley or scallions (spring onions), for garnish

In a large frying pan, heat the oil over medium-low heat. Add the *chay* peppers, onion, and garlic and sauté until softened, about 3 minutes. Add the tomato sauce (seasoned passata), salt, pepper, bay leaf, and raw sugar and cook until the sauce reduces, about 2 minutes. Crack the eggs over the sauce and cook, covered, over medium heat until the eggs firm, about 3 minutes. Serve hot, garnished with parsley or scallions (spring onions).

Note: This style of cooking eggs appears in various examples of classic literature, including Cecilia Valdés o la Loma del Ángel *by Cirilo Villaverde and* Paradiso *by José Lezama Lima.*

EGGS ON A VEGETABLE BED

Huevos sobre lecho de vegetales

PREPARATION TIME: 20 MINUTES
COOKING TIME: 20 MINUTES
SERVES: 4

★

Salt
½ cup (100 g) green beans, cut into 1 inch (2.5 cm) pieces
2 tablespoons vegetable oil
2 chay peppers or cubanelles, finely chopped
4 cloves garlic, finely chopped
1 small white onion, finely chopped
1 scallion (spring onion), finely chopped
½ cup (100 g) pumpkin, grated
4 eggs
¼ teaspoon ground black pepper
⅓ cup (30 g) finely chopped parsley

Bring a medium pot of lightly salted water to a boil. Add the green beans and cook for 8–10 minutes. Drain and set aside.

In a medium frying pan, heat the oil over medium-low heat. Add the *chay* peppers, garlic, onion, and scallions (spring onions) and sauté until softened, about 3 minutes. Add the pumpkin and green beans, and sauté for 2 minutes. Make 4 small, deep holes and add the eggs one at a time. Cover and cook over very low heat until the yolks are firm, about 10 minutes. Season with ½ teaspoon salt and the pepper. Serve very hot, garnished with finely chopped parsley.

Notes: Other vegetables, such as carrots, tomatoes, bell peppers, eggplant (aubergine), and potatoes can also be used instead of the pumpkin and green beans.

MIMOSA EGGS

Huevos mimosa

PREPARATION TIME: 25 MINUTES
COOKING TIME: 10 MINUTES
SERVES: 4

★

8 hard-boiled eggs
1 cup (230 g) cooked shrimp
(prawns)
3½ tablespoons mayonnaise,
store-bought or homemade
(page 318)
1 head lettuce, chopped

Peel and halve the eggs lengthwise. Remove the yolks and transfer them to a medium bowl. Add the shrimp (prawns) to the yolks and grind in a food grinder (or finely chop the shrimp and mix with the egg yolks using a fork if you don't have a food grinder). Add the mayonnaise and mix until smooth. Fill each egg white half with a small spoonful of the egg yolk and shrimp filling. Arrange on a serving platter garnished with the lettuce.

MEXICAN-STYLE EGGS

Huevos a la mejicana

PREPARATION TIME: 10 MINUTES
COOKING TIME: 15 MINUTES
SERVES: 4

★

2 large tomatoes
2 large carrots, peeled and sliced
diagonally
2 large green bell peppers
8 teaspoons vegetable oil
8 eggs
8 Corn Arepas (page 34)
Salt and ground black pepper
1 cup (90 g) chopped parsley

Bring a small pot of water to a boil. Cut an "x" into the skin at the blossom end of the tomatoes and submerge them in the boiling water for 1 minute. Transfer to a cutting board to cool, then remove the skin (peeling at the "x"). Halve, seed, and cut into strips.

Bring the same pot of water back to a boil. Add the carrots and cook until soft, 8–10 minutes. Remove and let cool, then slice.

Roast the bell peppers directly over the flame of a gas stove, turning regularly, until the skin blackens, about 5 minutes. Let cool, then rinse, peel, and cut into strips.

In a medium frying pan, heat 1 teaspoon of the oil over medium-low heat. Add 1 egg and cook until the yolk is firm, about 1½ minutes. Transfer to a plate. Cook the remaining 7 eggs in the same manner, adding 1 more teaspoon of oil for each egg, if necessary.

Divide the *arepas* among 4 plates. Top with a fried egg and garnish with the tomato, carrot, and bell pepper. Season with salt and pepper to taste and sprinkle the parsley on top.

Note: This dish can also be prepared with poached eggs (see page 274).

EGG AND VEGETABLE SCRAMBLE

Pisto a la cubana

PREPARATION TIME: 10 MINUTES
COOKING TIME: 10 MINUTES
SERVES: 6

★

3 tablespoons olive oil
2 medium white onions, diced
1 medium green bell pepper, diced
3 cloves garlic, finely chopped
1½ cups (345 g) cooked chicken
(see page 19)
6 eggs, whisked
1 cup (200 g) diced cooked
pumpkin
½ cup (125 g) tomato sauce
(seasoned passata)
Salt
1 bunch scallions (spring onions),
finely chopped

In a medium frying pan, heat the oil over medium-low heat. Add the onions, bell pepper, and garlic and sauté until the onion turns translucent, about 3 minutes. Add the chicken and cook until lightly browned, about 2 minutes. Add the eggs and stir. Add the pumpkin and tomato sauce (seasoned passata). Season to taste with salt and continue cooking, stirring regularly with a wooden spoon, until the sauce thickens, 2–4 minutes. Add the scallions (spring onions) just before removing from the heat, and serve hot.

POACHED EGGS

Huevos escalfados

PREPARATION TIME: 5 MINUTES
COOKING TIME: 25 MINUTES
SERVES: 4

★

3 tablespoons vinegar
8 eggs
3 tablespoons vegetable oil
6 tablespoons finely chopped
fresh basil
¾ cup (45 g) finely chopped
scallions (spring onions)
¾ cup (185 g) tomato sauce
(seasoned passata)
½ cup (4 fl oz/125 ml) vegetable
stock
⅓ cup (2 ½ fl oz/125 ml) dry white
wine
1½ teaspoon raw cane sugar
1½ teaspoon lime juice
1 teaspoon salt

Bring a small pot of water with the vinegar to a boil over medium-high heat. Crack 1 egg into the water and simmer until poached, 4–5 minutes (if the water begins to boil again, remove the pot from the stove). Scoop out the egg with a slotted spoon and quickly rinse in tepid water to remove the taste of the vinegar. Set aside. Poach the remaining 7 eggs in the same manner.

In a medium frying pan, heat the oil over medium heat. Add the basil and scallions (spring onions) and sauté until softened, about 2 minutes. Add the tomato sauce (seasoned passata), stock, wine, raw sugar, lime juice, and salt and cook over medium-low heat until the sauce reduces, about 5 minutes.

Serve with the tomato sauce on top.

SALADS

Ensaladas

In Cuba, salads are not considered a favorite food, though they are consumed somewhat regularly. The most popular ingredients are lettuce, avocado, and tomato. Following in popularity are cabbage, cucumbers, green beans, and roasted bell peppers. Because it is common to eat rice, beans, meat, and salad all on the same plate, sometimes the "salad" of the meal consists of just a sliced tomato or large piece of avocado with a few drops of oil on top (especially common during the summer months). Less common salad ingredients include radishes, bok choy, watercress, spinach, eggplant (aubergine), okra, cauliflower, broccoli, beets, and carrots. The majority of salad recipes found in typical Cuban cookbooks include some cooked ingredients and are often accompanied with mayonnaise, cheese, meat or sausages, fish, eggs, and pickled foods. An example is the classic pasta salad served at birthday parties and other festive occasions, and it includes mayonnaise, chicken, pineapple, and sausage or hot dog. Salads are generally seen as an optional side dish, although lettuce, radish, roasted pepper, and tomato salads are considered indispensable for Christmas and New Year's feasts.

Salads have historically not had a dominant role in the Cuban diet, but starting in the 1990s Cubans began consuming them more, partly because of the scarcity of other types of food during the economic crisis. There was also a dramatic increase in urban agriculture and the production of vegetables across the country due to new policies implemented by the government in response to the necessity. The State also made efforts to promote the consumption of more vegetables during this time. It was within this context that the

Eco-Restorán El Bambú was founded at the National Botanical Garden in Havana as the first ecological, vegetarian restaurant in Cuba. It functioned from 1992 to 2014, and during this time, was influential in increasing the variety of recipes, techniques, and salad consumption in the Cuban diet. Some examples of these influences are the use of grated raw pumpkin, edible flowers, seeds, fruit salads with dressing, and native plants, such as pigweed and sweet potato leaves. During this time, the use of aromatic plants, such as basil, parsley, fennel, dill, and scallions (spring onions), was also popularized. These ingredients became incorporated into the Cuban diet within the context of the Special Period, and while many of them were consumed less frequently when the economic situation allowed for more availability of other types of traditionally preferred food, there were some long-term impacts to the food culture brought on with the increased incorporation of salads and vegetables during the 1990s. Many of the recipes in this chapter were created at the Eco-Restorán El Bambú, and while they are not representative of the most traditional dishes of the Cuban diet, they are included here to demonstrate the variety of recipes at this specific time.

Some requirements for successful salads are: Ingredients should be carefully and thoroughly rinsed and cut uniformly, and cooked ingredients should be generally cooked to crisp-tender. Salads should be prepared just before serving, with the dressing prepared separately and not added until serving time. Cooked ingredients should be dressed while hot. And ideally salads should have a variety of colors.

SWEET AND SOUR SALAD

Ensalada agridulce

In a large salad bowl, arrange a layer of the cabbage, then a layer of the onion, and finally a layer of peppers. Sprinkle with the raw sugar.

In a small pot, combine the vinegar, soy sauce, oil, and ½ teaspoon salt and bring to a boil. Pour over the salad while still very hot. Let the salad cool, then refrigerate for about 4 hours. Mix and season to taste with salt before serving.

PREPARATION TIME: 20 MINUTES,
PLUS 4 HOURS CHILLING TIME
COOKING TIME: 5 MINUTES
SERVES: 4

2 cups (7 ounces/200 g) chopped cabbage
1 medium white onion, sliced into half-moons
2 medium green bell peppers, cut into strips
4 tablespoons raw cane sugar
⅓ cup (2½ fl oz/80 ml) vinegar
1 tablespoon soy sauce
⅓ cup (2½ fl oz/80 ml) vegetable oil
Salt

GREEN SALAD

Ensalada al verde

Bring a large pot of lightly salted water with the lime juice to a boil over medium-high heat. Add the nopales and cook until softened, 8–10 minutes. Drain well.

Meanwhile, in a small bowl, combine the grapefruit juice, oil, and 1 teaspoon salt.

In a large salad bowl, combine the spinach, pigweed (purslane), lettuce, nopales, and scallions (spring onions). Dress the salad with the grapefruit vinaigrette and mix well.

PREPARATION TIME: 20 MINUTES
COOKING TIME: 10 MINUTES
SERVES: 4–6

Salt
1 tablespoon lime juice or vinegar
3 nopales (or other edible cactus pads), spines removed, cut into strips
2 tablespoons grapefruit juice
2 tablespoons olive oil
6 oz (180 g) Malabar or Savoy spinach, thinly sliced
1 cup (60 g) coarsely chopped pigweed (purslane)
1 cup (60 g) shredded or torn lettuce
3 scallions (spring onions), finely chopped

BOK CHOY, CORN, AND TOMATO SALAD

Ensalada de acelga, maíz y tomate

PREPARATION TIME: 20 MINUTES
SERVES: 4

★

½ lb (240 g) bok choy, cut into
strips (about 3 cups)
1 large tomato, sliced
½ cup (120 g) cooked corn kernels
3 cloves garlic, finely chopped
1 teaspoon salt
1 tablespoon lime juice
2 tablespoons vegetable oil

In a large salad bowl, combine the bok choy, tomato, and corn.

In small bowl, combine the garlic, salt, lime juice, oil, and 1 tablespoon water. Pour the dressing over the salad and gently mix.

COUNTRY SALAD

Ensalada campesina

PREPARATION TIME: 20 MINUTES
COOKING TIME: 40 MINUTES
SERVES: 6

★

1 medium (6 oz/175 g) white or
yellow sweet potato
Salt
2 medium taro roots (7 oz/200
g each), peeled and cut into
medium chunks
7 oz (200 g) pumpkin,
cut into large pieces
1 medium white onion, diced
4 cloves garlic, finely chopped
2 leaves fresh Cuban oregano
(Mexican mint) or regular oregano,
slivered
2 tablespoons bitter orange juice
2 tablespoons vegetable oil
1 cup (160 g) cooked corn kernels
1 cup (200 g) cooked green beans,
cut into 1 inch (2.5 cm) pieces

Bring a medium pot of water to a boil. Add the whole sweet potato, cover, and cook until softened, 30–40 minutes. Let cool, then peel and cut into bite-size pieces.

Bring another medium pot of lightly salted water to a boil. Add the taro, cover, and cook until softened, about 10 minutes. Add the pumpkin and cook until softened, about 10 minutes. Drain and set aside to cool.

In a medium heatproof bowl, combine the onion, garlic, oregano, ½ teaspoon salt, and the orange juice. In a small frying pan, heat the oil over medium heat. Pour over the onion mixture.

Arrange the sweet potato, corn, taro, green beans, and pumpkin in rows on a serving dish. Pour the hot dressing over the salad and serve.

AVOCADO AND AROMATIC HERB SALAD

Ensalada de aguacate con aroma de hierbas

PREPARATION TIME: 25 MINUTES
SERVES: 4

★

5 cloves garlic, finely chopped
5 fresh oregano leaves, minced
1 tablespoon lime juice
½ teaspoon ground black pepper
1 teaspoon salt
2 tablespoons vegetable oil
2 tablespoons dried basil, or ¼ cup
(20 g) fresh basil, minced
2 tablespoons dried mint, or ¼ cup
(20 g) fresh mint, minced
2 avocados, sliced

In a small bowl, combine the garlic, oregano, lime juice, pepper, salt, and oil. Let sit for 10 minutes to infuse. Add the basil and mint.

Arrange the avocados on a serving plate and dress with the vinaigrette.

CLASSIC CABBAGE SALAD

Ensalada clásica de col

PREPARATION TIME: 30 MINUTES,
PLUS 2 HOURS CHILLING TIME
SERVES: 6

★

½ head green cabbage,
thinly sliced
1 medium white onion, thinly sliced
2 medium carrots, grated
3 tablespoons vinegar
2 teaspoons raw cane sugar
½ cup (115 g) mayonnaise, store-
bought or homemade (page 318)
1 teaspoon mild mustard
Salt

Place the cabbage in a large bowl and squeeze it firmly to soften. Add the onion and carrots and gently mix. Set aside.

In a small bowl, combine the vinegar and raw sugar. Whisk in the mayonnaise and mustard until thick. Salt to taste. Pour the dressing over the cabbage and mix well. Refrigerate for 2 hours before serving.

RICE SALAD
(VIVIAN COSTA STYLE)

Ensalada de arroz al estilo Vivian Costa

**PREPARATION TIME: 20 MINUTES,
PLUS 30 MINUTES ONION
MARINATING TIME AND 2 HOURS
CHILLING TIME
COOKING TIME: 15 MINUTES
SERVES: 6**

2 large green bell peppers
1 large white onion, diced
2 tablespoons vinegar
2 tablespoons vegetable oil
1 cup (230 g) finely chopped
cooked chicken (see page 19)
3 cloves garlic, finely chopped
2 tablespoons toasted
sesame seeds
Salt
2 cups (400 g) cooked rice
½ cup (55 g) grated carrot
Generous ½ cup (125 g)
mayonnaise, store-bought or
homemade (page 318)

This recipe was originally created by Vivian Costa Leal, a Cuban housewife and admirer of all types of home cooking.

Roast the bell peppers directly over the open flame of a stove burner (or under a hot broiler [grill] if you don't have a gas stove), rotating with a fork. Remove the burnt skin and rinse, then remove the stem and seeds and cut into strips. Set aside.

In a small bowl, combine the onion and vinegar and let marinate for at least 30 minutes. Drain and set aside. In a medium frying pan, heat the oil over medium heat. Add the chicken, garlic, and sesame seeds and sauté until the garlic becomes fragrant, about 3 minutes. Stir in ½ teaspoon salt. Remove from the heat and set aside to cool.

In a large bowl, combine the rice and half the bell peppers, onions, chicken mixture, grated carrot, and the mayonnaise. Season to taste with salt. Refrigerate for 2 hours. Serve cold, garnished with the remaining roasted pepper.

CAULIFLOWER
AND PARSLEY SALAD

Ensalada de coliflor al perejil

**PREPARATION TIME: 15 MINUTES
COOKING TIME: 10 MINUTES
SERVES: 4**

1 medium head cauliflower,
leaves trimmed
3 tablespoons chopped parsley
1 small green bell pepper, diced
1 hard-boiled egg, finely chopped
2 tablespoons vinegar
½ teaspoon salt
4 tablespoons vegetable oil

The urban community gardens that developed in the 1990s helped to popularize cauliflower among part of the Cuban population.

In a steamer basket over a pan of boiling water, cover and steam the whole head of cauliflower until softened, about 10 minutes. Separate the cauliflower into florets.

Meanwhile, in a small bowl, combine the parsley, bell pepper, egg, vinegar, and salt. Stir in the oil.

Arrange the warm cauliflower in a large salad bowl. Pour the dressing over and gently toss.

CABBAGE
AND RADISH SALAD

Ensalada de col y rábano

In a small bowl, combine the vinegar, oil, 2 tablespoons water, and salt.

Place the cabbage in a large salad bowl and squeeze it firmly to soften. Add the radishes, celery, and onion. Pour the dressing over and gently toss. Sprinkle with the cheese.

PREPARATION TIME: 20 MINUTES
SERVES: 6

2 tablespoons vinegar
3 tablespoons vegetable oil
1 teaspoon salt
1 medium head cabbage,
cut into strips
12 red radishes, sliced
1 stalk celery, finely chopped
1 medium white onion,
finely chopped
½ cup (58 g) grated Cuban white
cheese or queso fresco

RUSSIAN SALAD

Ensalada rusa

The original recipe was known in Cuba by the upper class before the Revolution. It included carrots, potatoes, peas, white beans, cauliflower, ham, lobster, capers, pickles, herring, and mayonnaise. Later, a simpler version was replicated in the USSR, and Cuban students who studied there adapted that recipe, shown here.

Bring a medium pot of lightly salted water to a boil. Add the potatoes, cover, and cook until soft, about 5 minutes. Scoop the potatoes out of the water and set aside to drain and cool.

In the same cooking water, cook the carrot over medium heat until soft, about 5 minutes. Drain and let cool.
In the same pot, combine the beets and 2 quarts (2 liters) water. Cook, covered, over medium heat until tender, 45 minutes to 1 hour 15 minutes. Remove and when cool enough to handle, peel and dice.

In a large bowl, combine the potatoes, carrot, beets, onion, chicken, eggs, and mayonnaise and gently toss. Add the pepper and 1 teaspoon salt. Garnish with the scallions (spring onions) and pickled peppers (if using). Refrigerate for 2 hours and serve cold.

PREPARATION TIME: 40 MINUTES,
PLUS 2 HOURS CHILLING TIME
COOKING TIME: 1 HOUR 20 MINUTES
SERVES: 4

Salt
10 oz (300 g) potatoes, peeled
and cut into medium chunks
1 medium carrot, diced
2 medium beets (4 oz/110 g each)
1 medium white onion,
finely chopped
1 cup (230 g) finely chopped
cooked chicken (see page 19)
2 hard-boiled eggs, peeled and
cut into pieces
4 tablespoons mayonnaise, store-
bought or homemade (page 318)
¼ teaspoon ground black pepper
½ cup (30 g) chopped scallions
(spring onions)
Pickled peppers (optional)

BEAN AND BELL PEPPER SALAD

Ensalada de frijoles con pimientos

PREPARATION TIME: 20 MINUTES
COOKING TIME: 10 MINUTES
SERVES: 4

★

1 medium white onion, diced
3 tablespoons vinegar
2 medium green bell peppers
2 tablespoons vegetable oil
2 cloves garlic, finely chopped
2 cups (480 g) cooked black or
red beans
½ teaspoon salt

In a medium bowl, combine the onion and vinegar and let sit for 15 minutes to marinate. Drain and set aside.

Roast the bell peppers directly over the open flame of a stove burner (or under a hot broiler [grill] if you don't have a gas stove), rotating with a fork. Remove the burnt skin and rinse, then remove the stem and seeds and cut into strips.

In a medium frying pan, heat the oil over medium heat. Add the garlic and peppers and sauté until fragrant, about 2 minutes.

Place the beans in a large salad bowl. Add the pepper mixture, onion, and salt.

SPINACH SALAD

Ensalada de espinaca

PREPARATION TIME: 15 MINUTES
SERVES: 6

★

4 tablespoons sesame seeds,
toasted
1 teaspoon salt
1 teaspoon soy sauce
3 tablespoons bitter orange juice
(see page 18)
2 tablespoons oil
1 large bunch (1 lb 2 oz/500 g)
spinach (see Note), chopped
3 small white onions, halved and
thinly sliced

In a small bowl, combine the sesame seeds, salt, soy sauce, orange juice, and oil.

In a large salad bowl, combine the spinach and onion and pour the dressing over top.

Note: The types of spinach used in Cuba are Malabar spinach (Basella rubra) and espinaca de Baracoa (Talinum triangulare), but any type of spinach can be used for this recipe.

GREEN BEAN
AND CORN SALAD

Ensalada de habichuelas con granos de maíz

PREPARATION TIME: 20 MINUTES
COOKING TIME: 45 MINUTES
SERVES: 6

★

Salt
1 lb 2 oz (500 g) green beans,
cut into ¾–1-inch (2–3 cm) lengths
2 medium ears field corn
1 small white onion, sliced into
half-moons
1 tablespoon lime juice
2 tablespoons vegetable oil

Bring a large pot of lightly salted water to a boil. Add the green beans and cook uncovered until crisp-tender, about 12 minutes. Drain and set aside.

Meanwhile, bring another large pot of lightly salted water to a boil. Add the corn and cook until soft, 30–40 minutes. Drain and let cool. Cut the kernels off the cobs.

In a large bowl, combine the green beans, corn, and onion. Drizzle with the lime juice and oil and gently toss. Season to taste with salt.

ORANGE AND ONION SALAD

Ensalada de naranja con cebolla

PREPARATION TIME: 20 MINUTES
SERVES: 4

★

1 tablespoon vinegar
1 tablespoon vegetable oil
½ teaspoon salt
¼ teaspoon black peppercorns,
crushed with a mortar and pestle
1 large white onion, thinly sliced
into rounds
4 large oranges, peeled, sliced,
and seeded
1 sprig Japanese mint (Mentha
arvensis; see Note) or other mint
Green pitted olives, for garnish
(optional)

In a small bowl, combine the vinegar, oil, salt, and crushed peppercorns.

Arrange the onion slices in a medium salad bowl. Top with the orange slices and drizzle with the vinaigrette. Garnish with the mint leaves and olives (if using).

Note: Japanese mint has small leaves and a very strong flavor. In Japan, it is used to produce the essential oil used to make menthol.

LETTUCE AND HIBISCUS SALAD

Ensalada de lechuga y marpacífico

PREPARATION TIME: 15 MINUTES

SERVES: 6

★

3 tablespoons grapefruit juice

1 tablespoon vegetable oil

1 teaspoon salt

3 heads lettuce , chopped or hand-torn

2 cups (60 g) fresh hibiscus flowers, petals separated

In a small bowl, combine the grapefruit juice, oil, and salt.

In a large bowl, combine the lettuce and hibiscus flowers. Drizzle with the grapefruit vinaigrette and gently toss.

POTATO, BOK CHOY, AND EGG SALAD

Ensalada de papa, acelga y huevo

PREPARATION TIME: 15 MINUTES

COOKING TIME: 20 MINUTES

SERVES: 4

★

Salt

4 potatoes (5 oz/150 g each), cut into ¾-inch (2 cm) chunks

2 tablespoons vinegar

2 tablespoons vegetable oil

½ teaspoon dried basil

1 cup (140 g) shredded cooked bok choy

2 hard-boiled eggs, thinly sliced

2 small white onions, cut into thin half-moons

Green pitted olives, for garnish (optional)

Bring a medium pot of lightly salted water to a boil. Add the potatoes, cover, and cook until soft, about 20 minutes. Drain and set aside.

Meanwhile, in a small bowl, combine the vinegar, oil, basil, and ½ teaspoon salt and gently stir.

In a large salad bowl, combine the potatoes and bok choy and toss gently. Pour the dressing over top and garnish with the eggs, sliced onions, and olives (if using).

Note: This salad can also be dressed with mayonnaise instead of the dressing.

POTATO AND EGG SALAD

Ensalada de papas con huevo

PREPARATION TIME: 25 MINUTES
COOKING TIME: 20 MINUTES
SERVES: 6

3½ lb (1.6 kg) large potatoes, cut into slices ⅓ inch (1 cm) thick
2 teaspoons salt
4 tablespoons vinegar
4 tablespoons olive oil
1 teaspoon mild mustard
¼ teaspoon ground black pepper
6 hard-boiled eggs, peeled and sliced
6 small white onions, sliced
⅓ cup (60 g) drained pitted green olives

In old recipes for this salad, mashed cooked egg yolks were added to the dressing.

In a medium pot, combine the potatoes, 1 teaspoon of the salt, and water to cover by 1 inch (2.5 cm). Bring to a boil over medium heat, cover and cook until firm-tender, about 20 minutes.

In a small bowl, combine the vinegar, olive oil, mustard, pepper, and remaining 1 teaspoon salt.

Arrange the potatoes in a large serving bowl and top with the eggs, onions, and olives. Drizzle with the vinaigrette and gently stir.

POTATO SALAD
WITH EGG AND FISH

Ensalada de papas con huevo y pescado

PREPARATION TIME: 25 MINUTES
COOKING TIME: 20 MINUTES
SERVES: 6

Salt
3½ lb (1.6 kg) large potatoes, cut into slices ⅓ inch (1 cm) thick
4 tablespoons vinegar
¼ teaspoon ground black pepper
4 tablespoons olive oil
6 hard-boiled eggs, peeled and sliced
6 small white onions, finely chopped
2 cans (4½ oz/120 g each) oil-packed sardines

This dish, influenced by Spanish cuisine, is common in Cuba. It was originally prepared with salt cod.

Bring a medium pot of lightly salted water to a boil. Add the potatoes, cover, and cook until firm-tender, about 20 minutes.

Meanwhile, in a small bowl, combine the vinegar, 1 teaspoon salt, the pepper, and oil.

In a large salad bowl, arrange the potatoes, then the eggs, onion, and drained sardines. Drizzle with the vinaigrette and gently mix.

Note: Canned tuna can be used instead of the canned sardines.

CUCUMBER SALAD
WITH YOGURT DRESSING

Ensalada de pepino con salsa de yogur

In a small bowl, combine the yogurt, oil, salt, garlic, and onion.

Arrange the cucumbers in a medium salad bowl. Drizzle with the yogurt dressing, garnish with parsley springs (if using), and serve.

PREPARATION TIME: 15 MINUTES
SERVES: 4

⅔ cup (165 g) whole-milk yogurt
2 tablespoons vegetable oil
½ teaspoon salt
2 cloves garlic, finely chopped
1 medium white onion, finely chopped, or ½ cup (30 grams) chopped scallions (spring onions)
2 small cucumbers (6 oz/160 g total), peeled lengthwise in alternating strips and thinly sliced crosswise
Parsley sprigs, for garnish (optional)

BELL PEPPER
AND TOMATO SALAD

Ensalada de pimiento y tomate

Roast the bell peppers directly over the flame of a gas stove (or under a hot broiler [grill] if you don't have a gas stove), turning regularly, until the skin blackens, about 5 minutes. Let cool, then rinse, peel, and cut into strips.

In a small bowl, combine the salt, sugar, pepper, lime juice, and olive oil.

In a large salad bowl, combine the roasted peppers, onion, and tomato. Drizzle with the vinaigrette and serve.

PREPARATION TIME: 20 MINUTES
COOKING TIME: 5 MINUTES
SERVES: 4

4 green bell peppers
½ teaspoon salt
½ teaspoon sugar
¼ teaspoon ground black pepper
1 tablespoon lime juice
2 tablespoons olive oil
1 small white onion, thinly sliced
1 large tomato, cut into thin wedges

CUCUMBER AND GRAPEFRUIT SALAD

Ensalada de pepino y toronja

PREPARATION TIME: 20 MINUTES
SERVES: 4

★

1 tablespoon vinegar
1 clove garlic, finely chopped
¾ teaspoon salt
⅛ teaspoon ground black pepper
¼ teaspoon sugar
2 tablespoons vegetable oil
1 small cucumber, peeled
in alternating strips, halved
lengthwise, and thinly sliced
2 medium grapefruits, supremed
1 bunch lettuce, torn
1 medium white onion, diced

In a small bowl, combine the vinegar, garlic, salt, pepper, sugar, and oil.

In a large salad bowl, combine the cucumber, grapefruit, lettuce, and onion. Drizzle with the vinaigrette and serve.

HOME-STYLE PASTA SALAD

Ensalada fría casera

PREPARATION TIME: 1 HOUR
10 MINUTES, PLUS 4 HOURS
CHILLING TIME
COOKING TIME: 40 MINUTES
SERVES: 8

★

Salt
2 packages (14 oz/400 g each)
elbow macaroni
1 cup (140 g) cubed pineapple
¼ cup (40 g) cubed papaya
¾ cup (165 g) raw cane sugar
2 tablespoons vegetable oil
1 cup (230 g) cooked chicken (see
page 19), cut into ½ inch
(1 cm) pieces
2 cloves garlic, finely chopped
1 large white onion, diced
½ cup (115 g) mayonnaise, store-
bought or homemade (page 318)
4 tablespoons tomato sauce
(seasoned passata)
2 tablespoons vinegar
Scallions (spring onions), pickled
peppers, olives, and/or hard-boiled
eggs, for serving

Bring a large pot of lightly salted water to a boil. Add the elbow macaroni and cook until slightly overcooked, about 15–18 minutes. Drain well and transfer to a large bowl. Let cool for 10 minutes.

In a medium pot, combine the pineapple, papaya, raw sugar, and ⅓ cup (2½ fl oz/80 ml) water. Cook over medium heat until syrupy, about 15 minutes. In a sieve set over a bowl, drain the fruit and reserve both the fruit and syrup.

In a medium frying pan, heat the oil over medium heat. Add the chicken and garlic and sauté for 3 minutes.

Add the onion, fruits, and chicken to the cooked pasta and gently toss. Add the mayonnaise, tomato sauce (seasoned passata), and 2 tablespoons of the reserved syrup or more to taste. Season to taste with salt, then add the vinegar and stir. Refrigerate until very cold, about 4 hours. Garnish with scallions (spring onions), pickled peppers, olives, and/or hard-boiled eggs and serve.

Note: Any cooked meat or fish can be substituted for the chicken.

BANANA-MINT SALAD

Ensalada de plátano a la menta

PREPARATION TIME: 10 MINUTES
SERVES: 6

★

1½ tablespoons lime juice
2 tablespoons honey
1 tablespoon finely chopped fresh
Japanese mint (Mentha arvensis)
or other mint, plus more for serving
6 medium bananas, sliced

This was a very popular salad at the Eco Restaurant El Bambú at the National Botanical Garden.

★

In a small bowl, combine the lime juice, honey, and mint. Arrange the bananas in a large salad bowl, drizzle with the dressing, and gently toss. Decorate with more mint leaves and serve.

Notes: Various types of bananas can be used, including burro, manzano, Gros Michael, and Vietnamese.

FESTIVE PASTA SALAD

Ensalada festiva

PREPARATION TIME: 25 MINUTES,
PLUS 4 HOURS CHILLING TIME
COOKING TIME: 1 HOUR 10 MINUTES
SERVES: 15

★

1 large boneless, skinless chicken
breast (10½ oz/300 g)
Salt
1½ packages (21 oz/600 g) elbow
macaroni
1 cup (200 g) sugar
2 cups (280 g) diced pineapple
3 medium white onions,
finely chopped
½ can (2 oz/55 g) oil-packed tuna
3 tablespoons green peas
30 pitted green olives, halved, plus
2 tablespoons brine
2 tablespoons ketchup
1½ cups (345 g) mayonnaise,
store-bought or homemade
(page 318)
1 tablespoon vinegar
¼ teaspoon ground white pepper
1 large pickled morrón pepper,
cut into strips, for garnish
2 hard-boiled eggs, cut into
pieces, for garnish

Pasta salads are typically prepared and served at birthday parties and other celebrations or festive days, such as weddings or even Christmas or New Year's Eve. Traditionally, the chicken is roasted in the oven or barbecued and the pasta is slightly overcooked.

★

In a medium pot, combine the chicken and water to cover by 1½ inches (3.8 cm). Season the water lightly with salt, cover, and simmer over medium heat until soft, about 50 minutes. Let cool, then finely chop.

Bring a large pot of lightly salted water to a boil. Add the elbow macaroni and cook, stirring regularly with a skimmer, until slightly overcooked (see Note), about 15–18 minutes. Drain well and transfer to a large bowl.

In a medium saucepan, stir together the sugar and ½ cup (4 fl oz/120 ml) water. Add the pineapple and bring to a boil over medium heat. Cook, stirring carefully, about 20 minutes. In a sieve set over a bowl, drain the pineapple, reserving both the pineapple and syrup.

Add the chopped chicken, pineapple, onions, tuna, peas, olives, ketchup, and mayonnaise to the cooked pasta and gently stir with a wooden spoon. Add 2 tablespoons of the pineapple syrup or more to taste, 2 tablespoons of the reserved olive brine, the vinegar, white pepper, and 2 teaspoons salt. Refrigerate for 4 hours. Adjust the acidity and salt to taste. Garnish with the pickled pepper and eggs and serve.

Note: Cubans have a general preference for overcooked foods. While other pastas can be cooked al dente, it is important to overcook the pasta in this dish so that all the flavors mix well— and to follow the authentic recipe.

BEET SALAD
WITH PLANTAIN SAUCE

Ensalada de remolacha con salsa de plátano

PREPARATION TIME: 20 MINUTES
SERVES: 6

★

1 ripe burro plantain, peeled
1 tablespoon lime juice
1 tablespoon raw cane sugar
2 scallions (spring onions),
finely chopped
½ teaspoon salt
4 medium beets, peeled and grated

In a blender, combine the plantain, lime juice, raw sugar, scallions (spring onions), and salt, and blend until thick and smooth.

Arrange the beets in a large salad bowl. Drizzle with one-third of the plantain sauce and gently toss. Pour the remaining sauce over the beets and serve.

COLD POTATO SALAD

Ensalada fría de papas

PREPARATION TIME: 30 MINUTES
COOKING TIME: 15 MINUTES
SERVES: 6

★

Salt
1 lb 5 oz (600 g) large potatoes,
peeled and diced
2 hard-boiled eggs, peeled and
thinly sliced
1 red bell pepper, diced
1 green bell pepper, diced
3 small white onions, diced
1 cup (140 g) diced glazed
pineapple
Generous ½ cup (125 g)
mayonnaise, store-bought
or homemade (page 318)
2 tablespoons sesame seeds
⅛ teaspoon ground black pepper
1 head lettuce, hand-torn
2 tablespoons finely chopped
parsley, for garnish
Tomatoes, pickled peppers, and
olives (optinal), for garnish

Bring a medium pot of lightly salted water to a boil. Add the potatoes, cover, and cook until soft, about 5 minutes. Drain and let cool.

In a large bowl, combine the potatoes, eggs, bell peppers, onions, and pineapple. Add the mayonnaise, sprinkle with the sesame seeds, and gently toss. Season with the pepper and salt to taste. Serve with lettuce and garnished with parsley, tomatoes, pickled peppers, and olives (if using).

TOMATO, AVOCADO, AND CHEESE SALAD

Ensalada de tomate, aguacate y queso

PREPARATION TIME: 20 MINUTES
SERVES: 4

★

½ teaspoon salt
2 tablespoons vinegar
½ teaspoon mild mustard
½ teaspoon raw cane sugar
1 tablespoon dried basil or the
leaves of 1 sprig fresh basil
2 tablespoons vegetable oil
3 medium tomatoes,
coarsely diced
1 large avocado, chopped
3½ oz (100 g) Cuban white cheese
or queso fresco, grated

In a small bowl, combine the salt, vinegar, mustard, raw sugar, basil, and oil.

In a large salad bowl, arrange the tomatoes, avocado, and cheese. Drizzle with the vinaigrette and serve.

WATERCRESS SALAD

Ensalada de berro

PREPARATION TIME: 25 MINUTES
SERVES: 4

★

3 tablespoons grapefruit juice
2 tablespoons vegetable oil
1 teaspoon salt
1 bunch watercress, cut into ¾-inch
(2 cm) pieces

In a small bowl, combine the grapefruit juice, oil, and salt. Let sit for 10 minutes to infuse.

In a large salad bowl, combine the watercress and the vinaigrette and gently toss.

TOMATO, ONION, AND BELL PEPPER SALAD

Ensalada de tomate, cebolla y pimiento

PREPARATION TIME: 15 MINUTES
SERVES: 4

★

¼ cup (15 g) finely chopped
scallions (spring onions)
½ teaspoon salt
½ teaspoon sugar
¼ teaspoon ground black pepper
1 tablespoon lime juice
2 tablespoons vegetable oil
3 large tomatoes, cut into wedges
1 large white onion,
sliced into half-moons
2 green bell peppers, cut into strips

In a small bowl, combine the scallions (spring onions), salt, sugar, black pepper, lime juice, and oil.

In a large salad bowl, arrange the tomatoes, onion, and bell peppers. Drizzle with the lime dressing and serve.

PIGWEED SALAD

Ensalada de verdolaga

PREPARATION TIME: 15 MINUTES
SERVES: 6–8

★

½ teaspoon mild mustard
1 tablespoon lime juice
½ teaspoon ground cumin
2 tablespoons vegetable oil
1 tablespoon salt
1 lb 2 oz (500 g) pigweed
(purslane), cut into pieces 1 inch
(2.5 cm) long
3 medium white onions—2 finely
diced and 1 thinly sliced

Cuban Anthropologist Fernando Ortiz wrote that African slaves introduced the consumption of *verdolaga* (pigweed) in Cuba, where it is a common weed. Pigweed (*Portulaca oleracea*) is also known as purslane, little hogweed, red root, and pursley. It can reach up to 16 inches (40 cm) in height.

★

In a small bowl, combine the mustard, lime juice, cumin, oil, and salt.

In a large salad bowl, toss together the pigweed (purslane) and finely diced onions. Drizzle with the lime dressing and garnish with the thinly sliced onion.

SAUCES AND DRESSINGS

Salsas y aliños

Cubans have a strong preference for sauce-heavy foods and because it is most customary to eat rice with beans, meat, vegetables, and salad all on the same plate, the term *mojar el arroz* or "wet the rice" (meaning drench rice with some kind of sauce or dressing) is relevant in this context. Often the beans, prepared with plenty of water, serve this purpose, but other times it is a juicy sauce that is spread over both the meat (or other main course) and all over the rice as well.

Many of the sauces found in both restaurants and homes are tomato-based, with the typical onions, pepper, and garlic for flavoring. The standard spices used are cumin, bay leaf, and oregano. While there is still little variety of herbs and spices in most Cuban homes, the private restaurants are increasingly experimenting with other flavors and seasonings, and thus contributing to new developments in the Cuban food culture. The sofrito (a sautéed mixture of onions, garlic, peppers, and tomatoes) is the most typical way to season a dish and can be added to beans, a sauce, or mixed with other ingredients. Mayonnaise is very popular with Cubans, so various mayonnaise-based spreads are also common.

Although salads are not as popular in Cuban cuisine, they are still an important part of the traditional diet. The dressings added to salads help increase their variety. The two basic elements of dressings—oil and an acidic ingredient—are complemented by aromatic plants and dried spices. It is generally recommended that dressings be prepared in the following order: first the salt; then the herbs, dried spices, and acidic ingredient; and finally, the oil. This allows the different tastes to dissolve in the acidic ingredient and gives the dressing a pronounced flavor.

CUBAN SAUCE

Salsa criolla

This is the most common sauce in Cuban cooking. It is typically used as an ingredient added to stews, soups, and beans. It is similar to a sofrito, which is cooked separately and then added to various dishes.

Bring a medium pot of water to a boil. Cut an "x" into the skin at the blossom end of the tomatoes and submerge them in the boiling water for 1 minute. Transfer to a cutting board to cool, then remove the skin (peeling at the "x"). Halve, seed, and finely chop.

In a medium frying pan, heat the oil over high heat. Add the *chay* peppers and sauté until softened, about 1 minute. Add the onion and garlic and cook until the onions turn translucent, about 2 minutes. Add the chopped tomatoes and sauté until reduced, about 3 minutes. Reduce the heat to medium-low, add the tomato sauce (seasoned passata), and cook for about 3 minutes. Add the wine, ¼ cup (2 fl oz/60 ml) water, the cumin, bay leaf, oregano, and salt. Bring to a boil and cook until thickened, about 5 minutes.

Note: Cachucha peppers can be used instead of chay peppers.

PREPARATION TIME: 15 MINUTES
COOKING TIME: 15 MINUTES
MAKES: 1¼ CUPS (10 FL OZ/300 ML)

2 large tomatoes
2 tablespoons vegetable oil
5 chay peppers or cubanelles, seeded and finely chopped
1 medium white onion, finely chopped
4 cloves garlic, finely chopped
½ cup (125 g) tomato sauce (seasoned passata)
2 tablespoons dry white wine
¼ teaspoon ground cumin
⅛ teaspoon ground bay leaf
⅛ teaspoon dried oregano
1 teaspoon salt

CUBAN DRESSING

Mojo criollo

With a mortar and pestle, crush the garlic into a paste. In a small bowl, mix the garlic paste with the bitter orange juice and salt. In a small frying pan, heat the oil over medium heat. Add the garlic/orange juice mixture, cover, and remove from the heat. Serve hot.

PREPARATION TIME: 10 MINUTES
COOKING TIME: 5 MINUTES
MAKES: ⅓ CUP (2½ FL OZ/75 ML)

10 cloves garlic, peeled
2 tablespoons bitter orange juice (see page 18)
½ teaspoon salt
2 tablespoons vegetable oil

SPICY SAUCE

Mojo picante

PREPARATION TIME: 10 MINUTES
MAKES: ⅓ CUP (2½ FL OZ/75 ML)

★

½ small white onion,
finely chopped
5 cloves garlic, finely chopped
¼ teaspoon salt
2 small hot chilies, such as
guaguao or habanero
4 tablespoons vinegar or bitter
orange juice (see page 18)

The traditional *mojo* recipe, known as *mojo simple*, is the following recipe without the hot peppers. Serve over fish, meat, and root vegetables.

★

In a medium bowl, combine the onion, garlic, salt, whole chilies, and vinegar. Mix well and let sit for at least 30 minutes before serving.

SPECIAL SWEET AND SOUR SAUCE

Salsa agridulce especial

PREPARATION TIME: 30 MINUTES
COOKING TIME: 15 MINUTES
MAKES: 2½ CUPS (20 FL OZ/600 ML)

★

1 small carrot, finely diced
2 tablespoons cornstarch
(cornflour)
¾ cup (6 fl oz/200 ml) vegetable
stock
2 tablespoons vegetable oil
½ small green bell pepper,
finely diced
1 small red bell pepper, finely diced
3½ oz (100 g) fresh pineapple,
finely diced
½ small onion, finely diced
2 teaspoons grated fresh ginger
3 small pickled cucumbers,
finely diced
6 tablespoons vinegar
6 tablespoons strawberry jam
or jelly
¼ cup (60 g) tomato paste
(tomato puree)
Salt

This sweet and sour sauce is commonly used in Chinese restaurants in Cuba and has become popularized by other chefs and in Cuban homes. Serve over roasted fish, Fried Wontons (page 49), Corn Arepas (page 34), boiled taro root, yuca (cassava), or sweet potatoes, and *frituras*.

★

Bring a small pot of water to a boil over medium heat. Add the carrot and cook until semi-soft, about 3 minutes. Drain and set aside.

In a small bowl, dilute the cornstarch (cornflour) in 6 tablespoons of the vegetable stock.

In a medium frying pan, heat the oil over medium heat. Add the carrot, bell peppers, pineapple, onion, ginger, and pickled cucumbers and sauté until softened, about 3 minutes. Add the vinegar and let cook until reduced, about 2 minutes. Add the jam or jelly, tomato paste (puree), the remaining 6 tablespoons stock, and cornstarch mixture and cook until thickened, 4–6 minutes. Remove from the heat and season to taste with salt.

Note: Another kind of berry jam or jelly can be used instead of strawberry.

SWEET AND SOUR GUAVA SAUCE

Salsa agridulce de guayaba

PREPARATION TIME: 12 MINUTES
MAKES: ¾ CUP (175 G)

★

¼ cup (85 g) Guava Marmalade
(page 336)
¼ cup (60 g) mayonnaise, store-
bought or homemade (page 318)
2 tablespoons vegetable oil
2 tablespoons vinegar
A few drops lime juice (optional)
¼ teaspoon salt
⅛ teaspoon ground black pepper
1 tablespoon chopped scallions
(spring onions) or parsley

Serve over fish, boiled root vegetables (such as yuca [cassava], taro root, and sweet potatoes), Steamed Vegetables (page 222), or Sautéed Vegetables (page 221).

★

In a small bowl, combine the guava marmalade and mayonnaise and gently mix until smooth. Mix in the oil, vinegar, lime juice (if using), salt, and pepper. Add the chopped scallions (spring onions).

CARROT-PEANUT SPREAD

Pasta de zanahoria al maní

PREPARATION TIME: 15 MINUTES
MAKES: 1 CUP (240 G)

★

1 large carrot, grated
3 cloves garlic, finely chopped
¼ cup (40 g) unsalted roasted
peanuts, coarsely crushed
Generous ½ cup (125 g)
mayonnaise, store-bought
or homemade (page 318)
½ teaspoon salt
¼ teaspoon ground black pepper

Use as a sandwich spread or serve with cooked vegetables, salads, roasted fish, or to accompany appetizers as a dip.

★

In a medium bowl, combine the carrot, garlic, peanuts, mayonnaise, salt, and pepper.

GREEN PEANUT SAUCE

Salsa verde al maní

PREPARATION TIME: 15 MINUTES
MAKES: 2 CUPS (475 G)

⭐

¼ cup (20 g) leaves fresh basil
1 medium onion, diced
¼ cup (40 g) unsalted roasted
peanuts
½ cup (4 fl oz/120 ml) olive oil
1 tablespoon lime juice
1 teaspoon raw cane sugar
2 cloves garlic, peeled but whole
1 teaspoon salt
⅛ teaspoon ground black pepper

Serve with fish, pastas, vegetables, and tubers, or spread
on crackers.

⭐

In a blender (see Note), combine the basil, onion, peanuts,
olive oil, lime juice, raw sugar, garlic, salt, pepper, and ⅓ cup
(2½ fl oz/80 ml) water and blend until even, a few seconds.
Adjust the thickness to your preference by adding more oil.

*Note: The traditional way to prepare this sauce is to crush the
solid ingredients in a large mortar with pestle.*

VEGETARIAN SANDWICH SPREAD

Pasta vegetariana para bocaditos

PREPARATION TIME: 15 MINUTES
COOKING TIME: 10 MINUTES
MAKES: 2 CUPS (475 G)

⭐

4 small green bell peppers,
chopped
1 medium white onion, chopped
5 cloves garlic, chopped
3 tablespoons tomato sauce
(seasoned passata)
3 tablespoons vinegar
3 tablespoons raw cane sugar
1 teaspoon salt
2 tablespoons all-purpose (plain)
flour
2 eggs, whisked
3 tablespoons vegetable oil

This recipe became very popular during the Special
Period, because it is both tasty and affordable, and it is
still common for people to make this recipe in their homes.
Spread over bread or crackers.

⭐

In a blender, combine the bell peppers, onion, garlic, tomato
sauce (seasoned passata), vinegar, raw sugar, salt, flour,
and eggs and blend. With the machine running, gradually
add the oil, blending until smooth.

Transfer the mixture to a small pot. Warm over low heat
and cook, stirring occasionally with a wooden spoon, until
thickened, 8–10 minutes. Remove and let cool. Store in
the refrigerator for up to 3 days.

HOMEMADE MAYONNAISE

Mayonesa casera

PREPARATION TIME: 10 MINUTES,
PLUS 1 HOUR CHILLING TIME
MAKES: 1 CUP (240 G)

★

1 egg, at room temperature
1 tablespoon white vinegar
1 teaspoon salt
½ teaspoon raw cane sugar
1 clove garlic, peeled
¾ cup (6 fl oz / 180 ml) vegetable oil

In a blender, combine the egg, vinegar, salt, sugar, and garlic. Begin to blend, without the top on, and very slowly stream in the oil. Continue blending until the mayonnaise thickens. Refrigerate until chilled, at least 1 hour.

Note: It is important that the egg be very fresh.

YUCA MAYONNAISE

Mayonesa de yuca

PREPARATION TIME: 10 MINUTES
MAKES: 2 CUPS (475 G)

★

Salt
2 lb (1 kg) yuca (cassava) root,
peeled, cut into 2 inch (5 cm)
long pieces
1 egg
6 cloves garlic, peeled but whole
3 tablespoons vinegar
1 teaspoon raw cane sugar
½ cup (4 fl oz /120 ml) vegetable oil

Serve with salads, cooked vegetables, or sandwiches.

★

Bring a large pot of lightly salted water to a boil. Add the yuca (cassava) and cook, covered, until soft, 1 hour. Drain and remove the fibrous vein.

In a blender, combine the yuca, egg, garlic, vinegar, 1 teaspoon salt, and raw sugar and blend until smooth. If the sauce is too thick to get smooth, add 1–2 tablespoons of water to loosen it. With the machine running, slowly drizzle in the oil, blending until thick.

MAYONNAISE WITH PEPPERS

Mayonesa con pimientos

PREPARATION TIME: 10 MINUTES
COOKING TIME: 5 MINUTES
MAKES: 1½ CUPS (350 G)

★

1 large red bell pepper
1 large green bell pepper
¾ cup (170 g) mayonnaise, store-
bought or homemade (page 318)

Serve with salads, breads, appetizers, or snacks.

★

Roast the bell peppers directly over the flame of a gas stove (or under a hot broiler [grill] if you don't have a gas stove), turning regularly, until the skin blackens, about 5 minutes. Let cool, then rinse, peel, and dice. Transfer to a medium bowl and add the mayonnaise.

HERB DRESSING

Aliño de hierbas

PREPARATION TIME: 10 MINUTES
MAKES: 1 CUP (8 FL OZ/240 ML)

★

1 stalk fresh celery, finely chopped
2 scallions (spring onions),
finely chopped
2 cloves garlic, finely chopped
1 sprig parsley, finely chopped
1 teaspoon salt
2 tablespoons lime juice
3 tablespoons olive oil

Serve over salads or boiled root vegetables, such as taro root, yuca (cassava), and sweet potato.

★

In a small bowl, combine the celery, scallions (spring onions), garlic, parsley, salt, lime juice, and ½ cup (4 fl oz/125 ml) water. Add the oil and stir.

ASIAN DRESSING

Aliño Oriental

PREPARATION TIME: 10 MINUTES
MAKES: 1 CUP (8 FL OZ/240 ML)

★

3 tablespoons lime juice
1 teaspoon mild mustard
½ teaspoon soy sauce
1 tablespoon honey
4 cloves garlic, finely chopped
1 teaspoon salt
½ cup (4 fl oz/120 ml) vegetable oil

Serve over salads or root vegetables, such as taro root, yuca (cassava), and sweet potato.

★

In a small bowl, combine the lime juice, mustard, soy sauce, and honey. Add the garlic and salt, then add the oil and mix well.

GUACAMOLE

Guacamole

PREPARATION TIME: 15 MINUTES
SERVES: 4

1 avocado, cut into medium-size chunks

2 small tomatoes, chopped

1 small white onion, chopped

2 chay peppers or cubanelles, chopped

2 small hot chilies or 1 teaspoon chili powder (optional)

1 tablespoon lime juice

1 tablespoon chopped fresh cilantro (coriander)

½ teaspoon salt

⅛ teaspoon ground black pepper

½ teaspoon raw cane sugar

This recipe comes from Mexican cuisine, but Cuban home cooks make it occasionally as a way to vary the preparation of avocado. It has become more popular in recent years, despite the fact that there is no presence of Mexican influence in Cuban cuisine. Serve with vegetables, bread, or breaded foods.

In a blender, combine the avocado, tomatoes, onion, *chay* peppers, chilies (if using), lime juice, cilantro (coriander), salt, pepper, and raw sugar and blend until smooth.

BÉCHAMEL SAUCE

Salsa bechamel

PREPARATION TIME: 5 MINUTES
COOKING TIME: 15 MINUTES
MAKES: 2 CUPS (17 FL OZ/500 ML)

★

2¼ cups (18 fl oz/540 ml) whole milk

3 tablespoons (45 g) unsalted butter

5 tablespoons all-purpose (plain) flour

1 teaspoon salt

⅛ teaspoon ground white pepper

⅛ teaspoon grated nutmeg

In a small pot, warm the milk over low heat. Set aside.

In a medium frying pan, melt the butter over medium heat. Add the flour all at once, remove from the heat, and stir with a wooden spoon to incorporate. Whisk in ¼ cup (2 fl oz/ 60 ml) of the warm milk into the flour mixture. Return the pan to medium heat and continue whisking about ¼ cup (2 fl oz/60 ml) of the warm milk at a time until all the liquid is incorporated. Bring the sauce to a simmer, then reduce the heat to medium-low and cook until thickened, stirring constantly to avoid lumps, 10–12 minutes. Add the salt, white pepper, and nutmeg. Remove from the heat and use immediately.

TOMATO SAUCE

Salsa de tomate

In a blender, puree the tomatoes until smooth. Pass the pureed tomatoes through a sieve. Measure out 3 cups (750 ml).

In a medium pan, heat 2 tablespoons of the olive oil over medium heat. Add the onion, garlic, and *chay* peppers and sweat the vegetables until the onions are slightly translucent, 2–3 minutes. Add the pureed tomatoes, the remaining 1 tablespoon oil, the paprika, raw sugar, vinegar, and wine. Bring the mixture to a boil, then reduce to a simmer and cook until reduced by about half, 25–30 minutes.

Set a fine-mesh strainer over a medium bowl and strain the sauce, pressing the vegetable solids with a spatula or a small ladle to force most of them through. Season with salt and black pepper to taste. Use immediately or cool completely before refrigerating for up to 3 days.

PREPARATION TIME: 20 MINUTES
COOKING TIME: 25 MINUTES
MAKES: 2 CUPS (450 G)

★

12 medium tomatoes, cored and cut into chunks
3 tablespoons olive oil
¼ medium white onion, diced
2 clove garlic, minced
2 chay peppers or cubanelles, seeded and diced
1 teaspoon paprika
1 teaspoon raw cane sugar
2 tablespoons white or apple cider vinegar
2 tablespoons dry white wine
Salt and ground black pepper

EGG SAUCE

Salsa de huevos

This sauce is also known as crème anglaise. Pour it over desserts and sweets.

★

In a medium bowl, combine the milk and cornstarch (cornflour) and whisk until dissolved. Add the egg yolks and mix. Strain through a fine-mesh sieve into a medium pot and add the sugar and the lime peel. Heat the mixture over low heat, stirring regularly with a wooden spoon, until thick enough to coat the back of a spoon, about 10 minutes (do not let the sauce boil at any point). Remove from the heat and add the vanilla. Remove the lime peel before serving. If not using right away, it should stay in a *bain-marie*.

PREPARATION TIME: 15 MINUTES
COOKING TIME: 10 MINUTES
MAKES: 2 CUPS (15 FL OZ/450 ML)

★

2 cups (16 fl oz/500 ml) whole milk
2 teaspoons cornstarch (cornflour)
6 egg yolks, beaten
¾ cup (150 g) sugar
1 strip lime peel
1 teaspoon vanilla extract

SIMPLE SYRUP

Almíbar ligero

In a saucepan, combine the sugar and ½ cup (4 fl oz/120 ml) water and bring to a simmer over medium-low heat until the sugar is dissolved, about 5 minutes. Remove from the heat and let cool before using.

COOKING TIME: 5 MINUTES
MAKES: 1 CUP (8 FL OZ/240 ML)

★

1 cup (200 g) sugar

SWEETS AND DESSERTS

Dulces y postres

Sweets and desserts have significant social, economic, and cultural roots in Cuba and are considered an important part of the typical diet. Some of the most traditional recipes date back to the Spanish influence, mixed with significant contributions from the slave population. Many master pastry chefs arrived in Cuba from Europe and Santo Domingo during the colonial period, and they taught domestic slaves to make cakes, cookies, candies, bonbons, and so on. Nuns in monasteries in Santa Clara also taught the recipes for various sweets and desserts to slaves, who then popularized them among the slave population. In 1860, the first pastry shops were opened in Cuba. Other dessert recipes were adopted at the time of the American presence during the first half of the twentieth century.

Cuban sweets are often very sweet; a preference that is consistent with the high consumption of sugar by the population. As part of the rations system, each Cuban individual receives *eight pounds* (3.5 kg) of sugar each month—five white and three brown—subsidized by the government. And many people eat it all.

A historical perspective shows how significant sugar has been in Cuba. During colonial times, the majority of agricultural lands was designated for sugar production, creating a large economic dependence. Later, during the years of the Republic, the mono-crop model continued, guided by American interests. At the time that the Revolutionary government took control, 82 percent of all fertile land was dedicated to one crop only, and 60 percent to sugar production. The Revolutionary government nationalized its land, and while agrarian reforms were implemented with the intention of seeking more food sovereignty, in practice, significant agricultural diversification did not take place. In the 1990s, Cuba restructured its agricultural systems in response to the economic crisis.

During the Special Period, sugar was even more significant as one of the few available ingredients during times of severe scarcities. Millions of Cubans regularly consumed *sopa de gallo* (Rooster Soup), the popular term for sugar water, as a snack or dessert. When the economic crisis caused shortages of everything else, there was still plenty of sugar on an island whose entire agricultural history had been dedicated to its production.

While the custom to drink plain sugar water has decreased among the population within the context of a better economic reality, the high consumption of sugar in general is still very prevalent. It is not rare for Cubans to add several spoonfuls of sugar to mango or another fruit juice. It is also more common to turn fruits into various desserts (such as those found in the following pages) than to consume them in their natural state. The typical way to serve coffee, the national drink, is as a strong espresso with plenty of sugar added. As you will see in the following chapter, many of the recipes call for large quantities of sugar, which can be reduced to taste.

Sweets are frequently sold at food stands, as one of the preferred options for the Cuban consumer. It is also common to see individuals walking around selling homemade sweets on the street. Some kind of marmalade or dessert is almost always included in the meals served at the *comedores* (school and work dining halls), showing how ingrained dessert is in the Cuban food culture.

Cuban desserts are usually divided into two categories: the *pastelería*, or pastry arts, which use flour, and include breads, cookies, and pies, and the *repostería*, which are based on sugar, egg, milk, and fruits.

TRADITIONAL DULCE DE LECHE WITH MILK CURD

Dulce de leche cortada (con yemas de huevo)

This is based on a traditional recipe, which includes egg yolks; more modern versions of *dulce de leche cortada* leave the egg yolks out. Milk curd is common in Cuban desserts. Due to the heat (and the lack of refrigeration in the past in the countryside), fresh milk curdles and, instead of throwing it away, it is used in this and other desserts. In rural zones, this dessert is made with milk from a cow that has recently given birth, so that the milk has colostrum in it. The colostrum makes the dulce de leche smoother and more flavorful.

★

In a glass pitcher, stir together the milk and sugar. Add the egg yolks, lime zest, lime juice, vanilla, salt, and cinnamon stick. Set aside for 30 minutes at room temperature to curdle the milk.

Pour the mixture into a medium pot and cook until it boils and curdles completely, 15 minutes. Reduce the heat to medium-low and cook, stirring occasionally with a wooden spoon, until the mixture turns a golden brown and the liquid reduces, about 1 hour 15 minutes to 1½ hours. Let cool slightly, then refrigerate for 2 hours (optional). Scoop into small bowls and serve cold or at room temperature.

PREPARATION TIME: 40 MINUTES
COOKING TIME: 1 HOUR 45 MINUTES
SERVES: 10

2 quarts (2 liters) whole milk
2 cups (400 g) sugar
4 egg yolks
1 teaspoon grated lime zest
1 teaspoon lime juice
¼ teaspoon vanilla extract
⅛ teaspoon salt
1 cinnamon stick

YUCA FLAN

Flan de yuca

PREPARATION TIME: 10 MINUTES,
PLUS 2 HOURS CHILLING TIME
COOKING TIME: 25 MINUTES
SERVES: 6

★

6 tablespoons (80 g) sugar
1 cup (110 g) grated yuca (cassava)
1 cup (8 fl oz/240 ml) Simple
Syrup (page 323)
3 eggs
¼ teaspoon grated nutmeg

This recipe has become very popular in Cuba in culinary competitions and parties.

★

In an 8 inch (20 cm) round cake pan or baking dish (preferably one that closes hermetically; see Note), stir together the sugar and 1 tablespoon cold water to evenly moisten. Bring to a boil over high heat and cook the sugar syrup until a light-amber caramel forms, 3–4 minutes. Swirl from side to side to coat the bottom with the caramelized sugar. Set aside to cool to room temperature.

In a bowl, mix together the grated yuca (cassava), simple syrup, eggs, and nutmeg. Pour the batter into the pan on top of the hardened, caramelized sugar and cover the pan tightly. It is very important to cover the pan tightly; if you do not have a pan that closes hermetically, cover tightly with foil, wax paper, or a plastic bag and put a rubber band around the pan.

Transfer the pan to a pressure cooker (see Note). Pour water halfway up the pan. Lock the lid and bring to pressure over medium-low heat. Cook at pressure until a toothpick inserted into the center of the flan comes out dry, about 25 minutes. Quick-release the pressure. Let cool, then refrigerate for 2 hours to chill.

To unmold, invert a large serving plate over the flan, then flip the pan and the plate together. Lift the cake pan away, leaving the flan and the melted caramel sauce on the serving plate.

Note: If you don't have a pressure cooker, follow the directions for Home-Style Flan (page 332), and cook the flan for 1 hour.

HOME-STYLE FLAN

Flan casero

**PREPARATION TIME: 15 MINUTES,
PLUS 3 HOURS CHILLING TIME
COOKING TIME: 1 HOUR
SERVES: 12**

★

6 tablespoons (80 g) plus 1 cup
(200 g) sugar
5 eggs
2 cups (180 g) whole dry milk
powder
½ teaspoon vanilla extract
Pinch of sea salt

In an 8 inch (20 cm) round 3½ inch (8 cm) deep cake pan or baking dish (preferably one that closes hermetically; see Note), stir together 6 tablespoons of the sugar and 1 tablespoon cold water to evenly moisten. Bring to a boil over high heat and cook the sugar syrup until a light-amber caramel forms, 3–4 minutes. Swirl from side to side to coat the bottom with the caramelized sugar. Set aside to cool to room temperature.

In a blender, combine the eggs, remaining 1 cup (205 g) sugar, 1½ cups (12 fl oz/375 ml) water, the powdered milk, vanilla, and salt and blend until smooth, about 30 seconds. Pour the batter into the cake pan with the caramel and cover the pan tightly. It is very important to cover the pan tightly; if you do not have a pan that closes hermetically, cover tightly with foil, wax paper, or a plastic bag and put a rubber band around the pan.

Transfer the pan to a pot wide enough to hold the cake pan with room on the sides and pour 1½ inches (4 cm) water (the water should come halfway up the sides of the cake pan). Cover the pot tightly and bring to a simmer over low heat. Steam the flan until set and just barely jiggly at the center, 1 hour to 1 hour 10 minutes. Remove the flan from the pot of water and let cool. Then refrigerate for at least 3 hours or overnight until well chilled.

To unmold, invert a large serving plate over the flan, then flip the pan and the plate together. Lift the cake pan away, leaving the flan and the melted caramel sauce on the serving plate.

Note: Pans with other measurements (including 5 inch/13 cm round pans with 5 inch/13 cm sides) are also commonly used in Cuba. Some people bake flans in recycled cans of various measurements.

PUMPKIN CINNAMON FLAN

Flan de calabaza a la canela

In an 8½ inch (22 cm) round cake pan or baking dish (preferably one that closes hermetically; see Note), stir together 6 tablespoons of the sugar and 1 tablespoon cold water to evenly moisten. Bring to a boil over high heat and cook the sugar syrup until a light-amber caramel forms, 3–4 minutes. Swirl from side to side to coat the bottom with the caramelized sugar. Set aside to cool to room temperature.

In a blender, combine the pumpkin puree, condensed milk, eggs, salt, vanilla, and cinnamon and blend until smooth. Pour the batter into the pan and cover the pan tightly. It is very important to cover the pan tightly; if you do not have a pan that closes hermetically, cover tightly with foil, wax paper, or a plastic bag and put a rubber band around the pan.

Transfer the pan to a pot wide enough to hold the cake pan with room on the sides and pour 1½ inches (4 cm) water (the water should come halfway up the sides of the cake pan). Cover the pot tightly, and bring to a simmer over low heat. Steam the flan until set and just barely jiggly at the center, 45–50 minutes. Remove the flan from the pot of water and let cool. Then refrigerate for at least 3 hours or overnight until well chilled.

To unmold, invert a large serving plate over the flan, then flip the pan and the plate together. Lift the cake pan away, leaving the flan and the melted caramel sauce on the serving plate. Garnish with candied pumpkin, honey, or other fruits dipped in a simple syrup.

Notes: *Pans with other measurements (including 5 inch/13 cm round pans with 5 inch/13 cm sides) are also commonly used in Cuba. Some people bake flans in recycled cans of various measurements.*

You can use fennel or anise in place of the cinnamon.

PREPARATION TIME: 20 MINUTES, PLUS 3 HOURS CHILLING TIME
COOKING TIME: 45–50 MINUTES
SERVES: 8–10

6 tablespoons (80g) sugar
1 cup (250 g) canned pumpkin puree
1 can (14 oz/396 g) sweetened condensed milk
5 eggs
¼ teaspoon salt
½ teaspoon vanilla extract
½ teaspoon ground cinnamon
Candied pumpkin, honey, or fruits (such as papaya, pineapple, or mango) dipped in Simple Syrup (page 323), for serving

FAMILY-STYLE RICE PUDDING

Arroz con leche familiar

**PREPARATION TIME: 10 MINUTES,
PLUS 2 HOURS CHILLING TIME
COOKING TIME: 1 HOUR 25 MINUTES
SERVES: 8**

1 cup (230 g) short-grain white
rice
1 cinnamon stick
Rind of 1 lime
1 can (14 oz/39g g) sweetened
condensed milk
1 can (12 fl oz/354 ml) evaporated
milk
¼ teaspoon salt
¾ cup (150 g) sugar
1½ teaspoons ground cinnamon

This is a very typical Cuban dessert, rooted in Spanish culinary traditions. The secret to this dessert is to cook the rice perfectly—until it is quite soft, but doesn't lose its form—and then add the milk. Otherwise, the casein in the milk would prevent the rice from continuing to soften.

★

In a large pot, combine the rice, cinnamon stick, lime rind, and 5½ cups (44 fl oz/1.3 liters) water. Cover and cook over medium heat until tender and fluffy, about 45 minutes. Add the sweetened condensed milk, evaporated milk, salt, and sugar and stir. Continue to cook, stirring occasionally so that the rice doesn't stick to the bottom, until the rice has absorbed the milk and sugar, about 30 minutes. Reduce the heat to low and cook, stirring constantly, until the rice pudding thickens, about 10 minutes, Pour it into a large serving dish while still hot, and sprinkle with cinnamon. Refrigerate for 2 hours. Serve cold on small dessert plates.

RICE PUDDING WITH FRUIT SYRUP

Arroz con leche y salsa de frutas

**PREPARATION TIME: 30 MINUTES,
PLUS 2 HOURS CHILLING TIME
COOKING TIME: 1 HOUR 15 MINUTES
SERVES: 6**

For the rice pudding:
½ cup plus 1 tablespoon (115 g)
short-grain rice
¼ teaspoon salt
Zest of 1 small lime
1 cup (200 g) sugar
4 cups (32 fl oz/950 ml) whole milk

For the fruit syrup:
½ cup (100 g) sugar
1 cup (160 g) diced fresh fruit,
such as papaya, mango, guava,
pineapple

Make the rice pudding: In a large saucepan, combine the rice, 3 cups (24 fl oz/750 ml) water, salt, and lime zest. Cover and cook over medium-low heat, until the rice is cooked and the water has evaporated, about 25 minutes. Stir in the sugar. Add the milk little by little and cook over medium heat, stirring regularly with a wooden spoon to prevent the pudding from sticking to the pan, until thick and creamy, 1 hour to 1 hour 15 minutes.

Meanwhile, make the fruit syrup: In a medium saucepan, combine the sugar, ¼ cup (2 fl oz/60 ml) water, and fruit. Bring to a simmer over medium heat and cook until the fruits are syrupy, about 15 minutes.

Add the fruit sauce to the rice pudding, stir, and cook until the pudding has absorbed the flavors of the fruit sauce, about 5 minutes. Refrigerate for 2 hours. Serve cold on small dessert plates.

COUNTRY-STYLE MARMALADE

Mermelada campestre 📷

PREPARATION TIME: 20 MINUTES
COOKING TIME: 55 MINUTES
SERVES: 4

★

2 medium white or yellow sweet
potatoes (1 lb 5 oz/600 g total),
peeled and cut into large pieces
9 oz (250 g) pumpkin, peeled and
cut into medium chunks
1½ cups (330 g) raw cane sugar
1 cup (120 g) grated fresh coconut
¼ teaspoon salt
¼ teaspoon vanilla extract

Despite the name marmalade, this is very different from
the spread used on toast. In Cuba, marmalade refers to
fruit pulp cooked in sugar. It is a dense liquid that is eaten
with a spoon.

★

Bring a medium pot of water to a boil. Add the sweet
potatoes. After 5 minutes, add the pumpkin and cook until
both are tender, about 15 minutes. Reserving the cooking
water, drain the sweet potato and pumpkin, and let both
vegetables cool down.

In a blender, combine the sweet potatoes, pumpkin, and
1½ cups (12 fl oz/355 ml) of the cooking water and blend
until smooth.

In a medium heavy-bottomed pot, combine the sweet
potato/pumpkin mixture, the raw sugar, coconut, and
salt and cook over low heat, stirring very regularly, until
thickened, about 20 minutes.

Remove from the heat, add the vanilla, and set aside to cool.
Serve in bowls.

GUAVA MARMALADE

Mermelada de guayaba

PREPARATION TIME: 20 MINUTES
COOKING TIME: 30 MINUTES
SERVES: 8

★

8 medium guavas (1 lb/10 oz/
750 g total)
2 cups (400 g) sugar (see Note)

This is considered a very typical Cuban dessert. Serve with
white cheese or cream cheese on top or on the side.

★

Wash the guavas and cut them into fourths. Put them in the
blender with 1 cup (8 fl oz/240 ml) water and mix. Pour into
a sieve set over a heavy-bottom pot and strain the seeds
out. Add the sugar and cook, stirring occasionally with
a wooden spoon, over medium-low heat until thickened,
about 30 minutes. Serve in bowls.

*Note: The amount of sugar in the traditional recipe can be
reduced if desired.*

BASIL-PUMPKIN MARMALADE

Mermelada de calabaza a la albahaca

**PREPARATION TIME: 30 MINUTES,
PLUS 2 HOURS CHILLING TIME
COOKING TIME: 15 MINUTES
SERVES: 4**

★

1½ lb (690 g) pumpkin, peeled and
cut into large pieces
Leaves of 4 sprigs basil, plus more
for garnish
1 cup (200 g) raw cane sugar
¼ teaspoon salt

In a medium pan, bring 2 cups (16 fl oz/500 ml) water to a boil. Add the pumpkin and sprigs of basil and simmer until the pumpkin is soft, about 15 minutes. Drain then mash to a puree with a fork.

In a large heavy-bottomed pot, combine the pumpkin puree, raw sugar, and salt and cook over low heat, stirring regularly with a wooden spoon, until you can draw a clear line through the mixture with the spoon, without it flowing immediately back to fill the gap, about 15 minutes. Remove from the heat, let cool, then refrigerate for at least 2 hours, until well chilled. Serve cold, garnished with a sprig of basil.

GUAVA HELMETS

Cascos de guayaba

**PREPARATION TIME: 20 MINUTES
COOKING TIME: 40 MINUTES
SERVES: 4**

★

5 large firm-ripe guavas
(3½ oz/100 g each)
1 cinnamon stick
1 cup (200 g) sugar

The final color of these guava shells ("helmets") depends on the type of guava used; the red guava will make a dark red "helmet," and the white guava will make a yellow one. The "helmets" can be filled with cream cheese.

★

Peel the guavas carefully, removing just a thin layer of skin. Halve them lengthwise and scoop out the pulp and seeds leaving a shell (the "helmet") with walls about ¾ inches (1 cm) thick. (Save the pulp to make marmalade.)

Put the guava shells in a medium pot and add water to cover by 1 inch (2.5 cm). Add the cinnamon, cover, and cook over medium-high heat until somewhat soft, about 10 minutes. Add the sugar and cook over medium heat, stirring occasionally with a wooden spoon, until the shells are completely soft, about 30 minutes.

Note: Another method is to soften the guava in boiling water and make a simple syrup (page 323) separately. Then heat the previously softened guava shells in the simple syrup for 5 minutes.

PINEAPPLE-MINT DESSERT

Dulce de piña a la menta

This recipe, a syrupy liquid served over the cooked fruit, is eaten like a chilled soup with a spoon. The syrup can be drained, if preferred, although the authentic Cuban style includes the syrup. Serve with a scoop of white cheese or cream cheese on the side.

★

Put the pineapple in a medium pot and add cold water to just cover. Bring to a boil over medium heat. Reduce to a simmer and cook until the pineapple is soft, about 15 minutes. Reserving ½ cup (4 fl oz/125 ml) of the cooking liquid, drain the pineapple and set aside.

In the same pot, combine the sugar and the reserved cooking liquid and bring to a boil over low heat. Add the pineapple, lime juice, salt, and mint leaves and let simmer for 5–7 minutes. Let cool, then refrigerate for at least 2 hours, until well chilled. Serve cold.

**PREPARATION TIME: 10 MINUTES,
PLUS 2 HOURS CHILLING TIME
COOKING TIME: 20 MINUTES
SERVES: 6**

★

2 cups (340 g) diced fresh pineapple
1½ cups (300 g) sugar
1 tablespoon lime juice
⅛ teaspoon salt
10 large leaves fresh spearmint

COCONUT DESSERT

Dulce de coco

In addition to being eaten like a chilled soup with a spoon, this recipe can also be used as a filling for *empanadas*, cakes, and pies.

★

In a medium pot, combine the sugar, ½ cup (4 fl oz/125 ml) water, and cinnamon stick and cook over medium heat for 5–7 minutes. Add the grated coconut and cook over medium-low heat for 10 minutes. Stir and set aside to cool. Serve at room temperature.

**PREPARATION TIME: 10 MINUTES
COOKING TIME: 20
SERVES: 4**

★

¾ cup (160 g) sugar
1 cinnamon stick
2 cups (240 g) fresh grated coconut (or unsweetened canned grated coconut)

SWEET POTATO-COCONUT DESSERT

Malarrabia con coco

**PREPARATION TIME: 10 MINUTES,
PLUS 2 HOURS CHILLING TIME
COOKING TIME: 30 MINUTES
SERVES: 6**

★

4 medium white or yellow sweet
potatoes (1¾ lb/800 g total),
peeled and finely diced
1 cup (8 fl oz/240 ml) Simple
Syrup (page 323)
1 cup (240 g) Coconut Dessert
(page 339)
4 bitter orange leaves
3 cinnamon sticks
White cheese or cream cheese,
for serving (optional)

The traditional version of this recipe is prepared with
sugarcane syrup instead of simple syrup.

★

Put the sweet potatoes in a medium pot and add cold water
to just cover. Cook, covered, over medium heat until semi-
soft, about 10 minutes. Add the simple syrup, the coconut
dessert, orange leaves, and cinnamon. Continue cooking
until the sweet potatoes completely soften, about
10–12 minutes. Let cool, then refrigerate for at least
2 hours (see Note). Serve cold with a generous scoop of
white cheese or cream cheese (if using).

*Note: It is common to eat this dessert at room temperature
in the countryside.*

SWEET POTATO WITH MILK CURD

Malarrabia con leche cortada

**PREPARATION TIME: 10 MINUTES,
2 HOURS CHILLING TIME (OPTIONAL)
COOKING TIME: 40 MINUTES
SERVES: 6**

★

2 medium white or yellow sweet
potatoes (1 lb 5 oz/600 g total),
peeled and cut into ¾ inch (2 cm)
pieces
2 cups (16 fl oz/500 ml) whole milk
¼ teaspoon salt
1 teaspoon lime juice
1 cup (200 g) raw cane sugar
4 bitter orange leaves
3 cinnamon sticks
White cheese or cream cheese,
for serving

Place the sweet potatoes in a medium pot with water to
just cover. Cook, covered, over medium heat until semi-soft,
about 10 minutes. Drain the water out of the pot (leaving
the potatoes in) and stir in the milk, salt, and lime juice.
Add the raw sugar, orange leaves, and cinnamon sticks.
Continue cooking until the milk curdles, about 30 minutes.
Cool, then refrigerate for at least 2 hours (optional). Serve
cold or at room temperature with a generous scoop of white
cheese or cream cheese.

SWEET POTATO-
SUGARCANE DESSERT

Malarrabia con leche y guarapo

**PREPARATION TIME: 10 MINUTES,
PLUS 2 HOURS CHILLING TIME
(OPTIONAL)
COOKING TIME: 1 HOUR 15 MINUTES
SERVES: 4**

1¾ cups (14 f loz/415 ml) sugarcane
water (sugarcane juice)
3 cups (430 g) peeled and diced
white or yellow sweet potato
(see Note)
1 cup (8 fl oz/240 ml) whole milk
1 cinnamon stick
1 teaspoon fine sea salt

In a small pot, bring the sugarcane juice to a boil over medium heat and cook at a low boil until reduced to a light syrup, 18–20 minutes. Skim the foam from the surface and set aside.

Meanwhile, in a medium pot, combine the sweet potatoes, 1 cup (8 fl oz/240 ml) water, the milk, cinnamon stick, and salt and bring to a boil over medium-high heat. Reduce to medium-low and cook, without stirring, until the sweet potatoes are very tender, 15–20 minutes.

Drain and return the sweet potatoes to the pot. Add the sugarcane syrup, return to medium heat, and simmer for 5 minutes. Let cool, then refrigerate for at least 2 hours (optional). Remove the cinnamon stick and serve cold or at room temperature.

Note: Keep the sweet potato in a bowl of water until you're ready to cook. This keeps it from darkening. Drain before using.

SWEET POTATO PUDDING WITH COCONUT

Boniatillo con coco

In a medium pot, combine the sweet potatoes with enough cold water to cover. Bring to a low boil over medium-high heat and cook until tender, 12–15 minutes. Drain, cool completely, then mash into a puree.

In a medium pot, combine the coconut with 3 cups (24 fl oz/710 ml) water and bring to a simmer over medium heat. Reduce the heat and simmer until the coconut softens, about 20 minutes. Drain, reserving ½ cup (4 fl oz/120 ml) cooking water, and transfer to a blender. Add the reserved cooking water and blend until smooth. Set aside.

In a large pot, combine the sugar, ¾ cup (6 fl oz/180 ml) water, and the cinnamon stick. Bring to a boil over medium heat and cook until the sugar dissolves, about 5 minutes. Add the sweet potato, the coconut, and the butter and cook over low heat, stirring constantly with a wooden spoon, until the mixture thickens and clumps together slightly as you mix, 20–25 minutes. Remove from the heat and stir in the salt. Let cool slightly before serving. Sprinkle with the ground cinnamon.

PREPARATION TIME: 20 MINUTES
COOKING TIME: 1 HOUR 5 MINUTES
SERVES: 8

3 medium white or yellow sweet potatoes, peeled and sliced
2 cups (180 g) unsweetened dried shredded coconut or grated fresh coconut (see page 20)
1½ cups (330 g) raw cane sugar
1 small cinnamon stick
1 tablespoon (15 g) butter
1 teaspoon salt
½ teaspoon ground cinnamon, for garnish

TOASTED COCONUT

Coco quemado

Preheat the oven to 400°F (200°C/Gas Mark 6). Grease a 9-inch (23 cm) square baking dish with the vegetable oil. In a small pot, combine 1 cup (8 fl oz/240 ml) water and the sugar and heat gently over medium heat until the sugar has dissolved completely. Bring to a boil and cook to make a simple sugar syrup, about 5 minutes. Remove from the heat and cool for 10 minutes.

In a medium pot, combine the grated coconut, egg yolks, cinnamon, wine, and simple syrup and stir. Bring to a simmer over medum heat and cook until the liquid in the bottom of the pan has been absorbed, about 10 minutes. Pour the mixture into the prepared pan and bake until golden brown on top and around the edges, 15–20 minutes. Cool, then cut into squares.

PREPARATION TIME: 15 MINUTES
COOKING TIME: 20 MINUTES
SERVES: 6

1 tablespoon vegetable oil
2 cups (400 g) sugar
4½ packed cups (1 lb/450 g) grated fresh coconut, left to air-dry for 1 hour before using
3 egg yolks, beaten
½ teaspoon ground cinnamon
2 tablespoons dry white wine

BREAD PUDDING
WITH PEANUT CARAMEL

Pudín con salsa de maní

PREPARATION TIME: 30 MINUTES
COOKING TIME: 1 HOUR
SERVES: 12

★

1 soft baguette (5 oz/150 g), crusts
removed and torn into pieces
2 cups (16 fl oz/480 ml) whole milk
1 cup (200 g) plus 6 tablespoons
(80 g) sugar
4 eggs, whisked
½ teaspoon salt
2 tablespoons (30 g) butter,
very soft
2 tablespoons dry white wine
½ teaspoon vanilla extract
Heaping ½ teaspoon ground
cinnamon
1 cup (140 g) unsalted roasted
peanuts

Pudding is considered a typical Cuban dessert. Because it is both delicious and affordable, it is very common in Cuban homes. Bread pudding can be made with coconut, glazed fruits, coffee, or corn, while other recipes replace the bread with ground or grated yuca (cassava).

In an 8 inch (20 in) round cake pan or baking dish (preferably one that closes hermetically; see Note), stir together 6 tablespoons of the sugar and 1 tablespoon cold water to evenly moisten. Bring to a boil over high heat and cook the sugar syrup until a light-amber caramel forms, 3–4 minutes. Swirl from side to side to coat the bottom with the caramelized sugar. Set aside to cool to room temperature.

In a blender, combine the bread, milk, ½ cup (100 g) of the sugar, the eggs, salt, butter, wine, vanilla, cinnamon, and ½ cup (70 g) of the peanuts and blend until smooth and thick. Transfer to the cake pan with the caramel and cover tightly. It is very important to cover the pan tightly; if you do not have a pan that closes hermetically, cover tightly with foil, wax paper, or a plastic bag and put a rubber band around the pan.

Transfer the pan to a pot wide enough to hold the cake pan and pour in 3 cups (24 fl oz/750 ml) water (the water should come halfway up the sides of the cake pan; see Note). Cover the pot tightly and bring to a simmer over low heat. Steam the pudding until just set and jiggly at the center, about 1 hour. Remove the pudding from the pot of water and let cool, then flip over onto a serving dish with a lip.

In a small pot, combine the remaining ½ cup (100 g) sugar and 1 tablespoon water and melt over medium heat. Let the sugar melt completely before it boils, then let it bubble to light golden brown, about 5–7 minutes. Remove from the heat and stir in the remaining ½ cup (70 g) peanuts. Spoon over the pudding and serve.

Notes: Pans with other measurements (including 5 inch/13 cm round pans with 5 inch/13 cm sides) are also commonly used in Cuba. Some people bake puddings in recycled cans of various measurements.

This can also be cooked in a pressure cooker with 2 cups (16 fl oz/500 ml) water in the bottom. It should take 20–25 minutes.

MILK-PEANUT CANDIES

Cremita de leche al maní

Grease an 8-inch (20 cm) square pan with butter.
In a medium pot, combine the sweetened condensed milk,
sugar, 1 cup (8 fl oz/240 ml) water, and salt and bring to
a boil over high heat. Reduce to medium heat and cook,
stirring from side to side with a wooden spoon, until the
mixture darkens to a light tan, thickens slightly so you can
see the bottom of the pot, and the bubbles become fat and
slow, 20–22 minutes. (To test if the batter is ready, as soon
as you can see the bottom of the pot, put a little ball of
the batter into a glass of cold water; if it's ready, it should
hold its form).

Remove from the heat and stir in 1 teaspoon butter, the
peanuts, and vanilla. Stir in one direction for 7–9 minutes
until the mixture thickens and turns less shiny. Transfer
to the prepared pan, smooth with a knife, and incise
1½ x 2½-inch (6 x 4 cm) rectangles on the surface with a
lightly oiled knife. Let cool completely, then cut the
cremitas into rectangles along the incised lines.

PREPARATION TIME: 20 MINUTES
COOKING TIME: 25 MINUTES
SERVES: 15

★

1 teaspoon (5 g) butter, plus more
for the pan
1 cup (8 fl oz/309 g/240 ml)
sweetened condensed milk
1 cup (200 g) sugar
¼ teaspoon salt
⅓ cup (40 g) toasted,
unsalted peanuts
¼ teaspoon vanilla extract

COCONUT PUDDING WITH FRUIT SAUCE

Pudín de coco con salsa de frutas

PREPARATION TIME: 15 MINUTES,
PLUS CHILLING TIME
COOKING TIME: 1 HOUR 20 MINUTES
SERVES: 6

8 tablespoons (100 g) sugar
1 cup (8 fl oz/240 ml) whole milk
½ cup (130 g) Coconut Dessert
(page 339)
2 cups (300 g) dried breadcrumbs
1 tablespoon (15 g) butter
2 eggs
½ teaspoon salt
¼ teaspoon ground cinnamon

For the fruit sauce:
4 tablespoons sugar
1 cup (160 g) diced seasonal fruits,
such as guava, papaya, mango,
pineapple, and so on

In an 8 inch (20 in) round cake pan or baking dish (preferably one that closes hermetically; see Note), stir together 6 tablespoons of the sugar and 1 tablespoon cold water to evenly moisten. Bring to a boil over high heat and cook the sugar syrup until a light-amber caramel forms, 3–4 minutes. Swirl from side to side to coat the bottom with the caramelized sugar. Set aside to cool to room temperature.

In a blender, combine the milk, coconut dessert, breadcrumbs, butter, eggs, the remaining 2 tablespoons sugar, salt, and cinnamon and blend until smooth and thick. Transfer to the cake pan with the caramel and cover tightly. It is very important to cover the pan tightly; if you do not have a pan that closes hermetically, cover tightly with foil, wax paper, or a plastic bag and put a rubber band around the pan.

Transfer the pan to a pot wide enough to hold the cake pan and pour in 3 cups (24 fl oz/750 ml) water (the water should come halfway up the sides of the cake pan; see Note). Cover the pot tightly and bring to a simmer over low heat. Steam the pudding until just set and jiggly at the center, about 1 hour. Remove the pudding from the pot of water and let cool, then flip over onto a serving dish with a lip.

To make the fruit sauce: In a small pot, mix the sugar, 3 tablespoons water, and the diced fruit and cook over medium heat until the fruits are glazed, about 15 minutes.

Serve the pudding cold with the fruit sauce on top.

Notes: Pans with other measurements (including 5 inch/13 cm round pans with 5 inch/13 cm sides) are also commonly used in Cuba. Some people bake puddings in recycled cans of various measurements.

This can also be cooked in a pressure cooker with 2 cups (16 fl oz/500 ml) water in the bottom. It should take 20 minutes.

VANILLA-CARAMEL CUSTARD

Natilla de vainilla decorada con caramelo

PREPARATION TIME: 25 MINUTES
COOKING TIME: 15 MINUTES
SERVES: 8

★

For the custard:
4¼ cups (34 fl oz/1 liter)
whole milk
½ cup (100 g) sugar
2 teaspoons vanilla extract
½ teaspoon salt
6 tablespoons cornstarch
(cornflour)

For the caramel:
1 cup (200 g) sugar

To make the custard: In a pot, stir together 3¼ cups (26 fl oz/ 750 ml) of the milk, the sugar, vanilla, and salt. In a bowl, dissolve the cornstarch (cornflour) in the remaining 1 cup (8 fl oz/240 ml) milk.

Place the pot over medium heat and bring to a boil. Add the cornstarch mixture and stir vigorously with a spatula or wooden spoon to avoid lumps and keep it from sticking. When the custard starts to bubble, remove from the heat. Serve in a large dessert bowl while hot.

To make the caramel: In a small heavy-bottomed pot, combine the sugar and 3 tablespoons water. Heat over medium heat until it turns golden brown, about 10 minutes. Wait until the caramel stops foaming before decorating the custard.

Drizzle the caramel over the custard, creating the design of your choice just before serving.

Note: You can also make small shapes with the caramel. Use a spoon to drizzle the hot caramel on lightly greased parchment paper. When they harden, separate them from the paper and place gently on top of the custard.

SWEET CHEESE

Quesito dulce

PREPARATION TIME: 15 MINUTES,
PLUS 3 HOURS CHILLING TIME
COOKING TIME: 50 MINUTES
SERVES: 8

6 tablespoons (80 g) sugar
1 can (14 oz/396 g) sweetened
condensed milk
1 teaspoon salt
4-5 tablespoons white vinegar

This is a very popular recipe in Cuban homes, due to its excellent combination of flavors.

★

In an 8 inch (20 cm) round cake pan or baking dish (preferably one that closes hermetically; see Note), stir together the sugar and 1 tablespoon cold water to evenly moisten. Bring to a boil over high heat and cook the sugar syrup until a light-amber caramel forms, 3-4 minutes. Swirl from side to side to coat the bottom with the caramelized sugar. Set aside to cool to room temperature.

In a medium bowl, combine the sweetened condensed milk, salt, and vinegar. Pour the batter into the cake pan with the caramel and cover the pan tightly. It is very important to cover the pan tightly; if you do not have a pan that closes hermetically, cover tightly with foil, wax paper, or a plastic bag and put a rubber band around the pan.

Transfer the pan to a pot wide enough to hold the cake pan with room on the sides and pour 1½ inches (4 cm) water (the water should come halfway up the sides of the cake pan). Cover the pot tightly and bring to a simmer over low heat. Steam the flan until set and just barely jiggly at the center, 50 minutes. Remove the flan from the pot of water and let cool. Then refrigerate for at least 3 hours or overnight until well chilled.

To unmold, invert a large serving plate ontop, then flip the pan and the plate together. Lift the cake pan away and serve.

Note: Pans with other measurements (including 5 inch/13 cm round pans with 5 inch/13 cm sides) are also commonly used in Cuba. Some people bake flans in recycled cans of various measurements.

TWO-TONE PUDDING

Natilla a dos tonos

In each of two small bowls, whisk together ½ cup (4 fl oz/ 120 ml) milk and 3 tablespoons cornstarch (cornflour) to dissolve.

In a medium pot, combine 1½ cups (12 fl oz/355 ml) of the milk, ¼ cup (50 g) of the sugar, ½ teaspoon of the salt, and the cocoa powder and bring to a boil over medium heat, about 5 minutes. Add one bowl of cornstarch mixture to the pot and cook, stirring vigorously with a whisk to avoid lumps or sticking to the bottom, until the pudding begins to bubble, about 1 minute. Remove from the heat, cover the surface with plastic wrap, and set aside.

In another medium pot, combine the remaining 1½ cups (12 fl oz/355 ml) milk, the remaining ¼ cup (50 g) sugar, remaining ½ teaspoon salt, and the vanilla and bring to a boil over medium heat. Add the remaining bowl of cornstarch mixture and cook, stirring vigorously with a whisk to avoid lumps or sticking to the bottom, until the custard begins to bubble, about 1 minute. Remove from the flame.

Pour ¼ cup (60 ml) of the chocolate pudding into one side of each of 8 dessert bowls while simultaneously pouring ¼ cup (60 ml) of the vanilla pudding into the other side of the dessert bowls so that the puddings meet in the middle. Cover with plastic wrap to touch the surface and let cool completely before serving.

PREPARATION TIME: 25 MINUTES
COOKING TIME: 15 MINUTES
SERVES: 8

4 cups (32 fl oz/950 ml) whole milk
6 tablespoons cornstarch (cornflour)
½ cup (100 g) sugar
1 teaspoon salt
2 tablespoons (30 g) cocoa powder
1 teaspoon vanilla extract

CHOCOLATE ALMOND CAKE

Negro en camisa

PREPARATION TIME: 40 MINUTES
COOKING TIME: 45 MINUTES
SERVES: 8

7 tablespoons plus 2 teaspoons
(115 g) butter, plus more for the
cake pan
1 dark chocolate bar (4 oz/115 g),
grated
⅔ cup (115 g) sugar
½ cup (115 g) toasted, crushed
almonds or peanuts,
4 eggs, separated
Egg Sauce (page 323)

The origin of this dessert is controversial. Some say it is from Venezuela, while others argue that it is French or Italian, since chocolate was not used in Venezuelan recipes until the twentieth century. It is found in old Cuban cookbooks and is considered a classic dessert. The direct translation of the title "A Black Guy in a Shirt" is outdated for modern times.

★

Preheat the oven to 375°F (190°C/Gas Mark 5). Grease a 6-inch (15 cm) round 3½ inch (9 cm) deep cake pan with butter.

In a large bowl, stir together the chocolate, butter, sugar, almonds, and egg yolks. In a separate bowl, with an electric mixer, beat the egg whites until they form peaks. Gently fold the whites into the chocolate/almond mixture. Scrape the batter into the cake pan and cover the pan tightly. It is very important to cover the pan tightly; if you do not have a pan that closes hermetically, cover tightly with foil, wax paper, or a plastic bag. Tie a rubber band around the pan.

Transfer the pan to a pot wide enough to hold the cake pan with room on the sides and pour hot water to come halfway up the sides of the cake pan. Bake until a toothpick inserted in the center comes out dry, about 45 minutes. Remove and let cool. Invert carefully and cool to room temperature.

Serve at room temperature with enough warm egg sauce on top to cover.

IMPOSSIBLE DESSERT

Dulce imposible

PREPARATION TIME: 30 MINUTES,
PLUS 1 HOUR RESTING TIME
AND 2 HOURS CHILLING TIME
COOKING TIME: 55 MINUTES
SERVES: 12

★

For the caramel:
¾ cup (150 g) sugar

For the flan:
3 eggs
4 tablespoons (40 g) whole milk
powder
¾ cup (150 g) sugar
1 teaspoon vanilla extract
¼ teaspoon salt
1 cup (8 fl oz/240 ml) whole milk

For the cake batter:
3 eggs
¾ cup (150 g) sugar
¼ teaspoon salt
1 teaspoon vanilla extract
1 cup (135 g) all-purpose (plain)
flour

This dessert has become very popular in recent years because the combination of cake and flan is well-loved by Cuban people. It is "impossible" because it is challenging to bake the cake on top of the flan without the batters mixing together. It can be served with a simple syrup (page 323) drizzled over the serving plate before flipping the cake and flan if desired.

★

Caramelize the sugar: In a 6-inch (15 cm) round 3½-inch (9 cm) deep pan, combine the sugar and 2 tablespoons water and cook very gently over low heat, without stirring, until the sugar is completely dissolved. Once the sugar has dissolved, increase the heat to medium and boil until a dark caramel, about 9 minutes. As it boils, dip a clean pastry brush into cold water and wash down the sides of the pan a few times. Carefully tilt the pan to spread the hot caramel over the bottom and lower part of the sides of the pan, then set aside to cool.

Make the flan: In a blender, combine the eggs, powdered milk, sugar, vanilla, salt, and liquid milk and blend until smooth. Strain into a medium bowl and set the batter aside for 1 hour.

Meanwhile, make the cake batter: In a large bowl, with an electric mixer, beat together the eggs and sugar until doubled in volume, about 10 minutes. Stir in the salt and vanilla. With a wooden spoon, gradually and gently mix in the flour until smooth. (The cake batter should be thick and creamy so that it floats over the flan mixture while being cooked.)

Pour the flan mixture into the caramel-lined pan, then pour the cake batter on top and cover the pan tightly. It is very important to cover the pan tightly; if you do not have a pan that closes hermetically, cover tightly with foil, wax paper, or a plastic bag and tie a rubber band around the pan.

Transfer the pan to a pressure cooker. Pour 2 cups (16 fl oz/ 475 ml) water into the pressure cooker. Lock the lid and bring to pressure over medium heat. Cook at pressure until a toothpick inserted into the center comes out dry, about 45 minutes. Quick-release the pressure. Let cool for 2 hours, then carefully invert onto a serving dish and serve.

YUCA FLAN CAKE

Tocinillo de yuca

Ileana Aguilar Aguilera from Artemisa, in Western Cuba, created this original recipe (half flan, half yuca [cassava] cake). It is not a traditional recipe, but uses typical ingredients.

In a 6-inch (15 cm) round 3½-inch (9 cm) deep pan, combine ½ cup (100 g) of the sugar and 2 tablespoons water and cook very gently over low heat, without stirring, until the sugar is completely dissolved. Once the sugar has dissolved, increase the heat to medium and boil until a dark caramel, about 5 minutes. As it boils, dip a clean pastry brush into cold water and wash down the sides of the pan a few times. Carefully tilt the pan to spread the hot caramel over the bottom and sides of the pan, then set aside to cool.

Wrap the yuca (cassava) in a clean tea towel and squeeze until the yuca is still moist, but some of the liquid has been drained. Transfer the yuca to a large bowl. Add the egg yolks, remaining 1 cup (200 g) sugar, the salt, vanilla, and bitter orange juice and mix well with a spoon.

In a medium bowl, with an electric mixer, beat the egg whites on high speed until thick and fluffy, but not dry, about 1 minute. Using a spatula, gently fold the egg whites into the yuca mixture until evenly distributed. Transfer to the pan with the caramelized sugar and cover tightly with foil. Transfer to a large pressure cooker with 2 cups (16 fl oz/ 500 ml) of water. Lock the lid and bring to pressure over medium heat. Cook at pressure until a toothpick inserted in the center comes out dry , about 45 minutes. Quick-release the pressure. Remove the pan and transfer to a large bowl with room temperature water, changing the water every 15 minutes until the *tocinillo de yuca* has cooled down significantly. Pour the simple syrup ontop (if using) and refrigerate for 4–5 hours. Invert the pan onto a plate just before serving.

PREPARATION TIME: 30 MINUTES, PLUS 5 HOURS CHILLING TIME
COOKING TIME: 45 MINUTES
SERVES: 10

★

1½ cup (300 g) sugar
2 medium fresh yuca (cassava) roots (12 oz/345 g total), peeled and grated
3 eggs, separated
¼ teaspoon salt
2 teaspoons vanilla extract
¼ cup (2 fl oz/60 ml) bitter orange juice (see page 18)
1 cup (8 fl oz/240 ml) Simple Syrup (page 323) or 3–4 tablespoons honey (optional)

WHITE BEAN DESSERT

Dulce de frijoles blancos

PREPARATION TIME: 15 MINUTES,
PLUS 6 HOURS BEAN SOAKING
TIME AND 2 HOURS CHILLING TIME
COOKING TIME: 1 HOUR 20 MINUTES
SERVES: 10

★

1 cup (220 g) dried white beans,
rinsed and soaked in water to
cover for 6 hours
1 large (1 lb/460 g) white or yellow
sweet potato, peeled and diced
1 can (14 oz/396 g) sweetened
condensed milk
⅛ teaspoon salt
1 cinnamon stick
2 tablespoons sugar
½ teaspoon vanilla extract

In the Eastern provinces, where this recipe is most common, coconut milk is also used. This dessert was traditionally shared among family and neighbors on Good Friday and is typically serveed with salted crackers.

In a pressure cooker (see Note), combine the beans 5 cups (40 fl oz/1.2 liters) water. Lock the lid and bring to pressure over medium heat. Cook at pressure until softened, about 50 minutes. Quick-release the pressure. Reserving 2 cups (16 fl oz/475 ml) of the cooking water, drain the beans. Transfer the beans and cooking water to a blender (see Note) and blend until smooth. Push the beans through a sieve.

Pour the beans into a heavy-bottomed pot. Add the sweet potato, sweetened condensed milk, salt, cinnamon, and sugar. Cover and cook over medium-low heat until the sweet potatoes have softened, about 30 minutes, stirring every 5 minutes so they don't stick to the bottom. When a creamy texture is achieved, add the vanilla. Set aside to cool, then refrigerate for 2 hours (optional). Serve hot or cold.

Notes: If you don't have a pressure cooker, cook the beans for 1 hour in a large pot with 3 cups (26 fl oz/750 ml) water, then follow the instructions as directed.

Sometimes the beans are added whole.

YUCA-RUM DELIGHT

Matahambre

Place the grated yuca (cassava) in a tea towel and squeeze well until most of the water is released. Spread out on a large sheet pan and let dry in the sun for 6 hours.

Sift the yuca in a sieve over a bowl to get a very fine flour, known as *catibía*. Measure out 1 cup (200 g) of the *catibía* and transfer to another bowl. Add the sugar and set aside. In a small pot, combine the shortening and 3 tablespoons water and melt over medium heat. Remove from the heat and set aside.

In a medium bowl, mix together the egg yolks, melted butter, rum, anise liqueur, cinnamon, salt, and anise seeds and stir well. Stir in the *catibía* mixture.

In another medium bowl, with an electric mixer, beat the egg whites on high speed until they start to form peaks, 1–2 minutes. Gently fold in the *catibía* mixture with a spatula. Add the melted shortening and mix.

Line the bottom of a large pot with a round of parchment paper. Pour the batter into the pot, sprinkle with the sesame seeds, and cook, covered, over low heat until a toothpick inserted in the center comes out dry, about 30 minutes. Remove and let cool until room temperature before inverting out of the pot.

**PREPARATION TIME: 40 MINUTES,
PLUS 6 HOURS DRYING TIME
COOKING TIME: 40 MINUTES
SERVES: 8**

2 large yuca (cassava) roots
(1 lb 5 oz/600 g total),
very finely grated
¾ cup (145 g) superfine (caster)
sugar
⅓ cup (60 g) vegetable shortening
4 egg yolks, lightly beaten
2 tablespoons (30 g) butter,
melted and cooled
1 tablespoon rum
½ tablespoon anise liqueur
¼ teaspoon ground cinnamon
¼ teaspoon salt
¼ teaspoon anise seeds, crushed
2 egg whites
2 tablespoons sesame seeds

SESAME FRENCH TOAST

Torrejas al ajonjolí

PREPARATION TIME: 25 MINUTES
COOKING TIME: 25 MINUTES
SERVES: 8

★

4 tablespoons granulated sugar
2 cinnamon sticks
2 cups (16 fl oz/500 ml) whole milk
2 tablespoons dry white wine
3 eggs, whisked
¼ teaspoon salt
1 tablespoon raw cane sugar
3 tablespoons sesame seeds, toasted
8 oz (230 g) soft baguette, cut into 8 slices
Vegetable oil, for frying

In a small pot, combine the granulated sugar, cinnamon, and 3 tablespoons water and bring to a simmer over medium heat until the sugar is dissolved, about 5 minutes. Remove the cinnamon sticks and set the simple syrup aside.

In a large bowl, combine the milk, ½ cup (4 fl oz/125 ml) water, the wine, eggs, salt, raw sugar, and sesame seeds. Dip the bread slices in the milk mixture and let the excess run off.

In a medium frying pan, heat 1 cup (8 fl oz/240 ml) oil over medium heat until very hot. Add the *torrejas* and fry until browned, about 1 minute on each side. Serve drizzled with the simple syrup.

Notes: Honey can be used instead of the simple syrup. Traditionally, the torrejas are first dipped in the milk mixture and then dipped in the eggs.

COCONUT MILK FRENCH TOAST

Torrejas con leche de coco

PREPARATION TIME: 15 MINUTES
COOKING TIME: 20 MINUTES
SERVES: 8

★

1 cup (8 fl oz/240 ml) coconut milk, store-bought or homemade (see Note)
½ cup (110 g) raw cane sugar
¼ teaspoon ground cinnamon
¼ teaspoon salt
2 tablespoons dry white wine
8 slices (½ inch/1.25 cm thick) white bread (about 7⅜ oz/211 g)
4 eggs, whisked
3 tablespoons vegetable oil, for frying
Honey or sugarcane syrup, for serving

In a medium pot, combine the coconut milk, raw sugar, cinnamon, and salt and heat over medium heat, whisking until the sugar dissolves, 2–3 minutes. Remove from the heat and let cool to room temperature. Transfer to a wide, shallow bowl and add the wine. One at a time, dip both sides of the bread slices in the coconut milk mixture, then in the eggs.

In a large nonstick frying pan, heat 1 tablespoon of the oil over medium-high heat until very hot. Add the *torrejas* and fry until browned, 1 minute on each side. Serve drizzled with sugarcane syrup or honey.

Note: To make coconut milk, blend 1 cup (75 g) grated fresh coconut with 1 cup (8 fl oz/240 ml) hot water in a blender. Strain the mixture through a sieve lined with cheesecloth, then squeeze the cheesecloth hard to get out as much coconut milk as possible.

PEANUT CANDIES

Bombones de maní

PREPARATION TIME: 1 HOUR 15 MINUTES
COOKING TIME: 10 MINUTES
MAKES: 16 CANDIES

★

1½ cups (250 g) skin-on roasted peanuts
⅔ cup (125 g) sugar

Grind the peanuts and sugar in a meat grinder on the smallest setting two times. Transfer half of the peanut mixture to a bowl. Add a little water (see Note), just enough to moisten, and mix with your hands. Add the remaining peanut mixture and continue carefully adding water so that the mixture stays compact and does not loosen.

Roll the mixture into 16 small balls and set them aside to dry on parchment paper.

Note: The process of wetting the ground peanuts is done with very little water, which should be added drop by drop. A small portion of the dry mixture should be set aside to adjust the texture throughout the process of moistening it.

CHOCOLATE ROLL

Salchichón de chocolate

PREPARATION TIME: 30 MINUTES, PLUS 6 HOURS CHILLING TIME
SERVES: 10

★

7 oz (200 g) dark chocolate, grated
1 cup (230 g) blanched almonds or peanuts, finely ground
6 tablespoons (130 g) sweetened condensed milk
1 tablespoon honey

This recipe was common among Cuban housewives in the 1950s, when desserts were commonly made in Cuban homes. At this time, new kitchen technologies were introduced and cooking shows became popular on television. After this period, in the 1960s, many women began working and some of the previously popular dessert recipes became less common.

In a large bowl, combine the chocolate, almonds, sweetened condensed milk, and honey and mix well. Transfer the mixture to a sheet of parchment paper and shape into 1 thick roll, then wrap the parchment paper around the chocolate, rolling and shaping to create a smooth sausage. Twist the ends. Refrigerate for 6 hours, then serve sliced.

Note: The chocolate bar can be substituted with cocoa powder.

TOASTED MERINGUES

Merenguitos dorados

Serve the *merenguitos* on their own or as an accompaniment for cakes or custards.

In a large bowl, beat the egg whites vigorously with a fork (or an electric mixer) until soft peaks form, about 3 minutes. Add 1 tablespoon of the sugar and continue beating until thick, shiny stiff peaks form. Keep beating in the sugar until all of the sugar is added. Dip the fork into the meringue and pull it out with about 1 heaping tablespoon meringue. Carefully hold the fork with the meringue over a medium flame, rotating it until a hardened layer forms on the outside, about 15 seconds. Remove the meringue from the fork by pushing it away with your finger or another fork and transfer to a dessert plate. Repeat until all of the meringue mixture is used.

PREPARATION TIME: 20 MINUTES
COOKING TIME: 10 MINUTES
MAKES: 20 MERINGUES

4 egg whites
4 tablespoons sugar

YOGURT CAKE

Panetela de yogur

Preheat the oven to 350°F (180°C/Gas Mark 4). Grease a 9-inch (23 cm) springform pan with oil, then line the bottom with a round of parchment paper.

In a large bowl, sift the flour and baking soda (bicarbonate). Add the raw sugar, salt, and lime zest and mix well.

In a medium bowl, combine the eggs, yogurt, 4 tablespoons oil, and the lime juice and gently stir. Add the yogurt mixture to the flour mixture and gently mix with a wooden spoon until smooth.

Transfer the batter to the prepared pan and bake until golden and risen and a toothpick inserted in the center comes out clean, about 30 minutes. Remove and let cool. Invert carefully and let cool to room temperature.

Notes: Any kind of yogurt can be used, including cow's milk, soy, flavored, and so on.

This cake can be decorated with frosting, custard, or glazed fruits.

PREPARATION TIME: 15 MINUTES
COOKING TIME: 30 MINUTES
SERVES: 12

4 tablespoons vegetable oil, plus more for the pan
1½ cups plus 2 tablespoons (240 g) all-purpose (plain) flour
1 teaspoon baking soda (bicarbonate of soda)
1 cup plus 1 tablespoon (220 g) raw cane sugar
¼ teaspoon salt
1 tablespoon grated lime zest
4 eggs, whisked
½ cup (125 g) whole-milk yogurt
4 tablespoons lime juice

SPRING DREAM CAKE

Panetela sueño de primavera

1⅔ cups (225 g) all-purpose (plain)
flour
1 teaspoon baking powder
2 tablespoons cornstarch
(cornflour)
4 egg yolks
3 egg whites
⅛ teaspoon salt
⅔ cup (125 g) sugar
⅓ cup (2½ fl oz/80 ml) whole milk
1 tablespoon vegetable oil, for
greasing
¾ cup (180 g) Glazed Green
Papaya in Simple Syrup (see Note)
¾ cup (180 g) Glazed Ripe Papaya
in Simple Syrup (see Note)
¾ cup (180 g) Glazed Pineapple
in Simple Syrup (see Note)
¾ cup (180 g) Coconut Dessert
(page 339)
1 cup (240 g) Guava Marmalade
(page 336)

This recipe won prizes in cooking competitions for the elderly hosted by the City Historian's Office and the University of Havana.

In a bowl, sift together the flour, baking powder, and cornstarch (cornflour) and set aside.

In a bowl, with an electric mixer, beat the egg yolks, egg whites, and salt and mix while gradually adding the sugar. Add the milk while continuing to mix. Gently stir in the flour mixture.

Preheat the oven to 350°F (180°C/Gas Mark 4). Grease a 10-inch (25 cm) round baking dish.

Pour the batter into the baking dish and bake until a toothpick inserted into the center comes out dry, about 25 minutes. Remove and let cool. Invert carefully and cool to room temperature.

Halve the cake horizontally into two layers. Brush some of the fruit syrup (to taste) over each layer. Spread two-thirds of the guava marmalade on one layer and place the other layer on top.

Spread the top and the sides of the cake with the rest of the guava marmalade. Make 3 vertical lines on the top of the cake with a spatula and another 3 lines at a 90-degree angle so they look like a grid. Mark a circle in the center with a glass or small bowl. Arrange the glazed fruits and coconut dessert separately in each section so that the colors contrast. Pour the leftover guava marmalade in the circle in the center. Serve.

Note: To make Glazed Fruits in Simple Syrup, cut 5 oz (150 g) ripe papaya, green papaya, or pineapple into ⅛-inch (4 mm) dice. In a small pan, combine the diced ripe papaya, green papaya, or pineapple, ½ cup (100 g) sugar, and ¼ cup (2 fl oz/60 ml) water. Cook over low heat until softened, 12 minutes for the green papaya and pineapple and 6 minutes for the ripe papaya. Remove and drain, reserving the syrup. Set aside the fruit and the syrup in separate containers.

YUCA-COCONUT GIFT

Tortilla de regalo

This is a very traditional dessert in Cuba, but is not commonly baked these days because of its complex preparation.

Wrap the yuca (cassava) in a tea towel and squeeze to remove most of the liquid. Transfer to a large pot and add the coconut milk, 2 cups (16 fl oz/475 ml) water, the sugar, cinnamon, and salt. Cook over medium heat, stirring constantly, until creamy, about 30 minutes.

Meanwhile, preheat the oven to 350°F (180°C/Gas Mark 4). Generously grease an 11-inch (28 cm) round cake pan with butter and set aside.

Whisk a little of the coconut milk mixture into the eggs to warm them, then transfer to the pot, stirring to avoid clumping. Remove the cinnamon stick, then add the lime zest, nutmeg, and 1 tablespoon (15 g) butter. Cook over low heat, stirring constantly, for 5 minutes. Remove from the heat and stir in the vanilla. Scrape the batter into the prepared cake pan and spread evenly with the back of a spoon. Sprinkle evenly with the sesame seeds and bake until browned, 45 minutes. Let cool, then cut into wedges.

Note: To make coconut milk, blend 1 lb (450 g) grated fresh coconut with 1 cup (8 fl oz/ 240 ml) hot water in a blender. Strain the mixture through a sieve lined with cheesecloth, then squeeze the cheesecloth hard to get out as much coconut milk as possible.

PREPARATION TIME: 1 HOUR 30 MINUTES
COOKING TIME: 1 HOUR 25 MINUTES
SERVES: 15–18

2 large yuca (cassava) roots (3 lb/ 1.38 kg total), peeled and grated
1 cup (8 fl oz/240 ml) coconut milk, store-bought or homemade (see Note)
3½ cups (700g) sugar
1 cinnamon stick
1 teaspoon salt
1 tablespoon (15 g) butter, plus more for the pan
2 eggs, lightly beaten
1 teaspoon grated lime zest
¼ teaspoon grated nutmeg
1 teaspoon vanilla extract
¾ cup (95 g) toasted sesame seeds

CAKE FRITTERS

Frituras con sabor a panetela

This dessert became popular in Havana during the Special Period because of its affordable ingredients. It is recommended to accompany teas.

Pour 2 inches (5 cm) oil into a large saucepan and heat the oil over high heat until very hot, about 356°F (180°C). Meanwhile, in a large bowl, combine the flour, sugar, baking powder, cinnamon, and salt. Make a well in the middle, then pour in the egg and milk and mix until thick.

Carefully drop tablespoons of the dough into the oil and fry until dark golden and puffed, 3–4 minutes. Remove with a slotted spoon and transfer to a plate lined with paper towels to absorb excess oil. Roll in more sugar or drench in syrup and serve.

PREPARATION TIME: 15 MINUTES
COOKING TIME: 20 MINUTES
SERVES: 8–10

Vegetable oil, for deep-frying
1 cup plus 2 tablespoon (160 g) all-purpose (plain) flour
3 tablespoons sugar
1 teaspoon baking powder
1 teaspoon ground cinnamon
Pinch of salt
1 egg, whisked
6 tablespoons milk
Sugar or Simple Syrup (page 323), for serving

FROSTED CAKE

Panetela con merengue y yema

**PREPARATION TIME: 30 MINUTES,
PLUS 6 HOURS COOLING TIME
COOKING TIME: 10 MINUTES
SERVES: 12**

1 plain round cake (9 oz/265 g) or
Spring Dream Cake (page 362)
¾ cup (6 fl oz/180 ml) Moscatel
wine (see Note)
6 eggs, separated
6 tablespoons powdered (icing)
sugar (see Note)
½ cup (100 g) plus 2 tablespoons
granulated sugar
½ teaspoon vanilla extract
1 tablespoon lime juice
1 teaspoon finely grated lime zest
Sprinkles or dried fruit (optional)

Preheat the oven to 375°F (190°C/Gas Mark 4).

Arrange the cake on a rimmed baking sheet and cut it into
12 wedges, while maintaining its shape. Using a skewer,
poke holes all over the cake, then slowly spoon the wine
over it little by little, until it has all been absorbed.

In a large bowl, with an electric mixer, beat the egg yolks
and powdered (icing) sugar until thick and foamy, about
5 minutes. Spread over the cake.

In a large bowl, with an electric mixer, beat the egg whites
until soft peaks form. Add the granulated sugar in three
additions, bringing the mixture to stiff peaks each time,
until a thick, fluffy meringue frosting forms. Add the vanilla,
lime juice, and lime zest, and beat again briefly. Using a
frosting spatula (palette knife), cover the cake with the
frosting, creating your preferred shape or form (see Note).
Bake until the frosting firms, is golden, and slightly burnt,
about 3–5 minutes. Decorate with sprinkles or dried fruits
(optional) and serve.

Notes: Moscatel wine is a sweet wine made in Cuba from raisins.

*It is difficult to find powdered (icing) sugar in Cuba, so most
home cooks just make their own in a blender by processing
regular granulated sugar to a fine powder.*

*In Cuba, cakes are abundantly frosted. The frosting can be
up to 1 inch (2.5 cm) high and it is common to create one or
several peaks.*

IMPERIAL PUDDING

Pudín imperial

Preheat the oven to 350°F (180°C/Gas Mark 4). Generously grease a 9-inch (23 cm) springform pan with butter, sprinkle with 1 tablespoon of the sugar, and spread the pieces of cake across the dish.

In a large bowl, combine the melted butter, eggs, milk, cinnamon, nutmeg, lime zest, and remaining 2 tablespoons sugar and mix well. Pour over the cake and let soak. Bake until puffed and golden and a toothpick inserted into the center of the pudding comes out dry, 1 hour. Let cool. Garnish with glazed fruits.

PREPARATION TIME: 15 MINUTES
COOKING TIME: 1 HOUR
SERVES: 8

2 tablespoons (30 g) butter, melted, plus more for the pan
3 tablespoons sugar
1 plain round cake (9 oz/265 g) or Spring Dream Cake (page 362), torn into pieces
4 eggs, whisked
3 cups (24 fl oz/750 ml) whole milk
Generous pinch of ground cinnamon
Generous pinch of nutmeg
1 teaspoon finely grated lime zest
Glazed Fruits in Simple Syrup (page 362), for serving

IMPERIAL DRUNK SOUP

Sopa borracha imperial

Put the cake pieces into a large glass bowl. In a medium bowl, beat 6 of the egg yolks together with the wine. Pour this over the cake and let sit until it is soaked in.

In a small pot, combine the sugar, cinnamon stick, and 2 cups water (16 fl oz/500 ml) and bring to a boil over high heat. Cook for 5 minutes. Set aside.

In a small bowl, beat the remaining 6 egg yolks. Bring the simple syrup back to a boil. Working with 2 or 3 pieces of cake at a time, dip them into the egg yolks using tongs and then drop them into the boiling syrup, turning once, until they harden, about 3 seconds. As you work, transfer them to a serving dish.

Notes: Sherry can be used instead of the wine.

Sprinkles can be added on top for decoration.

PREPARATION TIME: 40 MINUTES
COOKING TIME: 30 MINUTES
SERVES: 8

1 plain round cake (9 oz/265 g) or Spring Dream Cake (page 362), hand-torn into ¾ inch (1 cm) pieces
12 egg yolks
1 cup (8 lf oz/240 ml) Moscatel wine (see Note)
2½ cups (500 g) sugar
1 cinnamon stick

MARRIED CAKE

Sopa de casados

**PREPARATION TIME: 10 MINUTES,
PLUS CHILLING TIME
COOKING TIME: 25 MINUTES
SERVES: 15**

1 plain round cake (9 oz/265 g) or
Spring Dream Cake (page 362),
broken into pieces
3 eggs, separated
3 tablespoons dry white wine
2 cups (16 fl oz/475 ml) thick
simple syrup (see Note)
3 cups (24 fl oz/710 ml) whole milk
1 teaspoon ground cinnamon
Raisins, mint sprigs, or cinnamon
stick, for garnish

This recipe is from the beginning of the twentieth century, if not before, and shows a notable Spanish culinary influence.

★

Place the cake pieces in a medium pot. In a bowl, beat the egg whites until frothy, add the yolks, and continue beating. Add the wine, simple syrup, milk, and cinnamon. Beat to mix all the ingredients. Pour this mixture over the cake pieces.

Place over low heat and slowly bring to a boil, stirring occasionally with a wooden spoon, about 25 minutes. Transfer to a serving dish and let cool. Then refrigerate until well chilled. Serve cold and garnish with raisins, mint springs, or cinnamon sticks.

Note: The thick simple syrup is made the same way as regular simple syrup (page 323), but is cooked for an additional 7 minutes after it comes to a boil.

CHOCOLATE TRUFFLES

Trufas de chocolate

**PREPARATION TIME: 35 MINUTES,
PLUS 2 HOURS 30 MINUTES
CHILLING AND FIRMING TIME
MAKES: 26 TRUFFLES**

Vegetable oil, for greasing
4¼ oz (120 g) semisweet
chocolate, broken into pieces
20 chocolate cookies (5 oz/145 g
total)
⅓ cup (50 g) unsalted roasted
peanuts
3 tablespoons whipping cream
1 tablespoon coffee liqueur, such
as Kahlúa
¼ cup (30 g) unsweetened cocoa
powder, sifted
¼ cup (30 g) powdered (icing)
sugar, sifted

This recipe was very popular among housewives in the 1950s.

★

Lightly grease a 10 x 6 inch (25 x 15 cm) rectangular pan with oil.

In a large bowl set over a pan of simmering water, melt the chocolate. Remove the bowl from the pan.

In a food processor, combine the cookies and peanuts and pulse until finely chopped. Transfer to the bowl with the melted chocolate, add the cream and liqueur, and mix. Pour into the prepared pan and refrigerate until firm, 1–2 hours. Set up two bowls, one with the cocoa powder and the other with the powdered (icing) sugar. Wet your hands with just a little water and roll the chocolate mixture into 26 small balls. Roll half of the balls in the cocoa and the other half in the sugar and transfer to a tray lined with parchment paper. Refrigerate until firm and set, about 30 minutes.

MAMBÍ BREAD

Pan patato

This recipe has its roots in the Haitian immigration to the Eastern side of Cuba. It is found in the twenty-second volume of the *Complete Works of José Martí y Pérez*, the Cuban national hero and was used in the nineteenth century by the Mambises (Independence fighters) during the Ten Year War. Martí wrote, "*Pan-patato*: they would grate raw sweet potato, they mixed it with pumpkin, or cassava, or another *vianda*, or grated coconut; and after would add honey, or sugar, and vegetable shortening. It was good for four or six days. This way they could take advantage of sweet potato that had gone bad."

★

Preheat the oven to 350°F (180°C/Gas Mark 4). Grease a 10½ x 3 inch (27 x 8 cm) rectangular baking dish with sides 2¾ inches (7 cm) high with the vegetable oil.

In a large bowl, combine the sweet potato, coconut, sugar, vegetable shortening, and honey and mix. Transfer to the prepared baking dish and level the surface. Bake until a toothpick inserted into the center of the bread comes out clean, 30–40 minutes. Let cool in the pan. Flip the pan over and cut the bread into slices.

PREPARATION TIME: 30 MINUTES
COOKING TIME: 40 MINUTES
SERVES: 8

1 tablespoon vegetable oil
1 heaping cup (120 g) grated white or yellow sweet potato
1 cup packed (3½ oz/100 g) finely grated fresh coconut, left to air-dry for 1 hour before using
1 cup (200 g) sugar
2 tablespoons (30 g) vegetable shortening or butter
2 tablespoons honey

TRADITIONAL DOUGHNUTS

Buñuelos tradicionales o navideños

PREPARATION TIME: 45 MINUTES
COOKING TIME: 1 HOUR 30 MINUTES
SERVES: 10

For the dough:
1 lb 2 oz (500 g) white sweet potatoes, peeled and cut into chunks
3 medium yuca (cassava) roots (2 lb/900 g total), peeled and cut into chunks
1 tablespoon vanilla extract
1 tablespoon sugar
1 teaspoon salt
1 egg, whisked
1 cup (125 g) sifted all-purpose (plain) flour

For the cinnamon syrup:
2 cups (400 g) sugar
½ teaspoon lime juice
1 cinnamon stick

For the buñuelos:
All-purpose (plain) flour, for forming
Vegetable oil, for frying

These doughnuts, traditionally prepared on Christmas, can be formed as simple balls (like doughnut holes), but they are often formed into more elaborate shapes, like figure-eights or wreaths.

★

Make the dough: In a medium pot, combine the sweet potatoes and water to cover by ¾ inch (2 cm). Cover and cook until softened, about 30 minutes. In a separte medium pot, combine the yuca (cassava) and water to cover by 2 inches (5 cm). Cook, uncovered, until soft, about 1 hour. Drain and transfer the sweet potatoes and yuca to separate containers.

In a small saucepan, combine ¼ cup (2 fl oz/60 ml) water, the vanilla, and sugar and bring to a boil over medium heat and cook for 3 minutes. Set aside.

Grind the sweet potatoes and yuca through a meat grinder, or mash them into separate purees. Measure out 1 cup (200 g) sweet potato puree and 2 cups (400 g) yuca puree and put them on a smooth, floured surface. Mix them together, adding the water/vanilla/sugar mixture and salt. Add the whisked egg and continue to knead the dough, sprinkling the flour over the dough little by little while you knead it, until it is no longer sticky.

Make the cinnamon syrup: In a pot, combine the sugar, 1 cup (8 fl oz/240 ml) water, lime juice, and cinnamon stick and bring to a boil over medium heat, then cook for 5 more minutes. Remove from the heat and strain the syrup. Set aside to cool.

Make the buñuelos: Sprinkle the work surface with flour. Divide the dough into 10 portions. Roll each portion into a ball (like a doughnut hole), or roll into a cylinder to form into a figure 8 or a traditional doughnut shape.

Pour 2 inches (5 cm) oil into a heavy-bottomed pot or deep frying pan and heat over medium heat until very hot. Working in batches, fry the buñuelos until they are golden-brown, about 5 minutes. Drain on paper towels.

Serve them on a dessert plate with the simple syrup poured over them.

CHURROS

Churros 📷

PREPARATION TIME: 30 MINUTES

COOKING TIME: 1 HOUR 30 MINUTES

SERVES: 10

★

2 cups (270 g) all-purpose (plain) flour

2 cups (16 fl oz/500 ml) whole milk

1 teaspoon salt

2 eggs

Vegetable oil, for frying

Granulated or powdered (icing) sugar, for dusting

Sift the flour. In a heavy-bottomed medium pot, combine 1 cup (8 fl oz/240 ml) water, the milk, and salt and bring to a boil over medium heat. Add the flour all at once and stir forcefully with a large wooden spoon until it forms the texture of a thick paste.

Put the dough in a stainless steel bowl to let it cool for 5 minutes. Crack 1 egg into the dough, and knead it well to incorporate it. Add the second egg and knead again.

Pour 2 inches (5 cm) oil into a deep pot and heat it over medium heat until very hot. Fill the canister of a churro press or a piping bag fitted with a large star tip with dough. Press or pipe out churros 4 inches (10 cm) long and fry until browned, about 5 minutes. Drain on paper towels. Dust with sugar and serve hot.

HOMEMADE ICE CREAM

Helado casero

PREPARATION TIME: 30 MINUTES,

PLUS 16 HOURS FREEZING TIME

COOKING TIME: 15 MINUTES

SERVES: 8

★

1 cup (8 fl oz/240 ml) evaporated milk

2 tablespoons cornstarch (cornflour)

2¼ cups (18 fl oz/540 ml) whole milk

Generous pinch of salt

¾ cup (150 g) sugar

½ teaspoon vanilla extract

Freeze the evaporated milk in the can or in an ice cube tray until solid, about 6 hours.

In a small bowl, combine the cornstarch (cornflour), ¼ cup (2 fl oz/60 ml) of the milk, and the salt.

In a small pot, warm the remaining 2 cups (16 fl oz/480 ml) milk over low heat.

In a small pan, heat the sugar over medium heat and cook, without stirring, until patches of golden caramel appear. Swirl the bubbling caramel toward the dry sugar, until any dry patches have been absorbed. When the caramel is a dark copper, carefully add the warmed milk and stir with a wooden spoon. Continue stirring over low heat until the caramel dissolves again. Add the cornstarch mixture and stir. Cook until the mixture coats the back of the spoon, 5 minutes. Remove from the heat, stir in the vanilla, and let cool.

Break the frozen evaporated milk into chunks or empty out the ice cube tray, then transfer to a blender or food processor and blend until smooth. Add the caramel mixture and blend for a few seconds to mix. Pour into a 2 inch (5 cm) deep 2-quart (2-liter) freezer container and freeze until semi-frozen, about 4 hours. Remove and stir well, using a fork or electric hand mixer to break up the ice crystals. Return to the freezer and repeat this process 2 or 3 times until smooth. Return to the freezer and freeze until firm, about 4 hours. Serve in small bowls.

GUAVA SORBET

Sorbete de guayaba

**PREPARATION TIME: 20 MINUTES,
PLUS 4 HOURS FREEZING TIME
SERVES: 6**

★

½ small white or yellow sweet
potato (5 oz/150 g), peeled and
cut into chunks
4 tablespoons sugar
4 medium guavas (10½ oz/300 g
total), unpeeled, cut into chunks
⅔ cup (5 fl oz/150 ml) whole milk
¼ teaspoon salt
Mint leaves and pieces of guava,
for garnish

In a small pot, combine the sweet potato with water to cover by ¾ inch (2 cm). Cook, covered, until softened, about 20 minutes. Drain and set aside to cool.

In small saucepan, combine the sugar and 3 tablespoons water and boil for 5 minutes to make a simple syrup. Set aside to cool.

In a blender, combine the guava, cooked sweet potato, simple syrup, milk, and salt and blend well. Strain and put into a metal pie dish to partially freeze, about 2 hours With a fork, stir the mixture to break up the ice crystals. Repeat this process 3 times every 45 minutes to add some air.

Serve in ice cream dishes, decorated with mint leaves and pieces of guava.

Note: The guava can be substituted with papaya, mango, banana, and pineapple, among other fruits.

DRINKS

Bebidas

The hot climate of Cuba makes it necessary to consume plenty of liquids to quench one's thirst. Luckily, there is a large variety of drinks to satisfy this need. They can be hot or cold, but the latter are logically more common in Cuba—and very cold or almost frozen drinks are preferred. The popular *jugos* (juices made from fruits or vegetables with added water) and *zumos* (a pure form of liquid extracted from fruits or vegetables) can also be made with aromatic herbs, such as basil, rosemary, and mint. Fruit juices are much more common than vegetable juices. A third category is *refresco*, which can be translated as soda, but also refers to a watered-down juice. These are commonly prepared in homes and frequently found at street food stands.

The average home has a simple blender, but not a juicer that can separate the liquid and solid materials, so Cubans, by preference, strain their blended drinks. Some of the most common drinks in Cuba are tropical and citrus fruit juices, *guarapo* (sugarcane water), *pru oriental* (fermented roots and herbs), *batidos* (milkshakes), cocktails, coffee, beer, and rum. *Batidos* are made with ice cream, fruit, nuts or seeds (almond, peanut, sesame), or grains.

One element that stands out about traditional drinks in Cuba is that they are made from natural resources found on the island, in contrast to the food, much of which is imported. The large quantities of sugar added to drinks is consistent with Cubans' preferences, and dates back to when slaves were given sugarcane water to drink in the morning at the sugar plantations. The most internationally famous Cuban drinks, mojitos and daiquiris, are cocktails. The presence of fermented drinks, such as *sambumbia* (Fermented Corn Beverage, page 393),

pru oriental (Fermented Herb and Root Beverage, page 393), and garapiña (Fermented Pineapple Beverage, page 392), indicate the influence of the indigenous people of the island, while the consumption of *aguardiente* (a distilled alcoholic beverage made from sugarcane) shows the customs of African slaves between the sixteenth and nineteenth centuries.

Coffee is considered the national drink of Cuba and is an important ritual. Offering coffee in one's home is how Cubans show hospitality to others. The most common coffee maker found in a typical Cuban home is the steel, Italian percolator.

In the early years, hot chocolate, made from cacao from Baracoa, was the most common drink in Cuban homes. But when French colonizers immigrated to Cuba at the time of the Haitian Revolution in 1791, coffee production and exportation were developed. As a result, by the nineteenth century, coffee had displaced hot chocolate as the national drink—though it remains common for Cuban children to drink hot chocolate with breakfast.

While coffee may be the most typical drink to share with others, it is also common to offer a juice, smoothie, *refresco*, or another beverage to a visitor, especially an unexpected visitor. There may not be extra food to offer in an average Cuban home, but that doesn't prevent hosts from extending their hospitality with a drink alternative. Alcoholic beverages are elemental to many social interactions, whether the simple *aguardiente*, a refined rum, or a nice, cold beer on a hot day. The typical *brindis*, or toast, is made to and for health. As we say here, "*¡Salud!*"

SOURSOP JUICE

Jugo de guanábana

In a blender, combine the soursop pulp, honey, and 4 cups (32 fl oz/1 liter) water and blend until smooth. Adjust the sweetness to taste. Serve cold.

PREPARATION TIME: 5 MINUTES
SERVES: 4

3 cups (800 g) frozen seedless guanábana (soursop) pulp
2 tablespoons honey

BEET, WATERCRESS, AND ORANGE JUICE

Jugo de remolacha, naranja y berro

This drink was commonly prepared by grandmothers for their grandchildren as a way to boost their immune system. It is a tradition that dates back to the first half of the twentieth century.

In a blender, combine the beet, ice water, raw sugar, orange juice, and watercress and mix until smooth. Strain and serve over ice.

PREPARATION TIME: 15 MINUTES
SERVES: 4

1 medium beet (4 oz/110 g), peeled and cut into chunks
2 cups (16 fl oz/500 ml) ice water
3 tablespoons raw cane sugar, or 2 tablespoons honey
2 cups (16 fl oz/500 ml) orange juice
½ cup (27 g) chopped watercress

PAPAYA BANANA JUICE

Jugo con frutabomba y platanito

PREPARATION TIME: 15 MINUTES

SERVES: 4

★

5½ oz (160 g) papaya, peeled
and cut into large pieces
2 bananas, cut into large pieces
¼ cup (22 g) leaves fresh
spearmint
2 tablespoons honey
or sugarcane syrup

In a blender, combine the papaya, banana, spearmint, 1½ cups (12 fl oz/375 ml) water, and 1 cup (240 g) ice cubes and blend until smooth. Sweeten with the honey and serve cold.

VEGETABLE JUICE

Jugo de vegetales

PREPARATION TIME: 15 MINUTES

SERVES: 4

★

1⅓ cup (11 fl oz/330 ml) tomato
juice
2 oz (75 g) Malabar, Baracoa,
or Savoy spinach, hand-torn
⅔ cup (35 g) watercress
1 tablespoon lime juice
¼ teaspoon salt

In a blender, combine the tomato juice, spinach, watercress, lime juice, salt, and 1 cup (240 g) ice cubes and blend on high speed until smooth. Strain if desired and serve very cold.

SUMMER JUICE

Jugo de verano

PREPARATION TIME: 10 MINUTES
SERVES: 4

★

5½oz (170 g) fresh pineapple,
cut into medium chunks
5½ oz (170 g) cucumber,
cut into medium chunks
2 cup (16 fl oz/500ml) orange juice
Leaves of 6 sprigs fresh spearmint

In a blender, combine the pineapple, cucumber, orange juice, spearmint, and 1 cup (250 g) ice cubes and blend until smooth. Strain (if desired) and serve cold.

EIGHT-VEGETABLE JUICE

Jugo de ocho vegetales

PREPARATION TIME: 15 MINUTES,
PLUS 1 HOUR CHILLING TIME
COOKING TIME: 20 MINUTES
SERVES: 4

★

1 carrot, cut into medium chunks
1 small beet, cut into medium
chunks
1 small onion, cut into medium
chunks
5 large tomatoes (1¾ lb/800 g
total), cut into medium chunks
1 green bell pepper, cut into
medium pieces
2 oz (60 g) spinach leaves
Leaves of 1 stalk celery, chopped
1 sprig parsley
2 tablespoons lime juice
1 teaspoon salt

This juice is a homemade version of V8, the canned vegetable juice that was imported from the US and that became popular in Cuba starting in the 1950s.

★

In a large pot, combine the carrot, beet, onion, tomatoes, bell pepper, spinach, and 3¼ cups (26 fl oz/750 ml) water. Cover and cook over medium heat, stirring occasionally, until the vegetables soften, about 20 minutes. Add the celery and parsley just before removing from the heat. Remove and let cool, then transfer to a blender and blend until smooth. Strain and add the lime juice and salt. Refrigerate until chilled, at least 1 hour. Serve cold.

CUCUMBER AND PINEAPPLE JUICE WITH MINT

Jugo de pepino y piña a la menta

PREPARATION TIME: 15 MINUTES
SERVES: 4

★

2½ cups (21 fl oz/625 ml)
pineapple juice
1 medium cucumber, semi-peeled
with a fork, cut into chunks
Leaves of 1 sprig fresh spearmint,
plus more for garnish
Honey (optional)

Pour the pineapple juice into a blender. With the machine running, add the cucumber chunks, spearmint, and 1 cup (240 g) ice cubes little by little. Strain if desired and sweeten with honey (if using). Serve garnished with mint leaves.

FRUIT SMOOTHIE WITH GINGER

Batido de frutas al jengibre

PREPARATION TIME: 10 MINUTES
SERVES: 4

★

5½ oz (160 g) papaya, peeled
and cut into large chunks
2 small bananas, cut into large
chunks
⅓ inch (1 cm) fresh ginger,
finely chopped
½ cup (120 g) crushed ice
1 tablespoon honey
Pinch of salt (optional)

In a blender, combine the papaya, bananas, ginger, crushed ice, honey, salt (if using), and 1 cup (8 fl oz/240 ml) water and blend until smooth. Serve cold.

Note: Milk can be used instead of water.

MAMEY MILKSHAKE

Batido de mamey

PREPARATION TIME: 15 MINUTES

SERVES: 6

★

1 large mamey sapote (1¾ lb/800 g),
cut lengthwise, seed and white
fibers around seed cavity removed
½ cup (100 g) sugar, or to taste
¼ teaspoon salt
1 cup (240 g) crushed ice
3 cups (24 fl oz/750 ml) whole
milk

Using a spoon, scrape the pulp of the mamey (avoiding scraping the peel too much) into a blender. Add the sugar, salt, ice, and milk and blend until smooth. Strain (if desired) and serve cold.

Note: It is common to use sweetened condensed milk for this milkshake in Cuban homes, even though this alters the taste of the mamey. In this case, the sugar is left out and the milk is substituted with 2 cups (16 fl oz/500 ml) of water.

BANANA MILKSHAKE

Batido de plátano

PREPARATION TIME: 15 MINUTES

SERVES: 4

★

4 bananas, cut into small pieces
½ cup (100 g) sugar
¼ teaspoon salt
½ cup (120 g) crushed ice
3 cups (24 fl oz/750 ml) whole milk

In a blender, combine the bananas, sugar, salt, ice, and milk and blend until smooth. Serve cold.

Note: A few drops of lime juice can be added to prevent the milkshake from turning brown.

ORANGE JUICE WITH TOMATO

Zumo de naranja con tomate

PREPARATION TIME: 15 MINUTES
SERVES: 4

4 small tomatoes (about
3½ oz/100 g each), quartered
¼ cup (60 g) ice cubes
2 cups (16 fl oz/500 ml) orange
juice
1 tablespoon honey (optional)
¼ teaspoon salt
1 teaspoon grated orange zest

In a blender, combine the tomatoes and ice and blend until smooth. Strain into a large pitcher. Stir in the orange juice, honey (if using), and salt. Garnish with the orange zest.

SOURSOP MILKSHAKE

Champola de guanábana

PREPARATION TIME: 5 MINUTES
SERVES: 4

2 cups (520 g) fresh guanábana
(soursop) pulp
2 cups (16 fl oz/500 ml) whole milk
Sugar

According to a theory of anthropologist Fernando Ortiz, *champola* is the African word for a type of melon that could have been applied to the guanábana (soursop) by the African slaves. Another speculation is that *sampula*, the word in the Congo language that means to move quickly, is how *champola* was named. In Cuba, and other Latin American countries, this drink is called *guanabanada*.

In a large bowl, stir together the soursop pulp, milk, and sugar to taste. Strain into a large pitcher. Refrigerate until chilled and serve very cold over ice cubes (if desired).

TWO-COLOR LIMEADE

Limonada bicolor

This recipe was presented at a culinary event of the Association of Cuban Dieticians in 1953.

In a large pitcher, combine the coconut water, lime juice, and sugar. Pour into an ice-filled glass. Slowly pour in the beet juice over the back of a spoon, creating contrasting colors, and serve immediately.

Note: To make beet juice, blend ½ raw beet with ½ cup (4 fl oz/125 ml) water and strain.

PREPARATION TIME: 10 MINUTES
SERVES: 4

3 cup (25 fl oz/750 ml) coconut water
6 tablespoons lime juice
4 tablespoons sugar or honey
8 tablespoons beet juice, store-bought or homemade (see Note)

SUGARCANE WATER WITH LIME

Guarapo y limón

Guarapo (sugarcane water) is considered one of the most typical drinks in Cuba. It is prepared by squeezing the sugarcane with a *trapiche*, a machine with two cylinders that squeezes the whole sugarcanes to extract the juice. This drink turns dark and quickly tastes acidic, but there are many stands across the country (often near farmers' markets) where it is extracted fresh and served for immediate consumption. It is common to flavor it with lime juice.

In a large pitcher, combine the sugarcane water and lime juice. Pour into an ice-filled glass and serve cold.

PREPARATION TIME: 5 MINUTES
SERVES: 4

3 cup (25 fl oz/750 ml) sugarcane water (sugarcane juice)
4 tablespoons lime juice

ORANGE JUICE

Naranjada

PREPARATION TIME: 5 MINUTES

SERVES: 6

4 cups (32 fl oz/1 liter) orange juice

4 teaspoons sugar

1 cup (8 fl oz/240 ml) ice water

Orange slices, for garnish

This drink was traditionally made with sweet oranges in cities and bitter oranges in the rural areas. Samuel Hazard, an American writer who traveled to Cuba during the nineteenth century and recorded his observations about Cuban food culture, considered the *naranjada* the national drink of the time.

In a large pitcher, combine the orange juice, sugar, and ice water. Pour into ice-filled glasses and garnish with orange slices. Serve cold.

PINEAPPLE COCONUT JUICE

Refresco de piña y coco

PREPARATION TIME: 10 MINUTES

SERVES: 4

4 slices fresh pineapple (24 oz/ 120 g each), cut into small pieces

2 tablespoon lime juice

2 cup (400 g) grated fresh coconut (see Note)

½ cup (120 g) crushed ice

In a blender, combine the pineapple, lime juice, coconut, ice, and 1 cup (8 fl oz/ 249 ml) water and blend until smooth. Strain (see Note) and serve cold.

Notes: If fresh coconut is not available, dried coconut flakes can be mixed with 1½ cups of hot water to rehydrate and then drained.

The pineapple and coconut fibers that are strained out of the drink can be used in desserts or to decorate salads.

TAMARIND JUICE

Refresco de tamarindo

Mix the tamarind pulp with the sugar in a stainless steel container (tamarind is acidic). Add the water. Serve cold, preferably over ice.

PREPARATION TIME: 10 MINUTES
SERVES: 8

★

7 oz (200 g) tamarind concentrate
½ cup (100 g) sugar
6¾ cups (52 fl oz/1.6 liters)
ice water

MANGO JUICE

Refresco de mango

In a blender, combine the mango, sugar, and ice water and blend until smooth. Pour into glasses and serve cold.

Note: If the mangos are very ripe, it is not necessary to add sugar.

PREPARATION TIME: 5 MINUTES
SERVES: 4

★

2 cups (330 g) diced mango
2 tablespoons sugar (see Note)
2 cups (16 fl oz/500 ml) ice water

FERMENTED PINEAPPLE BEVERAGE

Garapiña

PREPARATION TIME: 10 MINUTES, PLUS 2 DAYS FERMENTING TIME

SERVES: 4

★

10 oz (280 g) pineapple rind, cut into ¾ inch (2 cm) pieces
½ cup (110 g) raw cane sugar

This drink is known as *garapiña* in Havana, but called *chicha* in the Eastern provinces.

★

In a 1½ quart (1½ liter) glass container, combine the pineapple rind and 2 tablespoons of the raw sugar, without stirring. Add 4 cups (32 fl oz/1 liter) water, cover with a thin cloth that allows the air to flow, and let ferment for 2 days. Add the remaining 6 tablespoons sugar and stir. Strain and serve very cold.

Note: Honey can be added instead of sugar at the end.

FERMENTED FRUIT BEVERAGE

Aliñado

PREPARATION TIME: 40 MINUTES, PLUS 5 MONTHS FERMENTING TIME

COOKING TIME: 15 MINUTES

MAKES: 26 QUARTS (25 LITERS)

★

3 lb (1.38 kg) prunes, pitted and cut into small pieces
2 lb (920 g) figs, cut into small pieces
6 medium apples, cored and cut into small pieces
5 lb (2.3 kg) raisins
1 gallon (3.8 liters) 90 proof alcohol
18 lb (8.280 kg) sugar
Juice of 25 medium oranges
Juice of 1 large pineapple

Originally from the Eastern provinces, it was said that as soon as a woman became pregnant, this preparation was made and fermented for nine months, to be drunk in celebration of the birth. One bottle was set aside until the child turned fifteen years old, at which point it would be drunk in celebration of that birthday. A more tropical preparation is made with sugarcane, prunes, grapes, pineapple, gooseberries, starfruit, and candied Cuban cherries. This traditional drink is still produced and sold, especially in Granma province.

In an 18 inch (46 cm) tall crock with a 12 inch (30 cm) diameter, combine the prunes, figs, apples, raisins, and alcohol. Cover with a cheese cloth and let ferment in a cool place with some ventilation for 2 months.

In a large pot, combine the sugar and 7 quarts (6.75 liters) water and bring to a simmer over medium heat until the sugar is dissolved. Remove and let cool, then add the orange and pineapple juices. Pour this mixture into the crock with the fermented fruits. Cover with cheese cloth and let ferment for at least 3 months. Strain and bottle.

FERMENTED CORN BEVERAGE

Sambumbia

Cuban anthropologist Fernando Ortiz wrote that in Cuba the term *sambumbia* has been used to describe anything with a bad taste. Some versions call for water, sugarcane syrup, and pepper; others call for toasted dried corn.

In a 4 quart (4 liter) glass container, combine the sugarcane syrup, corn, and 3 quarts (3 liters) water. Cover loosely and let ferment for 6 days. Serve straight or diluted with cold water.

PREPARATION TIME: 15 MINUTES, PLUS 6 DAYS FERMENTING TIME
MAKES: 4 QUARTS (3. 75 LITERS)

1 bottle (25 fl oz/750 ml) sugarcane syrup
¼ cob toasted (almost burned) dried corn

FERMENTED HERB AND ROOT BEVERAGE

Pru oriental

The roots and plants used in this recipe are indigenous to the Caribbean. See below for their scientific names and descriptions. To make this, you need what is called a "mother pru" (sort of like a sourdough starter). If you don't have a mother pru to start out, the mixture needs to be fermented for up to 1 week more. Pru is very foamy.

In a 7-gallon (26-liter) pot, bring 26 quarts (25 liters) water to a boil. Add the *jaboncillo, bejuco ubí, pimienta* leaves, ginger, *raíz de China,* and cinnamon and cook the pru until the water is dark, about 2 hours.

Strain the pru into a large stainless steel or wood container and let sit for 24 hours. Stir in the mother pru and raw sugar. Set aside for 72 hours. Reserve 1 quart (1 liter) as the mother pru for the next batch. Transfer to ½-quart (½-liter) plastic bottles, if preferred. Serve very cold.

Notes: Jaboncillo (Gouania polygama) *is a vine in the* Ramnáceas *family. Its inside is white, spongy, and bitter. Many people use it to clean their teeth. It is believed to have medicinal properties to cure wounds.*

Bejuco ubí (Cissus sicyoides) *is a plant in the* Vitáceas *family and has medicinal properties.*

Pimienta de Jamaica (Pimenta dioica, Pimenta officinalis) *is also known as* pimienta dulce, *sweet pepper, or allspice.*

Raíz de China (Smilax domingensis) *is a root that belongs to the* Esmiláceas *family.*

PREPARATION TIME: 30 MINUTES, PLUS 4 DAYS FERMENTING TIME
COOKING TIME: 2 HOURS
MAKES: 21 QUARTS (20 LITERS)

1 jaboncillo stem (see Note), bark removed and cut into small pieces
1 bejuco ubí root (see Note), bark removed
6 pimienta de Jamaica leaves (see Note)
1 oz (30 g) fresh ginger
1 raíz de China tuber (see Note), cut into small pieces
4 cinnamon sticks
4 cups (32 fl oz/1 liter) mother pru
10 cups (2.2 kg) raw cane sugar

COFFEE WITH MILK

Café con leche

PREPARATION TIME: 5 MINUTES
SERVES: 4

3½ cups (28 fl oz/840 ml) whole milk, boiled
½ cups (4 fl oz/ 120 ml) brewed coffee
Sugar (optional)

Café con leche is considered a typical Cuban breakfast, along with a bread roll with butter. In Havana, it is also common to drink it at night, accompanied with bread and butter. A common joke made by people from the countryside is that the only thing *habaneros* (people from Havana) eat is coffee with milk and bread with butter.

In a pitcher with a spout, combine the hot milk and coffee. If desired, sweeten with sugar to taste. Pour into coffee cups and serve hot.

Note: Many people add a pinch of salt.

HORSE-CART COFFEE

Café carretero

PREPARATION TIME: 5 MINUTES
SERVES: 1

1 tablespoon freshly ground coffee
1 teaspoon raw cane sugar

This preparation is common in the rural zones of the country, especially for people who work in the sugar plantations. Its name dates back to when coffee was brought around by horse cart for the employees of sugar plantations. It was tradionally served in the *jicara*, a shell made from the *güira* tree.

In a small saucepan, bring ½ cup (4 fl oz/120 ml) of water and the sugar to a boil. Add the ground coffee, stir, and let boil for 4–5 seconds. Turn off the flame and let sit at least 1 minute before serving (it's important to let the ground coffee settle to the bottom of the pan before serving, since it is not strained).

HOT CHOCOLATE

Chocolate caliente

Hot chocolate was the typical Cuban drink before coffee took its place. It is very common to drink hot chocolate at wakes.

In a medium saucepan, heat the milk over medium heat. Meanwhile, in a small saucepan, combine the cocoa powder and sugar and warm over low heat, stirring with a wooden spoon, until melted, about 2 minutes. Add the salt and ⅔ cup (5 fl oz/160 ml) hot water and continue to simmer for 10 minutes. Stir the cocoa mixture into the hot milk and serve hot.

PREPARATION TIME: 5 MINUTES
COOKING TIME: 15 MINUTES
SERVES: 4

4 cups (32 fl oz/1 liter) whole milk
4 tablespoons unsweetened cocoa powder
8 tablespoons (100 g) sugar
¼ teaspoon salt

ENERGIZING BREAKFAST DRINK

Desayuno energético

In a mug, combine the peanuts, powdered milk, and cocoa mix. Add the boiling water and stir with a spoon. Sweeten with the honey.

PREPARATION TIME: 5 MINUTES
SERVES: 1

2 tablespoons ground peanuts
2 tablespoons powdered milk
1 tablespoon cocoa mix
¾ cup (6 fl oz/180 ml) boiling water
1 teaspoon honey

MOJITO

Mojito

PREPARATION TIME: 5 MINUTES
MAKES: 1 COCKTAIL

★

1 generous tablespoon sugar
¼ fl oz (7 ml) lime juice
1½ fl oz (45 ml) aged white rum
3 fl oz (90 ml) sparkling water
1 sprig spearmint

The mojito, the most famous and typical of Cuban cocktails, originated in the restaurant-bar La Bodeguita del Medio near the baroque Cathedral in Old Havana.

★

In a chilled cocktail glass, combine the sugar and lime juice and stir until dissolved. Add the rum, 3 ice cubes, and sparkling water and stir. Garnish with the mint and serve with a small spoon or a straw.

Note: An alternative preparation is to combine the sugar, lime juice, and a little sparkling water in a previously chilled glass, then add the mint and crush the stem (without damaging the leaves) to release the juice from the mint. Add the ice, rum, and the remaining sparkling water and stir. Garnish with more mint leaves and serve.

RUM AND COKE

Cuba libre

PREPARATION TIME: 3 MINUTES
MAKES: 1 COCKTAIL

★

1½ fl oz (45 ml) aged white rum
6 fl oz (180 ml) Coca-Cola

Although there is some debate about the origins of the original Cuba Libre, it is generally traced back to Cuba's War for Independence in 1898, when Colonel Theodore Roosevelt and his regiment, known as the Rough Riders, along with thousands of other Americans, arrived in Cuba. American troops introduced Coca-Cola to Cuba, and it soon became a popular choice for Cubans and Americans alike.

It is also documented that in August of 1900, while celebrating victory at a bar in Havana, Captain Russell of the United States Army Signal Corps ordered his Cuban rum with a Coke, served with a wedge of fresh lime. This new combination sparked interest from the soldiers around him and soon the entire bar was drinking one. The Captain proposed a toast, *"¡Por Cuba libre!"* in celebration of a free Cuba. The words had special political significance and were frequently used by both Cubans and Americans. The name caught on quickly and has remained popular to this day, however Cuban scholars would argue that this origin story is controversial—considering that Cuba was not free, but rather under the United States' domination for another fifty-nine years after that occurence.

★

In a chilled 8 oz (240 ml) glass, combine 3 ice cubes and the rum. Fill the glass with the Coca-Cola and serve with a straw to stir.

CLASSIC DAIQUIRI

Daiquirí natural

PREPARATION TIME: 5 MINUTES
MAKES: 1 COCKTAIL

1 generous teaspoon sugar
¼ fl oz (7 ml) lime juice
1½ fl oz (45 ml) aged white rum

This is the original recipe for this famous Cuban cocktail. It was created in 1898 in Santiago de Cuba, and later in the bars of Havana thanks to the influence of bartender Emilio González (known as Maragato), before becoming known worldwide.

★

In a cocktail shaker, combine the sugar and lime juice and stir until dissolved. Add the rum and 3 ice cubes and shake. Strain into a chilled cocktail glass and serve.

Note: You can also add ½ fl oz (15 ml) maraschino liqueur.

FROZEN DAIQUIRI

Daiquirí frappé

PREPARATION TIME: 10 MINUTES
SERVES: 4

2 tablespoons sugar
1 fl oz (28 ml) lime juice
¼ teaspoon Maraschino liqueur
6 fl oz (180 ml) aged white rum
12 oz (120 g) crushed ice

Constantino Ribalaigua, the great bartender of the Floridita Bar in Havana during the 1920s, is given credit for the creation of this version of the drink. Ernest Hemingway received international fame for his frequent enjoyment of this drink at this bar.

★

In a blender, combine the sugar and lime juice and blend until dissolved. Add the Maraschino liqueur, rum, and ice and blend until smooth. Pour into chilled cocktail glasses and serve with two small straws in each glass.

CUBAN BLOODY MARY

Cubanito

**PREPARATION TIME: 5 MINUTES,
PLUS CHILLING TIME
SERVES: 6**

★

6 pinches salt
3 tablespoons lime juice
1 tablespoon Worcestershire sauce
1 cup plus 2 tablespoons
(9 fl oz/270 ml) aged white rum
2¼ cups (18 fl oz/540 ml) tomato
juice
¼ teaspoon Tabasco sauce
Lime slices, for garnish (optional)

This is the Cuban version of a Bloody Mary, which substitutes the vodka with rum.

★

In a pitcher, combine the salt, lime juice, Worcestershire sauce, and rum and stir until dissolved. Stir in the tomato juice and Tabasco sauce to taste. Serve over ice in chilled cocktail glasses, with a straw or a small spoon for stirring. Garnish with a lime slice if desired.

HONEY RUM DRINK

Canchánchara

**PREPARATION TIME: 5 MINUTES
MAKES: 1 COCKTAIL**

★

2 teaspoons honey
½ fl oz (15 ml) lime juice
1½ fl oz (45 ml) aguardiente

During the independence wars in the nineteenth century, the *mambises* (independence fighters) in the eastern countryside invented this drink to keep them warm during the night while facing food shortages and rough conditions in the mountains. This recipe includes ingredients that were easy for the *mambises* to acquire, such as the *aguardiente* (a distilled alcoholic beverage made from sugarcane). It was traditionally drunk in *jícaras*, the shell of the *güira* fruit, because this is what was available to them.

It is said that when consumed hot, this drink alleviates congestion and helps confront the coldest days of the Cuban winter. Ice was added to *canchánchara* in its modern adaptation.

★

In a chilled 8 oz (240 ml) glass, combine the honey and lime juice and stir until dissolved. Add the *aguardiente*, 2 tablespoons water, and 2 ice cubes and stir.

CUBAN EGGNOG

Crema de vie con leche en polvo

PREPARATION TIME: 10 MINUTES
SERVES: 12

1 cup (200 g) sugar
1 cup (96 g) powdered whole-milk
1 egg
1 teaspoon vanilla extract
¾ cup (6 fl oz/180 ml) white rum

In a blender, blend the sugar until finely ground. Add the powdered milk, egg, vanilla, white rum, and 1 cup (8 fl oz/240 ml) water and blend until creamy. Serve over ice in a cocktail glass.

Note: ⅔ cup (5 fl oz/150 ml) aguardiente (a distilled alcoholic beverage made from sugarcane) can be used instead of rum.

HAVANA SPECIAL

Habana especial

PREPARATION TIME: 5 MINUTES
MAKES: 1 COCKTAIL

1 teaspoon Maraschino liqueur
1½ fl oz (45 ml) pineapple juice
1½ fl oz (45 ml) aged white rum
Wedge of pineapple, for garnish

This recipe was created in the 1920s and is similar to the Mary Pickford (page 403), Almendares, and Havana cocktails. It is typically served in a champagne flute.

In an ice-filled cocktail shaker, combine the Maraschino, pineapple juice, and rum and shake until well chilled. Strain into a chilled flute with 1 ice cube. Serve garnished with a slice of pineapple.

SANTIAGO

Santiago

PREPARATION TIME: 10 MINUTES
SERVES: 4

¼ teaspoon Maraschino liqueur
2 fl oz (60 ml) grenadine syrup
1 fl oz (28 ml) lime juice
6 fl oz (180 ml) aged white rum
16 oz (480 g) crushed ice
Candied cherries, for garnish

This is one of the first cocktails created in Cuba. It was created in the 1920s as a tribute to Santiago de Cuba.

In a blender, combine the Maraschino, grenadine, lime juice, rum, and ice and blend until smooth. Pour into chilled cocktail glasses. Garnish with a candied cherry and serve with two small straws for stirring.

PINE TREE ISLAND

Isla de pinos

This cocktail is dedicated to the second largest island of Cuba's extended territory, which has had many names: Camargo, Guanaja, Cigüanea, La Evangelista, Santiago, Isla del Tesoro, Isla de las Cotorras, Isla de Pinos, and Isla de la Juventud.

In a cocktail shaker, combine the sugar (see Note) and grapefruit juice and shake until dissolved. Add the vermouth, rum, and 3 ice cubes and shake until well chilled. Strain into a chilled cocktail glass or an empty grapefruit half. Garnish with a grapefruit supreme and serve.

Note: In some recipes, sugar is not added.

PREPARATION TIME: 5 MINUTES
MAKES: 1 COCKTAIL

1 generous teaspoon sugar
1½ fl oz (45 ml) grapefruit juice
½ floz (15 ml) sweet vermouth
1 fl oz (30 ml) aged white rum
Grapefruit supreme, for serving

MARY PICKFORD

Mary Pickford

This Cuban cocktail was inspired by the famous American silent film actress. It was created in the bar at the Sevilla hotel, located on the Paseo del Prado in Havana.

In an ice-filled cocktail shaker, combine the grenadine, rum, and pineapple juice and shake until well chilled. Strain into a chilled glass. Serve garnished with a slice of pineapple and a candied cherry.

PREPARATION TIME: 5 MINUTES
MAKES: 1 COCKTAIL

1 teaspoon grenadine syrup
1½ fl oz (45 ml) aged white rum
1½ fl oz (45 ml) pineapple juice
Wedge of pineapple and candied cherry, for garnish

CHOCOLATE LIQUEUR AND RUM COCKTAIL

Mulata

PREPARATION TIME: 10 MINUTES

SERVES: 4

4 teaspoons sugar

1 fl oz (28 ml) lime juice

2 fl oz (60 ml) dark crème de cacao liqueur

4 fl oz (120 ml) aged (7-year) white rum

16 oz (480 g) crushed ice

Lime slices, for garnish

This cocktail was created by Cuban bartender José María Vázquez during the 1940s.

In a blender, combine the sugar and lime juice and blend until dissolved. Add the crème de cacao, rum, and ice and blend until smooth. Pour into chilled cocktail glasses. Garnish with a slice of lime and serve with two straws for stirring.

PIÑA COLADA

Piña colada

PREPARATION TIME: 10 MINUTES

SERVES: 4

12 oz (360 g) crushed ice

4 fl oz (120 ml) whipping cream

4 fl oz (120 ml) coconut liqueur

12 fl oz (360 ml) pineapple juice

6 fl oz (180 ml) white rum

Wedge of pineapple, for garnish

Legend says there was a famous pirate from Puerto Rico who made a drink out of pineapple, coconut, and rum to raise the morale of his crew. It is thought that the recipe was lost when the pirate was executed in the nineteenth century, but it was possibly passed on. Another story states that a famous bartender from the restaurant Barrachina in San Juan created the piña colada in 1963, when he mixed pineapple juice, coconut crème, sweetened condensed milk, and ice in a blender. There is a plaque in front of this restaurant that declares it the birthplace. Despite its Puerto Rican origin, this drink has become extremely popular in Cuba and is among its most well-loved cocktails.

In a blender, combine the ice, cream, coconut liqueur, pineapple juice, and rum and blend until smooth and even, about 10 seconds. Pour into chilled cocktail glasses. Garnish with a slice of pineapple and serve with a straw.

Note: You can also add a pinch of ground cinnamon before serving.

PRESIDENTE

Presidente

This cocktail was invented at the Vista Alegre bar in Havana and was named after General Mario García Menocal, president of Cuba for two terms (1913–1921). Bartenders offer two options: Presidente dulce with sweet vermouth and Presidente seco with dry vermouth. During the 1930s, the bar Sloppy Joe's in Old Havana used Noilly Prat vermouth, grenadine, and Curaçao, while El Floridita bar in Old Havana (famous for being one of Ernest Hemingway's favorite places when he lived in Cuba) used Chambéry vermouth and just Curaçao. In traditional preparations, the drink was made with more vermouth than rum; today it is made with more rum than vermouth.

In an ice-filled cocktail shaker, combine the vermouth, grenadine, and rum and shake until well chilled. Strain into a chilled cocktail glass with the candied cherry. Serve garnished with the orange peel.

PREPARATION TIME: 5 MINUTES
MAKES: 1 COCKTAIL

½ fl oz (15 ml) red vermouth
¼ fl oz (7 ml) grenadine syrup
1½ fl oz (45 ml) aged white rum
1 candied cherry
1 strip of orange peel, for garnish

GUEST CHEFS

CHEFS

chefs
invitados

Eileen Andrade

FINKA TABLE & TAP

14690 SW 26TH STREET
MIAMI, FL
USA

Eileen Andrade—the chef and owner of Finka Table & Tap and Amelia's 1931 in Miami, Florida—has worked in restaurants since age eighteen. She was born into a Cuban family of restaurateurs: Her grandparents emigrated from Cuba to Miami and opened Miami's landmark restaurant Islas Canarias in 1977, and her parents opened two more restaurants. When Andrade eventually opened her own places, she combined her Cuban heritage with her love for Asian cuisine to create the restaurants' Latin-Asian fusion cuisine.

FRIED CHICKPEAS

Garbanzos fritos

PREPARATION TIME: 30 MINUTES
COOKING TIME: 40 MINUTES
SERVES: 4

Olive oil
½ lb (225 g) bacon (streaky), chopped
4 cloves garlic, minced
1 Spanish onion, diced
1 green bell pepper, diced
1 red bell pepper, diced
4 slices smoked ham, chopped
2 Spanish chorizos, thickly sliced
3 bay leaves
1 cup (8 fl oz/240 ml) red wine
2 cans (15 oz/425 g each) chickpeas, drained
1 can (8 oz/225 g) tomato sauce (seasoned passata)
scant 7 tablespoons ketchup
2 tablespoons Worcestershire sauce
1 tablespoon sherry vinegar
½ teaspoon ground cumin
½ teaspoon salt
Vegetable oil, for deep-frying
1 tablespoon paprika
½ tablespoon chipotle powder

In a large pan, heat a drizzle of olive oil over medium-high heat. Add the bacon and sauté until browned but not crispy, 3 minutes. Remove and set aside.

In the same oil, sauté the garlic, onion, bell peppers, ham, chorizos, and bay leaves for 5 minutes. Add the wine, half of the drained chickpeas, the bacon, tomato sauce (seasoned passata), ketchup, Worcestershire sauce, vinegar, cumin, and salt and stir well over medium heat until thick, about 30 minutes.

Meanwhile, in a medium pot, heat 3 inches (8 cm) vegetable oil over high heat. Add the remaining chickpeas and deep-fry until golden, 2–3 minutes. Transfer to paper towels to drain excess oil and let sit for a few minutes. Transfer to a large bowl, add the paprika and chipotle powder, and toss. Serve the chickpea/tomato mixture garnished with the deep-fried chickpeas.

MIDNIGHT
BRISKET SANDWICHES

Brisket medianoche

Make the brisket: Preheat the oven to 550°F (290°C/Gas Mark 12). Rub the brisket with salt, cracked black pepper and red pepper flakes until fully coated. Place the brisket in a 20 x 12 inch (50 x 30 cm) baking dish and sear in the oven for 8 minutes.

Meanwhile, combine the liquid smoke, carrots, onion, celery, garlic, beer, wine, beef stock, thyme, bay leaves, coriander seeds, and peppercorns in a roasting pan. Once the brisket has seared, remove from the oven and lower the heat to 300°F (150°C/Gas Mark 2).

Place the brisket into the pan with the braising liquid. Cover tightly with foil and bake until fork tender, about 3 hours. Once the brisket is ready, remove from the braising liquid and shred apart with tongs.

Make the sandwiches: In a small bowl, whisk together the mustard, kimchi base, and wasabi paste.

Layer the shredded brisket onto the bottom halves of the *medianoche* (sweet bread rolls) and layer with ham and Swiss cheese. Place in a toaster oven at 350°F (180°C) to melt the cheese. Drizzle with wasabi-kimchi mustard, place the top bun over each sandwich, and serve.

PREPARATION TIME: 30 MINUTES
COOKING TIME: 3 HOURS
SERVES: 4

For the brisket:
2 lb (454 g) beef brisket
Salt and cracked black pepper
Korean red pepper flakes
¼ cup (50 ml) liquid smoke
8 oz (225 g) carrots, chopped
1 white onion, chopped
2 celery stalks, chopped
4 oz (115 g) minced garlic
1 cup (8 fl oz/240 ml) beer (lager)
1 cup (8 fl oz/240 ml) white wine
2 cups (16 fl oz/475 ml) beef stock
3 sprigs thyme
3 bay leaves
1 teaspoon coriander seeds
1 teaspoon black peppercorns

For the sandwiches:
generous ½ cup (120 g) mild mustard
generous ½ cup (120 g) kimchi base
1 tablespoon wasabi paste
4 medianoche breads (sweet bread rolls)
10 oz (285 g) sliced smoked ham
8 oz (225 g) sliced Swiss cheese

CINNAMON SUGAR FRITTERS

Buñuelos de canela

PREPARATION TIME: 30 MINUTES
COOKING TIME: 1 HOUR
MAKES: 25–30 BUÑUELOS

For the syrup:
2 cups (16 fl oz/475 ml)
Redemption rye
2 cups (400 g) granulated sugar
½ cup (4 fl oz/240 ml) Pernod
absinthe

For the whipped lemon cream:
1¾ cups (14 fl oz/415 ml) whipping
cream
5 tablespoons powdered (icing)
sugar
4 tablespoons fresh lemon juice

For the buñuelos:
5 lb (2.25 kg) yuca (cassava),
peeled and cut into thirds
1 lb (454 g) white sweet potato,
peeled and cut into thirds
4 cups (800 g) granulated sugar
3 star anise
2 eggs
1 tablespoon anise seed
Salt
1 cup (135 g) all-purpose (plain)
flour
Vegetable oil, for deep-frying
¼ cup (30 g) ground cinnamon

Make the syrup: In a medium pot, combine the rye, granulated sugar, and absinthe and heat over medium-low heat. Stir with a whisk until the sugar has dissolved. Let cool and refrigerate.

Make the whipped lemon cream: In a bowl, with a hand mixer, beat the whipping cream until it begins to thicken. Slowly add the powdered sugar and lemon juice while continuously beating until everything is evenly mixed. Refrigerate.

To make the buñuelos: In a large pot, combine the yuca (cassava), sweet potato, 2 cups (400 g) of the granulated sugar, the star anise, and enough water to cover. Bring to a boil and cook until tender but not soft, about 20 minutes. Drain the vegetables (discard the star anise).

Pass the yuca and boniato through a potato ricer into a bowl. Place in the refrigerator until cooled down.

Beat the eggs into the cooled mixture along with 1 cup (200 g) of the sugar, the anise seeds, and salt to taste. Add the flour and stir until the dough no longer sticks.

In a bowl, mix together the remaining 1 cup (200 g) sugar with the cinnamon.

Roll the buñuelos into a ball (like a doughnut hole), or roll into a cylinder to form into a figure 8 or a traditional doughnut shape. Pour 2 inches (5 cm) oil into a deep heavy-bottomed pot and heat to 350°F (180°C). Working in batches, fry the buñuelos until golden brown. Toss in cinnamon sugar while still hot and serve with syrup and the whipped cream.

Yamilet Magariño Andux

HAVANA
CUBA

Chef, teacher, and television cooking show host, Havana-born Yamilet Magariño Andux studied at the Escuela de Hotelería y Turismo and at the Culinary Federation in Havana, where she now teaches classes. She specializes in pastries, and has published several cookbooks.

WARM OCTOPUS SALAD

Ensaladilla tibia de pulpo

Cook the octopus: Fill a large pot with water, season with salt and add 5 of the garlic cloves, the bay leaf, and peppercorns. Bring to a boil. Add the octopus and submerge for 3 seconds. Remove and repeat two more times, then submerge and let cook until tender, about 30 minutes. Remove and let cool. Cut the tentacles off and into medium pieces. Discard the bodies.

In a large pot, heat the olive oil to 176°F (80°C). Add the remaining 3 garlic cloves (unpeeled, but smashed) and the chili and let infuse for 5 minutes. Remove from the heat and add the octopus. Cover and let marinate for 15 minutes.

Meanwhile, make the salad: Fill a medium pot with 3 cups (24 fl oz/ 710 ml) water. Add ¼ teaspoon salt, onion, and bell pepper and bring to a boil. Add the lentils and cook until tender but whole, about 15 minutes.

Reserving the oil, drain the octopus, cover, and set aside. Transfer the infused oil to a blender and add the mustard, lime juice, remaining ¼ teaspoon salt, and the parsley and blend until emulsified.

Preheat the oven to 335°F (170°C/Gas Mark 3). Using a rolling pin, flatten the slices of bread until very thin, then cut into rounds. Arrange on a baking sheet and transfer to the oven until golden, 3 minutes.

Transfer the warm lentils and the octopus to a bowl. Toss with the sauce. Serve with the toasts.

PREPARATION TIME: 30 MINUTES
COOKING TIME: 50 MINUTES
SERVES: 4

For the octopus:
Salt
8 cloves garlic
1 bay leaf
generous ¼ teaspoon peppercorns
2¼ lb (1 kg) octopus, cleaned
scant ½ cup (3½ fl oz/100 ml) olive oil
1 chili

For the salad:
½ teaspoon salt
½ onion
½ green bell pepper
1⅓ cups (250 g) lentils
5 teaspoons mild mustard
2 teaspoons lime juice
¼ bunch parsley

4 slices whole wheat (wholemeal) bread

QUAIL IN ITS HABITAT

Codorniz en su hábitat

PREPARATION TIME: 40 MINUTES
COOKING TIME: 35 MINUTES
SERVES: 4

For the quail:
¼ cup (2 fl oz/60 ml) olive oil, plus
more for cooking the quail
¼ cup (2 fl oz/60 ml) bitter orange
juice (see page 18)
3 tablespoons soy sauce
3 cloves garlic, peeled
¼ bunch cilantro (coriander)
5 fresh cachucha peppers, seeded
Salt, ground white pepper and
ground pink pepper
2 quails, halved down the middle
and backbone removed
10 scallions (spring onions), quartered
4¼ cups (34 fl oz/1 liter) garapiña
(Fermented Pineapple Beverage,
page 392) or pineapple juice

For assembly:
1½ cups Moors and Christians (page 107)
2 new potatoes, scooped into
round balls with a melon baller
1 teaspoon salt
3½ tablespoons (1¾ oz/50 g) butter
½ cup chopped parsley

For the bean sprouts:
6 medium tomatoes
2 tablespoons olive oil
1 teaspoon red wine vinegar
¼ teaspoon raw cane sugar
Salt and ground black pepper
½ teaspoon dried dill
3 tablespoons chives, chopped
2 leaves fresh basil, chopped
1 cup (100 g) bean sprouts

For the tortillas:
2 tablespoons olive oil
1 clove garlic
¼ red onion, chopped
½ red bell pepper, chopped
¼ green bell pepper, chopped
7 tablespoons tomato sauce
(seasoned passata)
6 oz (160 g) tender young corn kernels
2 oz (60 g) bacon (streaky), finely diced

Prepare the quail: In a blender, combine the ¼ cup (2 fl oz/ 60 ml) olive oil, bitter orange juice, soy sauce, garlic, cilantro (coriander), *cachucha* peppers, ¼ teaspoon salt, ¼ teaspoon white pepper, and ¼ teaspoon pink pepper and blend until smooth. Arrange the quail in a shallow bowl and cover with the liquid. Cover and marinate in the refrigerator for 1 hour. Reserving the marinade, drain the quail.

Preheat the oven to 350 (180°C/Gas Mark 4).

In a large Dutch oven (casserole), heat a drizzle of olive oil over medium heat. Add the scallions (spring onions) and sauté until browned, 2–3 minutes. Add the quail and cook until lightly browned. Add the *garapiña* and the reserved marinade. Cover, transfer to the oven, and bake until tender, 20 minutes. Remove the quail and return the liquid to the oven to reduce until thick.

Meanwhile, spread the *moros y cristianos* on a baking sheet and sprinkle with 2 tablespoons water. Transfer to the oven and let dry until crunchy, 15 minutes. Leave the oven on, but increase the temperature to 400 (200°C/Gas Mark 6).

In a medium pot, combine the potatoes, enough water to cover, and the salt and bring to a boil. Cook until tender, 10 minutes. Drain.

In a medium frying pan, heat the butter over medium heat. Add the potatoes and parsley and sauté for 2 minutes.

In a blender, blend the tomatoes until smooth. Strain into a medium pot and cook over medium heat until thickened, 5 minutes. Transfer to a medium bowl, add the olive oil and red wine vinegar and whisk until emulsified. Add the sugar, ¼ teaspoon salt, and black pepper to taste. Add the dill, chives, and basil and mix. Add the bean sprouts and toss.

Make the tortillas: In a medium frying pan, heat the olive oil over medium heat. Add the garlic, onion, and peppers, and sauté for 8 minutes. Add the tomato sauce (seasoned passata) and let simmer for 3 minutes. Let cool. Transfer to a blender, add the corn, and blend until smooth.

In a medium frying pan, fry the bacon (streaky). Remove and let cool, then finely dice and set aside. In the bacon fat, fry 1 tablespoon of the corn mixture to form little tortillas. Transfer the tortillas to the oven and bake until crispy, about 8 minutes. Let cool, then break into irregular pieces.

To serve, spread the *moros y cristianos* on the bottom of each plate and top with the potatoes and quail. Garnish with the tortillas, bacon, and bean sprouts. Serve with the sauce.

GUAVA SEMIFREDDO WITH CHEESE AND CINNAMON TILE COOKIES

Semi-frío de guayaba

con emulsión de queso y tejas de canela

Make the guava semifreddo: In a small bowl, soak the gelatin in cold water until soft, about 10 minutes. Drain well.

In a medium pot, heat the guava puree to 194°F (90°C). Add the gelatin and stir to melt.

In a medium bowl, with a hand mixer, beat the egg whites until soft peaks form. Slowly add the guava mixture in a steady stream and fold into the meringue until smooth but stiff. Refrigerate.

Make the cheese emulsion: In a small bowl, combine the raisins and rum and set aside to soak.

In a small pan, heat the evaporated milk and cream to 180°F (82°C). In a large heatproof bowl, whisk the egg yolks and sugar until smooth. Set the bowl over a pot of simmering water and add the warmed milk/cream mixture and continue to whisk in a figure-eight. Once you can see the bottom of the bowl, remove from the heat.

Stir in the vanilla and strain the mixture into a bowl. Refrigerate until well chilled. Vigorously beat in the cream cheese. Add the soaked raisins and stir. Freeze until it takes shape, at least 12 hours.

Make the cinnamon *tejas*: Preheat the oven to 340°F (170°C/ Gas Mark 3). Line a baking sheet with parchment paper. In a large bowl, sift the flour, powdered (icing) sugar, and cinnamon. Add the butter in pieces, followed by the egg whites, and mix until smooth. Place tablespoons of the mixture on the prepared baking sheet, making sure they are smooth. Bake until browned around the edges, about 8 minutes. Remove immediately with a spatula and place them over a rolling pin so they take the shape as they cool. To serve, fill the bottom of each glass with a layer of the cream cheese mixture, followed by the guava semifreddo. Garnish with the cinnamon cookies.

PREPARATION TIME: 30 MINUTES, PLUS 12 HOURS FREEZING TIME
COOKING TIME: 35 MINUTES
SERVES: 4

For the guava semifreddo:
3 sheets gelatin
12 oz (350 g) guava puree
5 tablespoons (75 g) egg whites (about 3 eggs)
½ cup plus 2 tablespoons (125 g) sugar

For the cheese emulsion:
generous ½ cup (100 g) raisins, finely chopped
¼ cup (2 fl oz/60 ml) añejo rum
1 cup (8 fl oz/250 ml) evaporated milk
1 cup (8 fl oz/250 ml) heavy (whipping) cream
5 egg yolks
6 tablespoons (80 g) sugar
1½ teaspoons vanilla extract
1 lb (460 g) cream cheese, at room temperature

For the cinnamon tejas:
¾ cup (100 g) all-purpose (plain) flour
generous ¾ cup (100 g) powdered (icing) sugar
2 teaspoons ground cinnamon
7 tablespoons (100 g) butter
scant 7 tablespoons (100 g) egg whites (about 4 eggs)

Ricardo Barreras

PILAR CUBAN EATERY

397 GREENE AVENUE
BROOKLYN, NY
USA

Ricardo Barreras was born in Miami to Cuban parents who emigrated from Camagüey in 1959. A former research psychologist, he opened Pilar Cuban Eatery with his wife in 2009. Pilar is dedicated to honoring and preserving classic Cuban cuisine, but from a modern and elevated approach. It has become both a neighborhood institution as well as a destination for those seeking authentic Cuban ingredients and preparations.

CREOLE SHRIMP

Camarones enchilados

PREPARATION TIME:
25–35 MINUTES
COOKING TIME: 20–25 MINUTES
SERVES: 4

1 cup (8 fl oz/240 ml) dry white wine
1½ lb (680 g) head-on extra-large shrimp (prawns), peeled and deveined, shells and heads reserved
½ cup (4 fl oz/120 ml) extra-virgin olive oil
1 medium Spanish onion, cut into medium dice (about 2 cups/320 g)
1 green bell pepper, cut into medium dice (about 1 cup/150 g)
3 cloves garlic, finely chopped
1 cup (225 g) tomato puree (passata)
1 teaspoon dried oregano
1 large bay leaf
Salt and ground black pepper
4 oz (115 g) roasted red peppers, for garnish
2 tablespoons chopped fresh parley, for garnish

In a small pot, combine 1 cup (8 fl oz/240 ml) water and the wine and bring to a boil. Add the shrimp (prawns) shells and heads and cook over medium heat for 5 minutes. Strain the stock and set aside.

In a large sauté pan, heat ¼ cup (2 fl oz/60 ml) of the olive oil over medium heat. Add the onion and bell pepper and sauté until translucent, 8–10 minutes. Add the garlic and cook 1 minute, making sure it does not brown. Add the shrimp stock, tomato puree (passata), oregano, bay leaf, and salt and pepper to taste and cook for 2 minutes. If the sauce is thick, add a few tablespoons of water. (The sauce should be the consistency of a marinara or basic tomato sauce.) Add the shrimp and cook over medium heat, stirring occasionally, until the shrimp curl up, 5–7 minutes. Add the remaining ¼ cup (2 fl oz/60 ml) olive oil and transfer immediately to a serving dish. Garnish with the roasted red peppers and parsley.

SAVORY CHICKEN PIE FROM CAMAGÜEY

Pastelón camagüeyano

Make the dough: Add ¼ cup (2 fl oz/60 ml) lukewarm water to a medium bowl, sprinkle with the yeast and 1 teaspoon of the sugar, and let sit for 10 minutes until a small layer of bubbles or foam appears.

In a separate bowl, combine the eggs, butter, lard, wine, and milk and whisk thoroughly. Incorporate the flour, the remaining sugar, the yeast mixture, and the salt with as little kneading as possible. Simply with the tips of your fingers make sure all dry and wet ingredients are incorporated and there are no major lumps. The dough should be quite tacky and sticky. Cover the bowl in plastic wrap (clingfilm) and let sit at room temperature for 30 minutes to 1 hour.

Make the sofrito: In a large sauté pan, heat the olive oil over medium heat. Add the onion and bell pepper and cook until translucent, 10 minutes. Add the garlic and stir for 1 minute. Remove from the pan and set aside.

Make the filling: Skin the chicken and salt liberally on both sides with 1 teaspoon salt and let sit for 10 minutes.

In the same large sauté pan, heat the olive oil over medium-high heat. When the oil is hot, add the chicken, without crowding the pan. Cook until lightly browned, about 4 minutes on each side. Add the wine, then add the sofrito, tomato puree (passata), bay leaf, oregano, cumin, and salt to taste. Cover and cook over over medium-low heat for 20 minutes. Add the olives, raisins, and roasted peppers and remove from the heat. Once cooled, remove the bones from the meat and shred, then return the shredded meat to the sauce.

Preheat the oven to 350°F (180°C/Gas Mark 4).

In a 12-inch (30 cm) round or square or 12 x 14-inch (30 x 36 cm) rectangular baking dish no deeper than 3 inches (7.5 cm), fill the bottom with the chicken mixture. Divide the dough into 2-ounce (56 g) pieces and flatten slightly to make a 2-inch (5 cm) disk roughly ¼ inch (6 mm) thick. Cover the entire top with the dough and smooth it out with a wet spatula.

Make the glaze: Whisk together the egg yolk and sugar and brush over the entirety of the surface.

Bake until the top is golden brown, 25–30 minutes.

PREPARATION TIME: 30–45 MINUTES
COOKING TIME: 25–30 MINUTES
SERVES: 8

★

For the dough:
1 packet active dry yeast
¾ cup (150 g) sugar
4 eggs, lightly whisked
1 stick (4 oz/115 g) butter,
at room temperature
4 oz (115 g) pork fat or lard
½ cup (4 fl oz/120 ml) dry white wine
¼ cup (2 fl oz/60 ml) whole milk
4 cups (540 g) all-purpose (plain) flour
2 teaspoons kosher salt

For the sofrito:
¼ cup (8 fl oz/120 ml) olive oil
2 cups (320 g) chopped white onion (about 1 medium)
1 cup (150 g) chopped green bell pepper (about 1 medium)
3 cloves garlic, crushed

For the filling:
4 lb (1.8 kg) bone-in, skin-on chicken, preferably a combination of chicken breast, legs, and thighs
Salt
¼ cup (8 fl oz/120 ml) olive oil
½ cup (8 fl oz/120 ml) dry white wine
½ cup (120 g) tomato puree (passata)
1 bay leaf
1 teaspoon dried oregano
¼ teaspoon ground cumin
1 cup (10 g) stuffed Manzanilla olives, sliced
2 tablespoons raisins
4 oz (115 g) roasted red peppers, cut into ¼ inch (6 mm) cubes

For the glaze:
1 egg yolk
1 tablespoon superfine (caster) sugar

GUAVA AND CREAM CHEESE PIE

Pastel de guayaba y queso

PREPARATION TIME: 40–60 MINUTES
COOKING TIME: 45 MINUTES
SERVES: 6

★

For the pie dough (shortcrust pastry):
10 oz (285 g) very cold unsalted butter
2½ cups (335 g) all-purpose (plain) flour
2 teaspoons sugar
1 teaspoon kosher salt
6 tablespoons cold water

For the guava and cream cheese filling:
8 oz (225 g) cream cheese, at room temperature
3 tablespoons sugar
8 oz (225 g) guava paste

For the glaze:
1 egg yolk
1 tablespoon superfine (caster) sugar

Make the pie dough (shortcrust pastry): Cube the butter and place back in the refrigerator. The butter should be very cold.

In a food processor, combine the flour, sugar, and salt. Add a few pieces of the butter and pulse a few times. Do this about four times until all the butter is incorporated. Do not overpulse. There should be pea-size chunks. Pour a few tablespoons of water at a time. When the mixture just becomes dough-like, do not pulse or add more water. It should be a loose dough, just starting to hold together, not a complete ball.

Divide the mixture into 2 balls and roll each out into a disk about 12 inches (30 cm) across. Do not knead the dough at all and handle it as little as possible so as not to melt the butter. Fit one disk of dough into a 9-inch (23 cm) pie plate. Place in the freezer for 1 hour to firm up. Reserve the remaining disk of dough for the top and place in the refrigerator for 1 hour.

Make the guava and cream cheese filling: Combine the cream cheese with the sugar and mix thoroughly. Cut the guava paste into strips no thicker than ¼ inch (6 mm). Preheat the oven to 350°F (180°C/Gas Mark 4).

Spread the cream cheese mixture over the bottom of the frozen pie shell (pastry case). Then place an even layer of guava strips on top of the cream cheese mixture. Place the top layer of pie dough (pastry) on top and trim the excess. Crimp the border.

Make the glaze: Whisk together the egg yolk and sugar. Brush the glaze all over the top of the pie, making sure to not leave any puddles or excess.

Cut 4 slits about 3 inches (7.5 cm) long from the center of the pie to the edges. Bake until browned, about 45 minutes.

Liuyen Álvarez Gallego

ATELIER

CALLE 5, BETWEEN PASEO Y CALLE 2, VEDADO
HAVANA
CUBA

Liuyen Álvarez Gallego was born in Havana in 1982. He has always been fascinated by cooking, and studied at the Culinary Federation, graduating in 1999. He has worked as the chef at the renowned Havana restaurant Atelier off and on since 2011.

SHRIMP, CUCUMBER, AND YOGURT SALAD

Ensalada de camarones con pepino y yogur

In a large bowl, combine the shrimp, cucumbers, culantro, yogurt, and olive oil. Season to taste with salt and pepper. Serve in a bowl and garnish with the arugula (rocket) and ground cumin.

PREPARATION TIME: 10 MINUTES
SERVES: 4

8½ oz (240 g) cooked shrimp, peeled
8½ oz (240 g) cucumbers, peeled, seeded, and cut into cubes
4 leaves culantro, slivered
½ cup (115 g) yogurt
2 tablespoons olive oil
Salt and ground black pepper
20 leaves wild arugula (rocket)
Cumin seeds, freshly ground

RED SNAPPER WITH PUREED POTATOES AND PESTO

Filete de pargo sobre puré de patatas al pesto

PREPARATION TIME: 30 MINUTES
COOKING TIME: 15 MINUTES
SERVES: 4

1 lb 7 oz (640 g) potatoes, peeled
and cut into small dice
Salt
½ cup (120 g) pesto
Juice of ½ lime
Ground black pepper
Milk, for drizzling (optional)
2¼ lb (1 kg) red snapper fillets
2 tablespoons olive oil, for frying
4 sprigs basil

In a large pot, combine the potatoes, enough water to cover, and salt. Bring to a boil and cook until tender, about 8 minutes. Drain, transfer to a food processor, and puree. Add the pesto, lime juice, and salt and pepper to taste. Add a drizzle of milk for a smoother consistency. Set aside.

Season the fish with salt and black pepper. In a frying pan, heat the olive oil over medium heat. Add the basil, then the fish and cook for 3 minutes on each side.

Divide the pureed potatoes among the plates and top with the fish. Garnish with the cooked basil.

LIME CREAM WITH BURNT MERINGUE

Crema de limón y merengue quemado

PREPARATION TIME: 10 MINUTES,
PLUS 30 MINUTES TO SIT
SERVES: 10

2 cups plus 2 tablespoons (17 fl oz/
500 ml) evaporated milk
1½ cups (12 fl oz/350 ml)
sweetened condensed milk
Pinch of salt
Grated lime zest of 4–6 limes
¼ cup (2 fl oz/60 ml) lime juice,
plus a few drops for the meringue
2 egg whites
4 tablespoons sugar
A few drops vanilla extract
1¾ oz (50 g) galletas maria (Marie
biscuits; see Note), finely crushed
Ground cinnamon, for sprinkling

In a large bowl, with a hand mixer, beat together the evaporated milk, condensed milk, salt, and lime zest. Add the ¼ cup (2 fl oz/60 ml) lime juice while continuing to beat. Transfer to wine glasses.

In a large bowl, with a hand mixer, beat the egg whites on high until soft peaks form. Slowly beat in the sugar, vanilla, and drops of lime juice. Beat until the meringue is smooth and the sugar has been fully incorporated.

Cover the tops of the lime cream with the crushed cookies and sprinkle with cinnamon. Top with the meringue and burn it with a blowtorch. Chill in the refrigerator for 30 minutes.

Note: If you can't find Marie biscuits, substitute any plain tea biscuit.

Luis Pous

ASIA DE CUBA
45 ST. MARTIN'S LANE
LONDON
UK

Havana native Luis Pous, studied at the National School of Culinary Arts in Havana, then in 1997 moved to Miami where he oversaw many award-winning restaurants. As executive chef for Asia de Cuba in

London, New York, and Abu Dhabi, Pous focuses on a contemporary menu that showcases the fusion of the Asian flavors of Havana's Chinatown (el Barrio Chino) and his traditional Cuban upbringing.

SWEET PLANTAIN OLD-FASHIONED

Maduros old-fashioned

In a saucepan, combine the sugar and ½ cup (4 fl oz/120 ml) water and bring to a simmer over low heat, stirring until the sugar is dissolved. Stop stirring and let simmer for 1 minute. Remove from the heat and let cool. Add the fried plantains and let steep for 2 hours. Strain the syrup through a fine-mesh sieve into a bowl, pressing on the plantains with a muddler to extract all the flavor. Store in the refrigerator for up to 1 month.

In a chilled cocktail glass, combine the rum, 1 teaspoon of the syrup, and bitters and stir. Add 1 large ice cube and stir. Serve.

PREPARATION TIME: 5 MINUTES, PLUS 2 HOURS STEEPING TIME
COOKING TIME: 5 MINUTES
MAKES: 1 COCKTAIL

1 cup (200 g) sugar
2 whole Fried Sweet Plantains (page 244)
1¾ fl oz (50 ml) Diplomático añejo (aged rum)
2 dashes Angostura bitters

CRAB EMPANADAS

Empanadas de cangrejo

PREPARATION TIME: 30 MINUTES
COOKING TIME: 10 MINUTES
MAKES: 20

2–3 tablespoons avocado
or canola oil
1 cup (150 g) finely diced Spanish
onion
1 teaspoon tomato paste
(tomato puree)
2 tablespoons all-purpose
(plain) flour
6 tablespoons (3 fl oz/90 ml)
light rum
2 ½ cups (460 g) finely diced
piquillo peppers
1½ cups (260 g) roasted corn
kernels
½ cup (20 g) chopped fresh
cilantro (coriander)
1 tablespoon cumin seeds,
toasted and ground
2 tablespoons fresh lime juice
1 lb (454 g) lump crabmeat
2 tablespoons olive oil
1 teaspoon cayenne pepper
Salt and ground black pepper
8 empanada discs (see Note)
Canola oil, for deep-frying
1 egg, whisked

In a large frying pan, heat the avocado oil over medium heat. Add the onion, reduce the heat to low, and sweat the onion until translucent, about 2 minutes. Add the tomato paste (puree) and cook for 1 minute. Add the flour and cook for 1 minute. Add the rum and deglaze. Add the piquillo peppers, corn, cilantro (coriander), cumin, lime juice, crabmeat, olive oil, and cayenne and let simmer for no more than 5 minutes. Season to taste with salt and black pepper. Transfer to a large rimmed baking sheet to cool to room temperature.

Spoon 2 ounces (57 g) of the crab filling onto each 4-inch (10 cm) empanada disk. Fold the dough in half and press to seal, using a fork to mark the edges.

Cook the empanadas, either by deep-frying or baking.
To deep-fry: Pour 4 inches of the oil into a large heavy-bottomed pot and bring the oil to 375°F (190°C). Working in batches, add the empanadas and deep-fry until golden brown, 4–5 minutes. Drain on paper towels.

To bake: Preheat the oven to 375°F (190°C/Gas Mark 5). Arrange the empanadas on a parchment-lined baking sheet. Brush the empanadas with the whisked egg and bake until golden brown, 10–12 minutes.

Note: You can buy premade disks of dough (such as the Goya brand) for making empanadas. The disks are 4 inches (10 cm) across and come in packs of 10 or more. You could also use the dough from empanadillas criollas (Cuban Turnovers, page 50).

HAVANA'S CHINATOWN STEAK

Steak del barrio chino

Make the fried boniato: Pour 3 inches (7.5 cm) of oil into a large heavy-bottomed pot and bring the oil to 250°F (120°C). Add the *boniato* and cook until fork-tender, about 15 minutes. Scoop out the *boniato*, reserving the oil in the pot. Set the *boniato* aside to cool.

Return the pot of oil to 375°F (190°C). Add the *boniato* and fry until crispy and golden brown, about 6 minutes.

Make the chipotle soy sauce: In a blender, combine the tamari, honey, chipotle, lime juice, and garlic and blend until smooth. With the blender running, slowly add the oil to emulsify.

In a medium bowl, combine the boniato with 6 tablespoons (3 fl oz/90 ml) of the chipotle soy sauce and toss.

Make the hearts of palm salad: In a large bowl, combine the hearts of palm, chili, onion, cilantro (coriander), and lime juice and toss. Season to taste with salt.

Preheat the oven to 400°F (200°C/Gas Mark 6).

Season the steaks with salt and pepper. In a large ovenproof frying pan, heat the oil over high heat. Add the steaks and sear for 3 minutes on each side. Transfer to the oven and cook for 10–15 minutes, depending on the doneness you want. Serve with the *boniato* and the hearts of palm salad.

PREPARATION TIME: 2 HOURS
COOKING TIME: 20 MINUTES
SERVES: 4

For the fried boniato:
Canola oil, for deep-frying
10 oz (300 g) white sweet potato, peeled and cut into irregular shapes

For the chipotle soy sauce:
1 cup (8 fl oz/240 ml) tamari
½ cup (170 g) honey
2 oz (56 g) chipotle in adobo sauce
1 tablespoon lime juice
6 cloves garlic, peeled
6 tablespoons canola oil

For the hearts of palm salad:
12 oz (340 g) fresh or canned hearts of palm, julienned
4½ tablespoons julienned Fresno chili
4½ tablespoons slivered red onion
½ cup (25 g) minced fresh cilantro (coriander)
6 tablespoons lime juice
Salt

For the steak:
4 aged New York strip steaks (sirloin steaks), about 7 oz/200 g each
Salt and ground black pepper
¼ cup (2 fl oz/60 ml) canola oil

Acela Matamoros Traba

CAMAGÜEY
CUBA

Born in Camagüey in central Cuba, Acela Matamoros Traba learned to cook from her mother, an excellent cook. She later studied at the Higher Institute of Food and Flavor Industry and is now a chef, teacher, author, and member of Slow Food International. Her cooking is inspired by international, Cuban, and Caribbean flavors.

PORT OF PRINCE COCKTAIL

Coctel Puerto Príncipe

PREPARATION TIME: 5 MINUTES
MAKES: 1 COCKTAIL

1½ teaspoons sugar
1 teaspoon Cuban oregano (Mexican mint) or regular oregano juice plus 1 sprig, for garnish
1½ fl oz (45 ml) Puerto Príncipe rum (see Note)
2½ fl oz (75 ml) coconut water
2½ fl oz (75 ml) pineapple juice

In an 8-ounce (240 ml) glass, combine the sugar and Cuban oregano juice. Stir with a spoon until dissolved, about 2 minutes. Add the rum and stir for 30 seconds, then add 3 ice cubes. Add the coconut water and pineapple juice and stir for 20 seconds. Serve garnished with the sprig of oregano.

Note: Cuba's famous Puerto Príncipe rum (made from sugarcane) is distilled in a factory in the city of Camagüey, which was formerly known as Santa María del Puerto del Príncipe, and today is simply called Puerto Príncipe—thus giving the rum its name.

YUCA WITH CUBAN CARNITAS

Papas de manioca cubierta con carnitas cubana

In a large pot, combine the yuca (cassava), enough water to cover, and 1 teaspoon salt. Bring to a boil and cook until tender, about 18 minutes. Drain and remove the fiber in the middle of the yuca.

Transfer to a bowl and mash with a fork, about 7 minutes. Add 6 cloves of the garlic and 2 teaspoons of the lime juice and continue to mash with a fork. Divide the mixture into 12 portions. Shape each portion into a 1 x ¾-inch (3 x 2 cm) rectangle. Set aside in a warm place.

In a frying pan, heat 4 teaspoons of the olive oil over medium heat for 2 minutes. Add 3 cloves of the garlic, 3 tablespoons of the diced onion, and the *cachucha* peppers and sauté for 2 minutes. Add the beef and continue cooking over high heat for 5 minutes. Add the cumin, ½ teaspoon salt, a generous ½ teaspoon black pepper, and the bitter orange juice and sauté for 2 minutes. Adjust the seasoning to taste.

In a frying pan, heat the remaining 2 teaspoons olive oil over medium heat. Add the bacon (streaky) and sauté for 3 minutes. Add the remaining 3 cloves garlic, the sliced onion, cilantro (coriander), beans, and salt and black pepper to taste and cook over low heat for 2 minutes.

In a bowl, mix together the avocado, tomato, the remaining 1 tablespoon finely diced onion and 1 teaspoon lime juice, and salt and pepper to taste.

To serve, arrange 3 yuca rectangles on each plate. Top one with the beef mixture, one with the bean mixture, and another with the avocado mixture. Garnish with finely chopped chives.

PREPARATION TIME: 23 MINUTES
COOKING TIME: 27 MINUTES
SERVES: 4

14 oz (400 g) yuca (cassava), peeled and cut into 3 inch pieces
Salt
12 cloves garlic, peeled
3 teaspoons lime juice
2 tablespoons olive oil
2 oz (55 g) onion—4 tablespoons finely diced, the remainder finely sliced
1 tablespoon thinly sliced cachucha peppers
4 oz (120 g) skirt steak (bavette), cooked and shredded
¼ teaspoon ground cumin
Ground black pepper
Juice of ½ bitter orange (see page 18)
1½ oz (40 g) bacon (streaky), thinly sliced
1 bunch cilantro (coriander)
scant ½ cup (120 g) cooked black beans
4 oz (120 g) avocado
scant ¼ cup diced tomato
1 bunch chives, finely chopped

CAMAGÜEY-STYLE STEWED SALT COD IN SWEET POTATO SHELLS

Guiso de bacalao en tinajón

de boniato estilo camagüeyano

**PREPARATION TIME: 25 MINUTES,
PLUS 30 MINUTES SOAKING TIME
COOKING TIME: 40 MINUTES
SERVES: 4**

1 lb (464 g) salt cod
2 tablespoons olive oil
6 cloves garlic, peeled
and crushed
2 oz (60 g) onion, thinly sliced
½ teaspoon ground white pepper
3 oz (80 g) tomato, thinly sliced
2 bunches parsley, chopped, plus
more for serving
1 leaf Cuban oregano
(Mexican mint) or regular oregano
1 bay leaf
½ teaspoon ground cumin
2½ tablespoons dry white wine
1 lb 4 oz (590 g) white or yellow
sweet potato, ends trimmed
¾ teaspoon salt
½ teaspoon sugar
1¼ cups (10 fl oz/300 ml)
vegetable oil

Soak the salt cod in water for 30 minutes, changing the water 3 or 4 times to remove the salt.

In a large pot, combine the cod and enough water to cover. Bring to a boil and cook until soft, 25 minutes. Remove and let cool. Remove the bones and the skin and gently crumble.

In a frying pan, heat the oil over medium heat for 5 minutes. Add the garlic, onion, cod, and pepper and sauté for 5 minutes. Add the tomato, parsley, oregano, and bay leaf. Sprinkle with the cumin, then add the wine. Continue cooking over high heat until the liquid is reduced, 10 minutes. Adjust the seasoning to taste.

In a large pot, combine 12 oz (360 g) of the sweet potatoes, enough water to cover, the salt, and sugar. Bring to a boil and cook until firm-tender, about 18 minutes. Drain and make a lengthwise incision, without cutting through the ends. Using a spoon, hollow out the sweet potato, leaving a ¼-inch (6 mm) shell. Set aside in a warm place.

Cut the remaining 8 oz (230 g) sweet potatoes into sticks ⅛ inch (2 mm) thick. In a medium pot, heat the vegetable oil over high heat. Add the sweet potato and deep-fry until golden and crunchy, about 2 minutes. Transfer the sweet potato crisps to paper towels to drain excess oil.

Arrange a sweet potato on each plate and fill each one with 1 cup (120 g) of the cod mixture. Serve with a sweet potato crisp and a sprig of parsley. Finish with the sauce from the cod mixture. Serve hot.

Note: Tinajones are very large, round clay receptacles that were used during Spanish colonial times for storing rainwater. They can still be found in the backyards of colonial homes or as a decoration in parks. They are a traditional symbol of Camagüey. Tinajas are a smaller version of the tinajones and are used to keep drinking water fresh inside houses.

GRAPEFRUIT PEEL PETALS WITH CUBAN WHITE CHEESE AND MINT

Petalos de cascos de toronja sobre queso blanco criollo y ramita de hierba buena

Remove the peel (with pith) from the grapefruits (reserve the flesh for another use). With a small spoon, make longitudinal incisions, scoop long oval shaped pieces from the white pith, and cut in quarters in order to create petals.

In a bowl, combine the grapefruit petals and enough water to cover. Change the water three times every 3 minutes to remove the bitterness. Transfer to a medium pot and cover with water. Bring to a boil over high heat and cook for about 10 minutes. Drain, add fresh water, bring to a boil again, and cook for 10 minutes. Repeat once more (total of three times) to remove the bitterness.

In a saucepan, combine the sugar, 7 tablespoons (3½ fl oz/ 100 ml) water, and the cinnamon stick. Cook over medium heat until a light syrup forms, about 15 minutes. Add the grapefruit petals and cook until softened, 12 minutes. Let cool.

Place the cheese on a serving dish and arrange the grapefruit petals on top. Garnish with a mint sprig in the middle. Serve chilled or at room temperature.

PREPARATION TIME: 1 HOUR
COOKING TIME: 1 HOUR
SERVES: 4

1 large grapefruit
(about 10 oz/300 g)
¾ cup (150 g) sugar
1 cinnamon stick
Cuban white cheese or queso
fresco, cut into 1 x ¾-inch
(3 x 2 cm) rectangles
Mint sprigs, for garnish

ajiaco bayamés 96
ajiaco de Puerto Príncipe 94, 95
albóndigas de res a la catalana 212
aliñado 392
aliño de hierbas 320, 321
aliño oriental 320
almíbar ligero 323
Andrade, Eileen 410–412
Andux, Yamilet Magariño 413–415
aporreado de pescado 162, 163
aporreado de pollo con boniato 180
aporreado de tasajo estilo habanero 203
arepas de maíz 34, 35
arepas rellenas 36
arepas
    corn arepas 34, 35
    stuffed arepas 36
Arimao River shrimp 158, 159
arroz a la camagüeyana 110, 111
arroz a la naranja con vegetales salteados 124, 125
arroz al curry 122
arroz amarillo 121
arroz con camarones secos 121
arroz con cerdo 103
arroz con frijol gandul y coco 123
arroz con leche familiar 334, 335
arroz con leche y salsa de frutas 334
arroz con maíz a la campesina 126, 127
arroz con maní y finas hierbas 128, 129
arroz con maní 128
arroz con papas 126
arroz con plátano maduro 120
arroz con pollo a la Chorrera 114, 115
arroz con pollo y vegetales 106
arroz con salsa de vegetales y pollo 112
arroz con vegetales 122
arroz congrí 102
arroz frito a la cubana 118, 119
arroz frito casero 117
arroz imperial con pollo 116
arroz pilaf exquisito 120
arroz salteado con vegetales 124
Asia de Cuba (London, UK) 421
Asian dressing 320
Atelier (Havana, Cuba) 419
aubergine see **eggplant**
avocado
    avocado and aromatic herb salad 284, 285
    guacamole 322
    tomato, avocado, and cheese salad 302, 303

bacalao con pan 56
bain-marie/baño de maría, about 18
ballotina de pollo 181
bananas
    banana milkshake 386
    banana-mint salad 298, 299
    papaya banana juice 380, 381
Barreras, Ricardo 416–418
batido de frutas al jengibre 384
batido de mamey 386, 387
batido de plátano 386
Bayamese stew 96
beans, dried see also **black beans; black-eyed peas; red beans; split peas**
    bean and bell pepper salad 288, 289
    Galician soup 82
    white bean dessert 356
beans, fresh
    green bean and corn salad 290, 291
    spicy green beans 249
béchamel sauce 322
beef, dried see **tasajo**
beef
    beef Stroganoff 202
    Camagüey-style meat and fruit salad 208
    Catalan-style beef meatballs 212
    corn and ground beef pudding 252
    Cuban ground beef 206, 207
    ground beef and capers 208, 209
    Havana-style ground beef 203

Havana-style salted dry beef 203
Havana's Chinatown steak 423
midnight brisket sandwiches 411
oxtail stew 214, 215
ropa vieja 204, 205
salted dry beef with sweet potato 206
Santiago-style pot roast 201
shredded beef 204, 205
stuffed bell peppers 224, 225
tender shredded beef 210, 211
yuca with Cuban carnitas 425
berenjena a la cubana 226
berenjena rebozada con pimiento 227
beverages see **drinks**
bistec de pollo encebollado 179
black beans
    black bean soup 74, 75
    Moors and Christians with sofrito 108, 109
    traditional Moors and Christians 107
black-eyed pea fritters 44
Bloody Mary, Cuban 400, 401
bocadito surtido 57
bocadito vegetariano 58
bolas de boniato y pescado 246
bolas de plátano rellenas 244
boliche mechado a la santiaguera 201
bolitas de pescado macabi 158
bombones de maní 360
boniatillo con coco 343
boniato frito 247
boniatos en tentación 248
borscht soup, Cuban 73
bread
    bread pudding with peanut caramel 344
    Cuban bread, about 19
brisket medianoche 411
brisket sandwiches, midnight 411
buñuelos de canela 412
buñuelos tradicionales o navideños 368, 369

café carretero 394
café con leche 394
cakes
    chocolate almond cake 352, 353
    chocolate roll 360
    frosted cake 364
    imperial pudding 365
    married cake 366
    spring dream cake 362
    yogurt cake 361
    yuca flan cake 355
calabaza agridulce 228
calamares en su tinta 156, 157
caldo gallego 82
caldosa tunera 84, 85
Camagüey-style meat and fruit salad 208
Camagüey-style rice 110, 111
Camagüey-style stewed salt cod in sweet potato shells 426
Camagüey, savory chicken pie from 417
camarones enchilados 416
camarones Río Arimao 158, 159
canchánchara 400
candy
    chocolate truffles 366
    milk-peanut candies 345
    peanut candies 360
carne de cerdo ripiá 192
carne de res a la Stroganov 202
cascos de guayaba 338
cassava see **yuca**
Catalan-style beef meatballs 212
cauliflower and parsley salad 286
cazuelita de pollo y verduras 189
ceviche, fish, with vegetables 38, 39
champola de guanábana 388
cheese see also **Cuban white cheese**
    cheese fritters 43
    chicken and cheese soup 92
    corn and cheese soup 89
    grilled cheese sandwich 56
    liseta mullet with cheese 165
    potatoes with cheese and Cuban oregano 242

chicharritas o mariquitas de plátano 40, 41
chicharrones 49
chicken
    braised chicken 184
    chicken and cheese soup 92
    chicken and rice soup 67
    chicken and sweet potato stew 180
    chicken cocktail 33
    chicken croquettes 48
    chicken in butter and soy sauce 177
    chicken noodle soup 67
    chicken rice stew 113
    chicken slices with coconut 188
    chicken steak with onions 179
    chicken tamale in a husk 254, 255
    chicken with fresh tomato sauce 179
    chicken with fruit 185
    cornmeal with chicken 83
    country-style chicken 178
    drunken chicken thighs 185
    garlic chicken 177
    Havana-style chicken stew 190
    imperial rice with chicken 116
    little pot of chicken and veggies 189
    marinated braised chicken with taro root 186, 187
    okra with plantain and chicken 228, 229
    orange chicken thighs 188
    pineapple chicken thighs 189
    queen-style chicken supremes 182, 183
    rice with chicken "a la Chorrera" 114, 115
    rice with chicken and vegetables 106
    rice with chicken-vegetable sauce 112
    savory chicken pie from Camagüey 417
    stuffed chicken 181
    tamale-stuffed chicken 190
    vegetable chicken chop suey 182
chickpeas
    chickpea soup 80
    fried chickpeas 250, 251, 410
chilindrón de chivo 213
chocolate caliente 395
chocolate
    chocolate almond cake 352, 353
    chocolate liqueur and rum cocktail 404
    chocolate roll 360
    chocolate truffles 366
    hot chocolate 395
chop suey de pescado 162
chop suey de vegetales y pollo 182
chop suey
    fish chop suey 162
    vegetable chicken chop suey 182
Chorrera, Fuente de la (restaurant) 114
churros 370, 371
cocktails see **drinks, alcoholic**
coco quemado 343
coconut
    chicken slices with coconut 188
    coconut dessert 339
    coconut milk French toast 358
    coconut pudding with fruit sauce 346, 347
    Mambí bread 367
    mashed taro root with coconut milk 240, 241
    pineapple coconut juice 390
    rice with pigeon peas and coconut 123
    sweet potato pudding with coconut 343
    sweet potato–coconut dessert 340, 341
    teti with fresh coconut milk 160
    toasted coconut 343
    yuca-coconut gift 363
cóctel de camarones 32
cóctel de frutas con jugo de guayaba 30

cóctel de frutas naturales 30, 31
cóctel de langosta 32
cóctel de pescado al limón 29
cóctel de pollo 33
cóctel Puerto Príncipe 424
coditos con pollo 142
coditos con vegetales y queso 140, 141
codorniz en su hábitat 414
coffee
    coffee with milk 394
    horse-cart coffee 394
col guisado con jamón 226
congrí oriental 104, 105
corn and cornmeal see also **maíz molido**
    bok choy, corn, and tomato salad 282, 283
    corn arepas 34, 35
    corn stew with pork 196, 197
    cornmeal with chicken 83
    cornmeal with crabs 86, 87
    cornmeal with pork 83
    country-style rice with corn 126, 127
    fermented corn beverage 393
    green bean and corn salad 290, 291
    savory corn fritters 44
    seafood tamale 88
    tamale casserole 88
crab
    cornmeal with crabs 86, 87
    crab empanadas 422
crackers
    cracker assortment 58
    cracker omelet 264
crema de arroz y apio 92
crema de calabaza y malanga 90, 91
crema de limón y merengue quemado 420
crema de maíz con queso 89
crema de malanga y maní 90
crema de malanga, papa y apio 89
crema de queso con pollo 92
crema de vie con leche en polvo 402
cremita de leche al maní 345
Creole shrimp 416
crepas rellenas 36
crepes, stuffed 36
croquetas de jamón 48
croquetas de pescado al perejil 46, 47
croquetas de pollo 48
croquettes
    chicken croquettes 48
    fish and parsley croquettes 46, 47
    ham croquettes 48
crudo de pescado con vegetales 38, 39
Cuba libre 396
Cuban Bloody Mary 400, 401
Cuban borscht soup 73
Cuban bread, about 19
Cuban cuisine, influences on 9–10 28, 64, 154, 328
Cuban dressing 311
Cuban eggnog 402
Cuban eggplant 226
Cuban fried rice 118, 119
Cuban frita 52, 53
Cuban ground beef 206, 207
Cuban lime 20
Cuban paella 130, 131
Cuban pig's feet 200
Cuban salmon with shrimp 156
Cuban sandwich 54, 55
Cuban sauce 311
Cuban turnovers 50, 51
Cuban white cheese 19
    cabbage and radish salad 287
    elbow macaroni with vegetables and cheese 140, 141
    grapefruit peel petals with Cuban white cheese and mint 427
    spaghetti and meatballs 137
    stuffed crepes 36
    tomato, avocado, and cheese salad 302, 303
cubanito 400, 401
custard see **pudding and custard**

daiquiri frappé 398
daiquiri natural 398, 399
daiquiri
    classic daiquiri 398, 399
    frozen daiquiri 398
desayuno energético 395
desserts see also **cakes; flan; fritters, sweet; ice cream and sorbet; pudding and custard; rice pudding**
    basil-pumpkin marmalade 338
    coconut dessert 339
    coconut milk French toast 358
    country-style marmalade 336, 337
    grapefruit peel petals with Cuban white cheese and mint 427
    guava and cream cheese pie 418
    guava helmets 338
    guava marmalade 336
    imperial drunk soup 365
    impossible dessert 354
    Mambi bread 367
    pineapple-mint dessert 339
    sesame French toast 358, 359
    sweet cheese 350
    sweet potato–sugarcane dessert 342
    toasted coconut 343
    toasted meringues 361
    traditional doughnuts 368, 369
    white bean dessert 356
    yuca-coconut gift 363
    yuca-rum delight 357
disco volador de queso 56
doughnuts see also **fritters, sweet**
    traditional doughnuts 368, 369
drink, alcoholic see also **fermented beverages**
    chocolate liqueur and rum cocktail 404
    classic daiquiri 398, 399
    Cuban Bloody Mary 400, 401
    Cuban eggnog 402
    frozen daiquiri 398
    Havana special 402
    honey rum drink 400
    Mary Pickford 403
    mojito 396, 397
    piña colada 404
    Pine Tree Island 403
    Port of Prince cocktail 424
    presidente 405
    rum and coke 396
    Santiago 402
    sweet plantain old-fashioned 421
drink, nonalcoholic see also **coffee; milkshakes**
    beet, watercress, and orange juice 379
    breakfast drink, energizing 395
    cucumber and pineapple juice with mint 384, 385
    eight-vegetable juice 382
    fruit smoothie with ginger 384
    hot chocolate 395
    mango juice 391
    orange juice 390
    orange juice with tomato 388
    papaya banana juice 380, 381
    pineapple coconut juice 390
    soursop juice 379
    sugarcane water with lime 389
    summer juice 382, 383
    tamarind juice 391
    two-color limeade 389
    vegetable juice 380
dulce de coco 339
dulce de frijoles blancos 356
dulce de leche cortada (con yemas de huevo) 329
dulce de leche, traditional, with milk curd 329
dulce de piña a la menta 339
dulce imposible 354
dumplings
    macabi fish dumplings 158
    sweet potato and fish dumplings 246

eggnog, Cuban 402
eggs
    cracker omelet 264
    egg and vegetable scramble 274
    egg sauce 323
    eggs "in their beds" 268, 269
    eggs on a vegetable bed 270
    grated potato omelet 263

imperial omelet 266
Mexican-style eggs 272
mimosa eggs 272, 273
omelet "lasagna" 267
omelet with a vegetable crown 263
omelet with fried ripe plantains 264, 265
onion and bell pepper omelet 262
poached eggs 274
potato and bell pepper omelet 262
potato and egg salad 294
potato salad with egg and fish 294
potato, bok choy, and egg salad 292
rum omelet 267
Santiago-style eggs 270, 271
sautéed vegetables and hard-boiled eggs 266
scrambled eggs with bell peppers 261
scrambled eggs with onion 260
Spanish tortilla 261
empanadas de cangrejo 422
empanadas, crab 422
empanadillas criollas 50, 51
empanaditas dulces 50
enchilado de langosta 155
enchilado de pescado 161
ensalada agridulce 281
ensalada al verde 281
ensalada campesina 282
ensalada clásica de col 284
ensalada de acelga, maíz y tomate 282, 283
ensalada de aguacate con aroma de hierbas 284, 285
ensalada de arroz al estilo Vivian Costa 286
ensalada de berro 302
ensalada de camarones con pepino y yogur 419
ensalada de col y rábano 287
ensalada de coliflor al perejil 286
ensalada de espinaca 288
ensalada de frijoles con pimientos 288, 289
ensalada de habichuelas con granos de maíz 290, 291
ensalada de lechuga y marpacífico 292, 293
ensalada de naranja con cebolla 290
ensalada de papa, acelga y huevo 292
ensalada de papas con huevo y pescado 294
ensalada de papas con huevo 294
ensalada de pepino con salsa de yogur 295
ensalada de pepino y toronja 296, 297
ensalada de pimiento y tomate 295
ensalada de plátano a la menta 298, 299
ensalada de remolacha con salsa de plátano 300, 301
ensalada de tomate, aguacate y queso 302, 303
ensalada de tomate, cebolla y pimiento 304, 305
ensalada de verdolaga 304
ensalada festiva 298
ensalada fría casera 296
ensalada fría de papas 300
ensalada primavera 33
ensalada rusa 287
ensaladilla tibia de pulpo 413
ensopada de pollo 113
escabeche 164
espaguetis con albondiguillas 137
espaguetis con pimiento y cebolla 137
espaguetis con salsa de vegetales 138, 139
espaguetis salteados 138
estofado de carne 196

fermented beverages
    fermented corn beverage 393
    fermented fruit beverage 392
    fermented herb and root beverage 393
    fermented pineapple beverage 392
filete costero al horno 166

filete de cerdo en cazuela 191
filete de pargo sobre puré de patatas al pesto 420
filete de pescado a la baracoense 170, 171
filete de pescado a la miel 170
filete de pescado tropical 166, 167
filete de pescado Turiguanó 168, 169
Finka Table & Tap (Miami, Florida) 410
fish see also **salt cod**
    breaded fish with fine herbs 174
    fish and parsley croquettes 46, 47
    fish ceviche with vegetables 38, 39
    fish chop suey 162
    fish cocktail with lime 29
    fish escabeche 164
    fish fillet from Baracoa 170, 171
    fish in pepper sauce 161
    fish in red sauce 172, 173
    fish with "dog" sauce 176
    fried liseta mullet 165
    fried red snapper 174, 175
    honey fish fillet 170
    liseta mullet with cheese 165
    macabi fish dumplings 158
    oven-baked coastal fillet 166
    red snapper with pureed potatoes and pesto 420
    seafood tamale 88
    shredded fish 162, 163
    spiced fish 168
    teti with fresh coconut milk 160
    tropical fish fillets 166, 167
    Turiguanó fish fillet 168, 169
flan casero 332
flan de calabaza a la canela 333
flan de yuca 330, 331
flan
    home-style flan 332
    pumpkin cinnamon flan 333
    yuca flan 330, 331
    yuca flan cake 355
fricasé de cerdo 191
frijoles agridulces 248
frijoles enchilados 252, 253
frita cubana 52, 53
fritters, savory see also **croquettes**
    black-eyed pea fritters 44
    cheese fritters 43
    pumpkin fritters 42
    salt cod fritters 45
    savory corn fritters 44
    taro root and sesame fritters 43
    taro root fritters 42
fritters, sweet see also **doughnuts**
    cake fritters 363
    churros 370, 371
    cinnamon sugar fritters 412
frituras con sabor a panetela 363
frituras de bacalao 45
frituras de calabaza 42
frituras de frijol carita 44
frituras de maíz saladas 44
frituras de malanga y ajonjolí 43
frituras de malanga 42
frituras de queso 43
frozen daiquiri 398
fruit cocktail
    fresh fruit cocktail 30, 31
    fruit cocktail with guava juice 30
fufú agridulce 232, 233
fufú de plátano 230

Galician soup 82
Gallego, Liuyen Álvarez 419–420
galleticas surtidas 58
gandul bean see **pigeon peas**
garapiña 392
garbanzo beans see **chickpeas**
garbanzos fritos 250, 251, 410
gnocchi
    sweet potato gnocchi 144, 145
    taro root gnocchi 144
goat in red sauce 213
grapefruit peel petals with Cuban white cheese and mint 427
green beans see **beans, fresh**
green split pea soup 78, 79
guacamole 322
guanábana see **soursop**
guarapo y limón 389
guava
    bread with guava paste 59
    fruit cocktail with guava juice 30

guava and cream cheese pie 418
guava helmets 338
guava marmalade 336
guava semifreddo with cheese and cinnamon tile cookies 415
guava sorbet 372, 373
sweet and sour guava sauce 314, 315
guiso a la guajira 249
guiso de bacalao en tinajón de boniato estilo camagüeyano 426
guiso de huevos con vegetales 266
guiso de maíz con cerdo 196, 197
guiso de vegetales 222

Habana especial 402
habichuelas picantes 249
harina de maíz con cangrejos 86, 87
harina de maíz con carne de cerdo 83
harina de maíz con pollo 83
Havana special 402
Havana-style chicken stew 190
Havana-style ground beef 203
Havana-style salted dry beef 203
Havana-style soup 65
Havana's Chinatown steak 423
helado casero 370
hibiscus, lettuce and, salad 292, 293
hígado a la italiana 204
horse-cart coffee 394
huevos a la mejicana 272
huevos en su lecho 268, 269
huevos escalfados 274
huevos fritos a la santiaguera 270, 271
huevos mimosa 272, 273
huevos sobre lecho de vegetales 270

ice cream and sorbet
    guava semifreddo with cheese and cinnamon tile cookies 415
    guava sorbet 372, 373
    homemade ice cream 370
impossible dessert 354
Isla de Pinos 403
Italian-style liver 204

Juan Izquierdo–style okra with shrimp 237
jugo con frutabomba y platanito 380, 381
jugo de guanábana 379
jugo de ocho vegetales 382
jugo de pepino y piña a la menta 384, 385
jugo de remolacha, naranja y berro 379
jugo de vegetales 380
jugo de verano 382, 383

langosta Varadero 155
Las Tunas–style stew 84, 85
lasagna, home-style 143
lasaña casera 143
limonada bicolor 389
liseta frita 165
liseta Nápoles 165
liver, Italian-style 204
lobster
    lobster cocktail 32
    lobster in pepper sauce 155
    Varadero lobster 155
lomito de cerdo al horno 194, 195
lonjas de pollo al coco 188

macabi fish dumplings 158
macaroni
    elbow macaroni with chicken 142
    elbow macaroni with vegetables and cheese 140, 141
    home-style pasta salad 296
machuquillo 236
maduros old-fashioned 421
maíz molido 20
    chicken tamale in a husk 254, 255
    corn and cheese soup 89
    corn and ground beef pudding 252
    tamale-stuffed chicken 190
malarrabia con coco 340, 341
malarrabia con leche 340
malarrabia con leche y guarapo 342
Mambi bread 367
mamey milkshake 386, 387
mango juice 391
mariposritas chinas 49

INDEX   **429**

Mary Pickford 403
masa de base sencilla 146
masas de cerdo fritas 193
masas de pescado enchiladas 172, 173
matahambre 357
mayonesa casera 318, 319
mayonesa con pimientos 318
mayonesa de yuca 318
mayonnaise
   homemade mayonnaise 318, 319
    mayonnaise with peppers 318
    yuca mayonnaise 318
meatballs
   Catalan-style beef meatballs 212
   spaghetti and meatballs 137
merenguitos dorados 361
meringues, toasted 361
mermelada campestre 336, 337
mermelada de calabaza a la albahaca 338
mermelada de guayaba 336
Mexican-style eggs 272
milkshakes
   banana milkshake 386
   mamey milkshake 386, 387
   soursop milkshake 388
mimosa eggs 272, 273
mojito 396, 397
mojo criollo 311
mojo picante 312, 313
Moors and Christians with sofrito 108, 109
Moors and Christians, traditional 107
Moros y cristianos con sofrito 108, 109
Moros y cristianos tradicional 107
mulata 404
muslos de pollo borrachos 185
muslos de pollo con naranja 188
muslos de pollo con piña 189

naranjada 390
natilla a dos tonos 351
natilla de vainilla decorada con caramelo 348, 349
negro en camisa 352, 353
ñoquis de boniato 144, 145
ñoquis de malanga 144

octopus salad, warm 413
olla de chícharos y vegetales 81
omelets *see* **eggs**
oranges
   beet, watercress, and orange juice 379
   orange and onion salad 290
   orange chicken thighs 188
   orange juice 390
   orange juice with tomato 388
   orange rice with sautéed vegetables 124, 125
   orange, bitter, about 18
   orange-flavored carrots 224
oxtail stew 214, 215

paella a la cubana 130, 131
paella, Cuban 130, 131
pan con lechón 57
pan con timba 59
pan patato 367
panatela con merengue y yema 364
panatela sueño de primavera 362
panatela de yogur 361
papa con pimiento y cebolla 242, 243
papas asadas con salteado de vegetales 239
papas con queso y orégano francés 242
papas en escabeche 246
papas rellenas 247
papaya banana juice 380, 381
parguito frito 174, 175
pasta *see also* **gnocchi; macaroni; spaghetti**
   festive pasta salad 298
   home-style lasagna 143
   home-style pasta salad 296
pasta de zanahoria al maní 314
pasta vegetariana para bocaditos 316
pastel de guayaba y queso 418
pastelón camagüeyano 417
patica de cerdo a la criolla 200
pescado empanado a las finas hierbas 174
pescado salsa perro 176
pescado sobre uso 168
picadillo a la criolla 206, 207

picadillo a la habanera 203
picadillo alcaparrado 208, 209
pierna de cerdo asada 198
pig's feet, Cuban 200
pigeon peas, rice with, and coconut 123
pigweed salad 304
Pilar Cuban Eatery (Brooklyn, New York) 416
pimientos rellenos 224, 225
piña colada 404
Pine Tree Island 403
pisto a la cubana 274
pizza de albahaca 148
pizza de cebolla 146, 147
pizza de pimiento 148, 149
pizza
   basil pizza 148
   bell pepper pizza 148, 149
   onion pizza 146, 147
   simple pizza dough 146
plantain *see also* **bananas**
   beet salad with plantain sauce 300, 301
   fried green plantains 38
   fried sweet plantains 244, 245
   green plantain chips 40, 41
   mashed plantains 230
   mashed plantains with pork 236
   okra with plantain and chicken 228, 229
   omelet with fried ripe plantains 264, 265
   plantain soup 66
   rice with fried ripe plantains 120
   stuffed fried plantains 40
   stuffed plantains 244
   sweet and sour mashed plantains and sweet potato 232, 233
   sweet plantain old-fashioned 421
   tostones 38
plátano maduro frito 244, 245
pollo a la barbacoa 177
pollo a la guajira 178
pollo al ajillo 177
pollo con frutas 185
pollo con salsa natural 179
pollo en fricasé con malanga 186, 187
pollo en fricasé 184
pollo guisado a la habanera 190
pollo relleno con tamal 190
pork *see also* **pig's feet**
   Bayamese stew 96
   braised pork 191
   bread with suckling pig 57
   Camagüey-style meat and fruit salad 208
   corn stew with pork 196, 197
   cornmeal with pork 83
   fried pork 193
   fried pork rinds 49
   mashed plantains with pork 236
   oven-roasted pork tenderloin 194, 195
   pork rolls 199
   pork steak in sauce 191
   pork stew 196
   rice and pork 103
   roasted pork leg 198
   shredded pork 192
   tamale casserole 88
Port of Prince cocktail 424
Port of Prince stew 94, 95
potaje de chícharos 78, 79
potaje de frijoles colorados 76, 77
potaje de frijoles negros 74, 75
potaje de garbanzos 80
potatoes
   cold potato salad 300
   grated potato omelet 263
   mashed potatoes 232
   potato and bell pepper omelet 262
   potato and egg salad 294
   potato salad in sweet and sour sauce 246
   potato salad with egg and fish 294
   potato, bok choy, and egg salad 292
   potatoes with cheese and Cuban oregano 242
   potatoes with peppers and onions 242, 243
   red snapper with pureed potatoes and pesto 420
   rice with potatoes 126
   roasted potatoes with sautéed vegetables 239

stuffed potatoes 247
   taro root, potato, and celery soup 89
Pous, Luis 421–423
prawns *see* **shrimp**
presidente 405
pressure cookers, in Cuban cooking 23
pru oriental 393
pudding and custard *see also* **flan; rice pudding**
   bread pudding with peanut caramel 344
   coconut pudding with fruit sauce 346, 347
   lime cream with burnt meringue 420
   sweet potato pudding with coconut 343
   sweet potato with milk curd 340
   sweet potato–coconut dessert 340, 341
   traditional dulce de leche with milk curd 329
   two-tone pudding 351
   vanilla-caramel custard 348, 349
pudín con salsa de maní 344
pudín de coco con salsa de frutas 346, 347
pudín de maíz relleno con picadillo 252
pudín imperial 365
pulpeta de carne de cerdo 199
puré de malanga con leche de coco 240, 241
puré de malanga, calabaza y acelga 236
puré de papas 232
purslane *see* **pigweed**

quail in its habitat 414
quesito dulce 350
queso blanco criollo 19
quimbombó con bolas de plátano y pollo 228, 229
quimbombó con camarones al estilo de Juan Izquierdo 237
Quiquia's soup 93

rabo de res encendido 214, 215
radish, cabbage and, salad 287
red beans
   country-style stew 249
   Eastern-style rice and beans 104, 105
   red bean soup 76, 77
   red beans and rice 102
   sweet and sour beans 248
refresco de mango 391
refresco de piña y coco 390
refresco de tamarindo 391
remolacha agridulce 230, 231
remolacha en escabeche 254
revoltillo con cebolla 260
revotillo con pimientos 261
rice *see also* **rice pudding**
   Camagüey-style rice 110, 111
   chicken and rice soup 67
   chicken rice stew 113
   country-style rice with corn 126, 127
   Cuban fried rice 118, 119
   Cuban paella 130, 131
   curry rice 122
   Eastern-style rice and beans 104, 105
   exquisite pilaf 120
   homemade fried rice 117
   imperial rice with chicken 116
   Moors and Christians with sofrito 108, 109
   orange rice with sautéed vegetables 124, 125
   red beans and rice 102
   rice and celery cream soup 92
   rice and pork 103
   rice and vegetables 122
   rice salad (Vivian Costa style) 286
   rice sautéed with vegetables 124
   rice with chicken "a la Chorrera" 114, 115
   rice with chicken and vegetables 106
   rice with chicken-vegetable sauce 112
   rice with dried shrimp 121
   rice with fried ripe plantains 120

rice with peanuts 128
   rice with peanuts and herbs 128, 129
   rice with pigeon peas and coconut 123
   rice with potatoes 126
   traditional Moors and Christians 107
   yellow rice 121
rice pudding
   family-style rice pudding 334, 335
   rice pudding with fruit syrup 334
ropa vieja 204, 205
rum and coke 396
rum omelet 267
Russian salad 287

salad dressing
   Asian dressing 320
   herb dressing 320, 321
salads
   avocado and aromatic herb salad 284, 285
   banana-mint salad 298, 299
   bean and bell pepper salad 288, 289
   beet salad in sweet and sour sauce 254
   beet salad with plantain sauce 300, 301
   bell pepper and tomato salad 295
   bok choy, corn, and tomato salad 282, 283
   cabbage and radish salad 287
   Camagüey-style meat and fruit salad 208
   cauliflower and parsley salad 286
   classic cabbage salad 284
   cold potato salad 300
   country salad 282
   cucumber and grapefruit salad 296, 297
   cucumber salad with yogurt dressing 295
   festive pasta salad 298
   green bean and corn salad 290, 291
   green salad 281
   home-style pasta salad 296
   lettuce and hibiscus salad 292, 293
   orange and onion salad 290
   pigweed salad 304
   potato and egg salad 294
   potato salad in sweet and sour sauce 246
   potato salad with egg and fish 294
   potato, bok choy, and egg salad 292
   rice salad (Vivian Costa style) 286
   Russian salad 287
   shrimp, cucumber, and yogurt salad 419
   spinach salad 288
   spring salad 33
   sweet and sour salad 281
   tomato, avocado, and cheese salad 302, 303
   tomato, onion, and bell pepper salad 304, 305
   warm octopus salad 413
   watercress salad 302
salchichón de chocolate 360
salmón con camarones a la cubana 156
salmon, Cuban, with shrimp 156
salpicón camagüeyano 208
salsa agridulce de guayaba 314, 315
salsa agridulce especial 312
salsa bechamel 322
salsa criolla 311
salsa de huevos 323
salsa de tomate 323
salsa verde al maní 316, 317
salt cod
   Camagüey-style stewed salt cod in sweet potato shells 426
   salt cod fritters 45
   salt cod sandwiches 56
sambumbia 393
sándwich cubano 54, 55
sandwiches
   Cuban frita 52, 53
   Cuban sandwich 54, 55
   grilled cheese sandwich 56
   midnight brisket sandwiches 411
   mixed snack 57
   salt cod sandwiches 56
   vegetarian sandwich spread 316

vegetarian snack 58
Santiago (cocktail) 402
Santiago-style eggs 270, *271*
Santiago-style pot roast 201
sapote *see* **mamey**
sauces, savory *see also* **mayonnaise;**
  salad dressing
  béchamel sauce 322
  Cuban dressing 311
  Cuban sauce 311
  green peanut sauce 316, *317*
  guacamole 322
  special sweet and sour sauce 312
  spicy sauce 312, *313*
  sweet and sour guava sauce 314,
  315
  tomato sauce 323
sauces, sweet
  egg sauce 323
semi-frío de guayaba con emulsión
  de queso y tejas de canela 415
semifreddo, guava, with cheese and
  cinnamon tile cookies 415
shrimp
  Arimao River shrimp 158, *159*
  Creole shrimp 416
  Cuban salmon with shrimp 156
  Juan Izquierdo-style okra with
  shrimp 237
  rice with dried shrimp 121
  shrimp cocktail 32
  shrimp, cucumber, and yogurt
  salad 419
sides, vegetable *see also* **salads**
  beans with peppers 252, *253*
  breaded eggplant with bell
  pepper 227
  caramelized sweet potatoes 248
  Cuban eggplant 226
  fried chickpeas 250, *251*
  fried sweet plantains 244, *245*
  fried sweet potato 247
  mashed plantain 230
  mashed potatoes 232
  mashed taro root with coconut
  milk 240, *241*
  orange-flavored carrots 224
  potatoes with cheese and Cuban
  oregano 242
  roasted potatoes with sautéed
  vegetables 239
  sautéed vegetables 221
  spicy green beans 249
  steamed vegetables 222, *223*
  stewed cabbage and ham 226
  sweet and sour beans 248
  sweet and sour beets 230, *231*
  sweet and sour mashed plantains
  and sweet potato 232, *233*

sweet and sour pumpkin 228
taro root, pumpkin, and bok choy
  puree 236
vegetable stew 222
vegetables with basil 221
yuca in sauce 234, *235*
simple syrup 323
sopa a la habanera 65
sopa borracha imperial 365
sopa borscht a la cubana 73
sopa china 70, *71*
sopa de cabeza de cherna 93
sopa de casados 366
sopa de cebolla 65
sopa de malanga, piña y pepino 68, 69
sopa de maní 72
sopa de plátanos 66
sopa de pollo con fideos 67
sopa de pollo y arroz 67
sopa de vegetales 68
sopa oriental 97
sopa Quiquia 93
sorbet *see* **ice cream and sorbet**
sorbete de guayaba 372, *373*
soups *see also* **stews**
  black bean soup 74, *75*
  chicken and cheese soup 92
  chicken and rice soup 67
  chicken noodle soup 67
  chickpea soup 80
  Chinese soup 70, *71*
  corn and cheese soup 89
  Cuban borscht soup 73
  Eastern-style soup 97
  Galician soup 82
  green split pea soup 78, *79*
  green split peas and vegetables 81
  Havana-style soup 65
  onion soup 65
  peanut soup 72
  plantain soup 66
  pumpkin and taro root cream
  soup 90, *91*
  Quiquia's soup 93
  red bean soup 76, *77*
  rice and celery cream soup 92
  stone bass head soup 93
  taro root and peanut soup 90
  taro root, pineapple, and
  cucumber soup 68, 69
  taro root, potato, and celery soup
  89
  vegetable soup 68
soursop
  soursop juice 379
  soursop milkshake 388
spaghetti
  sautéed spaghetti 138
  spaghetti and meatballs 137

spaghetti with pepper and onion
  137
spaghetti with vegetable sauce
  138, *139*
spinach salad 288
split peas
  green split pea soup 78, *79*
  green split peas and vegetables 81
spreads
  carrot-peanut spread 314
  vegetarian sandwich spread 316
squid in its ink 156, *157*
steak del barrio chino 423
stews
  Bayamese stew 96
  beef Stroganoff 202
  chicken and sweet potato stew
  180
  chicken rice stew 113
  corn stew with pork 196, *197*
  country-style stew 249
  Havana-style chicken stew 190
  oxtail stew 214, *215*
  pork stew 196
  Port of Prince stew 94, *95*
  Las Tunas-style stew 84, *85*
  vegetable stew 222
Stroganoff, beef 202
sweet potatoes
  caramelized sweet potatoes 248
  chicken and sweet potato stew 180
  fried sweet potato 247
  Mambi bread 367
  salted dry beef with sweet potato
  206
  sweet and sour mashed plantains
  and sweet potato 232, *233*
  sweet potato and fish dumplings
  246
  sweet potato gnocchi 144, *145*
  sweet potato pudding with
  coconut 343
  sweet potato with milk curd 340
  sweet potato-coconut dessert
  340, *341*
  sweet potato-sugarcane dessert
  342
sweets *see* **candy**

tamal a la marinera 88
tamal en cazuela 88
tamal en hojas con pollo 254, 255
tamarind juice 391
tambor de yuca 238
tapas de manioca cubierta con
  carnitas cubanas 425
tasajo con boniato 206
tetí con leche de coco 160
teti with fresh coconut milk 160

tocinillo de yuca 355
torrejas al ajonjolí 358, 359
torrejas con leche de coco 358
tortilla al ron 267
tortilla con cebolla y pimiento 262
tortilla con corona de vegetales 263
tortilla con plátano maduro frito
  264, 265
tortilla de galletas 264
tortilla de papa y pimiento 262
tortilla de papas ralladas 263
tortilla de regalo 363
tortilla española 261
tortilla imperial 266
tostones 38
tostones rellenos 40
Traba, Acela Matamoros 424-427
trufas de chocolate 366
truffles, chocolate 366
Turiguanó fish fillet 168, *169*
turnovers *see also* **empanadas**
  Cuban turnovers 50, *51*
  sweet turnovers 50

vaca frita 210, *211*
Varadero lobster 155
vegetable side dishes *see* **sides,**
  vegetable
vegetable soup 68
vegetales a la albahaca 221
vegetales al vapor 222, *223*
vegetales salteados 221

watercress
  beet, watercress, and orange juice
  379
  watercress salad 302
wontons, fried 49

yellow rice 121
yuca (cassava)
  Bayamese stew 96
  Las Tunas-style stew 84, *85*
  Port of Prince stew 94, *95*
  yuca "drum" casserole 238
  yuca flan 330, *331*
  yuca flan cake 355
  yuca in sauce 234, *235*
  yuca mayonnaise 318
  yuca with Cuban carnitas 425
  yuca-coconut gift 363
  yuca-rum delight 357
yuca con mojo 234, *235*

zanahoria a la naranja 224
zumo de naranja con tomate 388

BIBLIOGRAPHY

Acosta Hernández, María Luisa.
  Trucos culinarios ... de la sabiduría
  popular. Havana: Ed. Científico-
  técnica, 2010.
Bolívar Aróstegui, Natalia, and
  Carmen González Díaz de
  Villegas. *Mitos y leyendas de la*
  comida afrocubana. Havana: Ed.
  Ciencias Sociales, 1993.
Cárdenas Alpizar, Bartolo, and Laura
  Gil Recio. *Cocina criolla cubana.*
  Santiago de Cuba: Ed. Oriente,
  2006.
Collective of authors. *Cocina cubana*
  tradicional. Vol. 1. Havana: Ed.
  Balcón, 2014.
Fernández Monte, Eddy, and Santiago
  Gutiérrez Lezcano. *El sabor de la*
  cocina cubana. Santiago de Cuba:
  Ed. Oriente, 2014.
Figueroa, Vilda and José Lama.
  Cocina cubana con sabor.
  Havana: Proyecto Comunitario
  Conservación de Alimentos, 2010.
Funes-Monzote, Fernando. *Agricultura*
  con futuro. La alternativa
  agroecológica para Cuba.
  Matanzas: Estación Experimental
  "Indio Hatuey," University of
  Matanzas, 2009.

García García, Alicia, and Sergio
  García Díaz. *El Aljibe, un estilo*
  natural. Havana: Ed. SI-MAR, 2004.
González Gallardo, Luisa.
  Aproximación a la cocina china.
  Havana: Ed. Científico Técnica,
  2006.
¿Gusta, usted? Prontuario culinario y ...
  necesario. Havana: Imprenta Úcar,
  García, S.A., 1956.
Loredo, Adriana (Rosa Hilda Zell).
  Arroz con mango. Havana:
  Impresos Ramallo, 1952.
Magariño Andux, Yamilet. *Como para*
  chuparse los dedos. Havana: Selvi
  S.A., 2014.
Matamoros Traba, Acela, and Pedro R.
  Fabregat Prieto. *Cocina cubana y*
  coctelería. Havana: Ed. Científico
  Técnica, 2011.
Méndez Rodríguez-Arencibia,
  Jorge L. *Hablando con la boca*
  llena. Diccionario gastronómico.
  Havana: Ed. Boloña, 2012.
Ministerio del Comercio Interior:
  Normas de elaboración de
  productos alimenticios, 18 t. La
  Habana, (s/a).
Núñez González, Niurka, and Estrella
  González Noriega. *El cacao y*

el chocolate en Cuba. Havana:
  Centro de Antropología, 2005.
Reyes Gavilán y Moenck, María
  Antonieta. *Delicias de la mesa.*
  Manual de cocina y repostería.
  Havana: Ed. Cultural S.A., 1952.
Rodríguez Vázquez, Leandro.
  "Fundamentos filosóficos de la
  relación entre educación y cultura
  alimentarias en Cuba." Thesis for
  PhD in Philosophical Sciences.
  Havana, Instituto de Nutrición en
  Higiene de los Alimentos, 2010.
Roig y Mesa, Juan Tomás. *Diccionario*
  botánico de nombres vulgares
  cubanos, 2 t. Havana: Ed.
  Científico-Técnica, 1988.
San Miguel, Carmencita. *Recetas de*
  ayer. Havana: Instituto de Arte
  Culinario "San Miguel," 1959.
Rubiel Díaz, Miriam. *Cocinando maíz.*
  Havana. Selvi S.A., 2016.
Santos Pérez, Yeikel. *En la cocina de*
  Yeikel. Miami: Ed. Ibukku, 2017.
Smith Duquesne, Gilberto, and
  Fernando Fornet Piña. *Cocina*
  cubana tradicional. Havana: Ed.
  Científico-Técnica, 2009.
Tondre, Imogene. "El sector privado
  gastronómico y la cultura

alimentaria cubana: Estudio
  de caso." Thesis for master's
  degree in History and Philosophy.
  University of Havana, 2015.
Varona de Mora, Ernestina. *Manual de*
  la cocina moderna. Havana: Ed.
  Impresora Vega y Cia. S. L., 1955.
Vázquez Gálvez, Madelaine. *Cocina*
  ecológica en Cuba. Havana: Ed.
  José Martí, 2001.
Vázquez Gálvez, Madelaine. *Comer*
  contigo. Santiago de Cuba: Ed.
  Oriente, 2015.
Vázquez Gálvez, Madelaine, and
  Alejandro Montesinos Larrosa.
  Beber en el trópico cubano.
  Havana: Ed. Científico-Técnica,
  2011.
Villapol Andiarena, Nitza, and Martha
  Martínez. *Cocina al minuto.*
  Havana, (s/a).
Villapol Andiarena, Nitza. *Cocina al*
  minuto. Havana: Ed. Orbe, 1980.
Villapol Andiarena, Nitza. *Cocina*
  cubana. Havana: Ed. Científico-
  Técnica, 1992.